THE KEYS TO BREAD AND WINE

THE KEYS TO BREAD AND WINE

FAITH, NATURE, AND INFRASTRUCTURE IN LATE MEDIEVAL VALENCIA

ABIGAIL AGRESTA

CORNELL UNIVERSITY PRESS
Ithaca and London

First published 2022 by Cornell University Press

Librarians: A CIP catalog record for this book is available from the Library of Congress.

ISBN 9781501764172 (hardcover)
ISBN 9781501764196 (pdf)
ISBN 9781501764189 (epub)

To my mother, Jennifer Newton
And in memory of my father, Steven Agresta

Contents

ACKNOWLEDGMENTS

This project has been with me for almost the whole of my life as a professional scholar. In that time I have received help and support from many, many people, and it is my privilege to thank a few of them here.

My first debt is to the several labor unions of which I have been a member during the last decade, which have fought tirelessly for my rights as a scholar and for a more just academy: UNITE-HERE Local 33, the Public Service Alliance of Canada Local 901, and the Queen's University Faculty Association. I owe particular thanks to my friends, colleagues, and organizers at Local 33, who first showed me that a medieval historian may be concerned for the living as well as the dead.

Among the institutions that have supported the long work of this book, first and foremost are Yale University, Queen's University, and George Washington University. The archival research for this book was conducted with additional support from the European Society for Environmental History, the Fulbright Commission, and the Medieval Academy of America. My thanks also to Ferran Garcia Oliver for his advice on the various Valencian archives, and to the archivists of the Archivo de la Catedral de Valencia, the Archivo del Reino de Valencia, the Arxiu de la Corona d'Aragó, and particularly the Archivo Municipal de Valencia for their generosity and patience.

The guidance and encouragement of many mentors, colleagues, and friends—at Yale, at Queen's, at George Washington, and beyond—have been key to this project at every stage. These debts of gratitude are too numerous to count, but chief among them is to Paul Freedman. Through his example I have learned to be a better scholar, teacher, colleague, and cat lover, though it is probably only in the last of these that I could hope to match his renown. Thanks also to Alan Mikhail, Francesca Trivellato, and Anders Winroth, as well as to Guy Geltner, Monica Green, and Adnan Husain, who have given me invaluable feedback at various stages of this project. My thanks to Mahinder Kingra for his patience with this manuscript, and to the two anonymous reviewers for Cornell University Press. Thanks also to the editors Chris Woolgar at the *Journal of Medieval History*, which originally published part of chapter 3 as "Unfortunate Jews' and Urban Ugliness: The 1391 Assault on the *Jueria* of Valencia," *Journal of Medieval History* 43:3 (2017), 1–22, and Katherine Jansen and Sarah Spence at *Speculum*, where a version of chapter 6 was published as "From Purification to Protection: Plague Response in Late Medieval Valencia," *Speculum* 95:2 (April 2020), 371–395. Thanks as well to the anonymous reviewers at both journals for their feedback. My deepest gratitude goes to Stephen Bensch, who insisted on taking me seriously as a medievalist, and whose training in the classroom and the archives has proved invaluable in the years since. Special thanks to Sarah Ifft Decker, my medieval comrade of more than fifteen years; to Adam Franklin-Lyons for his generosity in documents and ideas; and to Hillary Taylor for her insight and companionship on both sides of the Atlantic.

My family has been unwavering in their encouragement, even during the periods when they were forbidden to ask how this project was going. Thanks to Ellen Heiman, Sarah Struble, and Matt Handverger for listening to my medieval monologues. Thanks to my husband, Eric Holzhauer, for copyediting this manuscript, for journeying with me to jobs and archives near and far, and for being the best partner I could have ever hoped to find. Your love and support have made this book possible.

The pages that follow are dedicated to my parents. My mother, Jennifer Newton, through her own enthusiasm led me to love the past, stories, and ultimately history. My father, Steven Agresta, had faith in my intellect long before I was able to form words, and his support for my academic pursuits remained unwavering until the day he died. I wish he could have seen this book.

Note on Names, Language, and Quotations

Language is a more contentious issue in Spain today than it was during the medieval Crown of Aragon. As has become customary in the scholarship of this region, I present names of people and places in Valencian- and Catalan-speaking places in Valencian or Catalan, except where a much more common English version exists (e.g. "Catalonia" rather than "Catalunya," and "Valencia" rather than "València"). Castilian is used only for the names of people and places within Castile. Extracts from archival documents appear in the footnotes in their original spelling, with minimal modern punctuation. Unless otherwise noted, all translations of quoted texts are my own. Modern Valencian is used in the main text, with two exceptions: the medieval Morvedre for the modern town of Sagunt, and the medieval Guadalaviar for the modern river Túria. Both of these modern names derive from Roman forms and were changed after the Middle Ages in an attempt to elevate the region's classical past over its Islamic heritage. For local landmarks, streets, and other places within the city of Valencia, geographical terms ("gate," "square," etc.) have been translated into English. Proper names, however, have been translated only when the meaning is significant and there is only one possible English translation (e.g., "Sea Gate"). The aim is for readers to be able to locate the places mentioned in the text both in the existing historiography and in the modern city.

The honorifics *En* (masculine) and *Na* (feminine), equivalent to the modern English "Mr." and "Mrs.," have been left untranslated, as has *Mossén*, an abbreviation of *Mon senyor* (My lord) used for higher-status persons, both clerical and lay. The names of the kings of the Crown of Aragon can be a source of confusion, since Pere IV of Aragon was also Pere III of Catalonia and Pere II of Valencia. The text therefore refers to monarchs by cognomen (for example, Pere the Ceremonious) rather than by number.

The term *reconquista*, coined to justify late medieval Castilian expansion, is avoided in favor of the more neutral *conquest*. *Andalusi* is used to refer to the (predominantly Muslim) people living under the rule of the caliphate of al-Andalus or its successor states. The municipal and royal governments that took over Valencia following the thirteenth-century conquest are referred to as Christian.[1] Muslims living in the Crown of Aragon are referred to as *mudéjars*, while forcibly converted Muslims and their descendants are called Moriscos. Forcibly converted Jews and their descendants are termed conversos. Both Moriscos and conversos are also sometimes referred to as New Christians. None of these three terms can fully define the faith practices of these people, which raise vexed and generally unanswerable questions; they refer instead to group identities defined and increasingly racialized by Christian authorities.

Late medieval Valencia, like most other parts of Europe in this period, used the Roman-derived currency system of *librae, solidi,* and *denarii,* or pounds, shillings, and pence, where one *libra* equaled twenty *solidi* and one *solidus* equaled twelve *denarii*. These are rendered in the text in modern Valencian/Catalan as *lliures, sous,* and *diners*. Valencia, Barcelona, and other places in the Crown of Aragon each had their own lliures, sous, and diners, which fluctuated in value relative to one another. The documents also occasionally note payments in *florins* (of Aragon) and *morabatins*, the latter being a term originally from Andalusi currency that could also signify the "morabetí alfonsi" first minted by Alfons VIII of Castile. These also fluctuated in value relative to Valencian currency. Relevant comparisons are given in the text where possible. All mention of lliures, sous, and diners are in Valencian currency unless otherwise noted.

---

1. The alternative term *feudal*, favored in Spanish-language scholarship, is both its own terminological can of worms and inappropriate for the urban context of this book.

THE KEYS TO BREAD AND WINE

Introduction

At the end of May 1413, the Dominican preacher Vicent Ferrer paused on his way out of the kingdom of Valencia to preach about God's role in natural disaster. The famous friar, already halfway to sainthood, was five years into a preaching tour of the Iberian Peninsula. He had spent the season of Lent in the capital, also called Valencia, and since the week after Easter had been winding his way north toward Aragon. He traveled with some three hundred followers, including flagellants with covered faces who confessed their sins aloud over the blasts of a trumpet.[1] So powerful was the effect of Ferrer's presence that city after city in the Crown of Aragon wrote the prescriptions of his sermons into law after he preached in their squares. The city of Valencia had passed such legislation on his last visit, and during this Lent the townspeople had proudly claimed the friar as one of their own.[2]

Shortly after leaving the city of Valencia, Ferrer and his followers broke their journey in a village in the north of the kingdom. It was a Monday, the first of the three minor Rogation Days that led up to Ascension Thursday, so when

---

1. Philip Daileader, *Saint Vincent Ferrer, His World and Life: Religion and Society in Late Medieval Europe* (New York: Palgrave Macmillan, 2016), 60, 93–97.

2. Katherine Lindeman, "Fighting Words: Vengeance, Jews, and Saint Vicent Ferrer in Late-Medieval Valencia," *Speculum* 91, no. 3 (2016): 690–694.

Ferrer stood up to preach in the town's narrow square, rogation was his theme.[3] Why, he asked, do "people in all Christian places" process through the streets asking God to relieve natural disasters? He answered himself with a parable:

> There was a rich and powerful lord who had a slave or servant woman and many sons and daughters small and large, [and] to [the slave woman] he had entrusted the keys to the bread and the wine and the fruits and to all the other things so that the children could not have any bread except by the hand of the slave. And at times [the slave woman] was very cruel, and did not wish to give the children of the lord either bread or wine. The children, not knowing what they were doing, turned to their father, who chastised the slave etc. Thus it is with us: the lord of the house, of this world, is our lord God . . . the legitimate children are the Christians, and the Jews and Moors and other infidels are bastards, and for that reason do not have the inheritance of paradise. . . . The slave and the servant, to whom God has entrusted the keys of bread and wine and other earthly things is nature, from the hands of whom we must have bread and wine and other earthly things. As God, our father, has ordained that at times [she] is excessively cruel to the children of the Lord, so that when we care to harvest much bread and good wine, etc., she does not wish it, and takes it from us, sending us hail, locust, droughts, and fog. For this reason we turn to the Lord our father, praying him and supplicating him to chastise and curb his servant, and order her to give us bread and wine and the things necessary to us.[4]

---

3. The Valencian text of this sermon can be found in Vicent Ferrer, *Sermons*, vol. 6, ed. Gret Schib (Barcelona: Editorial Barcino, 1988), 107–113. This version is taken from ACV, MS. 276, 233–237. A Latin translation of the sermon is also preserved in the Biblioteca de Catalunya, MS. 477, 20r–21v, under the heading "Sermo factus in eodem loco de Adzeneta feria 2a in rogacionibus, XXIX. Madij." For a description of this manuscript, see Josep Perarnau i Espelt, "La compilació de sermons de Sant Vicent Ferrer de Barcelona, Biblioteca de Catalunya, Ms. 477," *Arxiu de textos catalans antics* 4 (1985): 213–402. The other locations and dates recorded in MS 477 trace a trajectory from Morvedre north to Barcelona. These suggest that the Adzeneta in question was Atzeneta del Maestrat, which lies between Onda (mentioned immediately before), and Albocàsser (mentioned immediately after). The date of the sermon means that the year must be 1413, which also fits with what is known of Vicent's movements.

4. "Era hun senyor rich e poderós qui havia una cativa o serventa e molts fills e filles petits e grans, a la qual havie comanat les claus del pa e del vi e de les fruytes e de totes les altres coses, en tant quels fills no podien haver pa ne res sinó per mà de la esclava. E a vegades ere tan cruel, que no volie dar als fills del senyor pa ne vi. Los fills, no sabents què·s fessen, recorregueren a son pare, que corregís la cativa, etc. Axí és de nosaltres: el senyor de la casa, de aquest món, és sotre senyor Déus. . . . Los fills legitims són los cristians, car los juheus e moros e altres infels són borts, e per ço no han la heretat de paraís. . . . La cativa e la serventa, a la qual Déus ha comanat les claus del pa e del vi e de les altres coses terrenals és natura, per les mans de la qual a nosaltres cové de haver pa e vi e les altres coses terrenals, car axi ó ha ordenat Déus, pare nostre, que algunes vegades és massa cruel als fills del senyor, que quan cuydam collir molt pa e bon vi, etc., ella no·u vol, ans nos ó tol, que·ns tramet pedres, lagosta, secades e neules. Per açò no-

This analogy for the relationship between God, human beings, and nature was well outside the norm for medieval preaching. Surviving sermons usually describe natural disaster as the consequence of God's anger at human sin.[5] For Ferrer, however, religious identity was the crucial factor; the children of God were succored not according to their goodness but according to their faith. Jews and Muslims, as illegitimate children of God, had no right to the fruits of the natural world, nor any standing to seek divine aid.[6] Even nature shared this subordinate religious status; the word Ferrer used for "slave woman," *cativa*, was most often used to describe a captive Muslim who was sold into slavery.[7] In Ferrer's analogy, nature was an entity that could exert influence, but that influence was weak compared to the rightful dominion of God. Nature as an enslaved Muslim woman could have no legitimate power over Christians. She was caretaker rather than owner of the world's resources, and any withdrawal of her bounty was mere caprice. This image would have seemed particularly apt to a Valencian audience. Their own land, the kingdom of Valencia, had itself been captured from its Muslim rulers by the Christian king, Jaume of Aragon, in 1238 and continued to have large populations of Jews and Muslims. Ferrer's message was thus tailored to the descendants of crusaders, who saw in their landscape the triumph of their forefathers' conquest.

Government, Environment, and Religious Difference in Medieval Valencia

This book is about the relationship between God, human beings, and nature, as imagined by Ferrer's erstwhile hosts, the city council of Valencia. It is about who was thought to hold the keys to bread and wine, who had a right to them, and how they were used to unlock the potential of the land in and around the city from the early fourteenth century to the early sixteenth. While the city council rarely used the term *nature* to describe the environments and climatic forces with which it interacted, those interactions show that the council had

---

saltres recorrem al Senyor, pare nostre, pregant-lo e soplicant-lo que correguesque e refrene la serventa, e li man que·ns dó pa e vi e les coses necessàries a nosaltres." Ferrer, *Sermons*, 6:108–109.

5. Jussi Hanska, "Cessante causa cessat et effectus: Sin and Natural Disasters in Medieval Sermons," in *Roma, magistra mundi: Itineraria culturae medievalis. Mélanges offerts à Père L. E. Boyle à l'occasion de son 75e anniversaire*, part 3, ed. Jacqueline Hamesse (Louvain-la-Neuve, Belgium: Fédération Internationale des Instituts d'Etudes Médiévales, 1998), 141–153.

6. On Ferrer's anti-Judaism, see Lindeman, "Fighting Words," 690–723.

7. On the usage of this word, an archaic form of the modern Catalan *cativa* (masc. *captiu*), see Antoni Ferrer Abárzuza, "Captives or Slaves and Masters in Eivissa (Ibiza), 1235–1600," *Medieval Encounters* 22, no. 5 (2016): 569–579.

clear environmental priorities that remained consistent over long periods of time. From the late fourteenth century to the early fifteenth, the city council aspired to take control of its landscape, initiating infrastructure projects to address the area's environmental challenges. From the late 1420s on, however, the council turned away from this strategy. Instead of focusing on infrastructure projects, it began to respond to natural disasters with processions appealing for divine aid. This shift resulted, in part, from the success of its efforts to erase the city's Islamic and Jewish heritage. The council was thus following Ferrer's advice; its increasing claims to divine help were based on an increasing confidence in the city's Christian identity. While there is no proof that any of the councilmen heard this particular sermon, Ferrer's analogy reveals something significant about the landscape of his birth: Valencians' relationships with God and with nature were driven less by sin and fear than by a consciousness of their history of religious conquest.

The following chapters argue that the city council of Valencia's understanding of God's role in the natural world evolved in the course of its efforts to Christianize the city. The landscape around Valencia had for centuries been shaped by humans to suit human concerns. After its conquest, Valencia's Andalusi past was evident not only in the people who remained on the land but in the very landscape that made it a prize worth conquering: a network of canals that irrigated the arid land around the city, making it one of the richest agricultural areas in the Mediterranean. Projects to transform, expand, and improve on this constructed landscape began almost immediately after the conquest, but the city government only began to take a leading role in these efforts in the later fourteenth century. During this period of both governmental expansion and frequent natural disasters, the council proposed infrastructure projects in response to droughts and other environmental crises. Few of these projects were completed, but the council continued to propose new initiatives. At the same time, it sought to minimize the city's Andalusi heritage and moved in the aftermath of the 1391 riots to eliminate the city's Jewish quarter. Having rendered the urban landscape more visibly Christian, Valencia's leaders pulled back from infrastructure responses to natural disaster and focused instead on religious rituals that highlighted the city's Christian population.

Late medieval Valencia therefore reverses the usual narrative of technological progress. Most broadly, it demonstrates that human beings were making complex environmental choices well before the modern period. Faith in technological capability could and did coexist with faith in divine power in the environment. In the late fourteenth and early fifteenth centuries, the city government routinely responded to natural disaster not with prayer but with plans to "improve" the landscape and address future disaster. By the second quarter of the fifteenth century Valencia was entering what is traditionally considered its golden age; its political star was rising and it was fast overtaking Barcelona in commercial wealth. Despite its long history of environmental intervention, this increasingly wealthy society chose to respond to natural disasters more with ritual than with infrastructure.

This book thus makes two claims. First, governmental zeal for landscape improvement was not a modern phenomenon and did not necessarily increase toward the dawn of the modern period. Second, and conversely, religious appeals in response to natural disaster were not necessarily ancient traditions and did not necessarily decline over this same span of time. The municipal government of Valencia developed a pattern of proposing infrastructure projects and landscape improvement well before it developed a tradition of natural disaster ritual. These planned improvements targeted both environmental vulnerabilities and evidence of the city's Islamic heritage. Only after a half century of infrastructure planning and building did the council develop a robust tradition of pleas for divine aid. Religious and material approaches to the environment are by no means mutually exclusive, but in Valencia successive governments made different choices about how to use resources for natural disaster response. Once the projects of the previous decades had made the city of Valencia more visibly Christian, processions through that city increasingly served to emphasize its Christianity. As Ferrer would have put it, rogation processions reminded God that Valencian Christians were his legitimate children, to whom he had a duty of care.

That medieval people were capable of sophisticated manipulation of their environments is well known within the field of medieval environmental history, though less apparent in general scholarship. Of course, as archeological and paleoclimatological work has shown, human beings have been transforming the land, water, and air around them since prehistoric times.[8] By the Middle Ages, much of this transformation was deliberate. Scholars like Richard Hoffman and Paolo Squatriti have made abundantly clear that medieval people did not, as was once imagined, live in fearful balance with nature.[9]

8. José S. Carrión, Santiago Fernández, Penélope González-Sampériz, Graciela Gil-Romera, Ernestina Badal, Yolanda Carrión-Marco, Lourdes López-Merino, José A. López-Sáez, Elena Fierro, and Francesc Burjachs, "Expected Trends and Surprises in the Lateglacial and Holocene Vegetation History of the Iberian Peninsula and Balearic Islands." Review of Palaeobotany and Palynology 162, no. 3 (2010): 458–475; A. García-Alix, F. J. Jimenez-Espejo, J. A. Lozano, G. Jiménez-Moreno, F. Martinez-Ruiz, L. García-Sanjuán, G. Aranda Jiménez, E. García Alfonso, G. Ruiz-Puertas, and R. Scott Anderson, "Anthropogenic Impact and Lead Pollution throughout the Holocene in Southern Iberia." Science of the Total Environment 449 (2013): 451–460.
9. Richard C. Hoffmann, An Environmental History of Medieval Europe (Cambridge: Cambridge University Press, 2014); Paolo Squatriti, Water and Society in Early Medieval Italy, AD 400–1000 (Cambridge:

People across the continent shaped a wide variety of environments and eco-systems, from rivers to rabbit warrens, to suit their needs.[10]

The relationship between these efforts and religious belief is not always clear. In the half century since its publication, Lynn White's one-dimensional characterization of Christianity as an agent of environmental destruction has been repeatedly challenged.[11] In place of the White thesis, a more nuanced picture of how religious belief shaped environmental understanding is begin-ning to emerge from scholarship in different local contexts. Ellen Arnold's work on monks in the early medieval Ardennes reveals people who were alive to the symbolic power of their environments, while David Shyovitz's study of Ashkenazi intellectuals shows that their obsession with the supernatural was part of a keen interest in the reality of the natural world.[12] The work of Chris-tian Camenisch, Christopher Gerrard, David Petley, and Christian Rohr on natural disaster response has shown that medieval observers did not necessar-ily attribute earthquakes or other disasters to the power of an angry God; such events could be and often were interpreted as purely natural occurrences.[13]

Acceptance of divine power over the material world did not preclude keen observance of natural causation mechanisms. As yet there has been little in-quiry into when medieval people preferred religious responses over material

---

Cambridge University Press, 1998); Paolo Squatriti, *Landscape and Change in Early Medieval Italy: Chestnuts, Economy, and Culture* (Cambridge: Cambridge University Press, 2013). On the medieval fear of nature, see Vito Fumagalli, *Landscapes of Fear: Perceptions of Nature and the City in the Middle Ages* (Cambridge: Polity, 1994).

10. For surveys of this field, see Ellen Arnold, "An Introduction to Medieval Environmental His-tory," *History Compass* 6, no. 3 (2008): 898–916; Richard W. Unger, "Introduction: Hoffmann in the Historiography of Environmental History," in *Ecologies and Economies in Medieval and Early Modern History: Studies in Environmental History for Richard C. Hoffmann*, ed. Scott G. Bruce (Leiden: Brill, 2010), 1–24; Roberta Magnusson, "Medieval Urban Environmental History," *History Compass* 11, no. 3 (2013): 189–200, and Hoffman, *An Environmental History of Medieval Europe*.

11. Lynn White, "The Historical Roots of Our Ecologic Crisis," *Science*, n.s. 155, no. 3767 (1967): 1203–1207. Of the many responses and refutations, see, in particular, Jeremy Cohen, *"Be Fertile and In-crease, Fill the Earth and Master It": The Ancient and Medieval Career of a Biblical Text* (Ithaca, NY: Cornell University Press, 1989); Ellen Arnold, *Negotiating the Landscape: Environment and Monastic Identity in the Medieval Ardennes* (Philadelphia: University of Pennsylvania Press, 2013); and Elspeth Whitney, "Lynn White Jr.'s 'The Historical Roots of Our Ecologic Crisis' after 50 Years," *History Compass* 13, no. 8 (2015): 396–410.

12. Arnold, *Negotiating the Landscape*; David Shyovitz, *A Remembrance of His Wonders: Nature and the Supernatural in Medieval Ashkenaz* (Philadelphia: University of Pennsylvania Press, 2017).

13. Christian Camenisch and Christian Rohr, "When the Weather Turned Bad: The Research of Climate Impacts on Society and Economy during the Little Ice Age in Europe; An Overview." *Geograph-ical Research Letters* 44, no. 1 (2018): 99–114; Christopher M. Gerrard and David N. Petley, "A Risk Society? Environmental Hazards, Risk and Resilience in the Later Middle Ages in Europe," *Natural Hazards* 69, no. 1 (2013): 1051–1079; Christian Rohr, "Man and Natural Disaster in the Late Middle Ages: The Earth-quake in Carinthia and Northern Italy on 25 January 1348 and Its Perception," *Environment and History* 9, no. 2 (2003): 127–149.

ones, or why these interpretive frameworks could sometimes, but not always, coexist. The present book is concerned with humans' relationship to nonhuman nature: how the realities of governmental power and irregular weather patterns existed in imagination, and how ideas about the landscape shaped the landscape itself. In this sense it is a work of what Arnold has called "cultural environmental history." As Arnold has observed, many such histories existed, each locally distinct, and most remain to be mapped.[14]

Late medieval Valencia is a case study of how consciousness of religious identity could shape the governance of the environment in the medieval period. The relationships between environment and religious difference have been little explored in the existing scholarship, because most of that scholarship has focused on religiously homogeneous contexts.[15] Valencia's landscape and history thus make it a particularly useful place to investigate the relationship between religious identity, environment, and governmental power. The city was famous to contemporaries for both its religious diversity and its landscape of irrigation canals. Both of these features were legacies of Andalusi rule. After the eighth-century Islamic conquest, communities of Andalusi farmers had created networks of canals that distributed the water of the major rivers across the Valencian coastal plain into irrigated zones known as *hortas* (see chapter 1). In a Mediterranean known for infrequent rainfall, Valencia was, alongside the Nile and Po River valleys, one of very few places where water was plentiful.

After the thirteenth-century Christian conquest, this landscape shaped the long process of colonization. Since the hortas were maintained by those whose property fronted each canal, they required relatively dense settlement to remain productive. The conquerors could not, therefore, expel all the region's Muslim inhabitants, as was done in the drier areas of New Castile. Instead, the thirteenth and early fourteenth centuries saw a slower, more limited series of displacements of Muslim farmers by Christian ones as the settler population grew. Most Muslims had been pushed out of the richest irrigated lands by the mid-fourteenth century, but the population of the kingdom as a whole remained at least one-third Muslim through the end of the fifteenth century.[16] Significant Jewish and Muslim communities also emerged in the city of Valencia itself. Postconquest Valencia therefore became an interfaith society to a degree unmatched almost anywhere else in Iberia, and one of the only places in Christian Europe that was, in demographic terms, a land of three religions.

14. Arnold, *Negotiating the Landscape*, 3–14.
15. Shyovitz, *A Remembrance of His Wonders*, is a notable exception.
16. Josep Torró, "Els camperols musulmans del regne de València. De la conquesta a la conversió," *La rella* 23 (2010), 203.

While this society has fascinated modern historians, contemporary Christians saw it as a weakness. Fourteenth-century Franciscan writer Francesc Eiximenis warned the Valencian council that a population "mixed with diverse infidels . . . could produce innumerable perils for the public good."[17]

For much of the late nineteenth and twentieth centuries, many scholars, most famously Claudio Sánchez-Albornoz, shared Eiximenis's view, rejecting Islamic influence on Spanish national culture. It was in contrast to such positions that Américo Castro coined the term *convivencia* in the mid-twentieth century to signify an interfaith harmony that had, he believed, produced a blended culture in medieval Spain. As interfaith coexistence and its discontents have come to stand at the center of medieval Iberian historiography (particularly in English), convivencia has been alternately challenged, rejected, and reimagined to encompass not only harmonious but also ambivalent and even violent forms of interfaith interaction.[18] Several works have moved beyond accounts of communal and intercommunal life to examine the construction of religious identity in medieval Iberia. Olivia Remie Constable and Thomas Devaney, in particular, have laid bare the social and cultural energy devoted to imagining and maintaining boundaries between ruling and minority faiths. The terms of these boundaries shifted and buckled over time with the forced conversions of 1391, the growing paranoia that led to the establishment of the Spanish Inquisition, the Christian triumphalism of the conquest of Granada, and the forced conversions of Iberian Muslims, first in Granada and then in Valencia.[19]

This book shows how such boundaries shaped the construction of the Valencian landscape, which its Christian rulers saw as marked by an Islamic past and a religiously mixed present. Consciousness of religious status and religious history shaped the Valencian council's governance of its environment; the city

---

17. The original reads, "perquè esteu mesclats amb diversos infidels, raó per la qual es poden produir innombrables perills per la cosa pública." Francesc Eiximenis, *Regiment de la cosa publica*, ed. Lluís Blanes and Josep Palomero (Alzira, Spain: Edicions Bromera, 2009), 56.

18. On convivencia, see David Nirenberg, *Communities of Violence: Persecution of Minorities in the Middle Ages* (Princeton, NJ: Princeton University Press, 1996); Maya Soifer Irish, "Beyond Convivencia: Critical Reflections on the Historiography of Interfaith Relations in Christian Spain," *Journal of Medieval Iberian Studies* 1, no. 1 (2009): 19–35; Brian Catlos, "Contexto social y 'conveniencia' en la Corona de Aragón. Propuesta para un modelo de interacción entre grupos etno-religiosos minoritarios y mayoritarios," *Revista d'historia medieval* 12 (2002): 259–69; Jonathan Ray, "Beyond Tolerance and Persecution: Reassessing Our Approach to Medieval Convivencia," *Jewish Social Studies* 11, no. 2 (2005): 1–18; and Eric Lawlee, "Sephardic Intellectuals: Challenges and Creativity (1391–1492)," in *The Jew in Medieval Iberia*, ed. Jonathan Ray (Brighton, MA: Academic Studies Press, 2011), 352–394.

19. Olivia Remie Constable, *To Live Like a Moor: Christian Perceptions of Muslim Identity in Medieval and Early Modern Spain*, ed. Robin Vose (Philadelphia: University of Pennsylvania Press, 2018); Thomas Devaney, *Enemies in the Plaza: Urban Spectacle and the End of Spanish Frontier Culture, 1460–1492* (Philadelphia: University of Pennsylvania Press, 2015).

council took seriously Eiximenis's exhortation not to "permit [Islam] to be honored publicly, so that God does not become irritated against you, or against the land."[20] In the late fourteenth and early fifteenth centuries the council sought to remove Andalusi streets and houses from the city and seized the opportunity to eliminate the city's Jewish quarter in the aftermath of the 1391 assault. As the city prospered in the second quarter of the fifteenth century, its Christian identity became a more straightforward source of civic pride. In times of environmental crisis, therefore, the city council became more likely to invoke these associations by organizing processions that emphasized the Christianity of the city and its inhabitants. In that sense, rituals for natural disaster were, at least in part, products of religious violence.

The later Middle Ages were a period not only of shifting attitudes toward environments but also of climatic transition. The Mediterranean is an area particularly sensitive to climate change, and this period saw a notable shift, from what is known as the Medieval Climate Anomaly to the Little Ice Age. The latter began between 1300 and 1400 and continued through the mid-nineteenth century. Its effects were first felt in the northern part of the Iberian Peninsula and in its mountain ranges; only later did they reach the southern regions and the plains.[21] Most notable among these effects were colder temperatures and storms, though some climate proxies show an increase in a variety of extreme weather patterns in the fifteenth century: hot and cold, flooding and drought.[22] The Black Death also arrived in Europe in the mid-fourteenth century, and thereafter plague recurred in Valencia, as in other European cities, every couple of decades into the early modern period. Connections have also been drawn between plague and the changing climate.[23] The evidence does suggest that Valencians of the late fourteenth and fifteenth centuries were confronted with somewhat more frequent and more severe natural disasters than their thirteenth-century ancestors had been. But contemporaries would have been only dimly aware of these long-term trends, which would have been barely

---

20. "Cal que no els permeteu de cap manera honrar públicament el nom d'aquell malvat Mahoma, a fi que Déu no s'irrite contra vosaltres ni contra la terra." Eiximenis, *Regiment de la cosa publica*, 56.

21. Andrea Balbo et al., "Amplified Environmental Change from Land-Use and Climate Change in Medieval Minorca." *Land Degradation and Development* 29, no. 4 (2018): 1266; G. Benito et al., "Palaeoflood and Floodplain Records from Spain: Evidence for Long-Term Climate Variability and Environmental Changes," *Geomorphology* 101, no. 1 (2008): 68, 73.

22. Emilio Manrique and Angel Fernandez-Cancio, "Extreme Climatic Events in Dendoclimatic Reconstructions from Spain," *Climatic Change* 44, no. 1 (2000): 123–138; Ana Moreno eta, "Flood Response to Rainfall Variability during the Last 2000 al.Years Inferred from the Taravilla Lake Record (Central Iberian Range, Spain)," *Journal of Paleolimnology* 40, no. 3 (2008): 943–961.

23. Bruce Campbell, *The Great Transition: Climate, Disease and Society in the Late-Medieval World* (Cambridge: Cambridge University Press, 2016); Monica Green, "Black as Death," *Inference: International Review of Science* 4, no. 1, http://inference-review.com/article/black-as-death.

perceptible over the course of a single human lifetime.[24] The most severe cold of the Little Ice Age in the sixteenth and seventeenth centuries has been linked to conflict and catastrophe across the globe, but little such disruption occurred in late medieval Valencia.[25] The city government had at its disposal a variety of means with which to respond to perceived natural disasters. Its choice of responses was primarily a function of the cultural and political realities of governance in a religiously mixed society.

The Sources

The central figures in this story are the municipal councilmen of Valencia. For most of the period under consideration, the city was governed by six jurats (four citizens and two noblemen), and a larger, less powerful *consell* of representatives from the aristocracy, the parishes, and the guilds. The first government after the conquest had been an annually renewable *curia*, or *cort*, established by Jaume the Conqueror in 1239. A royal privilege of 1245 extended to the citizens of Valencia the provisional right to choose four jurats to govern the city in the king's name. The number and composition of the group of jurats changed several times before being fixed at six in 1321. The composition of the consell likewise fluctuated over time, but was dominated by men from the merchant class (*ma mija*, elected by parish), and men from the artisan class (*ma menor*, elected by guild). Aristocrats (*ma major*) were limited to a total of six representatives. As in other cities in this period, the ma menor was numerically dominant, but played little active role in governance, while power increasingly concentrated in the hands of the urban elite. Despite the restrictions on noblemen, the differences between the most powerful merchant families and the aristocracy were soon moot; they frequently intermarried and engaged in similar economic pursuits.[26]

In addition to the jurats and consell, the medieval municipal government came to include some forty other administrative posts, the most important of which were the *justicia criminal*, the *justicia civil*, the *mostaçaf*, and the *racio-*

24. John Haldon et al., "Demystifying Collapse: Climate, Environment, and Social Agency in Pre-modern Societies," *Millennium: Yearbook on the Culture and History of the First Millennium C.E.* 17, no. 1 (2020): 3–7.

25. Geoffrey Parker, *Global Crisis: War Climate Change and Catastrophe in the Seventeenth Century* (New Haven, CT: Yale University Press, 2013); Sam White, *The Climate of Rebellion in the Early Modern Ottoman Empire* (Cambridge: Cambridge University Press, 2011); Sam White, *A Cold Welcome: The Little Ice Age and Europe's Encounter with North America* (Cambridge, MA: Harvard University Press, 2017).

26. Rafael Narbona Vizcaíno, *Valencia, municipio medieval: Poder político y luchas ciudadanas, 1239–1418* (Valencia: Ajuntament de Valencia, 1995), 25–52.

nal.[27] The first two were judges of the criminal and civil courts, respectively. The office of the mostaçaf (also written as *mustasaf*) was an inheritance from Andalusi municipal administration, charged with guaranteeing the accuracy of the weights and measures used in the marketplace and enforcing other regulations on pricing and quality. It also fell to him to supervise the built environment of the city, including street cleaning, building maintenance, and construction permits; and to prosecute offenses against morality, such as blasphemy and working on holy days. Unfortunately for modern historians, the judgments of the mostaçaf were summary and given orally, with no written record made of the penalties imposed.[28] The racional, or city treasurer, gained increasing power in the council from the reign of Alfons the Magnanimous on, becoming in effect the representative of royal authority in the city government. In 1418 Alfons created the *consell secret*, consisting of the jurats, racional, and a few lesser officials, as the city government's new executive body. After the establishment of the consell secret, the full consell met less frequently; the jurats and racional were the real governors of the city.[29]

The term of office for jurats (and *consellers*) was only one year, but these officers controlled the selection of their successors, directly before 1283, and thereafter via lottery (*sort dels rodolins*), in which the names of candidates were written on scraps of paper, encased in wax, and then drawn at random from a basin of water. The current jurats and consell generated the list of candidates for the lottery in the late fourteenth and early fifteenth centuries, but by the mid-fifteenth century this task fell to the racional, who acted on behalf of the king.[30] Throughout much of this period, the same figures and the same families dominated the municipal government. According to Rafael Narbona Vizcaíno, about a dozen families, including the Escrivà, Ferrer, Marrades, and Palomar families, dominated the highest municipal offices, sometimes rotating between them.[31]

The argument that follows is based primarily on the records produced by the city council of Valencia between 1306 and 1519, now in the Archivo Municipal de Valencia. 1306 is the date of the earliest surviving records, while 1519

27. Narbona, *Valencia, municipio medieval*, 52.

28. Thomas F. Glick, "'Muhtasib' and 'Mustasaf': A Case Study of Institutional Diffusion," *Viator* 2 (1971): 59–82.

29. Rafael Narbona Vizcaíno, "Alfonso el Magnánimo, Valencia y el oficio de racional," in *La Corona d'Aragona ai tempi di Alfonso II el Magnanimo: I modelli politico-istituzionali, la circolazione degli uomini, delle idee, delle merci, gli influssi sulla società e sul costume*, vol. 1, *Modelli politico-istituzionali*, ed. Guido D'Agostino and Giulia Buffardi (Naples: Paparo, 2000), 595n4.

30. Narbona, "Alfonso el Magnánimo," 593–617.

31. Narbona, *Valencia, municipio medieval*, 25–99. See also Rafael Narbona Vizcaíno, "Cultura política y comunidad urbana: Valencia, siglos XIV–XV," *Edad Media: Revista de historia* 14 (2013): 171–211.

marked the start of the Revolt of the Brotherhoods (Germanies), a popular uprising that convulsed the kingdom and culminated in the forced conversions of many of the city's Muslims. For this period, the council produced books of acts (Manuals de Consells) that survive in an almost unbroken series from 1306 onward. Other series, including letters, accounts, and the operations of the Board of Walls and Sewers (Junta de Murs i Valls) survive in significant numbers from the later fourteenth century on. This book contends that the decisions of the city council, as preserved in these records, may be used to reconstruct attitudes toward the natural world that evolved over time. These records have been supplemented with selected royal, ecclesiastical, and notarial documents, as well as evidence of archeological and paleoclimatological investigations.

As the main sources for this study, council records have both strengths and limitations. First and foremost, the council was not always a unified entity. Individual members of this government must have differed in their aims and been subject to political and social pressures that can be only partly reconstructed today. The medieval council records rarely mention disagreement or the participants in internal debates. Many of the pieces of surviving legislation must be the result of compromise or conflict rather than consensus. During the late fourteenth and early fifteenth centuries, in particular, these urban elites were riven by factional conflicts. The different parties, known in Valencian as *bandositats*, were not divided along class lines; rather, members of all classes were linked together as members of one faction or another. These factions attacked their opponents by night in the street, assaulted their houses, and even employed mercenaries to gain the upper hand.[32] While the council repeatedly condemned the violence of the bandositats, the jurats, consellers, and racional were part of the social worlds that produced them. The details of these conflicts remain mostly unrecorded. With a few exceptions, their impact on the council's governing process cannot be accurately assessed.[33] As a direct effect of this disorder, of the civil war that preceded the Compromise of Caspe, and of the accession of the Trastámara dynasty, royal influence increased in the city council of Valencia (as elsewhere in the Crown of Aragon) over the course of the fifteenth century.[34] (This dynamic, and its impact on the council's responses to natural disaster, will be discussed in chapter 4.) Despite these changes, the decision makers in the council were fairly homogeneous in their class interests and tended to remain in power for some years.

---

32. Narbona, *Valencia, municipio medieval*, 97–99, 129–140.

33. For one such exception, see chapter 3 of this book.

34. Narbona, "Alfonso el Magnánimo"; Ernest Belenguer Cebrià, *Fernando el Catolico y la ciudad de Valencia* (Valencia: Publicacions de la Universitat de València, 2012).

Successive councils were remarkably consistent in their environmental policies over fairly long periods of time.

The council documents record the pronouncements of the rulers rather than the ruled and of Christians rather than non-Christians. The council's opinions on the natural world, and on the roles of God and human beings within it, would not have been the only ones in Valencia on these subjects, even if they are sometimes the only ones that have survived. Popular preachers' interpretations of natural disasters were often very different from that of the council, and both royal and ecclesiastical officials also played a part in the governance of the Valencian landscape. Faced with these various public actions, private individuals must have drawn their own conclusions. The Valencian council cannot, therefore, be taken to stand for Valencian society.

Although it was merely a part of a larger, more complex whole, the council is a particularly useful part to study. Its authority ranged over a fairly wide area, containing a variety of landscapes. The jurats and consellers were therefore in a position to make many more decisions about the environment and to generate much more documentation of those decisions than were most other members of Valencian society. As the council was able, in many instances, to compel participation in its chosen actions, even those who disagreed with its assumptions would have been forced to engage with them. Valencia's municipal records are unusually complete for an Iberian city in this period, allowing for a fuller and earlier picture than would be possible elsewhere. This view of municipal environmental projects complicates the historiographical narrative that such ambition was associated with the rise of the early modern state.[35] Finally, the fact that the councilmen were laymen, and not particularly well educated, sets them apart from previous studies on medieval clerical views of the natural world.[36] Few if any of them would have been familiar with scholarly theories about divine and natural causation mechanisms. Their decisions on the subject, therefore, may be understood as a blend of common knowledge, common sense, and political expediency. While hardly a perfect stand-in for the views of the average person (or even the average Christian) on the street, the councilmen's views on the natural world can be a source of insight into the society in which they lived.

35. See, for example, John T. Wing, *Roots of Empire: Forests and State Power in Early Modern Spain, c. 1500–1750* (Leiden: Brill, 2015).

36. Arnold, *Negotiating the Landscape*; Shyovitz, *A Remembrance of His Wonders*; John Howe, "Creating Symbolic Landscapes: Medieval Development of Sacred Space," in *Inventing Medieval Landscapes: Senses of Place in Western Europe*, ed. John Howe and Michael Wolfe (Gainesville: University Press of Florida, 2002), 208–223; Jussi Hanska, *Strategies of Sanity and Survival: Responses to Natural Disasters in the Middle Ages* (Helsinki: Finnish Literature Society, 2002).

Paleoclimatology has provided valuable new data to environmental historians, but these data also come with certain limitations. The historian and the paleoclimatologist tend to work on different scales and with different objectives. This book is, above all, interested in human perception of and response to environmental change, meaning that it is concerned with precisely dated local events—weather rather than climate. As Dagomar Degroot has noted, the human experience of climate change is and always has been mediated through weather. While climate change is barely perceptible over an individual lifetime, weather is constantly remarked on. Weather, however, is the noise that many paleoclimatologists seek to strain out from the signal of climate fluctuations.[37] It is also more difficult to reconstruct from most nonhuman climate proxies, few of which can be resolved even to an annual scale, and many of which are located far from population centers like the city of Valencia (see chapter 5). The results of paleoclimatological studies cannot therefore be used to check the accuracy of documentary records of climate events. Rather, the two types of evidence must be added together, in order to create a more nuanced picture of medieval conditions.

As has often been noted, no disaster is divorced from human action, and therefore no disaster is ever truly "natural."[38] The term *natural disaster* is also anachronistic for the medieval period. Unfortunately, the alternatives are no better. *Acts of God* is equally misleading in its assumptions about causation, and *disaster*, unmodified, would include wars and other events beyond the scope of this book. The term *natural disaster* is therefore used narrowly to refer to events that, whatever their ultimate cause, were perceived to arise out of and primarily affect the environment. This book considers natural disasters to be a matter as much of human culture as of nonhuman environment, and seeks to balance its sources and conclusions accordingly.

An Overview of the Chapters

The first half of this book is roughly chronological, while the second half is thematically organized around types of natural disaster. Chapter 1 presents

---

37. Dagomar Degroot, *The Frigid Golden Age: Climate Change, the Little Ice Age, and the Dutch Republic, 1560–1720* (Cambridge: Cambridge University Press, 2018); Mike Hulme, "Climate Change and Memory," in *Memory in the Twenty-First Century: New Critical Perspectives from the Arts, Humanities, and Sciences*, ed. Sebastian Groes (London: Palgrave Macmillan, 2016), 159–162.

38. On the problematic history of the term *natural disaster*, see Monica Juneha and Franz Mauelshagen, "Disasters and Pre-industrial Societies: Historiographic Trends and Comparative Perspectives," *Medieval History Journal* 10, nos. 1–2 (2007): 1–31; and Ted Steinberg, *Acts of God: The Unnatural History of Disaster in America* (Oxford: Oxford University Press, 2000).

an overview of human intervention in the Valencian landscape from the Islamic conquest through the early fourteenth century. The Valencian environment had for centuries been shaped to fit the demands of human societies; these demands intensified after the Christian conquest as settlers reimagined the functioning of the irrigated space. The city council of Valencia followed in this tradition, treating the landscape as a human construction dependent on human maintenance. Chapter 2 shows how the councils of the later fourteenth and early fifteenth centuries became more ambitious, beginning a series of interventions in the extramural landscape. Many of these were undertaken in response to natural disasters or perceived environmental problems. During this same period the councilmen also sought to reconstruct the city's intramural space, as is discussed in chapter 3. The council granted a series of permits to widen or eliminate the narrow, "Islamic" streets of the urban core while implementing a program of civic ritual celebrating the city's crusading past. In the aftermath of the anti-Jewish riots of 1391, the council used the same reasoning to lobby for the elimination of the city's Jewish quarter. By the early fifteenth century the extramural infrastructure projects had come to a halt, but the urban landscape had been rendered decidedly more Christian.

As chapter 4 examines, it was at this point that the council began to develop a routine of ritual appeals for divine aid during natural disaster. Starting in the late 1420s it organized increasing numbers of rogation processions in response to natural disaster. These urban rituals replaced extramural infrastructure projects as the council's main natural disaster responses, turning moments of environmental crisis into performances of Christian civic unity. While this shift occurred for all types of natural disasters, the council responded to each type somewhat differently. The remaining chapters examine these differences. Although drought, as examined in chapter 5, was by far the most common natural disaster, council documents describe droughts as the direct result of God's anger at humankind. The council sought to soothe this anger with collective rituals that reaffirmed the Christian community as the true social body of the city. By contrast, during plagues, as discussed in chapter 6, the council tended to link the crisis to specific groups of sinners. Plague responses, which first targeted corruption and then, by the later fifteenth century, contagion, tended to mirror social divisions in a way that responses to other natural disasters did not. Although floods and locusts—the subjects of chapter 7—both had clear biblical precedents as cases of divine punishment, the Valencian council did not usually treat them as such. The council documents never described floods as divine punishment before the late fifteenth century and expressed open uncertainty about locusts' divine origins. Biblical analogies proved less important to the council than the particular ways these crises played out in the Valencian environment.

The Valencian city council's relationship to the environment was thus conditioned far less by ignorance than by knowledge of the religious history and natural characteristics of Valencia's landscape. The relationship between faith, nature, and infrastructure, as the councilmen understood it, was one in which Christians held power. A technocratic approach to environmental crisis gave way to religious performance under these terms, adding a new twist to our understanding of the relationship between medieval Christianity and the natural world. As Lynn White has famously observed, Christianity sometimes fostered a narrative of human ownership of the natural world.[39] In Valencia, however, ritual performance of that narrative could prove an effective substitute for material intervention. The imagined relationship at the core of this book—that of the father, the children, and the slave woman—was intensely local, bound up in historical memory of the Christian conquest and the Valencian landscape. Nevertheless, it has implications for the study of religion and environment across the medieval world.

fewer outside invasions during this time - a small industrial revolution

---

39. White, "The Historical Roots of Our Ecologic Crisis," 1203–1207.

CHAPTER 1

The Works and Arts of Men
Irrigation and Environment

In his treatise on good Christian government dedicated to the jurats of Valencia in 1384, the Franciscan writer Francesc Eiximenis praised the city's extraordinary landscape: "Those who long possessed [this land] before said many times that if paradise were to be found on earth, it would be in the kingdom of Valencia. And, in truth, experience clearly teaches us that this is one of the most remarkable lands in the world, if we take account of all its virtues. [Among these is the fact that] here abound springs, rivers, and good waters with which the whole land is irrigated, and is therefore very fertile and beautiful."[1] The jurats of 1423, by contrast, framed this same landscape as a human construction:

> This city and its realm is narrow in its boundaries and belongings, and situated in a place that seems naturally starved of rain (which is very often the source of good fortune). For this reason the inhabitants of this city and realm have succor in irrigated lands, which because of the great heat of the sun that dries them and the other lands and because of the waters irrigating

---

1. "Els qui l'han posseïda abans durant molt de temps han dit que si algun paradís hi ha en la terra, en el regne de València es troba. I, en veritat, l'experiència ens ensenya clarament que aquesta és una de les més notables terres del món, si tenim en comptes totes les seues nobleses. . . . [A]cí abunden les fonts, els rius i molt bones aigües amb què es rega tota la terra, i així és més fèrtil i més bella." Eiximenis, *Regiment de la cosa publica*, 61–62.

them, that naturally diminish, would be made sterile and of little fruit were it not for the great and excellent works and ingenuity of the men cultivating them. And so nature is assisted by the works and arts of men.[2]

While Eiximenis, following a long tradition of urban encomia, praised Valencia as a natural marvel, its rulers could and often did treat their landscape as a product of human ingenuity. For them the second nature of the canal network conferred on the irrigated landscape the bulk of its "natural" advantages.[3] These passages also show how the construction of the horta was a matter both past and present. Although the jurats praised the creation of the irrigation structures, they neglected to mention that the original creators were, in Eiximenis's words, "those who long possessed [this land] before [us]." The "works and arts" of Andalusi farmers first built the horta, those of Christian settlers reshaped it in the years after the conquest, and constant maintenance both before and during the jurats' own time kept it in place on the landscape.

As originally constructed, the horta's irrigation system served to counter the risk of crop failure. After the conquest, however, the new rulers expanded this system to extract ever more agricultural capacity from the land. The city councils of the late medieval period sought to keep the horta and its canals functioning in both times of stability and times of crisis. Although enforcement was often a struggle, council regulation aimed to protect the vulnerable structures of this landscape and to maintain the integrity and health of the environments around the city.

Continuity and Change in the Valencian Landscape

The city of Valencia sits on one of the largest of a series of plains running down the Mediterranean coast of the Iberian Peninsula. The easternmost mountain ranges of the Sistema Ibérico rise to the north and west, and the foothills of the Baetic Cordillera begin farther to the south, beyond the Xúquer River. The Valencian plain itself is almost completely flat, sloping at a barely perceptible

---

2. "Aquesta ciutat e aquest Regne strets en lurs termes e pertinencies e situats en partida naturalment segon hom veu desijosa de les aygues del cel de les quals molt sovin ha e soste fortuna han ço es los habitants en aquells haven soccors de les terres irrigues les quals axi per la gran ardor del sol qui molt aquelles e les altres exuga com per les aygues vegants aquelles les quals naturalment les amagrexen serien fetes sterils & de pochs fruyts sino fossen los grans e soberchs treballs e enginys dels homens culturants aquelles. E axi la natura es subvenguda per los treballs e arts de les homens." AMV, g3-16, 98r–100v.

3. On the idea of second nature and infrastructure as "natural" advantage, see William Cronon, *Nature's Metropolis: Chicago and the Great West* (New York: W. W. Norton, 1991), 14–15, 56–57.

0.2 percent gradient toward the sea and broken only by a few isolated hillocks. The mountains block the Atlantic fronts that provide most of the region's rainfall; modern average annual precipitation in the city of Valencia and its environs is only about four hundred millimeters.[4] The plain is therefore watered almost entirely by the several rivers that flow out of the mountains. Of these, the Xúquer, forty kilometers south of Valencia, is the largest by a considerable margin. Valencia's own river is the Túria, which was known in the medieval period (and will be known in this book) as the Guadalaviar (from the Arabic *wadi al-abyad*, "white river"). Some sources suggest that in Valencia's early days as a Roman *colonia* the city was an island between two river channels, but by the later Andalusi period it stood, as it does today, on the southern bank of the Guadalaviar, some five kilometers inland from the sea.[5] All along the coast, currents from the Gulf of Valencia form dunes and sandbars, behind which have developed a chain of marshes interspersed with scrub forest (*devesa*). The largest of these marshes, just down the coast from the city, is known as the Albufera (lagoon) of Valencia. The lagoon itself was at this time surrounded by a rough oval of wetlands, extending south to the Xúquer, north to the Guadalaviar, and inland almost to the city walls.[6] The city thus stood at the meeting point of marsh, river, and plain (see map 1). To the east, the coastal wetlands were little cultivated before the fourteenth century and used primarily for pasture, hunting, and fishing. To the north, west, and south spread the irrigated fields of the horta, fading into dry-farmed fields and fallow land nearer the mountains.

The earliest irrigation structures in the province of Sharq al-Andalus, later known as the kingdom of Valencia, date from just after the Muslim conquest of 711. The Arab, Berber, and particularly Syrian settlers who arrived in Iberia brought irrigation techniques with them. As they settled the peninsula, they chose sites suitable for irrigation and began to build canals and other irrigation structures across valley floors.[7] Thomas Glick and others have shown that these irrigation systems were largely the work of communities of

---

4. Pilar Carmona and J. M. Ruiz, "Historical Morphogenesis of the Turia River Coastal Flood Plain in the Mediterranean Littoral of Spain," *Catena* 86, no. 3 (2011): 140–141; A. López Gómez, *Geografia de les terres valencianes* (Valencia: Papers Bàsics 3i4, 1977), 136–137.

5. Pilar Carmona González, "Geomorfología de la llanura de Valencia. El Río Turia y la ciudad," in *Historia de la ciudad*, vol. 2, *Territorio, sociedad y patrimonio*, ed. Sonia Dauksis Ortolá and Francesco Taberner Pastor (Valencia: Publicacions de la Universitat de València, 2002), 21.

6. Carles Sanchis Ibor, *Regadiu i canvi ambiental a l'albufera de València* (Valencia: Publicacions de la Universitat de València, 2001), 33–41.

7. María Carmen Trillo San José, "A Social Analysis of Irrigation in Al-Andalus: Nazari Granada (13th–15th Centuries)," *Journal of Medieval History* 31, no. 2 (2005): 170; Arnald Puy, "Land Selection for Irrigation in Al-Andalus, Spain (8th Century A.D.)," *Journal of Field Archaeology* 39, no. 1 (2014): 84–100.

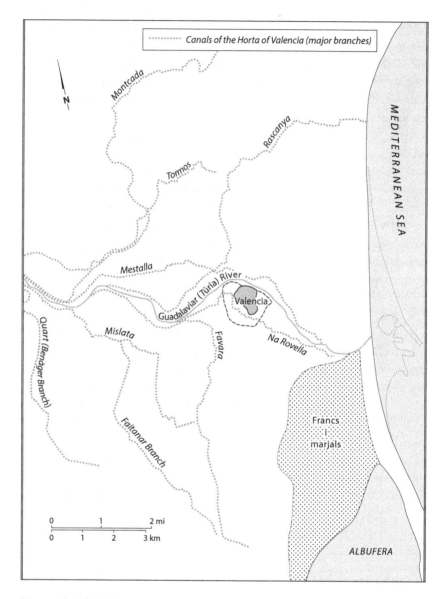

MAP 1. The Valencian horta

Andalusi farmers.[8] The first such systems were fed by wells, springs, or *qanats*—underground galleries that passed through a water table, into which the water

---

8. Thomas F. Glick, *Irrigation and Society in Medieval Valencia* (Cambridge, MA: Belknap Press of Harvard University Press, 1970); Miquel Barceló, Helena Kirchner, and Carmen Navarro, *El agua que no duerme: Fundamentos de la arquología hidráulica andalusí* (Granada: Sierra Nevada, 1996).

Natural water must be accessible [handwritten annotation]

filtered and flowed to the desired site.[9] Larger irrigated areas like the Valencian horta came later, taking their water from rivers by means of stone diversion dams (*açuts*, from the Arabic *sudd*), which directed part of the river flow into a main, or "mother," canal (*mare*). These main canals in turn flowed into secondary channels by means of small masonry divisors (*llenguas*, "tongues") that split the channel in a proportional manner.[10]

While the technologies involved were fairly simple, these systems were planned and would have required significant cooperation among kinship groups. Settlements in al-Andalus were located out of the way of the water channels in order to make the best quality land available for irrigation.[11] Powered only by gravity, irrigation canals must be designed so that water flows throughout the entire system at the appropriate speed: too fast and it will erode the banks, too slow and it will cease to flow altogether. Once the canals have been built, changes must remain within the initial parameters for the system to continue to function. This basic principle has allowed hydraulic archeologists to reconstruct the original design of many irrigation systems, which tended to remain quite stable over time.[12]

These systems nonetheless developed over the centuries. Irrigation in Valencia (or Balansiya, as it was known in Arabic) probably began with a number of smaller systems irrigated by springs and designed entirely by irrigators. In the tenth or eleventh centuries these smaller networks were connected to form a larger irrigated area: the horta. The Valencian horta was usually defined as the area irrigated by the eight canals taking water from the Guadalaviar (from upstream to downstream): Montcada, Quart (which included the branches of Benàger and Faitanar), Tormos, Mislata, Mestalla, Favara, Rascanya, and Na Rovella (see map 1). As was the case with other large urban hortas, merchants from Balansiya probably directed the construction so that the land could better supply the growing city.[13]

9. Thomas F. Glick and Helena Kirchner, "Hydraulic Systems and Technologies of Islamic Spain: History and Archaeology," in *Working with Water in Medieval Europe: Technology and Resource Use*, ed. Paolo Squatriti (Leiden: Brill, 2000), 305.

10. Glick, *Irrigation and Society*, 11, 175–177.

11. Trillo, "A Social Analysis of Irrigation," 167–168.

12. Helena Kirchner, "Original Design, Tribal Management and Modifications in Medieval Hydraulic Systems in the Balearic Islands (Spain)," *World Archaeology* 41, no. 1 (2009): 154–155.

13. Luis Pablo Martínez, "Els molins com a clau de l'articulació de l'horta medieval de València. La sentència de 1240 entre els moliners d'Alaxar i a comunitat de Rascanya," *Afers* 51 (2005): 390–392; Antoni Furió, "La domesticación del medio natural. Agricultura, ecología y economía en el País Valenciano en la baja Edad Media," in *El medio natural en la España medieval: Actas del I Congreso sobre Ecohistoria e Historia Medieval, celebrado en Cáceres, entre el 29 de noviembre y el 1 de diciembre de 2000*, ed. Julián Clemente Ramos (Badajoz, Spain: Universidad de Extremadura, Servicio de Publicaciones, 2001), 79.

Unlike their Christian neighbors to the north, the farmers who built and used the horta were autonomous peasants. They controlled their own land and the water rights attached to it through a kin-based property system. As Félix Retamero has argued, these farmers chose to irrigate not to maximize productivity but to minimize risk of environmental calamity. Andalusi peasants irrigated only the most fertile fields within their boundaries, which produced a wide variety of crops spread over two annual harvests with no need for fallow. This limited irrigation did not require all of the water diverted; the tail end of the canal returned excess back to the river. The remaining arable land was dry-farmed only intermittently, mostly left fallow to provide pasture, fuel, timber, and forage. Two harvests per year reduced the risk of crop failure, and the stable structure of the irrigation systems limited growth so that Andalusi water needs were unlikely to exceed the limits of the available supply.[14]

In the mid-thirteenth century the Christian king Jaume the Conqueror took control of these lands, incorporating them into the political entity known as the Crown of Aragon. In his autobiographical *Llibre dels fets*, Jaume recalled his campaign for Valencia as a feat that would secure his reputation as "the best king in the world."[15] Jaume's dreams of conquest, like those of his Aragonese and Catalan forebears, extended noble land holdings, royal dominions, and the boundaries of Christendom in one fell swoop. He was also able to exploit a moment of political disunity on the Valencian side of the border. Almohad rule over a united al-Andalus had collapsed in the aftermath of the Christian victory at Las Navas de Tolosa in 1212. The province of Sharq al-Andalus remained under the nominal control of an Almohad walī, Abū Zayd, but he was unpopular, under pressure from several rivals, and ultimately driven to negotiate with Jaume. As with Jaume's previous endeavors, the pope had declared the Valencia campaign a crusade, but it proceeded less as a conquest

---

14. Félix Retamero, "Irrigated Agriculture, Risk and Population: The Andalusi Hydraulic Systems of the Balearic Islands as a Case Study (Xth–XIIIth Century)," in *Marqueurs des paysages et systemes socio-économiques: Actes du colloque COST du Mans (7–9 décembre 2006)*, ed. Rita Compatangelo-Soussignan, Jean-René Bertrand, John Chapman, and Yves-Pierre Laffont (Rennes, France: Presses Universitaires du Rennes, 2008), 135–148; Félix Retamero and Helena Kirchner, "Becoming Islanders: Migration and Settlement in the Balearic Islands (10th–13th Centuries)," in *Agricultural and Pastoral Landscapes in Pre-industrial Society: Choices, Stability, Change*, ed. Félix Retamero, Inge Schjellerup, and Althea Davies (Oxford: Oxbow Books, 2016), 57–78; Josep Torró, "Field and Canal Building after the Conquest: Modifications to the Cultivated Ecosystem in the Kingdom of Valencia, ca. 1250–ca. 1350," in *Worlds of History and Economics: Essays in Honour of Andrew M. Watson*, ed. Brian Catlos (Valencia: Publicacions de la Universitat de València, 2009), 106.

15. "E, si aquela prenets, podets ben dir que sots lo meylor rey del món e aquel qui tant ha feyt." Jaume I of Aragon, *The Book of Deeds of James I of Aragon: A Translation of the Medieval Catalan "Llibre dels Fets,"* ed. and trans. Damian Smith and Helena Buffery (Aldershot, UK: Ashgate, 2003), chap. 129. Catalan text from Jaume I of Aragon, *Llibre dels fets del rei en Jaume*, vol. 2, ed. Jordi Bruguera (Barcelona: Editorial Barcino, 1991).

than as a series of negotiations. Most of the kingdom's cities and towns opened their gates to the Catalans in exchange for treaties that kept much of their population intact and guaranteed them certain privileges under the new regime, including the right to continue to follow their own faith, laws, and customs. Jaume did feel obliged to take the capital itself—by then under the control of Zayyān ibn Mardanīš—by force. After a siege of several months he entered the city of Valencia on October 9, 1238.[16]

With this victory Jaume ordered the Muslim population of the city expelled. The *Llibre dels fets* records that fifty thousand Muslims left the city of Valencia; while this figure is doubtless exaggerated, even a much smaller population displacement would have been significant.[17] Although overall the kingdom's annexation had been as much parley as crusade, the conquest of the city was immediately linked to the triumphant establishment of Christianity. This association would only strengthen in historical memory (see chapter 3). Outside the city walls, however, the aim of complete Christianization was in conflict with the functioning of the horta. On the one hand, to reward the king's followers and solidify the conquest, it was necessary to redistribute the land to Christian settlers. But maintaining the productivity of the land that made Valencia such a prize meant disrupting the irrigation system and its farmers as little as possible. These competing imperatives shaped Valencia's colonization. The conquerors celebrated the conversion of the city even as they stressed continuity in the irrigation system, insisting that water rights remain as they were "in the time of the Moors." Such rhetoric only partially masked the profound transformation of the landscape in the aftermath of the conquest.[18]

For many years, continuity rather than change was the focus of historical scholarship. Glick's 1969 *Irrigation and Society in Medieval Valencia*, which was the first to show that the hortas were Andalusi rather than Roman in origin, emphasized continuity of irrigation practice through the Christian conquest. In 1245, Muslim irrigation officials of Gandia, down the coast from Valencia, were ordered to describe, under oath, local customs of water distribution so that they might be adopted by new Christian cultivators.[19] The new kingdom's legal code, the Furs of Valencia, enshrined in statute that irrigation rights should be "just as in the past it was established and accustomed in the time of

16. Thomas W. Barton, *Victory's Shadow: Conquest and Governance in Medieval Catalonia* (Ithaca, NY: Cornell University Press, 2019), 220–231; Robert I. Burns and Paul E. Chevedden, *Negotiating Cultures: Bilingual Surrender Treaties in Muslim-Crusader Spain under James the Conqueror* (Leiden: Brill, 1999), 3–10.

17. Josep Torró, "Els camperols musulmans," 202.

18. Enric Guinot Rodríguez, "Una Historia de la huerta de Valencia," in *El patrimonio hidráulico del bajo Turia: L'horta de València*, ed. Jorge Hermosilla Pla (Valencia: Generalitat Valenciana, 2007), 60–98.

19. Glick, *Irrigation and Society*, 231–234.

the Saracens."[20] This phrase became a legal tradition equivalent to "time immemorial" in English law, which set the Christian conquest as the limit of legal memory and privileged rights seen as continuous from that date. Glick himself observed that this legal device did not imply any particular interest "in the specifics of the Islamic past." Nonetheless, he stressed the continuity of Andalusi irrigation techniques and terminology through the Christian conquest.[21] Miquel Barceló's investigations, which gave archeological confirmation to Glick's claims of Andalusi origin, also emphasized the irrigation systems' long-term stability.[22]

As Enric Guinot has observed, however, the Christian rhetoric of conquest posited an impossible combination of circumstances: complete replacement of the Andalusi population with Christian settlers, and, simultaneously, perfect continuity in irrigation practices. Over time, colonization did transform human relationships with the land.[23] Most Andalusi farmers remained on their land in the immediate aftermath of the conquest, but many were displaced over the following decades. At the start of the al-Azraq revolt (1247–58), King Jaume floated the idea of a complete expulsion of Valencia's Muslim inhabitants. The royal Muslim *aljamas* (officially organized minority communities) protested this proposal, as did nobles loath to lose their Muslim serfs. Jaume's eventual expulsion order in 1248 therefore applied only to those Muslims who "belonged" neither to the Crown nor to a lord. This and other actions in the aftermath of the al-Azraq revolt severely diminished the Valencian Muslim population. Real continuity of irrigation practice would have been extremely difficult in the context of such large-scale population displacement. As the kingdom was stabilized, moreover, new waves of Christian settlers arrived from the north to occupy the horta.

Despite these displacements, fully one-third of the kingdom's population remained Muslim through the late fifteenth century. Most of these *mudéjars* (Muslims under Christian rule) were removed to the dry-farmed river valleys of the kingdom's mountainous interior.[24] This happened slowly; the mudéjar farmers of Aldaia and Quart de Poblet, villages in the west of the Valencian horta, were not expelled from their lands until 1336. By the mid-fourteenth century the mudéjars who remained in the horta were concentrated in the ur-

20. The original reads, "segons que antiguament es e fo stablit e acostumat en temps de Sarrahins." Vicente Branchat, *Tradao de derechos y regalías que corresponden al real patrimonio en el reyno de Valencia y de la jurisdicción del intendente como subrogado en lugar del antiguo bayle general*, vol. 3 (Valencia, 1784), 276–77, quoted in Glick, *Irrigation and Society*, 234n24.

21. Glick, *Irrigation and Society*, 235–236.

22. Barceló, Kirchner, and Navarro, *El agua que no duerme*.

23. Guinot, "Una Historia de la huerta de Valencia," 74.

24. Torró, "Els camperols musulmans," 202–203.

ban *morerias* (Muslim quarters) of the city of Valencia and nearby Mislata and Paterna. Such morerias were often newly created after the conquest from a mix of internally displaced people. These communities had little institutional history or connection to an Andalusi past, and their inhabitants were mostly artisans and laborers who knew nothing of irrigation customs.[25]

After the conquest, royal officials distributed land and property to the king's followers in a process known as *repartiment*. Much of the kingdom was granted as large seigneurial lordships. But in the horta of Valencia itself, only the estates and villages farthest from the city were distributed in this way. The rest of the irrigated land was carved into smaller allodial properties (*heretats*), of between two and ten *jovades* each.[26] These plots were given to Christian commoners who (the crown hoped) would settle in the horta.[27] Many recipients seem to have sold or exchanged their lands in the first generation after the conquest, so a stable colonial population only arrived in the later thirteenth century.[28]

The dynamics of Christian colonization further reshaped the land. Christian settlers abandoned many Andalusi settlements, choosing either to found new villages or to cluster in a few walled towns. At first they used Andalusi toponyms, but in time many places were given Christian names.[29] The shape of the agricultural land also changed. As part of the repartiment, royal surveyors mapped out the properties to be distributed using Christian units of measurement to impose a rectilinear grid. Irrigated fields and channels resisted assimilation into the grid, but in places the shape of plots was altered to fit the number of jovades officials wished to assign.[30] The imposition of seigneurial lordship at the edges of the horta also changed land and water use.[31] Lords tended to

25. Guinot, "Una Historia de la huerta de Valencia," 72–74; Torró, "Els camperols musulmans," 204. The foundation date of the moreria of Valencia itself is unknown, as is the geographic origin of the people who lived there. Enric Guinot Rodríguez, "La conquesta i la colonització del regne de València per Jaume I. Balanç i noves perspectives," in *Jaume I: Commemoració del VIII centenari del naixement de Jaume I*, vol. 2, ed. María Teresa Ferrer i Mallol (Barcelona: Institut d'Estudis Catalans, 2013), 528.

26. One jovada was the area a team of oxen could plow in a day—approximately three hectares.

27. Enric Guinot Rodríguez, "El repartiment feudal de l'horta de València al segle XIII: Jerarquització social i reordenació del paisatge rural," in *Repartiments medievals a la Corona d'Aragó*, ed. Enric Guinot Rodríguez and Josep Torró (Valencia: Publicacions de la Universitat de València, 2007), 123.

28. Guinot, "La conquesta i la colonització del regne de València," 526.

29. Ferran García-Oliver, "L'espai transformat. El país Valencià de la colonización feudal," in Ferrer i Mallol, *Jaume I: Commemoració del VIII centenari del naixement*, 2:538–539.

30. Surveyors measured the dimensions of these plots in *cordas* and area in jovades. The corda was defined in Valencia as twenty spans of the king's arms, or 40.77 meters. Enric Guinot Rodríguez, "Arpenteurs en terres de conquête. La pratique de la mesure de la terre en pays valencien pendant le XIIIe siècle," *Expertise et valeur des choses au Moyen Age*, vol. 2, *Savoirs, écritures, pratiques*, ed. Laurent Feller and Ana Rodriguez (Madrid: Casa de Velázquez, 2016), 290–293. See also Torró, "Field and Canal Building."

31. Enric Guinot and Josep Torró, "Introducción: ¿Existe una hidráulica agraria 'feudal'?," in *Hidráulica agraria y sociedad feudal: Prácticas, técnicas, espacio*, ed. Enric Guinot and Josep Torró, (Valencia: Publicacions de la Universitat de València, 2012), 12. For a similar colonial transformation in the Baltic

adjust irrigation structures to prioritize milling over irrigation, because milling was a more immediate source of feudal revenue.[32] Peasants after the conquest tended to use irrigated lands primarily to improve the yields of crops that did not require irrigation—particularly wheat, in which rents were paid.[33]

As Enric Guinot and Josep Torró have shown, settlers also irrigated more intensively. In some cases they extended existing canals to water new agricultural areas, and in others they added branch canals within a horta so that no parcel of land went unirrigated. Because Andalusi irrigation systems tended to concentrate water on the best fields, irrigated plots were interspersed with dry-farmed fields and orchards. Repartiment officials designated all land as either irrigated (*regadiu*) or dry (*secà*). Regadiu, which was subject to higher taxes, included not only land currently irrigated but also land that could be irrigated in the future. The conquerors' bureaucratic vision of the Valencian landscape thus incentivized settlers to create a continuous carpet of irrigated fields within the boundaries of each horta.[34]

Where Andalusi canals had returned water to the river, the systems of the postconquest period tended to absorb all the water that they could take, though this was not without consequences. The Guadalaviar had been navigable up to the city walls in the Andalusi period, but postconquest irrigation diminished its flow until it became too shallow for boat traffic.[35] Meanwhile, water diverted to irrigation increasingly seeped into the Albufera, turning it from salt to fresh water.[36] As early as 1342, King Pere the Ceremonious enlisted a Valencian citizen, Guillem Fluvia, to redirect irrigation water from the Albufera back to the river so as not to harm the fish that brought revenue to the crown. These efforts were insufficient to counteract the influx of irrigation water into the Albufera. By the early modern period, as Carles Sanchis Ibor has shown, it was a freshwater lagoon.[37]

---

region, see Mariusz Lamentowicz, Katarzyna Marcisz, Piotr Guzowski, Mariusz Gałka, Andrei-Cosmin Diaconu, and Piotr Kołaczek, "How Joannites' Economy Eradicated Primeval Forest and Created Anthroecosystems in Medieval Central Europe." *Scientific Reports* 10, no. 18775 (2020), https://doi.org/10.1038/s41598-020-75692-4.

32. Glick and Kirchner, "Hydraulic Systems and Technologies of Islamic Spain," 324.

33. Furió, "La domesticación del medio natural," 84–85.

34. Torró, "Field and Canal Building," 83–101; Enric Guinot Rodriguez, "L'horta de Valencia a la baixa Edat Mitjana. De sistema hidràulica andalusi a feudal," *Afers* 51 (2005): 271–300.

35. Carmona and Ruiz, "Historical Morphogenesis of the Turia River," 141–142.

36. This shift to fresh water may have begun even before the conquest, as a result of intense flood activity during the Islamic period. Pilar Carmona, José-Miguel Ruiz Pérez, Ana-Maria Blázquez, María López-Belzunce, Santiago Riera, and Héctor Orengo, "Environmental Evolution and Mid-Late Holocene Climate Events in the Valencia Lagoon (Mediterranean Coast of Spain)," *The Holocene* 26, no. 11 (2016): 1750–1765.

37. Sanchis, *Regadiu i canvi ambiental a l'Albufera de València*, 81–82, 98, 106–112, 145.

Although their cumulative effects could be profound, most postconquest irrigation projects were small-scale initiatives undertaken by individual farmers or private lords. In the later thirteenth century the crown did sponsor two entirely new canals: at Alzira on the Xúquer and at Vila-real on the Millars River. These projects, particularly the Xúquer canal, were on a significantly larger scale than Andalusi irrigation had been. The Xúquer is so powerful and flood-prone that Andalusi farmers did not use it to irrigate at all. To harness such a flow, the New Canal of Alzira (later the Royal Xúquer Canal) required a much larger diversion dam. The canal was to bring water some thirty-five kilometers north, crossing the Magre River by means of a siphon. Between 1258 and 1274, however, only twenty-two kilometers were actually constructed. The final stretch, including the river crossing, was not completed until the eighteenth century.[38] As construction proceeded, the crown distributed newly valuable land along the canal route to colonists.[39] The canal on the Millars also spurred the foundation of a new town—Vila-real—just after construction began.[40]

Christian settlers also sought to extend the total area under cultivation. While Andalusi farmers had cultivated only the best land, thereby minimizing risk, Christian lords and their tenants sought to maximize income. The original Furs of Valencia gave the inhabitants the right to plant new fields, and in 1261 Jaume the Conqueror also granted the right to break ground in mountains, marshes, and riverbanks "that were not worked in the ancient times of the Saracens."[41] As Antoni Furió puts it, uncultivated lands began to be seen as "lands yet to be cultivated." In the mountains, much of this land was forest, which (as elsewhere in Europe in this period), settlers began to clear. In the coastal plain, the uncultivated land was marsh, exploited as a source of pasture and wild products like salt, soda ash, fish, and game. Many of the more than thirty marshlands along the Valencian coast continued to be used in this way after the conquest, but some were granted in small parcels to be drained for agricultural use. Although

38. Torró, "Field and Canal Building," 97–99.

39. See Robert I. Burns, ed., *Diplomatarium of the Crusader Kingdom of Valencia, The Registered Charters of Its Conqueror Jaume I, 1257–1276*, vol. 3, *Transition in Crusader Valencia: Years of Triumph, Years of War, 1264–1270* (Princeton, NJ: Princeton University Press, 2001), docs. 933, 939, 948, 950, 951, 967, 988.

40. Enric Guinot y Sergi Selma, "La construcción del paisaje en una huerta feudal: La Séquia Major de Vila-Real (siglos XIII–XV)," in *Hidráulica agraria y sociedad feudal: Prácticas, técnicas, espacio*, ed. Josep Torró and Enric Guinot (Valencia: Publicacions de la Universitat de València, 2012), 103–146.

41. The original reads, "en temps antich de sarrahins no·s solien laurar." *Furs de València* VII, ed. G. Colón and A. Garcia (Barcelona: Editoral Barcino, 1999), 165–167, quoted in Josep Torró, "Després dels musulmans: les primeres operacions colonitzadores al regne de València i la qüestió de les tècniques hidràuliques," in *Arqueologia medieval: La transformació de la frontera medieval musulmana*, ed. Flocel Sabaté Curull and Jesús Sucarrat (Lleida: Pagès, 2009), 96.

this process was slow and incomplete in many places (see chapter 2), it represented a shift in the use of the land under Christian rule.[42]

Glick famously described the Valencian conquest as a "neutron bomb scenario" in which the conquerors occupied the homes and fields of their vanished enemies. Subsequent research has shown that this was far from the case.[43] Over the course of several generations, nearly the entire mudéjar population was internally or externally displaced, shattering the continuity of irrigation practices. Nor did the Christian settlers simply pick up where their predecessors left off; rather, they began almost immediately to reshape the landscape to serve the needs of their new society.

The City Council in the Extramural Landscape

By the fourteenth century, the period of the earliest extant city council records, the landscape outside the city had for generations been shaped and reshaped according to the needs of its inhabitants. While Glick emphasizes the autonomy of irrigation communities from the city government, the council of Valencia did have an agenda in the horta. Councils of the late fourteenth and early fifteenth centuries took an active role in modifying certain parts of this environment and legislated to maintain infrastructure and remove hazards to human health. Although policing the horta often stretched the limits of the council's regulatory capacity, successive councils sought to preserve the health and productivity of the extramural space. As a result, the council documents stress the potential for human mismanagement to trigger a crisis in this constructed landscape.

Although the city's authority extended almost to the edges of the horta, irrigators themselves governed day-to-day matters of water distribution. The council intervened mainly as an advocate for the city in times of water shortage, but it also had oversight over the entire system. Irrigation was organized by canal; the space irrigated by each mother canal and its tributaries formed a self-governing community that included landholders, millers, and others with rights to the water. In the horta of Valencia, unlike in some other places in Iberia, rights to water were inalienable from rights to land; users paid a tax (*cequiatge*) for maintenance and met annually to elect officers and organize construction and repair. Once a year the water would be diverted out of the canal so that landholders could remove vegetation and detritus from their por-

---

42. Furió, "La domesticación del medio natural," 62–65.

43. Thomas F. Glick, *From Muslim Fortress to Christian Castle: Social and Cultural Change in Medieval Spain* (Manchester, UK: Manchester University Press, 1995), 166. See also Torró's critique of this phrase in "Field and Canal Building," 80–81.

tion of the channel.[44] The timing of this disruption could be contentious. In April 1415 the irrigators of Puçol, at the tail end of the Montcada canal, protested that such a diversion would exacerbate the effects of a drought, risking the loss of the harvest and the "ruin and depopulation" of the village.[45]

The officer in charge of maintenance, and of enforcing water regulations, was known as a *cequier*. He had authority along a single canal, and was by tradition one of its cultivators. The Furs of Valencia state that he and his assistants were to ensure "that no one dare steal water, nor disturb the canals, nor cut off the water of any canal, nor divert it through another, nor break down the main canals or branches." Glick's analysis of two surviving cequier fine books shows that while fine rates for these offenses were set high, actual fines collected were much lower, as cequiers tended to be sympathetic to the plight of irrigators.[46] In 1334 the city council issued a proclamation against those who "by their own authority have made . . . water channels into their properties . . . and in great damage to the other neighboring water users unlawfully divide and reduce the waters of the other users . . . [resulting in] conflicts, hatreds, ill will, and corruption of the waters, and what is more serious, woundings and deaths."[47] The council may have been exaggerating this last problem. Theft and waste of water were the most common offenses, but only a small fraction of incidents turned violent.[48]

The city's jurisdiction was strongest in the urban core, but did extend into the countryside. City and countryside were not entirely distinct; many townspeople, including some of the councilmen, also held land and were part of irrigation communities. The outer boundaries of urban jurisdiction—the "general contribution"—were roughly coterminous with the boundaries of the horta, but the city exercised more direct fiscal control over the "particular contribution," which consisted of the walled city and its closest suburban villages.[49] In much of the horta the city government intervened primarily through the position of *sobrecequier*. While each cequier was locally appointed, the sobrecequier,

44. Glick, *Irrigation and Society*, 12–14, 31, 34–37.

45. ARV, Gobernación 2208, Mano 19, 11r–v.

46. Glick, *Irrigation and Society*, 38–39, 52–64.

47. "Alguns persons per lur propria autoritat haien fets & facen correnties daygues per lurs heretats continuan de dia & de nuyt en gran dampnatge dels altres hereters circumvehins partaban mirvan les aygues als altres hereters contra la forma ordenada en Fur de Valencia. Per les quals correnties son appareylats contrasts odis & mals voluntats & corrupcio dels aygues & ço que seria pus greu nafres & morts." AMV, A-3, 94r–v.

48. In the Castelló fine books, taking "forbidden water" (*aygua vedada*) and "wasting water" (*lançar l'aygua a perdicio*) accounted for 29 and 17.3 percent of fines, respectively. Only 1.6 percent were for "taking water by force" (*levar l'aygua forcivolment*). Glick, *Irrigation and Society*, 54.

49. Vicente Melió, *La "Junta de Murs i Valls": Historia de las obras publicas en la Valencia del antiguo régimen, siglos XIV–XVIII* (Valencia: Consell Valencià de Cultura, 1991), 48–52.

or chief irrigation officer, was a municipal position. At some times the council appointed an individual to this office, while at others the jurats themselves assumed the role. Through the sobrecequier the council was able to exert authority over the regulation of the entire horta, but rarely involved itself in the affairs of individual canals.

During droughts the council did intervene in matters of water distribution in order to secure water for the city. As with normal water use, distribution in times of shortage was largely a matter of long-standing custom. When the water supply was insufficient for all users, a system of turns (*tanda*) was imposed, with each mother canal allowed to receive water from the river only on certain days. When it was another community's turn, the water would be diverted away from the head of that canal; when the tanda was theirs, it would be allowed to flow in. This offset the inevitable imbalance between upstream and downstream users; without the tanda, the upstream canals of Mislata, Montcada, Quart, and Tormos would use all the water before it reached the users of Favara, Mestalla, Rascanya, and Na Rovella (see map 1). The city government, in its role as sobrecequier, was instrumental in establishing the details of the tanda. In August 1313, for example, the city gave the four upstream canals seven *mulnars* of water from Monday morning to Friday evening. From Friday evening to Sunday evening, seven mulnars went to the downstream canals. The use of the mulnar, a unit equivalent to the water necessary to turn one mill wheel, shows the council's priorities in this distribution. Montcada, the canal on which most of the city's mills were located, was allotted three out of the seven mulnars, and the minor canal of En Pere Mercer was allowed to take water on both the upstream and the downstream days because the council deemed "the mills that have been constructed in that canal . . . of greater service to the city than almost all the other mills."[50] Idle mills were the city's most pressing concern during a drought, as lack of flour could cause famine in the city much more quickly than harvest failure. During very severe droughts, the council also sought water, grain, and flour from beyond the boundaries of the horta (see chapter 5).

When no drought threatened, council regulations were intended to preserve the space as a whole. While it was not involved in the daily policing of irrigation, the council was responsible for the maintenance of the horta's roads,

---

50. "Cafals dels molins que en aquella céquia són constrohits, los quals són a major servii de la ciutat que quasi tots los altres cafals de molins." The text says that the downstream canals will receive the water from Wednesday (*dimecres*) to Sunday rather than Friday (*divendres*) to Sunday, but I interpret that as a copying error. Since the purpose was to divide the water, overlapping time periods would not make sense in context. *El Primer Manual de Consells de la Ciutat de València (1306–1326)*, ed. Vicent Anyó Garcia (Valencia: Oficina de Publicacions de l'Ajuntament de Valencia, 2001), 93r–94v.

which mostly followed the layout of the canal network.[51] Roads that ran along canals sometimes suffered from the proximity. The council of 1360 forbade anyone cleaning a canal to heap the excavated slime (*tarquim*) on the roadbed. According to Glick's analysis, flooding the roads was the third most common offense for which cequiers levied fines.[52] Despite these efforts, in 1386 the council declared that "the roads frequently receive great damage by the fault of the cequiers and the irrigators, who do not take care that the water . . . does not spill or run in the roads." This, of course, burdened the city with the cost of repairs. The council therefore ordered the cequiers to collect the cost of repair from the perpetrators on top of the usual fine.[53] This measure proved difficult to enforce. Ten years later, the roads were still being ruined "by the fault of the irrigators and by the fault and negligence of the cequiers." To the council's frustration, the cequiers seemed to be sympathetic to the difficulty of irrigating without spilling water. As the *mostaçaf*, the municipal official charged with protecting the roads, was already "occupied with other affairs," the council appointed "a good person [to] have singular care and special charge" of the matter of water spillage. The new official's compensation would be drawn from the fines he collected.[54] This convenient plan hit a snag when the city was unable to recruit or retain a suitable individual to the unsalaried post. Once again, in 1417, "the roads [were] destroyed and the drainage ditches full of the water that the irrigators alongside the roads . . . [had thrown] on them." This time the council assigned the responsibility to the municipal inspector in charge of drinking troughs and the weekly flushing of the urban sewers. In addition to these duties, he was to walk the royal roads of the horta "once or twice a month," collecting fines that would supplement the salary he received from the city.[55] This arrangement, too, seems to have been ineffective; in 1450 the jurats complained to Prince Joan that the roads were once again ruined by water because the cequiers were "themselves landholders and cultivators participating in the abuse." Finally, the jurats passed enforcement off to the *racional*, or city treasurer, an increasingly powerful figure in city government who

51. AMV, A-18, 197v.

52. Glick, *Irrigation and Society*, 54.

53. "Quels dits Camins prenien sovin grans pejoraments a culpa de Cequiers & de Regants qui nos curaven guardar que les aygues dels Rechs no donassen o no discorreguessen en los camins." AMV, A-18, 181r–v.

54. "Avegades per culpa de regants & avegades per culpa & negligencia de cequier. E fos estat raonat que fora o seria cosa expedient & molt profitosa que aço en special fos comanat a una bona persona la qual hagues singular cura & special carrech daço." AMV, A-21, 40r. As Glick notes, cequiers were often irrigators themselves. *Irrigation and Society*, 37.

55. AMV, A-26, 217r–v.

may have had more resources to deal with the problem.[56] Such enforcement difficulties were fairly common for the council, which, like many urban governments, lacked the capacity to enforce its decrees throughout its territories. These regulatory efforts show that the council did at least claim the authority to police the horta and that it was particularly concerned with keeping infrastructure safe from harm.

Aside from the road network, the council also sought to regulate other hazards that threatened to damage the horta. Beekeeping and hunting were both forbidden there; bees were thought to harm the grape harvest, and hunting encouraged trampling the fields.[57] Hoofed domestic animals, however, posed the most serious threat. If allowed to graze an irrigated field, their hooves broke down the banks of the canals, thereby "blocking the running water . . . [so that] the water pools and destroys the cultivated lands and the harvests that are sown in them, and makes them marshy such that not only do they not produce crops, but they also infect the air, from which many damages and illnesses ensue in the city."[58] From the early fourteenth century on, the council declared the space of the horta off-limits to grazing animals: sheep, goats, cattle, horses, mules, donkeys, and pigs.[59] Before 1333 the penalty was the loss of the animal in question, but in July of that year the council declared this to be too "rigorous and weighty" and reduced the fine to six diners for each sheep and goat, and twelve (or one sou) for all other animals. The fines doubled if the animals was found at night.[60] This was still a hefty fine at a time when the daily wage for an unskilled laborer was roughly one sou for a woman and two for a man.[61] Municipal officials known as *guardians* were in charge of supervising animal activity in the horta. Although the guardians, unlike private guards, were supposed to be immune to bribes from herders, enforcing the rules remained a complicated business. This was even harder when the offend-

56. ARV, Real, 272, 143r, cited in Glick, *Irrigation and Society*, 21.

57. Beehives were forbidden only during July and August, when the grapes were ripe. AMV, A-1, 68v–71r; AMV, A-3, 12v–15v. See also María Antonia Carmona Ruiz, "La Apicultura Sevillana a Fines de la Edad Media," *Anuario de estudios medievales* 30, no. 1 (2000): 394–395. For the ban on hunting, see, for example, AMV, A-2, 64r–v.

58. "Les vaques qui son e han acostumar de estar en los brusquils enrunant les cequies e braçals de aquelles en enpathant les aygues decorrents vers lAlbufera e per no poder decorrer en aquella les dits aygues stan enbassades e guasten les terres que son stades reduhides a agricultura guastans aquelles e los splets que en aquelles son sembrats e axi son fets margalenques e tals que no solament no donen splet algu mas encara infectionen layre de que son subsegueixen a la dita Ciutat molts dans e malalties en gran dan de la cosa publica." AMV, A-43, 56r–v.

59. AMV, A-2, 10r; AMV, A-3, 208v; AMV, A-3, 62r–v.

60. AMV, A-3, 78v–79r.

61. This is the rate of pay for unskilled laborers in the earliest surviving account books of urban infrastructure projects (1380). AMV, d3-1.

ing animals belonged to other lords. In 1335 the city wrote to the archbishop of Zaragoza, lord of Paterna, complaining that not only was a man from Paterna pasturing animals in the horta but the *alcayt* (governor of the Muslim community) of Paterna had attacked those trying to enforce the ban on animals, leaving two Christians and one Muslim dead. The bishop claimed to be unaware that any such assault had taken place.[62]

The demand for pasturing near the city was largely driven by urban markets. As a concession to this demand, the city's butchers were allowed to keep up to fifty head of sheep in the horta to assure "a sufficient provision of mutton for the city's needs." The butchers were, however, to keep the beasts under constant guard and to pay for any damage that they caused.[63] Similar licenses were also occasionally granted to private citizens to keep goats in the horta so that the city would have a sufficient supply of milk.[64] The city granted even more pasture licenses in the Devesa, the scrub forest that extended south along the coast, between the marshes and the sea. As part of the Albufera, the Devesa belonged to the crown rather than to the city, but in 1335 the council invoked a thirteenth-century royal privilege permitting Valencian citizens to pasture there.[65] The Devesa was regulated as a kind of inverse of the horta; agriculture was forbidden, and the land was reserved for hunting, fishing, and pasture. As in the horta, hoofed animals damaged the landscape, breaking down the banks of the Albufera's natural waterways, churning up mud, and scaring away the fish from which the crown derived much its revenue.[66] The overseer of the Devesa attempted in 1341 to block Valencian citizens from pasturing there, but the council resisted this prohibition.[67] The Devesa was the outlet that allowed the horta to exist as a purely agricultural space.

In regulating the landscape around the city of Valencia, the council's other main objective was to avoid sources of disease. In Galenic medical theory, epidemic disease was the result of an external source of corruption—air, water, or food—affecting a number of bodies simultaneously. Corrupt air, or miasma, was the most common,[68] and could have a number of causes (as will be discussed in

62. AMV, g3-1, 54r–55r.

63. AMV, A-4, 51v.

64. AMV, g3-4, 6r; AMV, g3-7, 16r.

65. AMV, A-3, 118r–v.

66. Sanchis, *Regadiu i canvi ambiental a l'Albufera de València*, 42–43.

67. AMV, A-4, 38v, 133r–v, 328r–329v.

68. Jon Arrizabalaga, "Facing the Black Death: Perceptions and Reactions of University Medical Practitioners," in *Practical Medicine from Salerno to the Black Death*, ed. Luis García-Ballester, Roger French, Jon Arrizabalaga, and Andrew Cunningham (Cambridge: Cambridge University Press, 1994), 245; Carole Rawcliffe, *Urban Bodies: Communal Health in Late Medieval English Towns and Cities* (Woodbridge, UK: Boydell and Brewer, 2013), 55–115.

more detail in chapter 6), but the city council was primarily concerned with the most prosaic: decaying matter that corrupted the air around it and caused illness to those nearby. The greatest threat to health was stagnant water. As long as it was flowing, even dirty water was not a problem. The Na Rovella canal, which flowed through the city and provided water to the sewer system, was by all accounts filthy. It was known as the *molla de sang i foc* (depths of blood and fire) because it was used to clean the slaughterhouses and to fight fires.[69] Every week, from Saturday evening to Sunday evening, all of the water of Na Rovella was allowed to run through the sewer network, to flush away any obstructions and carry "corruptions and infections" away from the city.[70] Only if the water pooled and became stagnant (as when a canal was damaged) was it considered a health hazard.

Certain human activities actually required stagnant water, and the council sought to keep those as far as possible from the urban population. The most common was rice irrigation. Following Andalusi agricultural technique, medieval Valencians sowed seedlings in March and harvested the rice in September. In late spring they constructed channels (*correnties*) to direct water into the fields, and left it standing throughout the summer to irrigate the plants and discourage pests and weeds. The city government was less than pleased with this labor-saving cultivation method. Rice required much more water than any other crop, and this could, the council complained, increase irrigation disputes among neighbors and water runoff on the roads. And as if this were not enough, the stagnant water left on the fields through the hot summer was thought to be a source of disease in the horta. For these reasons the council repeatedly banned the practice of rice irrigation from 1335 on.[71] As with its other regulatory efforts, enforcement was an uphill battle. In 1388 the council attempted to ban even the sale of irrigated rice within the city, ordering that it be burned "like false merchandise." Less than a month later, however, the merchants of the city prevailed on the council to delay enforcement until the following year.[72] The sympathies of inspectors seem often to have lain with the farmers; in 1396 the council initiated a fine for corrupt inspectors who "for a price or for pity conceal[ed] . . . the making of correnties in rice fields."[73] While fourteenth-century councils stressed both disease and dis-

69. Carles Sanchis Ibor, "Acequia, Saneamiento y Trazados Urbanos in Valencia," in Dauksis and Taberner, *Historia de la Ciudad*, 2:93–95.

70. AMV, A-4, 412r.

71. AMV, A-3, 101v. Other bans can be found in 1341, AMV, A-4, 56r–v; and in 1360 (regarding Paterna), AMV, A-14, 6r–10r.

72. AMV, A-19, 24r, 25v–26r.

73. "Veedors elets al fet de les correnties dels arroços en anys passats haien commeses fraus celan o abcegan per preu o per prechs alcuns daquells." AMV, A-21, 50v.

order, by the late fifteenth century the councils banned correnties "to preserve this republic in health and so that infections of the air may be more easily
avoided."[74] Public health bans on rice irrigation continued through the early
sixteenth century.

Another profitable agricultural product, flax, also caused public health concerns. In order to extract usable linen fiber from the stalks of the flax plant,
the stalks had to be retted, or left submerged in water, until the rest of the
plant rotted away. This process created a noxious liquid that was lethal to
aquatic organisms. Cities all over medieval Europe banned or restricted flax
retting, often on public health grounds.[75] During the summer of 1376 the Valencian council expressed concern over the flax and hemp retting pools below
the royal palace, whence "stench and infection or corruption in damage to the
public good" came both to the palace and to the city. The number of retting
pools in this area had grown in recent years, and the stench in the summer
was said to be unbearable. The council therefore sought to limit the pools to
the number traditionally located there.[76]

The following year, royal bailiff Francesc Marrades, who stood to receive
some of the income from these pools, appeared before the council to protest
this limit. The accusations of stench and corruption were, he said, unjustified;
little stench emerged from the pools, and it was only noticeable to those very
nearby. He asserted, moreover, that there had been no infection in the city as a
result of the pools. In response, the council ordered that the site be inspected by
doctors to determine the truth of the case.[77] Here the council likely expected
validation of a common belief: flax pools were a known health hazard. A nui-
sance is in the eye of the beholder, however; the council's vigilance here was
doubtless due in part to its lack of direct financial stake in flax retting or rice
cultivation. Nonetheless, the council did prioritize the dangers of stagnant water
over these profitable activities, particularly in the immediate vicinity of the city.

Not everyone in the city, the horta, or the Devesa had the same aims for
the use of these spaces. The council's efforts to regulate according to its own

74. "Per preservar aquesta tan insigne republica en santitat e perque pus facilment les infeccions
dels ayres sien evitades." AMV, A-40, 212r–v.

75. Hoffman, An Environmental History of Medieval Europe, 226; see also, more generally, 64–265.
André Guillerme, The Age of Water: The Urban Environment in the North of France, A. D. 300–1800 (College Station: Texas A&M University Press, 1988), 100–101, suggests that flax retting was not environ-
mentally important. Richard Hoffman, "Economic Development and Aquatic Ecosystems in
Medieval Europe," American Historical Review 101, no. 3 (1996): 631–669, contradicts this. On surviving flax retting pools in Aragon, see Christopher M. Gerrard, "Contest and Co-operation: Strategies
for Medieval and Later Irrigation along the Upper Huecha Valley, Aragón, North-East Spain," Water
History 3, no. 1 (2011): 18.

76. "Pudor e infeccio o corrupcio en dan de la cosa publica." AMV, A-17, 65v.

77. AMV, A-17, 65v, 103v–104v.

agenda were, of course, assertions of urban authority into the countryside. As such they were quite frequently foiled by the council's limited capacity to police the area it sought to rule. What is noteworthy is less the council's success in regulating the horta than its ambition to do so, and how this ambition focused on the preservation of the horta's environment.

Long before the Christian conquest, the humans who lived around the city of Valencia shaped its landscape to suit their needs. The process of Christian colonization reshaped this rural landscape to suit the needs of a new society. Even before they sought to change the landscape themselves, their statutes treated it as a system vulnerable to human mismanagement. Rather than prioritizing profit, the council in many cases chose to limit the uses of the space in order to avoid damage to the system or threats to human health. Both degradation and disease resulted from human activities—often those that misdirected the flow of water over the land.

CHAPTER 2

Waters Dedicated to Some Purposes
New Infrastructure

Throughout the autumn and winter of 1371, no rain fell in the Valencian plain. The harvest was poor, and sickness was spreading in nearby villages.[1] In February, one of the councilmen reminded his colleagues of a privilege that the city had in its archive. Enrique II, who had recently seized the Castilian throne, had granted Valencia the right to "take and divert into the Guadalaviar, in whole or in part, the water of the Cabriol River," a tributary of the Xúquer River that flowed through Castile near the Guadalaviar watershed. The council agreed that this water would be useful and, besides, it was "of little value to obtain privileges and graces if they are not used." It therefore authorized a committee of four citizens, "together with masters or persons expert in such things," to go to the Cabriol at the city's expense "and see it with their own eyes and examine whether [the diversion] is possible to do and with what or how great expense."[2]

---

1. "En tot lautumpne prop passat e en linvern present no ha plogut per la qual rao se es mesa molt gran carestia de blats en la terra com per rao de malalties & mortaldats que son en alcuns partides circumvehins al dit Regne." AMV, A-16, 43v.

2. AMV, A-16, 62v–63r. The document refers only to "King Enric," but this must be Enrique II, the first member of the House of Trastámara, because Enrique I's reign was before the conquest of Valencia. The illegitimate son of Alfonso XI, Enrique II had only secured the throne three years earlier, after joining the War of the Two Peres on the Aragonese side had allowed to him to capture and kill his half-brother, Pedro the Cruel. This privilege may have been a nod to the role the city of Valencia played during that war.

This expedition was the first of a series of proposals in the late fourteenth and early fifteenth centuries to build infrastructure to address persistent environmental challenges. In 1372 Valencia was emerging from more than two decades of political crisis with a government much expanded in size and ambition. When a series of environmental crises struck the city in the 1370s, this government sprang into action. The councilmen planned major construction projects in response to crises in the extramural landscape. Most of these projects aimed to bring water where it was needed or remove it where it posed a threat to human activities. In that sense, the council sought not only to respond to environmental crisis but also to improve the landscape that it ruled.

This book makes a case for the significance of municipal governments like Valencia as environmental actors, and for a city-level approach to premodern environmental history. Several early modern environmental histories have associated infrastructure projects with the rise of state power and scientific expertise. Medieval governments are often treated as static prologues to these efforts, aspiring merely to regulation and repair.[3] A municipal view complicates this narrative. While many of its projects failed to come together, the Valencian council showed a marked enthusiasm for planning new canals and other infrastructure. On the local level, at least, zeal for improvement was very much a medieval phenomenon.[4]

Christian colonization in the thirteenth century had transformed Valencia's landscape, but the city council did not seek to direct this process before the late fourteenth century. Starting in the 1370s, however, the council began to propose infrastructure projects to reshape the environments under its rule. This flurry of projects was particular to the last quarter of the fourteenth century and the first quarter of the fifteenth; neither before nor after did the medieval council seek transformation on this scale. This is not, therefore, a story of the precocious modernity of the Valencian government. Although significant while it lasted, improvement was a strategy only pursued for a few decades, with mixed success.

Like the diversion of the Cabriol, most of these projects were begun in response to natural disaster. Facing short-term crises, these councils chose to initiate infrastructure projects designed to address environmental hazards.[5]

---

3. See, for example, Eric H. Ash, *The Draining of the Fens: Projectors, Popular Politics, and State Building in Early Modern England* (Baltimore: Johns Hopkins University Press, 2017), 10; and Wing, *Roots of Empire*, 25, 46–55.

4. Similar efforts have been documented elsewhere in Europe. See, for example, Michele Campopiano, "Rural Communities, Land Clearance and Water Management in the Po Valley in the Central and Late Middle Ages," *Journal of Medieval History* 39, no. 4 (2013): 377–393.

5. Areas near the North Sea responded similarly to problems with coastal flooding. See James A. Galloway, "Storm Flooding, Coastal Defence and Land Use around the Thames Estuary and Tidal

Such efforts may have been intended to protect the city from similar crises in the future. Changes to the landscape around the city also projected the council's power beyond the walls. This new approach to the extra-urban environment emerged in the context of Valencia's recovery from the crises of the mid-fourteenth century.

Crisis and Opportunity, 1347–1370

In the 1340s the city council was troubled by growing debts. The military expenses of King Pere the Ceremonious's 1344 annexation of the short-lived Kingdom of Mallorca, when added to the costs of defense against pirates, placed tremendous fiscal pressure on the Crown and its creditors.[6] The city of Valencia was among these creditors, having granted the king some 1,200,000 sous between 1339 and 1346. A series of bad harvests in 1343, 1344, and 1347 heightened the strain; chronicler Melchior Miralles termed 1347 "the year of the great hunger" (el any de gran fam).[7]

That same year also brought civil war. The annexation of Mallorca had been the first of a series of policy moves by which King Pere sought to concentrate authority into his own hands. The last straw for Valencia was the king's decision in March 1347 to make his daughter, Constança—rather than his brother, Jaume—his heir. Masculine succession was the custom in the Crown of Aragon, and this decision, taken as it was in the royal council rather than the Corts (the kingdom's parliamentary body) infuriated both nobility and urban elites. In their alarm at the king's abrogation of their traditional rights, Valencians proclaimed themselves to be "more captive than the Jews" (pus catius érem que juheus). Facing both debt and disenfranchisement, the city government led the formation of what is known as the Union of Valencia on June 1, 1347. This movement, made up of urban elites, revolted in support of Jaume, while much

River c. 1250–1450," Journal of Medieval History 35, no. 2 (2009), 171–188; and Tim Soens, "Flood Security in the Medieval and Early Modern North Sea Area: A Question of Entitlement?," Environment and History 19, no. 2 (2013): 209–232

6. "Introducció," in Diplomatari de la Unió del Regne de València (1347–1349), ed. Mateu Rodrigo Lizondo (Valencia: Fonts Historiques Valencianes, 2013), 13.

7. Mark D. Meyerson, "Victims and Players: The Attack of the Union of Valencia on the Jews of Morvedre," in Religion, Text and Society in Medieval Spain and Northern Europe: Essays in Honor of J. N. Hillgarth, ed. Thomas E. Burman, Mark D. Meyerson and Leah Shopkow (Toronto: Pontifical Institute of Medieval Studies), 2002, 70–102; Melchior Miralles, Crònica i dietari del capellà d'Alfons el Magnànim, ed. Mateu Rodrigo Lizondo (Valencia: Publicacions de la Universitat de València, 2011, 3.31, p. 150. The city council records are incomplete during this year, and make no mention of this famine, so we must rely on Miralles's account.

of the Valencian nobility (and some towns, including Xátiva) sided with the king.

The union won early victories against royal forces in late 1347. In the spring of 1348 the king attempted to negotiate from the castle of Morvedre, just to the north of the city of Valencia. Morvedre's rebel sympathizers handed the king over to the unionist leaders in Valencia in March. In May the Black Death arrived in the city. Fearing he would die in their care, the rebels released the king in early June. Pere then rallied his supporters and defeated the union forces, reentering Valencia on December 10, 1348. The king was extraordinarily harsh in his repression of the revolt; between those punished, those killed in battle, and those dead of plague, the ruling class of the city suffered almost a complete turnover. Nevertheless, the king remained wary of the council for some years thereafter.[8]

As early as 1342, the jurats had proposed constructing a new, expanded ring of walls around the city, replacing the outgrown preconquest defenses. The project was put on hold in the 1340s due to the city's crippling debts, but by late November 1351 the council began to organize financing and construction for a new moat (vall), to defend the "limits of the city that are not defended."[9] In mid-December, however, royal councilor Joan Escrivà informed the council that the king did not believe that the city needed new walls. Only three years after the revolt, Pere did not trust the city of Valencia not to betray him. He therefore ordered that any defensive works the city had begun in the suburbs "be immediately undone and broken down."[10]

Pressures both political and environmental soon changed the king's views on Valencian defenses. In the summer of 1356, as war with Castile loomed, he allowed repair of the old walls, the digging of a new moat, and eventually the creation of new walls.[11] These walls were still under construction on August 17, 1358, when one of the worst floods of the century struck Valencia.[12] Six days later, King Pere authorized the establishment of the Board of Walls and Sewers (Junta de Murs i Valls). The board was run by three administrators (obrers), one from each arm of the ruling classes (ecclesiastic, military, and

---

8. The king also destroyed the union's records, meaning that few city documents survive from the union period. See "Introducció," in Lizondo, *Diplomatari de la Unió*, 13–16; and Meyerson, "Victims and Players," 81–97.

9. This new construction, and the repair of the existing walls, was to be financed by a special tax on the city's inhabitants; AMV, A-4, 99r–99v;, A-10, 40r–41r. In early December the council also began to organize loans from prominent citizens to finance the project; AMV, A-10, 41r–45r.

10. AMV, A-10, 66r–67r; AMV, A-10, 58v–61r.

11. The king required the new defenses to encompass the royal palace, located opposite the city on the north bank of the river; AMV, A-13, 21r–22v, 26r–29r; AMV, A-13, Mano 3, 31v–32r.

12. AMV, A-13, Mano 3, 35v. See also chapter 7 of the present book.

royal), as well as municipal officials, including the jurats and *racional*. Financed independently through a series of taxes collected first in the "particular contribution" (the city and its suburbs), and later in the "general contribution" (the entire *horta*, or irrigated area around the city), its mission was to direct the city's public works, chiefly the repair and maintenance of the walls, the moats and sewers (valls), and the road network.[13]

The War of the Two Peres (so named for Kings Pedro the Cruel of Castile and Pere the Ceremonious of Aragon) began in 1356, but did not reach the city of Valencia until its final phases.[14] In December 1362 the council received a letter from Pere warning that Pedro's army was on its way. The new walls had to be finished immediately; Pere would take any hesitation as a sign of disloyalty. The council protested that it was trying its utmost to defend the city but could only do so much with the funds available.[15] The Castilians laid siege to Valencia twice, in May 1363 and February 1364, and both times the city held out until Pere arrived. These efforts served to reconcile city and king, putting to rest the lingering hostilities of the union period.[16]

Thus, as the war moved back into Castile in the later 1360s and finally concluded in 1375, Valencia had reason for optimism. The new walls had more than doubled the city's size, making it one of the largest in Europe. While much of that intramural space was still undeveloped, the city's population was fast recovering from the Black Death, as migrants from the rest of the kingdom flocked to the capital.[17] The establishment of the Board of Walls and Sewers, moreover, gave the municipal government the logistical capacity to engage in public works projects on a large scale.

The city council, which had up to this point restricted itself to regulation and maintenance, began to take a much more active approach to urban and suburban landscapes. As natural disasters revealed hazards in the environment around the city, the council proposed new infrastructure to relieve future pressure. Like the council's regulatory activity, these projects tended to focus on the placement (and replacement) of water on the land. A series of droughts led the council to begin initiatives to bring new water into the horta, while concerns about flood and disease prompted efforts to divert water away from inhabited areas.

---

13. Melió, *La "Junta de Murs i Valls,"* 39–49.

14. AMV, A-13, 33r–34r.

15. AMV, A-14, Mano 3, 24r–26v.

16. Immediately after the second siege, Pere gave the city criminal jurisdiction over neighboring Morvedre in recognition of its loyalty; *Libre de memories de diversos sucesos e fets memorables e de coses senyalades de la ciutat e regne de Valencia (1308–1644)*, vol. 1, ed. Salvador Carreres Zacarés (Valencia: Accion Bibliografica Valenciana, 1930), 73–74.

17. Agustín Rubio Vela, "Vicisitudes demográficas y área cultivada en la baja Edad Media. Consideraciónes sobre el caso valenciano," *Acta historica et archaeologica mediaevalia* 11–12 (1991): 264–265.

New Irrigation Canals

Drought was the clearest hazard on the Valencian plain, and the solution seemed simple: bring more water into the horta. Valencia's landscape was already designed around water redistribution (see chapter 1). Except in times of water scarcity, the council was rarely involved in the day-to-day maintenance of the horta. But starting in the 1370s the council became more ambitious in its efforts to bring new water sources into the horta. Yet this was easier said than done, particularly outside the boundaries of municipal authority. The committee dispatched in 1372 to examine the Cabriol was turned back at the city of Teruel "on account of the dispute that has long existed between Valencia and Teruel about the *montatge* [tax on transhumant flocks]."[18] Undeterred, the council appointed two jurats to make another attempt to survey the site. The journey did not take place until the summer of 1374, when the city was in the grip of another drought and suffering "great scarcity of food." On the last day of August the committee, including two "masters in the art of leveling," set out from the city "to see if the water of the [Cabriol] . . . could be taken and turned into the Guadalaviar River."[19] Levelers (*livelladors*) were surveyors specializing in hydraulic landscapes. Often skilled in masonry as well as surveying, they were employed to plan and construct new canals and extend existing watercourses.[20] An initial examination of the site may not have been promising, for nothing further was done until March 1376. Then, because of "the great drought that has been for a long time and is at present in the land, and the great decrease in the water that is in the Guadalaviar,"[21] the council again resolved to survey the area around the Cabriol. The object of this survey was not the river but rather a "lake of flowing water" near Santa Cruz de Moya, a village on the Castilian frontier.

This drought followed one of the worst droughts and famines of the century, which had begun in April 1374 and continued through the summer and fall, affecting not only Valencia but also Catalonia. Other adverse weather

---

18. That a trip to Teruel was necessary suggests that the intention was to divert the Cabriol into the Guadalaviar near the headwaters of both rivers, about thirty-seven kilometers northwest of Teruel. Although close to the border with Castile, this part of the river was no longer under Castilian control in the 1370s. A privilege from the Castilian king was probably necessary here because the Cabriol entered Castile some way downstream before flowing back into the kingdom of Valencia as a tributary of the Xúquer.

19. "Per regonexer & veure si laygua del dit Riu segons concessio que havem del Rey de Castilla proia esser presa & girada al Riu de Guadalaviar." AMV, I-8, 14r–14v.

20. Thomas F. Glick, "Levels and Levelers: Surveying Irrigation Canals in Medieval Valencia," *Technology and Culture* 9, no. 2 (1968): 165–180.

21. "La gran sequedat que es estada de lonch temps a ença e es de present en la terra e la gran minua daygua que es en lo dit Riu de Guadalaviar." AMV, A-17, 47v–48r.

caused harvests to fail across the western Mediterranean basin, causing widespread famine, as chronicler Melchior Miralles put it, "almost throughout the world."[22] Further droughts kept harvests in 1375 and 1376 low. Famine was felt most acutely among the urban poor, but shortages were more quickly resolved in the cities than in rural areas. The economic and coercive power of municipal governments, combined with a fear of bread riots, generally led city councils to obtain relief for their intramural population by any means necessary (see chapter 5).[23]

It was during the height of the drought, in the autumn of 1374, that the jurats first raised the possibility of bringing water into the struggling horta from the south rather than from the headwaters of the Guadalaviar. It had been suggested to them "by some notable persons and by some masters expert in the matter . . . that it was possible to bring water from the Xúquer River near Tous and carry it by means of a newly constructed canal to this Guadalaviar River . . . which could irrigate many places that are not now irrigated, and could give increase to the water of this river, and thus profit to the city and the horta—the more so in times of drought, such as that of the present and some others in the past."[24] Tous was a town on the Xúquer, some forty kilometers south of the Valencian horta (see map 2). Although the plan seems to have been to run part of the route along existing canals, this is the first record of the Valencian council undertaking a project on such a scale.

The council agreed to fund the initial survey and appointed a committee to oversee the project. Aware "that the project is very arduous and of great cost and labor," the council wished it to be "well examined and inspected both by persons expert in the arts of geometry and surveying and by other learned and discreet persons to know or arbitrate if and how said work might come to completion and at what cost."[25] As the project would be "better and more maturely known and arbitrated by a greater master than by a lesser," the council hired eight livelladors for the project: two from Barcelona, two from Manresa,

---

22. The original reads, "la segona fam, la qual fonch general quasi per tot lo mon"; Miralles, *Crònica i dietari*, 3.31, p. 150.

23. Adam Franklin-Lyons and Marie A. Kelleher, "Framing Mediterranean Famine: Food Crisis in Fourteenth-Century Barcelona," *Speculum* 97:1 (2022).

24. "E fon proposat en lo dit Consell per los dits honrats Jurats que per alcunes notables persones e per alcuns maestres en aço experts los era estat dit que possible cosa era traure aygua del Riu de Xuquer . . . de ques porien regar moltes partides que ara nos reguen e poria dar creximent a laygua daquest Riu a daqui profit a la Ciutat e a la orta majorment a temps de seccades segons es lo present temps e alcuns altres ja passats." AMV, A-16, 225r. For the initial survey, see AMV, I-8, 12r.

25. "Lo dit consell attenent quel dit fet es molt ardue e de gran cost e trevall e ques coue ans dalcun començament daquell que sia be examinant e regonegut axi per persones expertes en art de geometria e de livell com per altres sauies e discretes persones per saber o arbitrar si e com la dita obra pora venir a perfectio e ab quin o qual e quant cost." AMV, A-17, 20r–v.

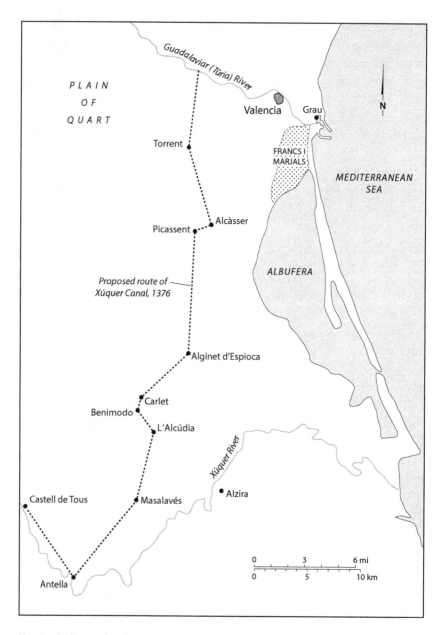

PLAIN OF QUART

Guadalaviar (Túria) River

Valencia

Grau

Torrent

FRANCS I MARJALS

MEDITERRANEAN SEA

Alcàsser

Picassent

Proposed route of Xúquer Canal, 1376

ALBUFERA

Alginet d'Espioca

Carlet

Benimodo

L'Alcúdia

Xúquer River

Castell de Tous

Masalavés

Alzira

Antella

N

0   3   6 mi
0   5   10 km

MAP 2. Projects undertaken in the Valencian horta

and four from Valencia itself.[26] As Josep Torró has observed, none of the hydraulic projects undertaken after the conquest were directed by a Valencian Muslim surveyor; Valencian Christians preferred Catalan or Occitan experts.[27] The surveyors completed their work by early 1376, and on February 11 related to the council that they had

> inspected and leveled and measured the whole work . . . beginning near and above said Castle of Tous on the land or plain of the river, and continu[ing] through the Tous valley up to the *açut* [stone diversion dam] of the Royal [Xúquer] Canal. . . . And from there they continued through mountains and through ravines and through plains, always with their levels, both stride levels and turning boards, and with the route and measure of the Royal Canal as long as it lasted. . . . And they found according to said levels and measures that starting the planned canal near and above the Castle of Tous it would or could come and carry or bring water from the Xúquer River . . . flowing into the Guadalaviar River above Manises but below the *açut* of Montcada.[28]

The experts assigned this canal the astronomical price tag of between thirty-five and forty thousand lliures (about ten times what the council would spend two decades later to drain the marshes near the city). After much debate, the council concluded that such a project required not only royal permission, but also an agreement with the other stakeholders to share both the costs and the new water.[29]

After the drought ended in the autumn of 1376 and food prices in the Crown of Aragon returned to normal, the project seems to have lost momentum.[30] Thomas Glick assumes that it faced opposition from King Pere, but the delay

---

26. The original reads, "lo dit fet mils e pus madurament pora esser vist o conegut o arbitrat per major ombre de maestres que per menor." AMV, A-17, 20r–v.

27. Torró, "Field and Canal Building," 102–103.

28. "Regonegut e fer regonexer e livellar e mesurar tot aquest fet e los lochs del açut e de la cequia faedor e faedora començan prop e sobre lo dit Castell de Thous en lo sol o pla del dit Riu e continuan per la vayll de Thous tro al açut de la cequia del Rey que us pren del dit Riu e rega en lo termes de la Ciutat de Xativa e de la via dAlgezira. E dalli avant continuan per muntanyes e per barranchs e per plants tota vegada ab livells axi dentreguart com de pas per hoc encara ab la via e mesura de la dita cequia del Rey aytant com durava. E trobaven segons los dits livells e mesures quels dita faedora cequia prenent aquella prop e sobre lo dit Castell de Thous venia o venir podia e traure e menar aygua del dit Riu de Xuquer passan sobre los lochs dAntella, de Raçalay, de la Alcudia, de Benimodel, de Carlet, de Alginet dEspioca, de Picacen, dAlcacer, de Torrent, e engravar en lo dit Riu de Godalaviar sobre lo loch de Manises empero deius laçut de Montcada." AMV, A-17, 38v–41r.

29. AMV, A-17, 38v–41r.

30. Adam Franklin-Lyons, *Shortage and Famine in the Late Medieval Crown of Aragon* (State College: Pennsylvania State University Press, 2022; in press). On precipitation patterns and drought perception in the fourteenth and fifteenth centuries, see chapter 5 of this book.

could as easily have come from the existing users of the Xúquer, the landowners along the route, or indeed the Valencian council itself. Pere's successor, King Joan the Hunter, eventually granted a privilege for the canal in 1393, but with no shortage of water throughout the 1380s and 1390s, the council did nothing further. Only with the start of the next drought, in the spring of 1400, did the council renew its effort to share the costs of the project. The jurats wrote to Hug, the bishop of Valencia, proposing that the church assign part of its revenues in the regions to be served by the canal to its construction, which would, presumably, be repaid by the greater productivity of the land.[31] A similar arrangement had been made for the restoration of the marshes in 1386, but the bishop was apparently unimpressed by this latest attempt. In July 1401, En Pere Lazer, notary and concerned citizen, made a plea for the Xúquer Canal project:

> Because of the frequency of successive droughts the city has a great poverty of water, from the sterility of which a great part of the harvest is lost, and [we] must secure provisions of flour from other places because the mills do not have enough water [to run], from which the city is seeing insupportable uproar and clamor, [he proposed] that the agreement to [construct] the canal from the Xúquer River to come to the Plain of Quart and irrigate it and from there flow into the Guadalaviar River of said city be continued and put in good order, seeing that the surveying has already been done.[32]

Once again this project was described as a response to a drought, even though the construction would almost certainly last longer than the drought itself. The council took up Pere Lazer's proposal and made another effort to obtain the cooperation of the other landholders. That same day the jurats wrote again to the bishop, informing him of the revival of the project and inviting him to a meeting to be held two weeks later, on August 5, at the Convent of Santa Maria del Carme (eventually changed to August 8 at Torres Torres). Invitations were also sent to Brother Berenguer March, head of the military Order of Montesa; the cathedral chapter of Valencia; and a number of secular nobles with influence in the area.[33] This meeting does not appear to have been

---

31. Glick, *Irrigation and Society*, 109, 326n10.

32. "Com per frequentacio de spesses secades la Ciutat haia gran penuria daygues en tant que per esterilitat daquelles gran partida dels splets se perden & ha a fer provisions de farines daltres parts per ço com los molins no han bastament daygues de que la Ciutat ve a importables rumors & brogits per tal provei quel tracte del traure de la cequia del Riu de Xuquer que deu venir al Pla de Quart & regar aquell & daqui engravar en lo Riu de Godalaviar de la dita Ciutat sia continuat & mes en alcun bon punt hauts & vists los livelles ja temps ha fets daquella." AMV, A-22, 120v–121r.

33. AMV, g3-7, 151r, 154r–155r.

a success; letters written after the event indicate that few of those invited chose to attend.[34] Nor had a conclusion been reached by September, according to the letters the council sent to their representatives at the royal court.[35] On October 15 the council wrote again to their representatives asking for "a copy of the survey [*livell*] of the water that is to be brought from the Xúquer River." Nothing further, however, was heard from that quarter.[36]

This plan came to nothing, probably because the city council was unable either to command sufficient resources to complete the project on its own or to secure the cooperation of other powerful stakeholders. The advantages to the city of an injection of water from the Xúquer would have been quite clear, particularly in times of drought. The advantages to landholders along the route were less apparent, as it would have been clear to all concerned that the city would try to monopolize this source of water during times of scarcity. Powerful as they were within the city limits, brokering regional infrastructure projects may have been beyond the councilmen.

Droughts continued to trouble Valencians, and just two years later, in November 1403, the treasurer of the Order of Montesa appeared before the council with two of his brethren and "made honest supplications, petitions, and prayers" that the council assist the landholders of the southern horta in "their intent" to construct a canal from the Xúquer. This time the proposal was to start the canal at Canó, in Alzira (see map 2).[37] In April 1404 the council debated the matter and concluded that "if the thing could be completed it would be very profitable . . . [but] it must be attempted with little expense so as not to commit the city to great and fruitless expenses." A small trial canal would be built first to test the feasibility of the project. The city would pay for half of the cost of the trial canal, and at least half of the full-size canal if it was constructed, in exchange for a claim on at least half the water it would bring to the horta.[38] The test canal may have been due to doubts about the route, which would skirt the high water table of the Albufera lagoon. It also limited the council's investment in a project that it did not control. By October 1404 the jurats were writing to remind Missèr Joffre de Tous that the region's landholders were bound to pay the other half of the test canal.[39]

By December the town of Alzira was holding up the groundbreaking. Valencia had sent messengers informing the town of the city's right to the water,

---

34. AMV, g3-7, 166r–v.
35. AMV, g3-7, 178v–179r, 187v.
36. AMV, g3-7, 203r.
37. AMV, A-22, 268v.
38. AMV, A-22, 288v.
39. AMV, g3-8, 81v.

but the town was "delaying [its response] in great expense to the city." Therefore the council determined that, after one final warning, it would ask the lieutenant governor of Valencia to go with two porters to the building site and
himself "execute the royal provision and order there to be made the break or
opening through which the water will be taken . . . with punishments to be
handed out by the governor to said town if they disrupt the work in any way."
The porters would remain to guard the site after the lieutenant left so that the
townspeople could not sabotage the project.[40]

Construction took the better part of two years; by October 1406 the trial
canal reached halfway to the Guadalaviar. By then, the council reported, "the
trial appeared to show to some that convenient water could not be had from
there as the city had desired." So as "not to spend money without result," the
council authorized "some of the honorable jurats and twelve of the worthy
councilors of the parishes, together with persons expert in such things, to go
see and inspect if the trial [canal] might be continued or changed to another,
better and feasible route."[41] Shortly thereafter a severe flood on the Xúquer
destroyed Alzira's walls and bridges; the canal may also have been damaged
or the inspections interrupted.[42]

By then the drought period had ended, and the project was not mentioned
again until the next drought occurred in 1413. In June of that year the city hired
a livellador to resurvey the original 1376 route near Tous (see map 2).[43] In
July 1413 the council was again considering the Canó project, which "some argue would bring great profit to the city and its inhabitants and very little expense because the knights and others through whose lands it would pass have
contributed to it."[44] That same summer the council also revisited the possibility
of bringing water from the lake near Santa Cruz de Moya, another project originally proposed in 1376. On June 23 it authorized an inspection of the site, and
a month later it formed a committee to negotiate for the rights to the water of

---

40. "Lo lochtinent de Governador de la Ciutat & Regne daquella que ensemps ab dos porters vaia al
loch on se deu pendre la dita aygua & present ell exseguin la provisio reyal se faca & man fer lo trench o
ubertura per on se deu pendre la dita aygua appellada del Cano ab manaments penals faedors per lo dit
lochtinent a la dita vila que no perturben la dita obra en alcuna manera. E fet aço romanguen los porters
lla a guardar que la continuacio de la dita obra no sia torbada & per executar les penes si comeses seran &
fer altres manaments de part del dit lochtinent ab imposicio de maiors pens." AMV, A-22, 328v–329r.

41. "Alcuns dels honorables jurats e .xii. prohomens consellers de les parroquies ab persones expertes en tals actes anassen veure e regonexer si lo dit ensaig fahia seguir o mudar en altra part factible
e mellor." AMV, A-23, 92v.

42. AMV, A-23, 96r–v.

43. AMV, A-25, 202r.

44. "Derrerament fon deduit en consell com per alcuns sia estat raonat que facilment se poria
hauer e fer dur al Riu de Godalaviar de la aygua de Xuquer de Algezira per lo Cano. E que daço re-
dundaria gran profit a la Ciutat e a sus habitators e fort poque despesa car han hi a contribuit los cavallers e altres heretats a vicus per on passara." AMV, A-25, 252r–v.

the lake.[45] By May 1415 the council concluded that it could bring water either from Santa Cruz or from the Xúquer, but not both.[46] A party that included jurat Lois Granollers and Brother Isambert, a master livellador, travelled to Tous "to see, survey, and know in what part of the Xúquer River . . . water might be brought . . . to the city most easily and with least expense."[47] They must have found a satisfactory route, because in September 1415 the council formally authorized the jurats to arrange the construction of a canal from the Xúquer to the Valencian horta.[48] This is, however, the last record of the project.

After 1415 the council's enthusiasm for new canals waned. No new projects were proposed for more than forty years (although, as chapter 5 will show, droughts continued to occur). In October 1456, in the midst of another drought, the jurats wrote to the authorities of Teruel that two citizens of Valencia were coming to examine the lake near the village of Tortajada, with an eye to channeling all the water into the Guadalaviar. In early 1457 the council sought and obtained a royal privilege to take this water, and in March the jurats wrote again to Teruel, declaring that although they had profound respect for the local government, conflict over this matter was unnecessary.[49] The water of the Tortajada lake, they declared, "was not useful nor served you or any of your uses." While "the waters that are dedicated to some uses or purposes have been given to the property to irrigate them . . . those that have never been put into use from the place from whence they spring, as this one has not, do not belong to anyone in particular."[50] Ownership of water was for the Valencian council inextricably linked to human use and human irrigation structures. This point notwithstanding, the project seems to have foundered on the details of the settlement between the two communities.[51]

On one final occasion the council flirted with a new irrigation project. In June 1479 the jurats wrote to the king that a man named Pere Ripol had appeared before the council. A native of Perpignan, Ripol was said to be "very

---

45. AMV, A-25, 237r–237v; AMV, A-25, 248v.

46. AMV, A-26, 13r.

47. "Per veure livellar & saber en qual part del Riu de Xuquer pus lengament e ab menys despesa quanta aygua se poria traure del dit Riu & venir a la Ciutat." AMV, J-39, 21r–v.

48. AMV, A-26, 65v.

49. For correspondence about the royal privilege, see AMV, g3-23, 76r, 78r, 86v.

50. "La dita aygua no era util o no servia a vos o amprius algu vostre o dels aldees, e que jatssia les aygues que son dedicades a alguns usos o amprius fossen donades als herets e regants de les dites aygues empero aquells que no eren stades james dermades les lochs on havien naixença axi com es aquesta no eren de de alguna universitat o de particulars." AMV, g3-23, 90r–91r.

51. The Valencian council agreed to build a bridge over the new canal wherever the community of Teruel wanted it, but refused to be responsible for its maintenance. The jurats likewise found "very impertinent" Teruel's insistence that the workforce on the project be entirely local. Negotiations continued until August 1457, but then disappear from the records. AMV, g3-23, 102r, 104r–104v, 108v–109r.

ingenious, with singular industry in drawing water and giving irrigation to lands that do not have it." His skills were particularly enticing, as the council was still vexed by the problem of "great scarcity of water, [and] lands that for lack of it remain uncultivated." In particular, it fretted over the Plain of Quart, the area to the southwest of the city that would have been irrigated by the Xúquer Canal (see map 2), which "would produce many harvests if it could be irrigated, and would give great happiness and abundance to this city . . . which for the greater part of the year is so populous that it must provision itself by sea . . . and it would therefore relieve us of the worry of provisioning ourselves from foreign parts." Pere Ripol promised to make this dream a reality, asking in return only that the king name him "master of waters," giving him authority to use his "many secrets and artifices" to irrigate the land. The pitch, as related by the council, seems almost too good to be true; either they or the king must ultimately have thought better of it, because nothing more was heard of Pere Ripol and his projects.[52] Plans to bring water from the Xúquer were periodically revived throughout the early modern period until one was finally completed by the Duke of Híjar in the eighteenth century.[53]

"Canal fever" in the medieval city of Valencia thus lasted from about 1370 to 1415. Before this period the council made no efforts to extend the infrastructure of the horta, and afterward such attempts were few and somewhat halfhearted. The council initiated each of these new canal projects during a period of drought, and in many cases referred explicitly to drought as the impetus. As chapter 5 will discuss in greater detail, a drought is in the eye of the beholder: a period of perceived water scarcity rather than particular precipitation totals. The present discussion has attributed projects to drought only when the council's own records mention it. It can be difficult to know precisely when droughts began and ended, or how severe they were relative to one another. Perceived drought was clearly a factor motivating the councils of the late fourteenth and early fifteenth centuries to undertake canal projects. But these must have been more than short-term relief efforts, since their construction (even if implemented) would almost certainly have outlasted the water shortages that prompted them. The Valencian council may have expected further

---

52. "En algunes parts de aquests vostres Regnes deça ha molta fretura daygues des terres que no poder sen haver resten incultes. . . . Entre algunes parts de vostres Regnes tenim una partida aci que per aquesta vostre ciutat ques diu del Pla de Quart hon si ffarien molts esplets si rech se podia hauer eforsa daria gran ffelicitat & abundancia a aquesta ciutat . . . lo qual la major part del any per esser tan populosa feht de provehir per mar." AMV, g3-29, 134r–135r.

53. Glick, *Irrigation and Society*, 110–112. In 1507 the council authorized private citizen En Pere Valenti to attempt the project. AMV, A-53, 296r–298r.

droughts in the future. As discussed in the introduction to this book, research suggests that the transition from the fairly warm and dry Medieval Climate Anomaly to the fairly cold and wet Little Ice Age began to be felt in Iberia sometime in the fourteenth century. This transition was characterized by variable precipitation, including both droughts and rains, but such effects were probably not intense enough to be obvious to contemporary observers.[54]

Early modern governments often regulated environments out of fears of resource scarcity. Even if the fears were exaggerated, the regulation served to increase the reach and power of the state.[55] Likewise, Tim Soens has shown that premodern infrastructure investment was never merely a reaction to natural disaster.[56] The Valencian council saw droughts as a threat throughout the later medieval period, but its particular zeal for infrastructure to address that threat was likely due to the new ambitions of the city government in the late fourteenth and early fifteenth centuries. In the decades after the creation of the Board of Walls and Sewers, successive councils took a proactive approach to the problem of water scarcity. Almost every perceived drought in these years sparked a proposal to bring new water into the irrigation system. That these efforts involved the projection of the city's power into neighboring jurisdictions can only have added to the appeal.

In any case, none of the irrigation canal projects were successfully completed. Their abandonments are poorly documented, but funding difficulties and disputes with neighboring landholders were probably factors, to say nothing of the technical challenges. Proposing projects is always easier than completing them, and the councils may have lost the initiative once each drought had passed. It is impossible to know how seriously the council took the initial proposals, but it does seem to have believed these projects were logistically possible.

"Many and Infinite Swamps"

The council's zeal for new projects extended to other initiatives as well. In the midst of municipal canal fever, in 1386 the jurats and *prohomes* (worthy men)

---

54. M. Oliva et al., "The Little Ice Age in Iberian Mountains," *Earth-Science Reviews* 177 (2018): 175–208.

55. On early modern forestry and fears of timber shortage, see Wing, *Roots of Empire*, 19–20, 28; and Karl Appuhn, *A Forest on the Sea: Environmental Expertise in Renaissance Venice* (Baltimore: Johns Hopkins University Press, 2009).

56. Tim Soens, "Floods and Money: Funding Drainage and Flood Control in Coastal Flanders from the Thirteenth to the Sixteenth Centuries," *Continuity and Change* 26, no. 3 (2011): 333–365.

of the Valencia council signed an accord with the bishop and cathedral chapter to restore an area of land belonging to the cathedral:

> Within the horta and boundaries of the City of Valencia a great area below the places of Russafa and Alfafar . . . has become marshy and deserted, particularly through the ruin of canals, branch canals, and drainage ditches, which for lack of people, who have diminished in number and in strength on account of the wars and plagues and other past adversities, have not been cleaned or kept in repair as they ought and as was customary in the past. And this is of great harm to the public good, not only because of the crops that have thus been and are being lost, but also because of the infection that ensues, and the more so because of the great extent of the marshy and deserted area, which is more than a league long and half, or at least a third, of a league wide.[57]

This area, known as the francs i marjals (free lands and marshes), was the northernmost fringe of the Albufera wetlands.[58] It extended north from the lagoon almost to the river, and west from the coastal dunes to the outskirts of the city (see map 2). As Antoni Furió has observed, marsh, not forest, was the main type of wild landscape along the medieval Mediterranean coast. Christian settlers tended from the start to see these marginal areas as "lands yet to be cultivated," and the Crown supported that vision.[59] As early as 1267 Jaume the Conqueror confirmed one Guillem Neuia's ownership over "the area you have worked in the marsh and in uncultivated land" on the Albufera road leading south from the city of Valencia.[60] For the most part, however, the marshes continued to be used, as they were before the conquest, for pasture, hunting, fishing, and as a source for such products as saltwort; plants in the genus *Aizoon* (which, when burned, yield soda ash used in soap and glassmaking); kermes beetles (for crimson dye); rushes; and grasses.[61]

---

57. "Com en la orta o terme de la Ciutat de Valencia una gran partida deius los lochs de Roçafa e dAlfofar e daltres fos e sia tornada marjalença e erma specialment per enruinament dels cequies e braçals e escorredors de les aygues qui per fretura de les gents aminuades en nombre e en poder per occasio de guerres & de mortaldats & daltres adversitats passats no son estats mundats ne tenguts en condret segons degren e solien antigament. E aço fos e sia gran dan de la cosa publica no tantsolament per los esplets qui si son perduts & perden ans encara per la infeccio que sen segueix e majorment per la gran tenguda de la dita partida marjalença e erma com tenga de lonch mes de una legua & dample mija o almenys terça poch mes o menys." ACV, Libro 3518, 167(bis)r–170r; the translation herein references Glick, *Irrigation and Society*, 99–100.

58. These marshes were "free" in the sense that they were legally outside of the horta, with its strict system of land and water rights.

59. Antoni Furió, "La domesticación del medio natural," 62.

60. ACA, Real Cancilleria, Registro 15, 68v, cited in Torró, "Field and Canal Building," 92.

61. Sanchis, *Regadiu i canvi ambiental*, 81; García-Oliver, "L'espai transformat," 545–549.

In the early fourteenth century, population pressure in the rest of the horta led some to attempt to cultivate these lands.[62] By 1342 one citizen, Guillem de Fluvia, was—at the king's command—constructing drainage canals in the area.[63] He quickly incurred the wrath of its major landlords, the bishop and chapter of Valencia cathedral, who complained that these new canals "direct[ed] water through places in which it was never accustomed to be directed," creating marshland in some areas even as they drained it in others. "It [was] not plausible," the clerics insisted, "that the lord king would wish to return . . . good land already fruitful and producing wheat to marsh in order to make fruitful and productive another piece of marsh that is not certain nor hopeful."[64]

Would-be cultivators of the francs i marjals quickly encountered the area's persistent drainage problems. As the cathedral chapter observed, channels built to drain tended to leak water into the areas through which they passed.[65] Once dry, moreover, the peaty soil of the marshes lost about half its volume, causing the new land to sink. To make matters worse, the sandbars along the Valencian coast, which had created the marshes in the first place, had a tendency to shift and block canals from draining into the sea.[66] Although farmers and landlords made inroads into the marshes in the late thirteenth and early fourteenth centuries, the pockets of drained land were at constant risk of reversion. For the most part, the francs i marjals remained too wet to cultivate easily.

The Black Death of 1348 caused the population of the horta to drop sharply, eliminating pressure to cultivate the marshes. Parcels of land increasingly fell vacant, and with no one maintaining the leaky canals, these parcels reverted to marshland. The agricultural population of the horta never returned to its fourteenth-century peak, although the urban population continued to grow, buoyed by immigration from as far afield as Castile.[67] The new push to reclaim

---

62. "La gran estretura de pastures per les muntanyes e marjals que son molt escaliabes e panificades." AMV, A-1, 145v, cited in Rubio Vela, "Vicisitudes demográficas," 261.

63. A transcription of the king's command to Guillem is published in Sáinz de la Maza Lasoli, "Noticias Documentadas sobre la Albufera," 151.

64. "En Guillem de Ffluvia novellament ha feytes & no ces continuament de fer cequies noves per menar algunes aygues per los lochs en james no foreti acostumades de menar . . . no solament dampiffi[] les dites terres e censal passan per aquelles la cequia . . . abre fluitat daygues les quals noy son acostumades de venir per les quals aygues com nols do nils puxa donar exida bena ni comial les dites terres & censal se començen a perdre negar & consumar & per tamps tornara a marjal & no es versemblant quel dit senor rey la terra bona & ja pacifficada & fructificcant vulle tornar ni metre en a marjal per fructar & panificar altre marjal el qual no es cert ne sperança." ACV, Pergaminos, 5597.

65. Glick, Irrigation and Society, 98.

66. Torró, "Field and Canal Building," 94; "Tierras ganadas: Aterrazamiento de pendientes y desecación de marjales en la colonización cristiana del territorio valenciano," in Por una arqueología agraria: Perspectivas de investigación sobre espacios de cultivo en las sociedades medievales hispánicas, ed. Helena Kirchner (Oxford: Archaeopress, 2010), 163.

67. Rubio Vela, "Vicisitudes demográficas," 267–268, 264.

the marshes in the later fourteenth century came not from settlers but from the city council.

On January 15, 1375, the council proposed "that the canals and branch canals of the marshy areas of the horta of the city be cleared out and cleaned, and those owning property fronting on said canals and branch canals, and all others who are obliged be made to do this . . . because it is expedient and necessary and profitable to the public good."[68] The lands would then be settled with the "many and diverse foreigners" then in the city. This was at the height of the great drought and famine of 1374–76, and just weeks earlier, in late December 1374, people in the city had begun to die of plague.[69] In this context, the project in the marshes was to be undertaken for two reasons: "to conserve the health of the city," which was threatened by the stagnant water of the marshes, and "to plant with wheat many lands in those parts . . . by means of which, with God's help, we may be aided in the present necessity and famine." These lands would be "very good for wheat of high and low quality," but "on account of the ruin of the aforesaid canals and branch canals have been lost and are deserted."[70] In securing these aims, the council would also remove migrants from the city, where they might cause bread riots, back to the countryside, where they could produce bread.

As with the new irrigation canals, this proposal was phrased as a response to a current crisis. The council did not plan to undertake the work of restoring the francs i marjals themselves. Instead, the *cequiers* (canal officials) would compel the area's landholders to restore and maintain the area's canals, as was the custom in the rest of the horta. In a dry year like 1374, this may have seemed feasible. Once the rains returned, however, it would have been clear that the marshes were not like the rest of the horta. Drainage canals required far more maintenance than irrigation canals, and there were fewer landholders to do it.

In 1384, during the next major plague, the jurats and prohomes of the council undertook an inspection of "the marshes of all those parts, in order to make some drainage ditches there to remove stagnant waters from the city, which apparently cause infection in said city and its horta, so that, dried out, the lands

---

68. "Que les cequies e braçals de les partides marjalenques de la orta de la dita Ciutat fossen e sien escurades e mundades e que a aço a fer sien destrets los frontalers de les dites cequies e braçals e tot altres qui tenguts hi sien per los Cequiers o per aquells de ques pertanga com aço sia expedient e necessari e profitos a la cosa publica." AMV, A-16, 250r.

69. AMV, A-16, 241r; AMV A-16, 250v–251v.

70. "Per conservacio de sanitat vullas per traure e panificar moltes terres de les dites partides les quals per enrunament de les dites cequies e braçals se son perdudes e estan ermes e serien e son molt bones per a blats grossos menuts per los quals ab la ajuda de Deu poria esser soccorregut a la present necessitat e fam e majorment com a present en la dit Ciutat haia moltes diverses persons estrangers que laurarien e panificarien volenterosament les dites terres." AMV, A-16, 250r.

might be planted with wheat and cultivated, as they were accustomed to be in ancient times."[71] Again the rhetorical stress was on ruin and redemption.[72] In truth, the francs i marjals had only ever been under cultivation for a few decades a generation or two earlier, and there were serious problems with drainage even then. Like many rulers of wetlands, the council also chose to ignore their existing economic value as pasture and as a source of marketable products.[73] It instead presented the marshes as ruined horta waiting to be restored.

Two years later, in 1386, the council finally drafted the accord with the bishop and chapter of the cathedral of Valencia. This document stressed the decline of the marshes from an earlier state of population and cultivation, and also acknowledged that restoration "[could] not be well done without great work and expense, according to what has been seen and inspected." The work would be funded by the rents and tithes owed on the area, which the bishop and chapter agreed to cede for ten years while the council undertook the repair work. The council, for its part, agreed to "rebuild and clean the canals and drainage ditches of said lands, . . . rebuild the bridges that go over them," and through its officials take perpetual charge of the maintenance of both bridges and canals. Those owning property in the area had to declare themselves to the council so that they could be held accountable for their share of the maintenance; if they did not do so by the appointed time, they would lose the right to that land, which the jurats could redistribute as they saw fit. Rice was not to be planted, and each cultivator was enjoined to plant willows, poplars, and vines on the borders of his fields to prevent erosion of the canal banks.[74] Despite the emphasis on the liability of the landholders, this agreement significantly increased the council's involvement in maintenance and reconstruction of a part of the horta. The ten-year time frame suggests that the signers saw this responsibility as temporary. Once restored, the marshes were meant to maintain themselves as the rest of the horta did, with the labor and taxes of their own inhabitants. Although drafted in 1386, the accord was not actually signed until November 1389.[75] Construction began with the next

71. "Per regonéxer les marjals de totes aquelles partides, per fer allí alguns escorredors per lunyar de la ciutat aygues adormides, qui versemblant donen infecció en la dita ciuta e orta daquella, per tal que, dessecades, les terres poguessen ésser panificades e plantades, segons que en temps antich ho solien ésser." AMV, I-13, 48r, quoted in Rubio Vela, "Vicisitudes demográficas," 272.

72. Similar language was later used about the English Fens. See Ash, The Draining of the Fens, 8–9.

73. Faisal Husain, "In the Bellies of the Marshes: Water and Power in the Countryside of Ottoman Baghdad," Environmental History 19, no. 4 (2014): 638–664; Ash, The Draining of the Fens, 8–9.

74. ACV, Libro 3518, 167(bis)r–170r.

75. It was sent for royal approval in the summer of 1386 and received approval by October. AMV, I-16, 7v, 13r–13v. In May 1387 the agreement was postponed until Michaelmas; agreement was reached in June 1388, and it was signed in November 1389. AMV, A-18, 222r; AMV, A-19, 10r, 86r.

building season, on February 8, 1390, under the direction of the Board of Walls and Sewers. A workforce of up to thirty men per day cleaned and repaired each canal in turn. The project was completed in August 1393 at a total cost of 78,228 sous, 5 diners.[76]

Before the work was even complete it was at risk of further damage. In March 1390 the city reached a settlement with one Joan Comte to demolish a mill he owned on the En Fluvia Canal that was "impeding the free [drainage] of . . . water" in the marshes.[77] In early 1391 the council appointed two guardians to keep humans and livestock from damaging the fields "and especially the canals, drainage ditches, and branch canals" then being restored.[78] By 1396 the cultivators of the marshes complained to the council that their newly resettled fields were suffering "great damage and especially neglect . . . on the part of the . . . city." The city, it was claimed, had "ceased or delayed the building of bridges over the canals in the marshes, for want of which bridges the bulls and other beasts large and small . . . cross the canals and branch canals and ruin and destroy them, blocking the course of the water so that it backs up into their property and makes it revert to its previous marshy state."[79] The complaint re-iterated the council's pledges in the original accord, including a pledge to grant one hundred lliures each year for the maintenance of the marshes and their infrastructure. The council concluded that the project remained immensely valuable to the public good "not only for the harvest of wheat from the land, but still more profitable for the health of the places and villages and parts around the marshes." Experience had shown, moreover, "that excavating and draining said marshes and cutting and straightening their canals is very costly to the city. And it would be an inconvenient thing and a great sin and crime to let [the marsh] be lost and reduced to its previous bad state."[80] The council therefore

---

76. AMV, d3-2, 339v–340v.

77. AMV, I-18, 28r.

78. AMV, A-19, 192v.

79. "Elles en lurs possessions tretes & cultivades en les dits marjals prenien gran dan & senyalada-ment en desidea & tarda de la part de la universitat de la dita Ciutat per cessar o tardar de fer ponts & pontons de les cequies de les dites marjals per fretura dels quals ponts & pontons los bous & altres besties major & menors pasturants en les dits dits marjals traversaven per les dits cequies & braçals & enrunaven & destrouien aquelles embargants lo cos de les aygues de manera que aquelles regolfaven en lurs possessions & aquelles fahien tornar al primer estament marjalench." AMV, A-20, 296r–296v.

80. "E per ço . . . lo dit Consell haud sobre aço raonament & acord attenent que tenir en condret les dits marjals era & tornava en gran profit de la cosa publica de la dita Ciutat no tant solament per la col-lita dels blats ques fa en les terres daquelles ans pus profitosament per la sanitat dels lochs & alqueries & partides convehins als dits marjals hoc encara de la partida de la dita Ciutat que mira o es vers aquelles segons que experiencia ha demonstrat & de mostra majorment con sia cert que traure & exugar les dits marjals & escuzar & endreçar les cequies daquelles costen de grans diners a la universitat de la dita Ciutat. E seria cosa inconvenient & de gran peccat & carrech lexar ho perdre & reduir al mal o stament primer." AMV, A-20, 296r–296v.

paid the one hundred lliures so that the environment of the marshes would be preserved from further degradation.[81]

Both council and cultivators admitted the extreme difficulty of maintaining the marshes as arable land while simultaneously recommitting to doing so. The marshes were inherently unstable, constantly on the verge of ruin. Although the aim was to integrate this area into the rest of the horta, water behaved differently in the marshes than elsewhere. In the horta, water was primarily a resource, and only secondarily a cause of land degradation and disease (see chapter 1). In the francs i marjals, by contrast, water was constantly threatening to mix with land, returning to what the council saw as an unproductive and infectious state that threatened the city's health, growth, and prosperity. To allow the land to revert in this way would be, in the council's words, "a great sin and crime." The health and prosperity of the city were based on human control of the land, and it was the council's duty to maintain and extend that control.

Over the course of the next century the council struggled to maintain the marshes as an agricultural environment. In June 1399 the council reported that there had been "great disputes" over the cleaning of the Castello Canal in the marshes, but that ultimately it was to be cleaned at the city's expense, "for the public good of the city and particularly for its health."[82] In 1401 the council paid En Francesc Aragones twenty gold florins for his work cleaning and repairing this canal.[83] In 1403 the council funded the construction of a canal to drain water from the En Fluvia Canal into the Albufera.[84] Three years later that canal was already deteriorating—so much so that Albufera landholder Jaume Dominguez complained on behalf of the king and queen (to whom the Albufera belonged) that the new canal "was in ruins and badly treated by animals and livestock."[85] In 1436 the council warned that the canals were again "in a terrible state from the waters not flowing, from which follows ill health to the people of the city and those outside it, and many and infinite swamps . . . almost up to the city walls, which [resulted in] the loss of many lands that could be cultivated and sown, and if a remedy could not be found, the city might be . . . in want of wheat." To address this apparent crisis the council approved the construction of another new canal, beginning above Castello d'en Arruffat

81. AMV, I-21, 26r, 30r.

82. "Per lo be de la cosa publica de la dita Ciutat e senyaladament per la sanitat daquella." AMV, A-21, 269v.

83. AMV, A-22, 63v–64r.

84. AMV, J-30, 51v.

85. "La dita cequia era stada en runada & malmenada per besties e per bestiars." AMV, A-23, 48r–48v.

and draining the water of the marshes into the sea.[86] Unfortunately, in December 1439 the mouth of the newly completed canal was ruined "by fortune and bad weather" such that the canal could no longer drain. The cequier requested emergency funds to repair this and other nonfunctional canals, lest the marshes "return to what they were before."[87] Less than two years later, however, the council claimed that "the health of the people of the city" was again at stake. A section of the En Fluvia Canal, which drained from the marshes into the river, needed to be widened "so that the . . . waters could run freely." En Barthomeu de Casanova, a livellador from Xátiva,[88] was employed in May 1442 to "level the waters of the marshes"—that is, to determine the difference in elevation between the top and bottom of the En Fluvia Canal so that it might be widened without disrupting the system.[89]

In May 1444 the council intervened again to address the perceived health hazard. Having consulted with experts, it decided to build yet another new canal in the marshes, beginning "in a certain part of the Bishop's Canal—that is, in the most unhealthy part of the marshes, below the canal called "of Castello"." From there it would cut across the fields to drain into "the unhealthy part of the canal called 'of En Fluvia' near the river."[90] The council continued to prefer outside Christian experts to local ones; construction would be undertaken by "certain Gascon masters who are now in the city at the pleasure . . . of the honorable jurats."[91]

On April 30 the council declared the completion of this "great canal" in the marshes "by which without any doubt the waters of said marshes will be able to run very freely and by which [the marshes] will undoubtedly be able to be well dried out." The announcement presents this project as an unqualified triumph, whereby the city would "from that time forward be able to be fruitful," and "the health of the people" would be protected from "bad infections, illnesses, and other inconveniences." In addition to the canal, two "very beau-

---

86. "Les marjals de la Ciutat staven en avol punt per no haver on discorrer les aygues de que sen seguia insania a les gents de la dita Ciutat & als defora hoc & molts & infinits ayguamolls hi hauia fins prop los murs de aquella la qual cosa era perdicio de moltes terres que nos podien conservar ne panificar e si remey si donaua no staria per aventura la Ciutat algunes vegades en congoxa de blats lo qual remey era fer una cequia començant damunt Castello dEn Arruffat fins a la mar." AMV, A-31, 73v.

87. "Sino les dits marjals tornarien en ço que primer eren." The council preferred to fund the repairs from the ordinary maintenance budget. AMV, A-32, 128r.

88. AMV, A-32, 17bisv–18bisr.

89. Glick, "Levels and Levelers," 165–180.

90. "En certa part de la cequia appellada del Bisbe que es en la part pus insana dels almarjals deça la cequia appellada de Castello & deu anar dreta via traversant per certs camps engravar en la part insana de la cequia appellada dEn Fluvia prop lo Riu." AMV, A-32, 201bisv–202bisr.

91. "Certs maestres gascos que son en la dita Ciutat a beneplacit . . . dels dits honorables jurats." AMV, A-32, 201bisv–202bisr.

tiful" bridges had also been built, "by which bulls, cows and other animals and livestock can cross without ruining it."[92] Three more would follow, "similar or greater to those already constructed." The council lavished praise not only on the project but also on its participants. The construction had been completed "with the abundance of great labor, care, solicitude, and industry" of one Perot Mercader, apparently a paragon of civic virtue "who had worked only for reverence of God and the honor of the . . . city, without wishing or demanding any remuneration." Furthermore, "a good man named En Pere Veixo leveled said canal many times and prudently tested [it] . . . because he was an intelligent and practical man in such things."[93] The council also asserted that this work had been accomplished with no dissension among property holders, all of whom had been "paid and satisfied" for the land used to construct the canal.

Over the next several years, however, the council had to make some adjustments to keep such users happy. In September 1445, a mere five months after the canal was completed, the council directed the Board of Walls and Sewers to construct a cement channel to bring water to users who had lost access to irrigation on account of the new canal.[94] In 1447 one of these users, En Bernat Gomiç, was compensated for water damage to his fields. Those cleaning the canal had "thrown the water of the canal over the lands of said farm, on

92. On livestock and grazing in the Valencian horta, see chapter 1 of the present book.

93. "Que en certa partida dels almarjals appellada de Castello den Arruffat era stada principiada e feta novament una gran cequia per la qual sens dubte algu les aygues de les dits almarjals porien decorrer molt delliurament e per aquella no es dubte se porien aquelles be exingar. De la qual cosa se seguiria molt gran beneffici & utilitat a la dita Ciutat axi per que aquells part daci avant porien fructificar com per la sanitat de les gents. Com fos cert que si les dites almarjals no hauien on se escorreguessen seria occasio de seguir se tot lo contrari ço es males infeccions malalties & altres inconvenients a les gents e les terres romandrien ermes & aras procurarien e cultivarien en evident utilitat de la cosa publica de la dita Ciutat & singulars de aquella. La qual començaua en la cequia appellada de Castello prop la casa appellada den Brasa e traversava les cequies appellades del Caualler & del Bisbe e dos camins publichs per lo hun dels quals se va a la Albufera & a marjals e per laltre a Cullera e fahia la via de la punta den Silvestre traversant per lo mig de moltes possessions e apres engrava en la cequia appellada den Fluvia en una arboreda assais prop lo Riu de Guadalaviar. Es verdad que en la dita cequia per beneffici de aquella eren necessaries alguns ponts per los quals poguessen passar los bous vaques & altres besties & bestiars per ço que no enrunassen aquella. Dels qua ne eren ja fets los dos molt bells e ni restauen a fer tres en certs lochs de la dita cequia consemblants o maiors dels que jay eren fets. No volien empero obmetre ans notificauen al dit honorable Consell que la dita cequia era stada feta & acabada ab sobres de grans treballs cura e sollicitud & industria del honorable Mosser Perot mercader lo qual hi hauia treballat per sola Reverencia de Deu & honor de la dita Ciutat sens que non volia ne demanava remuneracio alguna. Era veritat que hun bon home appellat en Petro Vexo hauia livellat la dita cequia per moltes vegades cert assaig ques era fet per raho de aquella que continuament per que era home entes & pratich en tals coses hauia entes & treballat en lo fer & fabricar de la dita cequia tenint esment & sollicitant los maestres e treballant en aquella hauia per ço pregat a ells dits honorables jurats & consell fos contentat de ço que dit es en aquella forma & manera quels plauria." AMV, A-33, 92r–93v.

94. AMV, A-33, 139v–140r.

account of which he could not sow the lands, and those already sown were lost."[95]

The council remained invested in the francs i marjals as agricultural land. A 1448 ban on grazing livestock specifically targeted "the lands that are sown with wheat [panificades] or beginning to be sown in the marshes."[96] The holders of that land, however, seem to have been less enthusiastic about farming it. In 1448 the council issued a proclamation that all landholders in the northern part of the marshes must within ten days clean all the canals on which their property fronted. Delinquents would pay double the cost if the city had to perform the cleaning.[97] Such threats do not seem to have been effective at shifting maintenance responsibility; over the next several years a number of the canals in the marshes continued to be cleaned, sometimes repeatedly, at the city's expense.[98] In the spring of 1452 the council issued a proclamation that anyone holding uncultivated land in the marshes must cultivate it within fifteen days.[99] In 1464 it declared that "many [landholders] have not done so, for which reason the honorable jurats notify all landholders that whoever has not cultivated and cared for [their lands] has one month to begin doing so."[100] In 1472 one of the first acts of the new cequier, Pere Navarro, was to enjoin landholders to farm their "uncultivated and deserted lands."[101] In April 1475 Navarro took more drastic measures: "So that the city might be kept in health, and because of the infection . . . of the uncultivated lands situated in the limits of the marshes," everyone holding land in the area must immediately begin to care for it as was appropriate, including bridge and canal maintenance. Any lands found deserted and uncultivated after fifteen days would be seized by the city and redistributed to "other persons who would care for them."[102] Even this measure was not the end of the problem; the council reissued the proclamation in 1477.[103] In 1482 the council again banned livestock in the marshes, complaining,

---

95. "Per hauer girada laygua de la dita cequia sobre les terres de la dita alqueria per causa de la qual no poch sembrar les dites terres ans les sembrades se perderen." AMV, A-33, 276v.

96. "Les terres que son en los dits marials panifficades o principiades panificar." AMV, A-34, 112r–113r. For similar bans in the horta as a whole, see chapter 1 of the present book.

97. AMV, A-34, 123v.

98. See AMV, A-34, 271v; AMV, A-35, 87r, 94r; AMV, A-35, 201r, 294r, 295v, 329v; and AMV, A-36, 28r.

99. AMV, A-35, 176r.

100. "Com en dies passats sien stades fetes diverses crides notificant a tots los hereters de les dites marjals que cascu colturas e tengues en condret les terres quey posseexen & molts de aquells non haien curat fer pertal los dits honorables jurats notifiquen a tots los dits hereters que colturat & procurat no han que dins hun mes del present dia a avant compt comencen a procurear & colturar les dites possessions & hereters que colturades no son en continuen de fer axi com deven es deu fer." AMV, A-37, 117bisr.

101. AMV, A-39, 170v.

102. "Per qua la dita Ciutat sia en sanitat conservada e per causa de la infeccio de la infeccio [sic] de les terres incultes situades en los limits de les margals preservada." AMV, A-40, 191r.

103. AMV, A-41, 64v.

The cows that are and have been accustomed to be in the thickets [of the marshes are] ruining the canals and branch canals and blocking the waters running towards the Albufera and, not being able to run into [the Albufera], they stand stagnant and destroy the lands that are put under cultivation, wasting them and the crops that are sown in them and thus [the lands] are made marshy and such that not only do they not give any harvest but they also infect the air, which causes many damages and illnesses to occur in the city in great damage to the public good.[104]

Despite these efforts, the francs i marjals never attracted enough settlers to become a self-regulating part of the horta, and the council struggled to maintain it as an agricultural space. City-sponsored canal building in the marshes lasted from 1375 to 1444, and subsequent councils continued to regulate to preserve the infrastructure and the city's investment. This investment was repeatedly justified as a defense of the city against the twin specters of famine and disease. Private cultivation of the marshes in the early fourteenth century was a consequence of population pressure, but the municipal project of the late fourteenth and early fifteenth centuries was driven more by the council's ambitions to improve the extramural landscape.

Water at the Port

Just as stagnant water brought disease, flowing water could bring health. Elimination of the one and provision of the other could at times be closely linked. During this period the council addressed the health and functioning of the city's seaport, known as the Grau, located at the river's mouth (see map 2). The interventions combined civic and private initiative, and, like the reform of the francs i marjals, blended health concerns with civic pride, in this case tied to the Grau's role in Valencian commerce.

The Grau was vulnerable to the river's shifting course, which was somewhat unstable near the ocean. In January 1390 the council observed that "for some years, the Guadalaviar River has been eroding the banks in the area

---

104. "Per los grans dans que aquells fan en la dita orta e boalar en les terres axi cultes com incultes e senyaladament en la Margal. Les vaques qui son e han acostumar destar en los brusquils enrunant les cequies e braçals daquelles e empatant les aygues decorrents vers lAlbufera. E per no poder decorrer en aquella les dits aygues stan enbassades e guasten les terres que son stades reduhides a agricultura guastans aquelles e los splets que en aquelles son sembrats e axi son fets margalenques. E tals que no solament no donen splet algu mas encara infectionen layre de que son subsegueixen a la dita Ciutat molts dans e malalties en gran dan de la cosa publica daquesta Ciutat molts dans e malalties en gran dan de la cosa publica daquesta Ciutat." AMV, A-43, 56r–56v.

around the Grau little by little, to such an extent that all observers and advisers agree that if a flood should occur, it would come over the Grau and destroy it entirely or in large part, if some remedy is not, with God's help, devised." The council therefore concluded that the jurats, accompanied by "worthy men expert in such matters," should "see and inspect the matter by eye and decide if and how it might be rectified and built to better advantage."[105] In August 1392 it was proposed that "for fear of a flood that could damage the houses of the Grau . . . it would be good and profitable to move the flow of the water of the Guadalaviar River away from the Grau." A diversion would be made near En Silvestre Point so that the river would run a longer course south toward the Albufera before reaching the sea. This was, in fact, the river's original course; it had shifted toward the Grau sometime before the late fourteenth century.[106]

The project to "turn . . . flow of the water of the Guadalaviar River at En Silvestre Point in a straight line to the sea" was completed sometime before August 1394. By then, however, "some of the inhabitants and residents of the Grau have said that because of the ceasing of said flow [of the river], some of the waters of the canals run from there down into the riverbed in the place where they were accustomed to flow, pool there, and can cause infection in those places. And experience has shown this through the excessive illnesses among the inhabitants of the Grau." As with the marshes, the council saw a clear connection between pools of stagnant water and disease among those who lived nearby. The inhabitants of the Grau concluded that they had traded the risk of floods for death from disease, and "prayed that the council, for the good of [their] health . . . return the flow of the water of the river to the place . . . where it first was." Recalling that the original move of the river "was done at the . . . request of many in the Grau," the council declined to sponsor its return. It did permit the Grau residents to reroute the river at their own expense, provided that the materials used in the original diversion were returned to the city for reuse.[107] Having learned from this mistake, the council

105. "Que dalcuns anys a ença laygua del Riu de Godalaviar poch a poch roent les Ribes a la part devers lo Grau havia presa tal volta que a arbitre de tots los veents & avisants era dispositio si diluvii daygues esdevenia a venir sobre lo Grau de la Mar e enderrocar aquell en tot o en gran partida si remey no si prema ajudant deu . . . quels honrats jurats de la Ciutat appellats & hauts a si aquells prohomes en semblants coses experts de qui vist los sera veien & regoneguen a ull la cosa & arbitren si & com se pora drecar & adobar a mellar avanatage daquella & de la Ciutat." AMV, A-19, 95v.

106. Carmona , "Geomorfología de la Llanura de Valencia," 25.

107. "Com alcun temps es passat lo Consell de la dita Ciutat e de part lur alcuns dels jurats daquella als quals fo comes cuydants fer be & profit haguessen girat lo decorriment de laygua del Riu de Guadalviar a la punta den Silvestre a dreta linea tro a la mar per la Rambla a la part della del Riu vers la dita punta, en axi que hauien levat o tolt lo dit deccoriment daygua a la part deço del Grau. E ara alcuns dels habitadors & vehins del dit Grau haguessen dit que per lo cessament del dit decorriment alcuns aygues

of 1403 responded coolly to a proposal to excavate a shipping channel from the coast to the city walls. The councilmen wished to investigate "first if it is possible to do, and then if it is durable or destructible by flood, and if destructible if it will cause infection."[108] The proposal went no further.

Water problems continued to trouble the Grau. In 1409, the jurats reported that a private citizen had successfully excavated a pair of canals to drain "the stagnant water in the plain and marsh between the river and the town of the Grau," for which the council compensated him 200 florins. It warned, however, that the Grau was becoming depopulated "on account of the scarcity of good water and the abundance of bad water that the townspeople drink, taking it from a very bad-tasting spring that was in the marsh." This spring was not only foul but was also insufficient to supply the ships and other vessels that came and went from the port. The city therefore proposed to bring "good, healthy, and continuous water . . . to the Grau by pipes, where a beautiful fountain was to be built, with abundant water for all the people and vessels." This water was to be conveyed from a spring "below Russafa" (a village just south of the city) through the marshes by canal and across the river in pipes to the Grau.[109] The project would be funded through taxes collected at the port. Provision of drinking water was only partly a public matter in Valencia: while the city constructed several fountains and drinking troughs (*abeuradors*), most of the inhabitants seem to have used wells, as was generally the case in European cities before the modern period.[110]

By August 1412 the Grau fountain was in urgent need of funds. All the money previously raised had been spent to bring the supply canal from the source to the river, but without "a great deal of money" it could not be extended across the river to the Grau. As the project remained "good and necessary to the

---

de cequies discorrens dalli auall en lo Riu en lo loch per on aquell solia decorrer sembassaven aqui es podrien & davan infectio en aquelles partides. E allo havia demostra experencia per massa malalties dels habitadors del dit Grau. E per ço de part lur fos pregat al present Consell que per be de sanitat volguessen tornar lo dit discorriment daygua de Riu per lo loch & en la manera que de primer era. Lo dit Consell hauda sobre aço deliberacio attenents segons fo alli raonat quel dit mudament era estat fet a dita & instancia de molts del dit Grau & vehins be que creegues lo dit Consell que ho hauien cuydat fer per bona intencio pero puys experiencia mostrava lo dit. Al dit Consell plahia & atorga que si lo habitadors & vehins del dit Grau volran quel dit retornament daygua sia fet a lurs despeses ques faça a la beneyta hora pero que les cavallades de fust que la donchs la Ciutat hi feu sien & romanguen de & a la dita Ciutat & a obs daquella." AMV, A-20, 191r–191v.

108. "Primerament si es possible de fer, en apres si es durable o destrouible per ruina, & on no sia destrouible si dara infeccio." AMV, A-22, 244r.

109. The project also included a covered arcade to protect merchandise from rain and storms. See AMV, A-28, 62v; and AMV, A-24, 162v–163r.

110. Agathe Euzen and Jean-Paul Haghe, "What Kind of Water Is Good Enough to Drink? The Evolution of Perceptions about Drinking Water in Paris from Modern to Contemporary Period," *Water History* 4 (2012): 235.

people of the Grau, who are being infected by bad and corrupted water," the council paid to finish the fountain.[111] It was complete by 1416, when the council instituted an inspection process; three times a year several of the port officials would walk the route from the spring to the fountain, to see if the canal required any repair, or if anyone had planted trees or vines too close to the pipes.[112]

This arrangement seems to have functioned for several years, but in June 1424 another crisis brought En Joan Bayona, administrator of the fountain, before the council. The pipes supplying the water had been "broken and filled in" by a flood of the Guadalaviar River, "since the [pipes] crossed the riverbed." The destruction was so severe that En Joan was hard pressed to repair it promptly without great expense, and in the meantime no water was flowing to the Grau. Those who were paying taxes toward the maintenance of the fountain had ceased to pay while it was not flowing, leaving the fountain without funds. En Joan proposed that water be brought from a different spring, farther from the Grau but on the same side of the river.[113] Since the water could run for much of the distance in the old pipes, the total cost would be a mere 1,000 florins. The council agreed to this "and no more."[114] By August the council had appointed a city administrator (*sindic*) as manager of the project funds, and by February 1425 the fountain was well over budget and leaking water all over the Grau. Payments for work and maintenance on the Grau fountain continued through 1451.[115] Providing a supply of fresh, healthy water to the Grau was considered crucial to the survival of the port and therefore to the city's commerce. The city continued to take responsibility for supplying that water even as the project became more difficult, complicated and expensive.

A series of political and military crises between 1347 and 1370 damaged both the physical fabric of the city and its credibility with the king, but Valencia emerged strengthened from these crises. The city's resistance during the Cas-

---

111. "Es bona e necessaria als habitadors del Grau qui per aygues males e corruptes se infeccionen." AMV, A-25, 88v–88r, 93v–94r.

112. AMV, A-26, 128v.

113. En Johan describes a spring near a mill "called d'En Burguera and afterward d'En Pere Despuig." This was probably the mill known as the Mill of Pilades or of Peguera, which belonged to the Despuig family in the fifteenth century. It was located on the Algirós branch of the Mestalla Canal, which ran along the north bank of the river. According to Enric Guinot Rodriguez and Sergi Selma Castell, *Les séquies de l'horta nord de València: Mestall, Rascanya i Tormos* (Valencia: Generalitat Valenciana, Conselleria d'Agricultura, Pesca i Alimentació, 2005), 196, the mill stood in the location now occupied by Valencia's public pool, about 750 meters downstream from the royal palace and 350 meters upstream from the Sea Bridge (Pont del Mar).

114. AMV, A-28, 61v–62r.

115. See AMV, A-31, 232v–233r; AMV, A-32, 132v–133r; AMV, A-34, 27v–28r, 33v, 174r, 192v, 272r; AMV, A-35, 127v; AMV, A-36, 154bisr; and AMV, A-38, 33r–33v.

tilian sieges had restored it to royal favor. The successful completion of the new ring of walls in the early 1360s more than doubled the area of the city, and the creation of the Board of Walls and Sewers increased the council's capacity to take on future projects. As the war drew to a close, therefore, the council began to use these capabilities to intervene in the landscape that it ruled. Councils responded to the crises of the early 1370s (particularly the famine of 1374) with plans to rearrange the hydrology around the city: draining stagnant water and bringing fresh water in from outside the horta. For the next four decades, until around 1420, councils responded to natural disaster (and threats of it) by initiating hydraulic projects designed to address vulnerabilities in the landscape. These projects were proposed piecemeal rather than as part of an overarching plan. Nonetheless, successive councils proposed similar moves repeatedly over this period. As repeating phenomena, these projects are indicative of enduring priorities among this generation of the city's ruling class. The Valencian example shows how medieval municipal governments could aspire to reshape their landscapes.

Much of this was aspiration rather than execution. Councils between 1370 and 1420 showed an unusual zeal for initiating landscape improvement. Like most governments, they proposed more projects than they planned, planned more than they executed, and completed very few indeed. Most seem to have foundered on jurisdictional or funding limitations—problems common to municipal authorities. Since the Valencian council rotated officers annually, it must also have struggled to maintain momentum. Energy for irrigation projects in particular appears to have flagged once each drought was over. That few new projects were proposed after 1420 may have been partly a function of these previous failures. Changes in the urban layout and the composition of the city government also led the councils of the 1420s onward to embrace religious ritual rather than infrastructure as their primary disaster response.

The rise and fall of infrastructure projects in Valencia shows that a shift toward technological solutions was not irreversible. For the Valencian council, these hydraulic efforts were one set of tools in a much larger tool kit that could be picked up and abandoned as the situation required. Before 1420, councils seem to have found these projects perfect vehicles for their new aspirations to prosperity and civic prestige. As we will see, these aspirations also had an aggressively Christian flavor.

CHAPTER 3

For the Beautification of the City
Christian Urban Reform

On October 9, 1338, the Feast of Sant Dionís, the city council celebrated "the centennial of the taking of the city of Valencia . . . which the most high Lord King Jaume of Aragon of blessed memory took . . . from the hands of the infidels and liberated to faithful Christians, so that the name of Our Lord Jesus Christ and of the Blessed Virgin his mother and of the saints of paradise might be blessed and praised here."[1] A procession of "worthy men and people of the city, [carrying] crosses" wound through the streets from the Cathedral of Valencia to the city gates and out to the Monastery of Sant Vicent Martir, an early Christian martyr "who to maintain and exalt the Catholic faith willingly endured and suffered martyrdom and [allowed] his blood to be spilled and suffered death in the aforesaid city" of Valencia.[2] Vicent was the city's patron saint, and his monastery one of its oldest Christian sites. A site of Mozarabic devotion supposedly constructed over the martyr's original tomb, the monastery and hospital were established by Jaume the Conqueror soon after the

---

1. "Lo centenar dayns se compliria de la preso de la Ciutat de Valencia . . . la qual lo molt alt senyor en Jacme de bona memoria rey dArago pres & trasch de mans dels infeels & liura aquella a feels cristians per tal qual nom del nostre Senyor Jehu Xrist e de la benaventurada Verge mare sua & dels sants de paradis hi fos benehit e loat." AMV, A-3, 245v–246r.

2. "Lo qual per mantenir & exalçar la fe catholica volch sostenir a sufrir martiri & la sua sanch esser estampada & mort sufrir en la dita Ciutat." AMV, A-3, 245v.

conquest.[3] Vicent was, therefore, one of the city's few claims to a Christian past that extended before 1238.

The symbolism of the centenary procession was not subtle. Like Fourth of July celebrations would later be in the young United States, this event was intended to foster a memory of Valencia's illustrious foundation. The council further declared that the procession would be held annually on October 9 "for all time" (as it is still in Valencia today).[4] Subsequent generations of councilmen took this tradition to heart. The newly ambitious councils of the 1370s redoubled their efforts to live up to the city's crusading heritage. They not only elaborated the city's calendar of Christian civic ritual but sought to transform the city's very fabric in order to obliterate its Andalusi past and religiously mixed present.

City rulers across medieval Europe strove for perfection in their urban spaces. Urban spaces were, in James Scott's phrase, more governable "miniatures" that could stand in for broader ambitions.[5] Medieval culture also inherited from classical antiquity a sense of the city's symbolic weight. The idea of the city as "microcosm of the universe and macrocosm of 'man'" derived from Plato's *Timaeus*, although Aristotle made similar use of macro- and microcosms. As this idea was translated into medieval Christian culture, it centered on Jerusalem, the ideal city that stood for Christendom and the body of Christ.[6] This symbolism was more complex, however, when the city in question was not entirely Christian.

Their Andalusi heritage notwithstanding, the cities and towns of Valencia had, since the conquest, symbolized the conversion of the kingdom as a whole. As Jaume the Conqueror took city after city, he banished the Muslim population beyond the walls and converted the intramural mosques into churches.[7] While the internal displacement of the rural Muslim population was often slow (see chapter 1), the cities could be rendered ostensibly Christian almost immediately. In the city of Valencia, settlers replaced the repurposed mosques with newly built churches by the end of the thirteenth century. The city around them was not so easily transformed.

---

3. Robert I. Burns, "Un monasterio hospital del siglo XIII: San Vicente de Valencia," *Anuario de estudios medievales* 4 (1967): 75–108.

4. AMV, A-3, 247r.

5. James C. Scott, *Seeing Like a State: How Certain Schemes to Improve the Human Condition Have Failed* (New Haven, CT: Yale University Press, 1999), 257–261.

6. Keith D. Lilley, *City and Cosmos: The Medieval World in Urban Form* (London: Reaktion Books, 2009), 7–8, 20.

7. Felipe Fernández-Armesto, *Before Columbus: Exploration and Colonization from the Mediterranean to the Atlantic, 1229–1492* (Philadelphia: University of Pennsylvania Press, 1987), 81–83.

This was partly because Valencia also included officially organized communities (*aljamas*) of Jews and Muslims. While cities across Christian Iberia housed minority religious communities, the relationships between those communities and their municipalities could be fraught. Most urban aljamas in the Crown of Aragon, including Valencia's *jueria* (Jewish quarter) and *moreria* (Moorish quarter), belonged to the king, which limited the authority of increasingly ambitious city governments. At once protected by the king and at his mercy, royal aljamas were, as a number of scholars have noted, both symbols of royal authority and local targets for antiroyalist sentiment.[8] A number of Jewish aljamas were attacked during the Black Death of 1348 (see chapter 6), and still more in the wave of violence that swept across Spain in the summer of 1391. Before and between those years, religiously motivated violence was comparatively rare, local, and limited in scope.[9]

Lack of violence does not, of course, mean harmonious coexistence. The ambitious councils of the 1370s sought to erase both the city of Valencia's Islamic heritage and, where possible, its religious minority neighborhoods. At the same time that these councils were initiating infrastructure projects in the suburbs, they began also to direct the construction of a more thoroughly Christian urban space. City officials focused their efforts on the layout of the streets and on Christian performances that moved along those streets. After the anti-Jewish riots of 1391, moreover, Valencia's Jewish community also became a casualty of the councilmen's vision of an ideal Christian city.

Rebuilding the Christian City

Francesc Eiximenis best articulated the problem that concerned the council in the later fourteenth century: "[The city of Valencia] is still quasi-Moorish, since it was recovered only recently, [and] for that reason [the city council] must attend to the walls, the sewers, the streets, the squares . . . such that the Christian

8. The extensive scholarship on kings and Jewish communities includes Yom Tov Assis, *Jewish Economy in the Medieval Crown of Aragon, 1213–1327* (Leiden: Brill, 1997); William Chester Jordan, *The French Monarchy and the Jews: From Philip Augustus to the Last Capetians* (Philadelphia: University of Pennsylvania Press, 1989); Thomas Barton, *Contested Treasure: Jews and Authority in the Crown of Aragon* (University Park: Pennsylvania State University Press, 2015); and Benjamin Gampel, *Anti-Jewish Riots in the Crown of Aragon and the Royal Response, 1391–1392* (Cambridge: Cambridge University Press, 2016).

9. See Nirenberg, *Communities of Violence*; Mark D. Meyerson, *A Jewish Renaissance in Fifteenth-Century Spain* (Princeton, NJ: Princeton University Press, 2004); and Mark D. Meyerson, *Jews in an Iberian Frontier Kingdom: Society Economy and Politics in Morvedre, 1248–1391* (Leiden: Brill, 2004).

government and the Christian way of life prevails everywhere."[10] Eiximenis spent much of his adult life in Valencia, and in 1384 dedicated his *Regiment de la cosa pública* to the city's jurats. They in turn kept a copy of this text in the council chamber. The *Regiment*, therefore, while not the work of the councilmen, closely mirrors their thinking about urban problems in the later fourteenth century.[11] The jurats were well aware of the problem Eiximenis identified. In a 1393 letter the council reflected on several decades of urban reform, noting that "this city was built by Moors in their custom, narrow and wretched, with many narrow crooked streets and other deformities . . . for some years now every day it receives improvements and embellishments, thank God."[12]

Despite the city's "conversion" after Jaume's conquest, Valencia's Islamic past remained visually evident in a way that, to the council, compromised its Christian present.[13] The urban core, within the original eleventh-century walls, was densely built in a manner understood at the time to be typical of an Islamic city (*madîna*).[14] A few main thoroughfares branched off into a multitude of dead-end alleys (known as *azucachs*, from the Arabic *zuqâq*), each of which would, under Andalusi rule, have housed a particular clan group.[15] After the conquest, Christian settlers occupied this urban core with few major changes. As the population grew in the early fourteenth century, settlers also built new developments, known as *poblas*, extending outward from the walls. These poblas consisted of one or more rectilinear blocks of new buildings,

---

10. "Perquè, com la ciutat és encara quasi morisca per haver estat recuperada fa poc, convé que poseu atenció en la reparació dels murs, fossats, carrers i places . . . de manera que el govern cristià i la forma de vida cristiana prevalga pertot." Eiximenis, *Regiment de la cosa pública*, 57–58.

11. Albert Hauf, Vicent Martines, and Elena Sánchez, "Introduction," in Francesc Eiximenis, *Lo regiment de la cosa pública en el Dotzè del Crestià*, trans. Vicent Martines and María Justiniano (Madrid: Centrio de Linguistica Aplicada Atenea, 2009), 22–23; Narbona , *Valencia, municipio medieval*, 14.

12. "Aquesta ciutat fo edificada per moros a lur costum, estreta e mesquina, ab molts carrer estrets voltats e altres deformitats, e com dalcuns anys a ençà pren tots dies melloraments e embelliments, a Déu mercé." In *Epistolari de la València medieval*, ed. Agustín Rubio Vela and Antoni Ferrando (Valencia: Insitut de Filologia Valenciana / Publicacions de l'Abadia de Montserrat, 1998), 86.

13. On the Christian-inflected urbanism of late medieval Valencia, see José Hinojosa Montalvo, *Una ciutat gran i populosa: Toponimia y urbanismo en la Valencia medieval* (Valencia: Ayuntamiento de Valencia, 2014), 21–30; and Antoni Furió and Juan Vicente García Marsilla, "La ville entre deux cultures: Valence et son urbanisme entre Islam et féodalité," in *La forme de la ville de l'Antiquité à la Renaissance*, ed. Stéphane Bourdin, Michel Paoli, and Anne Reltgen-Tallon (Rennes, France: Presses Universitaires de Rennes, 2015), 37–55.

14. On the evolution of such street plans, see Richard W. Bulliet, *The Camel and the Wheel*, 2nd ed. (New York: Columbia University Press, 1990), 223–227; and Hugh Kennedy, "From Polis to Madina: Urban Change in Late Antique and Early Islamic Syria," *Past and Present* 106 (1985): 3–27.

15. Josep Torró and Enric Guinot, "De la *madîna* a la ciutat. Les pobles del sud i la urbanització dels extramurs de València (1270–1370)," *Saitabi* 51–52 (2001–2): 56; Hinojosa Montalvo, *Una ciutat gran i populosa*, 20–21.

with facades fronting on streets wide and straight enough to allow wheeled traffic. The earliest was known as the Pobla de l'Almoina, built just after 1300, but they were usually named after their developers (for example En Bellvis, Na Carcassona, and Berenguer Dalmau), for whom the poblas were sources of rental income. A few poblas were built within the walls on space cleared through demolition, but for the most part they were constructed on former agricultural land.[16] Like contemporary settlement of the marshes (see chapter 2) these were private initiatives that rode a wave of population growth in the early fourteenth century.

The completion of the expanded ring of walls in 1356 brought these islands of development into the city proper (see map 3). The new city of the later fourteenth century therefore contained two distinct zones: the Andalusi-era core and, surrounding it, a ring of developments built by and for Christian settlers. This outer area was laid out with relatively wide and straight streets between roughly rectangular blocks. While its piecemeal development precluded a true rectilinear grid, it stood in contrast to the old city, where the street plan was still that of the Andalusi madîna. Although Valencia's actual Muslim community had been relegated to a neighborhood outside these walls, the "Islamic" street plan was harder to rearrange.

Eiximenis, following Augustine, believed that the material city should reflect the beauty and order of the celestial city. A geometric grid of "great and wide" main streets and "straight and beautiful" secondary streets should lead in clear and logical fashion from the gates to the cathedral at the center. Eiximenis here drew on the concept of the divine order of the heavenly Jerusalem; his ideal city was Christian to its very cobblestones.[17] Eiximenis was not alone in his desire for straighter streets; all across Europe, founders of new towns from the twelfth century onward favored orthogonal street plans.[18] This included the new towns founded in the kingdom of Valencia since the conquest: Almenara, Nules, Soneixa, and Vila-real were all laid out on a grid.[19]

16. Concha Camps and Josep Torró, "Baños, hornos y pueblas. La pobla de Vila-Rasa y la reordenación urbana de Valencia en el siglo XIV," in Dauksis and Taberner, eds., Historia de la Ciudad, 2:141–143.

17. "Carrer gran e ample travessant tota la ciutat de part a part . . . carrers drets e bells de cascun dels portals menys principals." Francesc Eiximenis, Dotzè del Crestià, chap. 110, quoted in David Guixeras, "L'urbanisme al Dotzè del Crestià," Mot so razo 8 (2009), 82–83.

18. Lilley, City and Cosmos, 62–71; A. E. J. Morris, History of Urban Form before the Industrial Revolution, 3rd ed. (Harlow, UK: Season Education, 1994), 119–143. For a number of local case studies, see Anngret Simms and Howard B. Clarke, eds., Lords and Towns in Medieval Europe: The European Historic Towns Atlas Project (Farnham, UK: Ashgate, 2015).

19. Soledad Vila, La ciudad de Eiximenis. Un proyecto teórico de urbanismo en el siglo XIV (Valencia: Diputació de Valencia, 1984), 118.

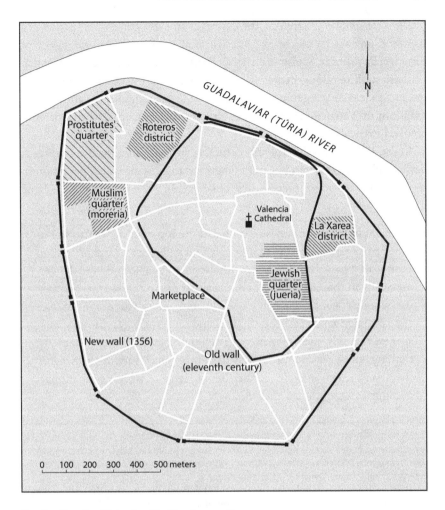

MAP 3. The city of Valencia with old and new walls

Existing cities also took steps in this period to widen and straighten intramural streets.[20] Although more frequently associated with early modern and

---

20. Such efforts are particularly well documented in Italy. For Siena, see Fabrizio Nevola, *Siena: Constructing the Renaissance City* (New Haven, CT: Yale University Press, 2007), 18. For Bologna, see Francesca Bocchi, "Shaping the City: Urban Planning and Physical Structures," in *A Companion to Medieval and Renaissance Bologna*, ed. Sarah Rubin Blanshei (Leiden: Brill, 2018), 73–74. For efforts focused on central piazzas, see Areli Marina, *The Italian Piazza Transformed: Parma in the Communal Age* (University Park: Pennsylvania State University Press, 2012). For Spain, see note 22 below and also María Eva Gutiérrez Millán, "La ciudad de Salamanca entre los siglos XIII y XV: Una eficaz planificación no escrita," in *L'edilizia prima della rivoluzione industriale secc. XIII–XVIII: Atti della 'Trenta Seiesima Settimana di Studi' 26–30 aprile 2004* (Prato, Italy: Istituto Internazionale di Storia Economica F.

modern sensibilities, therefore, the desire for an orthogonal street plan was a common one across medieval Christian municipalities.[21] But the legacy of conquest in Valencia, as elsewhere in southern Iberia, shaped this desire in particularly stark religious terms.[22] Both Eiximenis and the council applied Augustinian ideas of the geometric city of God to the religious situation of the kingdom of Valencia: coding wide, straight streets Christian and narrow, crooked streets Islamic.

In the 1370s, alongside the infrastructure projects described in chapter 2, newly ambitious councils began to take steps to close or widen preconquest streets and to demolish preconquest buildings. In 1377, the council declared that

> there are in the city many streets that at the top or at the corners or in other parts are so narrow that people and still more beasts of burden cannot well pass through them without great trouble and even danger, especially in the time of the grape harvest. And other streets in which the Moorish [morisques] wall or walls of some houses jut out more than the Christian walls of other houses and in other ways are very misshapen and ugly and are indirect in their passage. And others that have nothing but twists and turns to them or through closure of the head of them very much impede or hurt the business of people and animals coming and going along them.[23]

Datini, 2005), 365–381; Beatriz Arizona Bolumburu, "Formation et évolution du tissues urban dans le pays basque: L'exemple du Guipuzcoa," in *La ville au Moyen Age: Actes du 120e Congrès National des Sociétés Historiques et Scientifiques, Section d'Histoire Médiévale et de Philologie, Aix-en-Provence, 23–29 octobre 1995*, vol. 1, *Ville et espace* (Paris: CTHS, 1998), 41–50.

21. Wim Boerefijn, "About the Ideal Layout of the City Street in the Twelfth to Sixteenth Centuries: The Myth of the Renaissance in Town Building," *Journal of Urban History* 42, no. 5 (2016): 938–952. For examples of this association, see Morris, *History of Urban Form*, esp. 157–163; and Scott, *Seeing Like a State*, 53–63.

22. On similar efforts in the cities of Andalucía, conquered around the same time as Valencia, see Antonio Collantes de Terán Sánchez, "Espacio urbano y sociedad en la Andalucía bajomedieval: De la ciudad andalusí a la castellana," in *Morphologie et identité sociale dans la ville médiévale hispanique*, ed. Flocel Sabaté and Christian Guilleré (Chambéry, France: Université de Savoie, 2012), 173–192; José Manuel Escobar Camacho, "Córdoba en la baja Edad Media: La red viera de una ciudad mudéjar," *Boletín de la Real Academia de Córdoba de Ciencias, Bellas Letras y Nobles Artes* 138 (2000): 9–56; Pedro Jiménez Castillo and Julio Navarro Palazón, "El urbanismo islámico y su transformación después de la conquista cristiana: El caso de Murcia," in *La ciudad medieval: De la casa al tejido urbano; Actas del primer curso de Historia y Urbanismo Medieval organizado por la Universidad de Castilla-La Mancha*, ed. Jean Passini (Cuenca, Spain: Ediciones de la Universidad de Castilla–La Mancha, 2001), 71–129.

23. "En la dita Ciutat hauia diverses carrers dels quals alcuns en los caps o cantonales o altres partices daquells han tanta estretura que sens gran affayn e encara perill les gents e majorment les besties de tragi senyaladament a temps de venemes no poden bonament passar per aquells altres ni ha que per paret o parets morisques dalcuns alberchs daquells carrers les qual ixen o estan mes a enfora que les parets xpianesques dels altres alberchs e en altres maneres han gran deformitat o legea hon

As was the case for notaries in Marseilles during the same period, the Valencian council focused not on the visual regularity of the streets when viewed from above but rather on the experience of walking through them.[24] This experience, it concluded, was marred by evidence of Islamic heritage; the council consistently used words like *letg* (ugly) and *diforme* (twisted or misshapen) to describe Andalusi-era structures. In 1380 the council compensated En Anthoni Tibalt for the demolition of a wooden walkway and exterior staircase attached to a house he owned in Temple Square, because "the walkway and stairs were ancient and Moorish, and gave great deformity to the square, in which . . . when the king's court . . . is in the city, there are many royal officials and functionaries and other foreign persons."[25] Such relics were considered an embarrassment to the new Christian city.

Starting in the early 1370s, the council began to issue permits for property owners to close *azucachs* (dead-end alleys) on the grounds of avoiding trash (*inmundicies*) and criminal behavior.[26] In 1373 the council granted a favor "in reverence . . . to the church of Sant Salvador" that an azucach near the church be closed "to avoid rubbish and other inconvenient things."[27] In 1374 an alley (*carrero*) that ran from the moat to the Church of the Holy Cross was closed on account of "the filth that . . . was thrown into [it] and the stench that issued from it."[28] In 1388, the council allowed the residents of a certain "alley or azucach" to close it with a wooden gate, in order to avoid "throwing or putting filth into it . . . and opportunities for night-time hiding places."[29] Likewise, an azucach running alongside the Convent of Santa Magdalena was allowed to be closed in December 1391 because if it were allowed to stay open it "might be a hiding place of evil men, especially at night."[30] Whether or not the councilmen

---

encara desauinentea de passatge. E altres ni ha que per voles o girades daquells. O per tancament dels caps daquells embarguen o laguien molt lespatxament del anar de les gents e de les besties e de venir a lur terme." AMV, A-17, 157r–v.

24. Daniel Lord Smail, *Imaginary Cartographies: Possession and Identity in Late Medieval Marseille* (Ithaca, NY: Cornell University Press, 1999).

25. "Los quals andamis e escalera eren de temps antich e moriscs e dauen gran deformitat a la dita plaça en la qual comunament e majorment a temps que la cort del Senyor Rey o del Senyor Duch sia en aquesta Ciutat ha posaderies e confluencia de molts curials e daltres persones estranyes." AMV, Clavaria I-11, 15v.

26. See, for example, AMV, A-16, 173r, 179v; and A-17, 11r, 30v–31r, 118r.

27. "En reverencia e favor de la ecclesia de Sent Salvador . . . per esquivar inmundicies e altres coses inconvenients." AMV, A-16, 173r.

28. "Per les sutzures que en lo dit carrero eren lançades e per la pudor que en exia." AMV, A-16, 229v.

29. "No lancen o lançar o metre facen alcunes sutzures dins aquell, com per esquivar aço & occasions de amagatalls de nit en lo dit carrero se atorch la present tanqua." AMV, A-19, 14v–15r.

30. "Stant ubert lo dit carrero era o fora amagatayll de mals homes specialment de nit." AMV, A-19, 275v–276r.

really believed in the criminal potential of such spaces, this rhetoric appears repeatedly as a means to justify closing them. In 1390, part of an azucach that opened onto the Street of the Silversmiths (Argenteria) was granted to one En Francesc d'Arques to expand his house.[31] On May 4, 1397, it was asserted before the council that a certain "little azucach or alley that is between the houses of the honorable En Joan of Torre Grossa and the lady Na Maria, wife of the late En Francesc Piquer in the parish of Sant Salvador . . . was a hiding place and occasion for evil."[32] The council ordered that the place be inspected to see if this was true, and if it could be closed without prejudice to any property owners. On May 9 the city administrator (*sindic*) En Vicent Queralt reported that he had seen the alley and spoken with En Joan, Na Maria, and the other neighbors, and was of the opinion that "this azucach cannot serve any good except as a hiding place and occasion for evil." The jurats therefore concluded that it should be closed for the public good.[33] Although the council's priorities are clear in these documents, the projects were often initiated in response to petitions from property owners. Property rights were a greater constraint on the council in the city than in the suburbs, so infrastructure reforms were sometimes more piecemeal there than outside the city walls.

At the same time, the council undertook to widen through streets, claiming that wider, straighter streets would make the city more beautiful.[34] In 1376 the council purchased and partly demolished a "Moorish house" near the Church of Sant Lorenç in order to widen the street "for the beauty of the city."[35] In 1377 the city appointed a committee to oversee the widening of Great Sant Nicolau Street (today the Carrer dels Cavallers), and "a street that goes from near the Church of Sant Tomàs to the Church of Sant Joan of the Hospital near the Jueria."[36] In 1383, the council decided to demolish the Boatella Gate in the Andalusi city wall, with all its "angles and corners" and associated buildings, so that the main street leading the Monastery of Sant Vicent Martir could be straightened and made wider. In 1392 the council claimed that a new street near the Church of Sant Jordí had been built "to avoid turns and

---

31. AMV, A-19, 180r–v.

32. "Un petit azucach o carrero sens exida lo qual es entre los . . . alberchs del honrat En Johan de Torre Grossa & de la dona Na Maria muller çaenrere d'En Francesc Piquer defunct situats en la parroquia de Sent Salvador de la dita ciutat afferman quell dit azucach o carrero era amagatall & occasion e mal." AMV, A-21, 87v.

33. "Quel dit azucach no pot servir a res de be sino amagatall o a occasio de mal." AMV, A-21, 87v, 90v–91r.

34. See, for example, AMV, A-16, 118r–v.

35. AMV, A-17, 77r.

36. "Lo carrer major de Sent Nicholau appellat dels Cavallers per esguart del cap damunt daquell e .i. carrer per lo qual parten prop de la ecclesia de Sent Thomas va hom a la ecclesia de Sent Johan de l'Espital prop la Juheria e alcuns altres carrers." AMV, A-17, 157r–v.

tortuousness and delay in streets and passages, and for the consequent public profit and beauty of the city."³⁷ ᴄ٭٭ ᵥₑₐᵤₜᵢfᵤₗ ₘₒᵥₑₘₑₙₜ

In some parts of the city such beautiful openness was seen as a zero-sum proposition. In 1382 the council considered opening a new street between the marketplace and the Street of the Secondhand Clothes Dealers (Pelleria), running through the old wall, but concluded that it would narrow the existing street (Carrer de la Porta Nova or New Gate Street) that transected the wall in this part of town. To do this would destroy "one of the greatest and most beautiful things that the city has, and [a thing] for which it is famous among many in foreign parts, that is, the great press of people [going] through New Gate Street . . . near and in view of its loggia of merchants." This sight, according to the council, was a "great marvel [to] foreign merchants, and others . . . so much so that it is praised in all parts by a great multitude of people." Narrowing the street would apparently "take away its beauty and fame, and that of the city,"³⁸ and on these grounds the council rejected the project.

Civic Christianity

The project to open and straighten the city streets was intimately connected to one of their uses: celebrating the city's Christianity, and particularly its crusading legacy. Just before the Feast of Corpus Christi in 1390 the council ordered an "old and ruinous Moorish overhang" (embant vell morisch & roinos) in the Street of Sant Martí torn down not only because it was hazardous but because "it was extremely ugly on account of its great lowness . . . and what is more grave, when the processions in the days of Corpus Christi and Sant Jordí and Sant Dionís are done in the city, all of which are accustomed to pass by the street, it would happen that that those carrying the crosses and the pennants would have to stay well away from said overhang, lest they cause it to fall."³⁹ This language stresses the Christian processional role of city streets and

---

37. "Per esquivar voltes & tortuositats & tarda de carrers & de passatges & per conseguent profit publich & bellea de la dita ciutat." AMV, A-20, 25r.

38. "Es vist esser proveit e veday quel dit pas e carrer no sia ubert . . . quel dit pas e carrer nou bos devia fer . . . tolliment de una de les maiors e pus belles coses que la dita Ciutat ha e per les quals aquella en part lunydanes ha gran fama specialment de gran e molt poble ço es lo gran e molt espes passatge de gents del carrer de la Portanova de la dita Ciutat prop e en vista de la lotja dels mercaders daquella no sens gran maravella dels mercaders estrangers e altres qui alli estan en tant quel dit passatge es loat en tots parts de gran multitud de gents. . . . E si lo dit pas e carrer nou era ubert e fet aminuara molt al dita passatge de Portanova e lotja e tolria la dita bellea e fama daquell e de la Ciutat." AMV, A-17, 290r–v.

39. "Que en la carrer maior e prop la ecclesia de Sent Martí de la dita Ciutat hauia dos obradors ab embant vell morisch & roinos . . . lo qual embant era no tantsolament perillos per la sua vellea & dispositio de ruina com soven ne cayguessen rajoles ans encara estava fort letg per la sua gran baxea

sets up Andalusi-era buildings as impediments to that sacred purpose. As Thomas Devaney has shown, urban rituals were key to the construction of frontier ideology in late medieval Castile; though farther from the frontier, Valencia was similarly invested in a Christianizing ritual narrative.[40]

Processions had been relatively infrequent in Valencia in the early fourteenth century (see chapter 4), but the councils of the early 1370s brought new energy into annual celebrations of the city's Christianity. The first official Corpus Christi procession in the city had been held in 1355 (around the same time that the feast appeared elsewhere in Spain), but the intervening years had seen only small processions at the parish level.[41] In 1372 the council took control of the feast, declaring a single, city-wide procession and fines for participating in any competing celebration.[42] That same summer the council attempted to establish another feast dedicated to the city's Christian heritage. In mid-July, the jurats announced that on the upcoming Feast of Santa Anna (July 27), "and from then on every year in perpetuity," the city would celebrate the anniversary of the death of King Jaume the Conqueror, that "most excellent, holy and virtuous Lord King . . . who conquered and took this city and all its kingdom from the hands of infidels."[43] The initiative had the support of the current king, Pere the Ceremonious, who was also interested in establishing an anniversary for his illustrious forebear.[44] This attempt to jump-start a religious cult around the Aragonese crusader king echoed those of his contemporaries Fernando III of Castile and Louis IX of France. Although Jaume was revered in the city and authorities at all levels regularly referred to him as a saint, no official cult was ever established.[45] The anniversary service was held in 1372,

en tant que tot lo dit carrer qui era notable nestava despareçat & ço que pus greu era quant les processons en los dies de Corpore Xpi & de Sent Jordi & de Sent Dionis se fahien en la dita Ciutat les quals totes solen passar e passen per lo dit carrer covenia quels portants les creus & los penons se appartassen be del dit embant en altra manera molts a destruyt hi daven en fahien caure." AMV, A-19, 117r–v.

40. Devaney, Enemies in the Plaza.

41. Francis George Very, The Spanish Corpus Christi Procession: A Literary and Folkloric Study (Valencia: Tipografía Moderna, 1962), 4–5.

42. AMV, A-16, 77r, 87r–87v.

43. AMV, A-16, 96r–96v, 98v.

44. The city's announcement, however, does not seem to have been in direct response to a royal command. In 1372 the king wrote a letter asking the council to establish this anniversary, but it was dated July 15 in Barcelona, and could not have reached the council by the following day, when the decision was recorded in the books of acts (Manuals de Consells). The text of the council's announcement states that king and council had discussed the matter in times past. See Agustín Rubio Vela, "Jaume I. La imagen del monarca en la Valencia de los siglos XIV y XV," in El rei Jaume I: Fets, actes i paraules, ed. Germà Colón Domènech and Tomàs Martínez Romero (Barcelona: Fundacio Germà Colón Domènech / Publicaions de l'Abadia de Montserrat, 2008), 140–141.

45. Rubio Vela, "Jaume I. La imagen del monarca," 129–155. On Jaume's lack of saintly qualifications, see Robert I. Burns, "The Spiritual Life of James the Conqueror, King of Aragon-Catalonia, 1208–1276: Portrait and Self-Portrait," Catholic Historical Review 62, no. 1 (1976): 5.

but afterward seems to have disappeared without a trace. At precisely the moment that the council began to be concerned about the reform of the city and the renovation of the extramural landscape, it also began to promote Corpus Christi (and, briefly, Jaume's anniversary) as a celebration of Christian identity. The councils of the 1370s were developing a tradition of civic religious performance intended to highlight Valencia's Christianity that was similar to those developed in other cities during the later Middle Ages.[46] Such rituals took on a particular charge along the Iberian frontier, where Christianity was less of a settled issue.[47]

The route of the Corpus Christi procession of 1372 betrays the council's anxieties about the confessional geography of the city. It covered much of the same ground as the first Corpus Christi procession in 1355, but with significant changes. In 1355 the procession had traced a rough circle counterclockwise around the city, leaving the cathedral via the Apostles' Door and passing outside the old walls through the Gate of the Moreria (opposite the main gate of the moreria itself), turning east through the marketplace and back inside the walls at the Boatella Gate. From there the procession passed in front of the main gate of the jueria and back around to the cathedral, entering by the opposite door, near the bishop's palace (see map 4). This circular movement, first outside and then back inside the walls, is similar to Corpus Christi routes recorded elsewhere in Europe, which tended to make symbolic circuits of their cities and to pass through significant places like the market square.[48]

In 1372 the procession left the cathedral from the opposite side, near the bishop's palace. It then wound clockwise around the front of the cathedral toward the Church of Sant Nicolau, and made a sharp left down the Bosseria to pass through the market with only a glance at the moreria. It then continued counterclockwise around the city center before crossing its own path to reenter the

46. See, for example, Andrew Brown, *Civic Ceremony and Religion in Medieval Bruges, c. 1300–1520* (Cambridge: Cambridge University Press, 2011); Mervyn James, "Ritual, Drama and Social Body in the Late Medieval English Town," *Past and Present* 93 (1983): 3–29; Edward Muir, *Civic Ritual in Renaissance Venice* (Princeton, NJ: Princeton University Press, 1981); and Barbara A. Hanawalt, *Ceremony and Civility: Civic Culture in Late Medieval London* (Oxford: Oxford University Press, 2017).

47. On civic ritual elsewhere on the Iberian frontier, see Devaney, *Enemies in the Plaza*; David Coleman, *Creating Christian Granada: Society and Religious Culture in an Old-World Frontier City, 1492–1600* (Ithaca, NY: Cornell University Press, 2003); and A. Katie Harris, *From Muslim to Christian Granada: Inventing a City's Past in Early Modern Spain* (Baltimore: Johns Hopkins University Press, 2007).

48. Charles Zika, "Hosts, Processions and Pilgrimages: Controlling the Sacred in Fifteenth-Century Germany," *Past and Present* 118 (1988): 38–40. See also Lilley, *City and Cosmos*, 158–184, and Thomas A. Boogaart II, "'Our Saviour's Blood: Procession and Community in Late Medieval Bruges," in *Moving Subjects: Processional Performance in the Middle Ages and the Renaissance*, ed. Kathleen Ashely and Wim Hüsken (Amsterdam: Brill, 2001), 69–116.

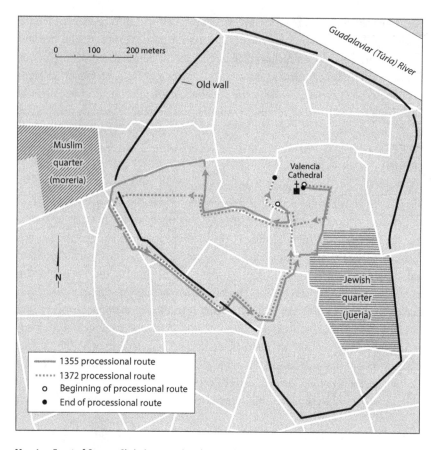

Map 4. Feast of Corpus Christi processional routes in 1355 and 1372

cathedral at the Apostles' Door, avoiding the Jewish quarter altogether (see map 4). Where the 1355 procession made a circle, therefore, the 1372 procession covered similar ground in a figure eight, avoiding both the jueria and the moreria.

Between 1355 and 1372, of course, the city's geography had changed. In 1355 the moreria had been outside the walls and the jueria on the urban fringe. Both quarters conformed to notions of appropriate social order, with each faith in its proper place. The completion of the new ring of walls in 1358, however, put both well within the city limits. Avoidance would not be a permanent strategy. As the council began to legislate its project of Christian urban reform in the 1370s, streets on the Corpus Christi processional route received particular attention. Great Sant Nicolau Street, which was slated for expansion in 1377, was on the 1355 processional route, and the street that went from the Church of Sant Tomàs to the Church of Sant Joan of the Hospital, also to be expanded, was probably adjacent to it.[49] The Corpus Christi route of 1372 avoided both, but by 1384, the procession was back to a circular trajectory: along the newly widened Great Sant Nicolau Street to the moreria, through the marketplace and the "marvelous" New Gate Street to the newly renovated Boatella Gate, along Sant Martí Street to the main gate of the jueria, and from there back to the cathedral.

Corpus Christi and the other processions organized in Valencia probably excluded Jews and Muslims, in contrast to the more ecumenical processions that took place in other Iberian cities. While minority religious communities were closely linked to royal power, their roles in municipal rituals varied widely. The city of Saragossa forbade Jews and Muslims from watching Corpus Christi processions, even from their own homes. The city of Murcia, on the other hand, expected both Jews and Muslims to participate in Corpus Christi celebrations.[50] In Valencia, Jews and Muslims took part in the ceremonies that marked royal entrances to the city. When Mata de Armagnac, the new wife of the future King Joan the Hunter, made her first entrance into Valencia in 1373, the council made sure to accommodate "the Jews and the Moors of the city who come out to receive the lady, in their best garments as they have been accustomed to do."[51] Valencia's civic processions, by contrast, seem to have been exclusively Christian. The text of rogation announcements from the 1340s declares the city's desire to move God through "the prayers of faithful Christians" and invite "all Christian men and women" (tot cristia e crisitiana) to participate.[52] In most of its general proclamations, the council spoke of "all and sundry persons of whatever religion [ley], condition, or class."[53] The text of Corpus Christi proclamations omitted mention of different religions when discussing those taking part in the procession itself: "clerics and lay men and women of whatever age, condition, or class they might be."[54] This omission might not be significant, but the same proclamation enjoined those of "whatever religion, condition, or class" who lived along the processional route to clean the street in front of their houses. Whether non-Christians watched these processions is less clear. A thirteenth-century law required Jews and Muslims to either hide themselves or kneel in the presence of the Eucharist, and

---

49. AMV, A-17, 157r–v.

50. Devaney, Enemies in the Plaza, 154–155.

51. "Los juheus e los moros de la Ciutat que isquen reebre cascuns per si la dita Senyora ab lurs mellors apparellaments segons han acostumat." AMV, A-16, 159v.

52. AMV, A-4, 179r.

53. For an example of this phrasing, see AMV, A-17, 197v–198r.

54. "Clergues com lechs homens & dones de qualsevol edat condicio o estament sien." AMV, A-18, 39v–40r.

a council statement from 1385 makes clear that some made a habit of ducking down streets or into nearby houses at the sound of the bell that announced processions.[55] By the late fifteenth century, when Corpus Christi processions had become much more elaborate, Muslims would travel in from the countryside to watch them.[56]

The bell was not the only sound that marked the geography of the city's religious performance. Much to the dismay of city officials, the soundscape continued to include Muslim calls to prayer. Verbal calls made from a minaret had been banned since the early days of the conquest, but in Valencia the use of a horn (*nafill*) or other instrument seems to have been customary from at least the early fourteenth century onward. The city government made periodic attempts to ban the horn in the moreria. In a petition to the *Corts* (the kingdom's parliamentary body) on the subject in 1371, it claimed that the sound of the horn was a "great disgrace to the holy Christian faith and [a great] displeasure to all faithful Christians," particularly at dusk, when the horn interrupted the bell announcing Christian evening prayers. The king rejected this petition, so the horn was probably still heard in the city in the later fourteenth century.[57]

The Jueria

The Jewish quarter became a particular focus of the council's concern in the later fourteenth century. In 1393, in the course of a dispute with the order of the Hospitalers, whose convent was adjacent to the Jewish quarter, the jurats recalled that some years earlier they had, at great expense, opened "a street or azucach that descended from the street of Sant Tomàs to Sant Joan of the Hospital, as it was all populated with Jews—having thrown out the Christians who used to be there—and from the head of this azucach through to the street there was no more space, just some old and putrid spaces of great ugli-

55. AMV, A-18, 83r–v.

56. See, for example, an excerpt from the trial of Açen Musa, which describes Muslims from the village of Alacuas traveling into the city to watch the Corpus Christi procession. ARV, Baile General, Registro 1431, 64v–99r; translated in *Medieval Iberia: Readings from Christian, Muslim, and Jewish Sources*, 2nd ed., ed. Olivia Remie Constable (Philadelphia: University of Pennsylvania Press, 2012), 491–493.

57. "Gran vituperi de la sancta ley chrisitana e desplaer de tots los feels christians majorment car los moros o lurs alfaquins tenen axí prest lo sonar de la dita nafil al vespre que tantost que·l primer toch del seny de la oració és fet, sens esperar de acabar los altres tochs, la dita nafil de continent quasi responent sona." ACA, Real Cancilleria, Registro 1508, 25v–26r; reproduced in Maria Teresa Ferrer i Mallol, *Els sarraïns de la Corona Catalano-Aragonesa en el segle XIV: Segregació i discriminació* (Barcelona: Consell Superior d'Investigacions Científiques, 1987), doc. 98, p. 308. On calls to prayer in the Crown of Aragon, see Olivia Remie Constable, "Regulating Religious Noise: The Council of Vienne, the Mosque Call and Muslim Pilgrimage in the Late Medieval Mediterranean World," *Medieval Encounters* 16, no. 1 (2010): 64–95.

ness, without any profit . . . [or] fruit except to rats and spiders."[58] While the streets in the rest of the city were being widened, the council sought to wall in Valencian Jews. As was the case elsewhere in Europe, marginalized communities were increasingly associated in fourteenth-century Valencia with criminality and disease.[59] Like the body of a single individual, an urban body required both the maintenance of flow and the isolation of hazards. Both humans and cities were nourished by movement: humors through veins, and traffic along streets. If excess waste matter accumulated in the body's extremities, however, it would putrefy and lead to disease, just as the detritus in blind alleyways led to crime. Yet these interdependent bodies also needed to be protected, lest infection in one part pose a risk to the whole.[60] In Eiximenis's ideal city, the sinful and the insalubrious elements—the "hospitals, leprosaria, brothels and gambling houses, and the outflow of sewers"—were to be placed on the margins, downwind from the center, so that neither the wind nor chance encounters would infect the larger city.[61] The containment of indigent beggars and of prostitutes was an ongoing preoccupation of the council in these years (see chapter 6). The jueria and the moreria, meanwhile, were places where the city's Christians went to engage in illicit gambling, a sin that corrupted and ruined men from good families.[62] In 1375 the council complained to the queen that its jurisdiction over the city's Jews was insufficient to punish gambling-related offenses properly.[63] In May 1390 the council sought to crack down on gambling houses throughout the city, and particularly in the Jewish and Muslim quarters.[64]

While the prostitutes' quarter and the moreria were located more or less where Eiximenis said they should be, far from the center and on the lee of

58. ".I. carrer o azucach qui devalla del carrer de Sent Thomàs vers Sent Johan de l'Espital, com fos tot poblat de juheus—foragitats los christians, de qui solia ésser—e del cap daquell azucach tro al dit carrer jusà no hagués pus espay, sinó alcuns patis vells e podrits e de gran legea, sens tot profit de Sent Johan de l'Espital, qui no fahien fruyt sinó a rates e aranyes." In Rubio Vela and Ferrando, Epistolari, 86.

59. See Rawcliffe, Urban Bodies, 54–104; Brian Pullan, "Plague and Perceptions of the Poor in Early Modern Italy," in Epidemics and Ideas: Essays on the Historical Perception of Pestilence, ed. Terence Ranger and Paul Slack (Cambridge: Cambridge University Press, 1992), 101–123.

60. Carole Rawcliffe, "The Concept of Health in Late Medieval Society," in Interazioni fra economia e ambiente biologico nell'Europa preindustriale, secc. XIII–XVIII, ed. Simonetta Cavaciocchi (Florence: Firenze University Press, 2010), 318; Rawcliffe, Urban Bodies, 54–60. Janna Coomans, Community, Urban Health and Environment in the Late Medieval Low Countries (Cambridge: Cambridge University Press, 2021), 32, 254–268.

61. "Espitals, llocs de llebrosos, bordells e tafureries e escorriments de clavegueres," Eiximenis, Dotzé del Crestià, chap. 110, quoted in Guixeras, "L'urbanisme al Dotzè del Crestià," 84.

62. Hinojosa Montalvo, Jews of the Kingdom of Valencia, 121. See, for example, AMV, A-16, 47v–48r. On the dangers of gambling in general, see chapter 6 of the present book.

63. AMV, g3-3, 136r–v.

64. AMV, A-19, 135v–136r.

Valencia's easterly winds, the jueria presented a problem.[65] Since it, unlike the moreria, predated the Christian conquest, it had always been located within the original city walls, very close to the city center (see map 3). With the completion of the new ring of walls, even the Jewish cemetery was inside the city.[66] In 1363, soon after the walls were built, the council ordered that the gravestones from this cemetery be removed and repurposed as a dam for a mill that was to be built in the area. The text of this piece of legislation claims only that mills would bring "honor" to the city, but the council clearly also wished to minimize Jewish presence within the walls.[67]

Still worse, from the council's perspective, was that by the late fourteenth century the Jewish community of Valencia had outgrown its old boundaries. The War of the Two Peres had also spurred Jewish immigration from the other towns of kingdom to the capital. As early as the 1371 Corts of Valencia, delegates from the cities complained that Jews were living outside the boundaries of their quarters. A royal command to maintain "separate and closed" Jewish quarters in every town in the kingdom apparently had limited effect, because the issue was raised again at the Corts of 1380. Despite these prohibitions, Jews continued to live and work in the parishes surrounding the Jewish quarter. In 1381 the Church of Sant Tomàs sought to fund its renovations through a tax on the Jews living in the parish. Complaints about Jews living in Christian parishes and Christians in the jueria persisted throughout the 1380s.[68] Mixing was also a concern in the moreria in these years. Royal decrees alternated between affirming the right of Christians (including converts and their descendants) to live in the moreria and ordering these Christians to abandon the quarter.[69]

The council had attempted to maintain separation between Christians, Jews, and Muslims throughout the fourteenth century, but these regulations became more frequent in the decade or so leading up to 1391. In 1383, and again in 1384 and 1391, the council reiterated restrictions forbidding Christian women

---

65. On how Eiximenis's ideal winds differ from Vitruvius and correspond to the Valencian climate, see Vila, *La ciudad de Eiximenis*, 93.

66. The Jews of Valencia would not necessarily have approved of this situation either; cemeteries outside the walls were customary for Jewish communities in this region. See Miquel Pujol i Canelles, "El fossar dels jueus de Castelló d'Empúries," *Annals de l'Institut d'Estudis Empordanesos* 36 (2003): 49.

67. AMV, A-14, 7v–9r. A similar appropriation of Jewish gravestones as construction materials took place in Tortosa in 1368. Albert Curto Homedes, "Topografia del call jueu de Tortosa," *Recerca* 3 (1999): 15.

68. "Apartats e closes." ACA, Real Cancilleria, Registro 811, 8v–9, quoted in Meyerson, *Jews in an Iberian Frontier Kingdom*, 267–269.

69. Christians were ordered to abandon the quarter in May 1346, but the order was revoked in August 1346. Their right to remain was affirmed in 1371 and 1372, but they were ordered to leave again in 1384. See Ferrer i Mallol, *Els sarraïns de la Corona Catalano-Aragonesa*, doc. 56, p. 264; doc. 99, pp. 308–311; doc. 100, pp. 312–315; and doc. 111, pp. 325–326.

from entering Jewish homes. Christians were also forbidden from eating with Jews and from attending Jewish weddings.[70] Although these prohibitions suggest a degree of neighborly intimacy, geographic integration had a darker side. On the eve of Easter 1380, in the Parish of Sant Tomàs, a Christian child was killed by a falling stone. Christian witnesses were quick to blame two Jewish tailors whose window opened onto the street. On the basis of their dubious testimony, one of the tailors was tortured, condemned, and executed for murder. As Ferran Garcia-Oliver notes, although the liturgical timing doubtless influenced the outcome of this incident, tensions within this mixed and transient neighborhood played a significant role.[71]

At the Corts of 1389, the city's representatives requested (and the king approved) the complete closure of the Jewish quarter, to be achieved by extending its boundaries to include more of the area where Jews were already living. This was an extremely contentious issue within the Christian community; the jurats elected the following year would ultimately accuse these representatives of treason, and their expansion of the Jewish quarter would be one of the issues cited. While interfaith mixing in these neighborhoods had been a concern for more than a decade, the enclosure of the quarter created a blockage in the heart of the Christian city.[72] The enclosure work began on March 8, 1390, and continued until early July 1391.[73] Almost immediately there were complaints that the closure made that part of the city difficult to navigate, cutting off access to the river and to the port at the river's mouth. The Dominicans, whose convent stood in La Xarea, between the old walls and the river, demanded that "as the council was accustomed . . . to opening streets and making passages for the beautification of the city," it correct this problem with a new street.[74] The council opened two new streets: one just north of the expanded jueria, and another running straight through it.[75] These do not seem to have fully resolved the problem.[76] In fact, the difficulty was unresolvable; the

---

70. AMV, A-18, 13r, 32v–33r; A-19, 200v.

71. Ferran Garcia-Oliver, "Quan la justícia és venjança, contra un jueu," *Anuario de estudios medievales* 43, no. 2 (2013): 577–608.

72. Rafael Narbona Vizcaíno, "El trienio negro: Valencia, 1389–1391. Turbulencias cohetáneas al asalto de la judería," *En la España medieval* 35 (2012): 194, 184–187.

73. Marilda Azulay and Estrella Israel, *La Valencia judía: Espacios, límites y vivencias hasta la expulsión* (Valencia: Consel Valencià de Cultura, 2009), 234.

74. "Com lo consell . . . hagues acostumat . . . per embellir la dita ciutat obrir carreres & fer passatges & altres obres." AMV, A-19, 145v–146r.

75. Doc. 12 in Rubio Vela and Ferrando, *Epistolari*, 85–86; AMV, A-19, 231r–v. See also the map in Narbona, "El trienio negro," 185.

76. Hinojosa Montalvo, *Jews of the Kingdom of Valencia*, 23, suggests that popular anger at the extension of the Jewish quarter was a motive for the riot of 1391 and that Dominican friars themselves took part in the attack. He does not give the source of this information.

council's vision of a harmonious Christian city required openness, but also the isolation of harmful elements. In the Jewish quarter, furthering one of these aims could come only at the expense of the other.

On Sunday, July 9, 1391, a mob assaulted Valencia's newly expanded jueria, killed at least one hundred of its inhabitants and forcibly converted most of the others. This was one of a number of such riots all across Spain that summer, inspired by the preaching in Sevilla of the archdeacon of Écija, Ferrán Martinez. These riots, and their significance for Iberian *convivencia* (interfaith coexistence) more broadly, have been the focus of much historical debate. Most of the surviving details of the Valencian assault come from documents produced by the Valencian council and show that the council shaped its narrative of the assault to serve its urban reform goals.[77]

The council reported that the commotion began around midday. A group of youths carrying crosses began to march toward the gates of the Jewish quarter in imitation of a religious procession, shouting that the Jews must be baptized or die. The gates were open because Sunday was a working day within the quarter. The Christian residents of the city were in the habit of taking advantage of this; in 1386 the council had had to forbid Christians from selling their own wares in the jueria.[78] On this Sunday a crowd began to gather, and the Jews closed the gates, though not before some youths had gotten inside. The jurats' first account of the attack, written the same day, reported that the youths provoked a fight within the gates. The city officials then lost control of the situation, standing helplessly by as the crowd outside invaded and sacked the jueria, looting its treasures and killing or forcibly converting its inhabitants.

In later letters, however, the jurats reframed the narrative to deflect blame for the violence. These more polished letters emphasize the innocence of the youthful procession and fixate on the moment when the Jews closed the gates. Once the gates were closed, the jurats insisted, a rumor grew among the crowd outside that the Jews were killing the youths behind the jueria's walls. City officials ordered the Jews to open the gates, both to show the crowd that no murder was taking place and so that the officials themselves could ride through and secure the streets of the Jewish quarter. This command is presented as a decisive action to restore public order: "We [the jurats], with the good men who were there, all on horseback, would have gone through and secured all the streets and best houses of the Jewish quarter and driven out the people or

---

77. For a fuller discussion of this incident, see Abigail Agresta, "'Unfortunate Jews' and Urban Ugliness: Crafting a Narrative of the 1391 Assault on the Jueria of Valencia," *Journal of Medieval History* 43, no. 3 (2017): 1–22; David Nirenberg, *Neighboring Faiths: Christianity, Islam, and Judaism in the Middle Ages and Today* (Chicago: University of Chicago Press, 2015), 75–88; and Gampel, *Anti-Jewish Riots*.

78. AMV, A-18, 135v.

struck or killed those who would not be driven out, and nothing would have been stolen or destroyed, or at least much less."[79] But instead "the unfortunate Jews, doubting from fear or for whatever other reason, did not want to open the gate, and so the clamor grew. And via the roofs of adjacent Christian houses and via the old sewer the crowd got into the Jewish quarter that [Prince Martí] and jurats and officials could not enter or see."[80] In the ensuing struggle, the jurats reported, the Jews killed a Christian and cut the finger off another. At the sight of corpse and finger the crowd went berserk, and "in a short space of time the whole quarter was sacked, and some one hundred Jews were killed."[81] The jurats thus created a narrative in which the violence of 1391 could be blamed on the Jews themselves, and in particular on their quarter and its walls. If the jueria were not enclosed, and if the Jews did not control the opening and closing of the gate, then the city officials could have done their duty and the crowd would not have been inflamed by rumors of Jewish violence.

None of the other surviving narratives of the 1391 assault focus on this particular moment.[82] That it should be the crucial one for the councilmen makes sense only in the context of their ongoing preoccupation with Christian urban reform. In Eiximenis's ideal city, the streets were straight and wide, the layout open and legible, and the unsavory elements banished to the margins and the private spaces. The very existence of a Jewish quarter, in which Christians gambled away their fortunes and bought and sold on Sundays, ran counter to the council's reform goals. In the council's narrative of July 9, the Jews acted out the same role that their quarter was perceived to play in the city's urban plan. By refusing to open the gates they blocked the free flow of public order through the city.

To the council, the solution was as obvious as it was convenient; the obstacle needed to be eliminated, and the space of the jueria reintegrated into

---

79. "E si los juheus haguessen ubertes les portes axi com lo duch los manava e los officials axi mateix foren sen seguides versemblant dues coses. La una que la gent haguera vist o hauda presumpcio que no fo ver de la mort dels minyons, e dels altres cristians e foras assossegada. E laltra quel duch els officials e nosaltres ab los homens de be que eren ab tots ells e nos a cavall haguerem descorreguts e establerts tots los carrers e alberchs mellors de la juheria, e haguerem fet exir la fent ferin o encara matan ne alcunes que exir non volgueseen, e no si haguera robat ne guastat res o almenys fora poch." AMV, g3-5, 23r.

80. "Los juheus desastruchs duptants de peior o per quesque fos no volgueren obrir & per aço la remor cresque. E molts per terrats dalberchs de cristians contigues a la juheria & alcuns per lo vayll veyll deius lo pont & tanque daquell esvairen la dita juheria quels dits senyor & officials & jurats & altres bons homens noy pogueren entrar ni vedar." AMV, A-19, 243r.

81. "E en poc espay de temps la dita juheria fon dissipada & robada morts daqui en lesvaiment quesque cent juheus entre uns & altres en diverses & maneres." AMV, A-19, 243r.

82. Prince Martí, the ranking official present during the attack, claimed in his report to his brother Joan I that the gates to the jueria were closed on his orders. ACA, Cancilleria, Registro 2093, 119r–120r. The letter is also reproduced in Jaume Riera i Sans, "Los tumultos contra las juderias de la Corona de Aragón en 1391," *Cuadernos de la historia* 8 (1977): 220–221.

the Christian body of the city. In the aftermath of the 1391 assault, the council continued to describe the enclosed jueria as a space of violence and disorder. Already on August 19, the council had written to inform the king that it planned to remove the remaining Jews from the city, to isolate them from the new converts. With the Jews gone, "the closures of the former jueria are without purpose and cause passersby great difficulty, and also engender great sins and crimes because the closures [create] large and deep hiding places."[83] In subsequent letters, the jurats clarified that "on account of the closures [of the jueria] infinite crimes are committed there, including those relating to women, gaming, and theft, and diverse quarrels and disturbances, and before the justice or his lieutenant has reached the place of the disturbance, all the malefactors have already gone."[84] The jurats described the jueria as a kind of large-scale azucach: a dead-end space that fostered criminal activity. The council therefore sought permission to tear down the walls of the quarter and reintegrate it into the Christian city.[85]

On October 2, 1392, King Joan and Queen Violant ordered Valencia's jueria officially dissolved, and "all of the blocks and closures made in the old and new juerias . . . all torn down and opened, and further all gates large and small that have entry into the jueria be entirely demolished and all the entrances be without any impediment public streets without any sign of closure or gate."[86] Although the monarchs sought to reestablish a Jewish quarter in Valencia, by 1403 the council had obtained royal permission never to have Jews in the city again.[87] While there is no evidence that the council began the attack of 1391, it certainly used the violence to further its own ends.

---

83. "Les tanques de la caenrere juheria no sien obs e les gents ne passen gran envig hoc encara que per los grans o pregons amagatalls que hic son per occasio de les dites tanques sen genren e facen grans peccats e mals." AMV, g3-5, 44r.

84. "Per occasio de les tanques se fan alli infinits delictes de fembres e de jochs e de ladronicis e diverses baralles e remors e ans que justicia o lochtinent haia circuit o plegat al loch de la remor ja son fuyts tots los malfeytors." AMV, g3-5, 49v. See also Hinojosa Montalvo, *Jews of the Kingdom of Valencia*, 261–262. In 1394 the council complained that prostitutes were frequenting the former Jewish quarter. AMV, A-20, 196v.

85. The council may have begun to demolish the walls before seeking permission; José Rodrigo y Pertegás, *La judería de Valencia* (Valencia: París-Valencia, 1992 [orig. 1913]), 10, observes that in September 1391 the city paid to have a "Moorish wall" on the street of En Cristòfol Soler torn down. In his opinion, the wall must have formed part of the enclosure of both old and new jueria.

86. Nirenberg, *Neighboring Faiths*, 75–88. The document dissolving the Jewish quarter is ACA, Cancillera, Registro 1905, 32v, issued at Sant Cugat del Vallés. It is partially reproduced in Azulay and Israel, *La Valencia judía*, 245 and also in Rodrigo y Pertegás, *La judería de Valencia*, 16–17.

87. Azulay and Israel, *La Valencia judía*, 279. Hinojosa Montalvo, *Jews of the Kingdom of Valencia*, doc. 270. On Jewish assistance to Judaizing conversos, see Meyerson, *A Jewish Renaissance*, 200–214.

The Fifteenth Century

References to buildings as "ugly" and "Moorish" grew fewer in the years after 1391, but subsequent councils did still seek to "beautify" the city and to widen the streets to accommodate civic rituals.[88] In 1413 the Street of the Beltmakers (Corregeria) proved too narrow for the spectacles planned for the royal entry of King Fernando of Antequera, so the council demolished some houses to create space.[89] Even after this stopgap measure this street remained "very twisted and very narrow" (*molt diforme e molt estret*). In the summer of 1416 the council undertook to widen both it and the Street of the Linen Clothmakers (Draperia de Lli), also on the usual processional route.[90] At the same time, the council restricted construction of projections and overhangs on the streets "of the royal entries and through which pass the processions of Corpus Christi, Sant Jordí, and Sant Dionís." So as not to impede such processions, people could not build extensions from their house facades lower than twenty-five *palms* (about 5.5 meters), and no ground-level projection could extend farther than three *palms* (about sixty-six centimeters) into the street.[91] In the following decades, councils initiated projects to widen several more streets in the urban center.[92] In 1444, one jurat, Galçan de Montsorin, declared to the council that while the Serrans Gate was "very beautiful and . . . renowned throughout the world, the Street of Sant Barthomeu [which led from the gate to the city center] did not correspond to it." This street (now known as Serrans Street), along which "the festivals and solemnities . . . or the entries of the Lord King and Queen . . . continually passed" was "narrow, twisted, and ugly on account of the overhangs and in other ways." The council undertook the demolition of these overhangs and purchased adjacent properties in order to widen the street.[93] The council of 1448 undertook a similar effort to

---

88. See Amadeo Serra Desfilis, "El 'consell' de Valencia y el 'embelliment de la ciutat,' 1412–1460," in *Primer Congreso de Historia del Arte Valenciano: Actas, mayo 1992* (Valencia: Conselleria de Cultura, Educació i Ciència, 1993), 75–79.

89. AMV, A-25, 193r; AMV, A-25, 340v–341r.

90. AMV, A-26, 141r–141v, 161–161v.

91. AMV, A-26, 178r–179r.

92. Examples include the Street of the Corts in 1417, the Street of the Second-Hand Clothiers (Carrer de la Pelleria) in 1422, and the Street of Sant Cristofol in 1431. AMV, A-26, 232v–233v; AMV, A-27, 363v–364r; AMV, A-29, Mano 2, 114r–v.

93. "Lo Portal dels Serrans era molt bell e notable e nomenat per tot lo mon. Lo carrer de Sent Berthomeu de la dita Ciutat no corresponia a aquell . . . les festes e solempnitats que la Ciutat a costuma fer en les entrades dels Senyors Reys e Reyna los quals continuament entren per los dits portal e carrer de Sent Bertholmeu . . . qui segon es dit es stret difforme e leig per les dites exides e en altra manera." AMV, A-32, Mano 2, 194v–195r.

open up the space around the Apostles' Door of the cathedral, where most rogation processions began.[94]

Street widening was an expensive, logistically challenging effort, usually undertaken only for the most ritually significant thoroughfares. An opportunity for larger-scale urban reform came on the night of March 16, 1447, when the worst fire in the city's history broke out in the market district. By the time the flames were extinguished the following day, forty-six houses had been destroyed and ten people had been killed. This was the only disaster in the history of the medieval city that destroyed a significant number of buildings, and therefore one of the only opportunities to rebuild a significant portion of the city center.[95] As Carmel Ferragud and Juan Vicente García Marsilla have shown, the council took advantage of that newly open space to rework the street plan in the affected neighborhood. In the two years after the fire, the city authorized more than one hundred expropriations to eliminate azucachs, overhangs, and other "remains of Islamic urbanism" in this neighborhood.[96] Seeking to continue these efforts beyond the damaged area, the council in 1448 allocated a budget of "at least 10,000 sous" to be spent annually on "demolition of projections and railings for the beautification of the city."[97] Such demolitions continued into the sixteenth century.[98]

As James Scott has observed in his classic *Seeing Like a State*, the quest for geographic order and legibility has a long association with ambitious governance. Those in power often seek both to impose an orthogonal urban plan and to demolish the narrow streets of autonomous urban neighborhoods. Baron Haussmann sought to render nineteenth-century Paris not only beautiful but impossible to barricade. The Valencian council's efforts to sweep away the "criminality" of the azucachs and the Jewish quarter show clear resonances with these later efforts. Scott himself, however, used a medieval city (Bruges) as his counterexample of the illegibility and disorder that resulted from a lack of urban planning.[99] Medieval urban reform is often barely visible by mod-

---

94. AMV, A-34, 126v–127r. For more on rogation processions, see chapter 4 of the present book.

95. An earthquake occurred in the city on December 18, 1396, but according to the council no buildings fell. AMV, A-21, 115r.

96. Carmel Ferragud and Juan Vicente García Marsilla, "The Great Fire of Medieval Valencia (1447)," *Urban History* 43, no. 4 (2015): 15–16.

97. AMV, A-34, 88v–89r. Compare the *Ufficiali sopra l'ornato* in Siena, founded in 1458 with the objective of beautifying the city through the removal of overhangs and balconies; Nevola, *Siena*, 98–101.

98. See, among many examples, the demolition of overhangs in Hazelnut Street (Carrer de les Avellanes) in 1495; or along the Corpus Christi route in 1511. AMV, A-48, 227v–228r; AMV, A-55, 28r.

99. Scott, *Seeing Like a State*, 53–63.

ern standards; the straightened and widened streets of Valencia's city center today appear quaintly narrow and meandering.

By the council's own standards, their efforts seem to have been a success. Valencia in the fifteenth century had become much more visibly Christian. Opinions would, of course, have differed about whether it was Christian enough. In 1455 another mob attacked Valencia's moreria, though casualties were few because the inhabitants had enough warning to flee.[100] In 1481 the council began construction on the city's most famous medieval structure, the Silk Exchange (Llotja de la Seda). As has often been noted, the Silk Exchange epitomized the confidence of the mercantile elite as it basked in the prosperity of Valencia's golden age.[101] If the Silk Exchange was the full flowering of that confidence, changes to the street plan sparked its early growth. In the late fourteenth and early fifteenth centuries, the council established a visible Christian identity in and through the city streets. Over the course of the later fifteenth century it began also to perform this identity in response to natural disaster.

100. For a full account of this attack, see Manuel Ruzafa García, "Façen-se cristians los moros o muyren," in *Violència i marginació en la societat medieval*, ed. Paulino Iriadiel (Valencia: Publicacions de la Universitat de València, 1990), 87–110.

101. Ramón Ferrer Navarro, "La lonja: Paradigma del comercio medieval valenciano," in *La Lonja: Un monumento del II para el III milenio*, ed. Salvador Lara Ortega (Valencia: Ajuntament de Valencia, 2000) 31–39.

CHAPTER 4

Divine Mercy and Help

Natural Disaster and the Rise of Rogation Processions

When the jurats assembled in the Valencia city council chamber on a Friday morning in November 1383, their first order of business was to wrap up an investigation of a wall collapse that had occurred several days earlier. Only when that was concluded did the council turn to the second item on its agenda: plague. "According to the report and assertion of doctors," there had been "some signs" that a plague was imminent in the city. This was cause not for panic but for deliberate action. In such a circumstance, the council concluded, "nothing is so fitting as to have recourse to divine mercy and help." It therefore ordered that "devoted processions and prayers be made, masses celebrated, and other meritorious works be performed."[1]

Natural disasters—be they plagues, droughts, floods, or locust swarms—were fairly frequent on council agendas in the fourteenth and fifteenth centuries. The councilmen of these years found a variety of "fitting" responses. Some of these responses were material, aimed at the causes and consequences of the disaster on the landscape (see chapters 1–2). Others were religious: in-

---

1. "Item lo dit consell attenent que alcuns senyals apparen de esser prestament general mortaldat en la dita Ciutat vullas car ja es en alcuns partides circumvehins vullas car ja alcuns en la dita Ciutat son morts pochs dies ha de malaltia de glanola & de febra pestilencial segons relacio & assercio de metges. E en tal cas res no sia tan covinent com recorrer a la divinal misericordia e ajuda per tal lo dit consell deliberadament & concordant provei & ordena que per aquesta rao fossen fetes devotes processos & orons celebrations de misses & altres meritories obres." AMV, A-18, 16v–17r.

tended to influence God, whose will was the ultimate cause of every crisis. The Valencian government made use of both material and religious responses to natural disaster during the late medieval period. The councils of the late fourteenth and early fifteenth centuries tended to favor material responses over religious ones, though these same councils also established an annual calendar of ritual events celebrating the city's Christian heritage (see chapter 3).

From the early 1420s on, councils began to layer increasing numbers of natural disaster rituals over this annual processional calendar. These disaster rituals took the form of rogation processions in which the city's Christians prayed publicly for divine mercy. As the city's political star began to rise in the later 1420s, rogation processions allowed the council to structure the urban experience of disaster around celebrations of Christian identity. As rogations multiplied, the extramural infrastructure projects (see chapter 2) dwindled. This shift in disaster response followed clearly from the urban reforms of the fourteenth century, which were designed in part to facilitate Christian ritual (see chapter 3). The new focus on disaster ritual also occurred alongside changes to the makeup and structure of city government, and was part of a growing emphasis on civic ritual across Europe in the fifteenth century. Most important, the rise of rogation processions as a response to natural disaster signaled a shift in the council's approach to governing its unruly environment. This shift was visible across all types of disaster, though each type had its own particular dynamics. From the 1420s onward, Valencian councils tended to promote ritual responses to natural disaster rather than technological ones. The city came to focus its energy and funds less on improvements to its landscape and more on rituals that emphasized the Christianity of its people. In so doing it echoed the Dominican preacher Vicent Ferrer's interpretation of natural disasters as evils from which only Christians deserved to be saved (see the introduction to this book). Triumphant Christianity, with its implicit erasure of the city's religious minorities, came by the mid-fifteenth century to be the main remedy for Valencia's environmental ills.

God and Nature

In the later Middle Ages, God's role in the natural world could be interpreted several ways. Intellectuals universally accepted that divine power lay behind, and occasionally overrode, the mechanisms of nature. This did not, of course, preclude interest in these mechanisms for their own sake. As Albert the Great put it, "We say that these things occur by the will of God, who governs the world, as a punishment for the evildoing of men. But we still say that God does these things on account of a natural cause, of which he who confers motion on all things is himself the first mover."[2]

Medieval academic meteorology was based on the premise that variations in weather were the result of the complex movements of planets and stars, just as more regular variations of climate and seasons were the result of the relative positions of the earth and the sun. Following Aristotle, meteorological study encompassed all natural phenomena below the sphere of the moon. Celestial movements could prompt corresponding shifts in the elements of air, water, fire, and earth in this terrestrial realm, causing winds, rain, droughts, corrupted air (miasmas), and earthquakes.[3] Biblical precedent existed for such a systemic understanding of meteorological phenomena, so medieval commentators tended, like Albert, to harmonize them into a divinely ordered universe.[4] Natural disasters were thus divine in the sense that they reflected God's will, but they occurred through material mechanisms. At the most sophisticated scientific level, divine and natural causes of disaster could not be separated. God was both present in and removed from every natural event.

Outside the universities, however, observers do seem to have made choices about whether or not to emphasize God's agency in natural disaster. Preachers across Europe regularly connected local natural disasters with local sins.[5] Laypeople sometimes agreed with them, but at other times they treated disasters as random misfortunes, with no mention of divine intervention.[6] Contemporaries were aware of the contrast between these positions. When the Arno River flooded Florence in 1333, chronicler Giovanni Villani reported "a great debate . . . in Florence on the subject of the inundation: whether it occurred by the judgment of God or in the course of nature."[7] Below the

2. Albert the Great, *On the Causes of the Properties of the Elements (Liber de Causis Proprietatum Elementorum)*, trans. Irven M. Resnick (Milwaukee, WI: Marquette University Press: 2010), 71–77.

3. On Aristotle's *Meteorologica*, see Malcolm Wilson, *Structure and Method in Artistotle's "Meteorologica": A More Disorderly Nature* (Cambridge: Cambridge University Press, 2013). On medieval interpretations, see Joëlle Ducos, "Théorie et pratique de la météorologie médiévale. Albert le Grand et Jean Buridan," in *Le temps qu'il fait au Moyen-Age: Phénomènes atmosphériques dans la littérature, la pensée scientifique et religieuse*, ed. Claude Thomasset and Joëlle Ducos (Paris: Press de l'Université de Paris-Sorbonne, 1998), 45–58; Resianne Fontaine, "Exhalations and Other Meteorological Themes," in *The Cambridge History of Jewish Philosophy: From Antiquity through the Seventeenth Century*, ed. Steven Nadler and T. M. Rudavsky (Cambridge: Cambridge University Press, 2009), 434–450.

4. See Anne Lawrence-Mathers, *Medieval Meteorology: Forecasting the Weather from Aristotle to the Almanac* (Cambridge: Cambridge University Press, 2020), esp. 3–6.

5. Hanska, "Cessante causa cessat et effectus." On Vicent Ferrer's sermons in Valencia, see Agustín Rubio Vela, "Las epidemias de peste en la ciudad de Valencia durante el siglo XV. Nuevas aportaciones," *Estudis castellonencs* 6 (1994–95), 1181.

6. Rohr, "Man and Natural Disaster"; Gerrard and Petley, "A Risk Society?"

7. Laurence Moulinier and Odile Redon, "L'inondation de 1333 à Florence. Récit et hypothèses de Giovanni Villani," *Médiévales* 36 (1999): 91–104.

university level, then, there was a choice to be made about whether to empha-size divine will or the workings of nature. This book has already discussed the logic with which the Valencian council approached dealing with the environ-ment on a material level. As we shall see, the council also employed a logic of divine power and the natural world. This was rarely an either/or proposition; material responses regularly coexisted with religious ones, and the Valencian council records show variations of emphasis. Given that it was possible to stress either the proximate or the ultimate causes of any natural disaster, the Valen-cian authorities chose in some cases to emphasize God's role with religious rituals and in other cases chose to leave out any mention of the divine. Choos-ing a response to natural disaster did not necessarily entail giving an explicit causative explanation, but public announcements and actions would have in-fluenced the narrative of the event. While official responses to natural dis-aster do not directly reflect the councilmen's understanding of the natural world, the council's choices can show how it sought to frame different dis-asters at different moments.

It is above all significant that the council had choices. Medieval pleas for divine aid in the fact of natural disaster have rarely been considered phenom-ena in need of explanation. Lacking any technological or scientific means to explain natural disaster, medieval people supposedly had no recourse but prayer. Climate historians Javier Martin-Vide and Mariano Barriendos Vallvé suppose that "the existence of [religious] ceremonies for environmental rea-sons is easily explained by the absence of any alternative course of actions left to the communities when they were faced with strong environmental variation."[8] In many places, few records of natural disaster response survive from the Middle Ages, so early modern religious practices have been imposed in retrospect to connect with fragmentary medieval evidence, creating the ap-pearance of a uniform tradition.[9] The relatively complete survival of the fourteenth- and fifteenth-century Valencian council records is unusual for Ibe-rian cities. This complete record series shows that requests for divine aid and the use of rogations did develop as new customs in the later Middle Ages.

8. Javier Martin-Vide and Mariano Barriendos Vallvé, "The Use of Rogation Ceremony Records in Climatic Reconstruction: A Case Study from Catalonia (Spain)," *Climatic Change* 30, no. 2 (1995): 204.

9. See William A. Christian, *Local Religion in Sixteenth-Century Spain* (Princeton, NJ: Princeton University Press, 1981). See also a number of studies using rogation ceremonies as environmental proxies, including Martin-Vide and Barriendos, "The Use of Rogation Ceremony Records," 201–221; Mariano Barriendos, "Climate Change in the Iberian Peninsula: Indicator of Rogation Ceremonies (16th–19th Centuries)," *Revue d'histoire moderne et contemporaine* 57 (2010): 131–159; and Fernando Domínguez-Castro et al., "Reconstruction of Drought Episodes for Central Spain from Rogation Ceremonies Recorded at the Toledo Cathedral from 1506 to 1900: A Methodological Approach," *Global and Planetary Change* 63 (2008): 234.

Although rogation processions employ elements of an early medieval ritual form, their use in medieval Valencia shifted dramatically over the course of a few decades.[10] Conducting multiple extraordinary rogation processions for a single natural disaster was less ancient rite than "invented tradition."[11] In medieval Valencia, the invention of the rogation tradition was tied to the council's efforts at Christianizing the city.

Early Rogation Processions

In fourteenth-century Valencia, religious response to natural disaster was limited, and rogation processions were relatively rare events. With a few exceptions, rogation processions followed a common form. A crier in the council's employ walked the streets accompanied by drums and trumpets to announce the event. He informed the townspeople that workplaces were to be closed during the procession, and enjoined all good Christian men and women to gather in the cathedral at the appropriate time (usually the following day) "to pray to our all-powerful Lord God and to the Blessed Virgin Our Lady Santa Maria his mother and to all the celestial court that our savior Jesus Christ not look at our faults but rather by his great mercy and piety give us [an end to the disaster]."[12] There, attired "honestly" and carrying lit candles in their hands, these good Christians would follow the clergy from the cathedral to another church or monastery and back by another route.[13] No matter how long the walk or how narrow the street, they were to walk without crowding or speaking to one another, praying that God, the Virgin and all the saints would intercede on the city's behalf. In theory the procession included

---

10. Rogation processions tend to be associated with Bishop Mamertus of Vienne, who purportedly instituted the celebration of Rogation Days in 474, or with Pope Gregory the Great's call for processions against plague in 590. See, for example, Andrew Brown, "Devotion and Emotion: Creating the Devout Body in Late Medieval Bruges," *Digital Philology* 1, no. 2 (2012): 228n. 13. In fact, as Nathan J. Ristuccia, *Christianization and Commonwealth in Early Medieval Europe: A Ritual Interpretation* (Oxford: Oxford University Press, 2018), has shown, early medieval rogations themselves have a similarly complex history.

11. Teofilo F. Ruiz, *A King Travels: Festive Traditions in Late Medieval and Early Modern Spain* (Princeton, NJ: Princeton University Press, 2012), 113, uses "invented tradition" to describe early modern Spanish urban ritual. Ruiz takes the term, of course, from Eric Hobsbawm, "Introduction: Inventing Traditions," in *The Invention of Tradition*, ed. Eric Hobsbawm and Terence Ranger (Cambridge: Cambridge University Press, 1992), 2.

12. "Per pregar al Nostre Senyor Deus tot poderos & a la Verge Benavendurada Nostre Dona Santa Maria mare sua & a tota la cort celestial qual salvador Jehu Xrist no volen esguardar als nostres defalliments mas per la sua gran misericordia & pietat no nulla donar ros & pluja." AMV, A-4, 179r.

13. AMV, A-16, 260r–v. In some processions at least, the city paid for the candles. AMV, A-32, 80v.

the entire Christian population of the city, although the number of actual participants may have been much smaller.[14]

Rogation processions were the joint responsibility of the municipal and episcopal authorities. The bishop and cathedral chapter organized the liturgy for the processions and set the date to fit into the existing liturgical calendar, but the decision to hold a rogation procession (and the responsibility to pay for it) belonged to the city council.[15] While the processions were liturgical in form, therefore, they were also operations of the municipal government.

The first recorded procession for natural disaster relief was in response to a drought in March 1343. Records survive of a total of five rogation processions organized in Valencia before 1370: four in response to drought and one in response to locusts. The locust procession announcement did not specify a destination, but all four of the drought processions went to the Monastery of Sant Vicent (see map 5). As was noted in chapter 3, Sant Vicent was an early Christian martyr, and his suburban monastery one of the city's oldest Christian sites. A procession to Sant Vicent meant traveling out of the city and back through a half kilometer of open countryside. This would have given early rogation processions the feel of pilgrimages.

The city councils of the 1370s established a cycle of annual feasts celebrating the city's Christian heritage (see chapter 3). Rogation processions continued to be rare during this period, but their changing form shows a resonance with the goals of these annual feasts. From the 1370s on, rogation processions in Valencia tended to be urban rather than extramural affairs. The Monastery of Sant Vicent became less common as a destination, replaced in popularity by sites within the city itself: the Chapel of Santa Maria de Gràcia in the Convent of Sant Agustí, the Convent of Santa Maria del Carme, and—later—the Chapel of Santa Maria de la Misericordia in the Convent of Sant Domènec. All three were Marian sites constructed outside the city in the early postconquest period, and all three now stood just inside the new Christian walls (see map 5). Unlike Sant Vicent, they would have served to emphasize the city's colonial Christian present rather than its ancient Christian past. The Chapel of Santa Maria de Gràcia and the Convent of Santa Maria del Carme began to be used for rogation processions in the 1370s, once the completion of new walls located them within the new urban space. The Chapel of Santa Maria de la Misericordia, however, was not a processional destination until after 1391.

---

14. An account entry for a procession in 1456 gives a count of twenty-eight prelates, two young subdeacons, and twenty youths (*fadrins*) among the marchers, although this may not have been an exhaustive list of participants. AMV, q.q. 4, 125r.

15. Martin-Vide and Barriendos, "The Use of Rogation Ceremony Records," 205–207.

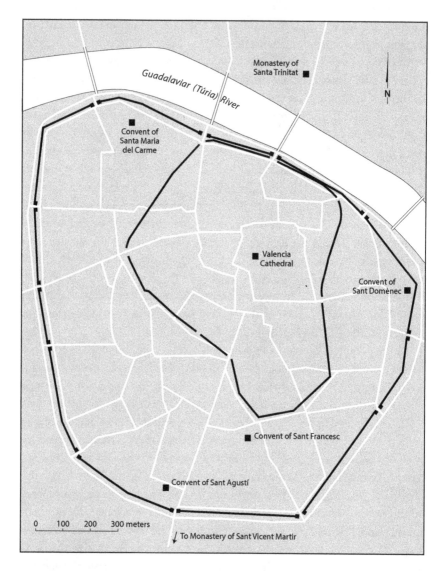

MAP 5. Primary rogation procession destinations in the city of Valencia

The Convent of Sant Domènec was located on the other side of the *jueria* (Jewish quarter) from the cathedral, so a procession to the chapel would have had to pass by or through it. The first procession that did take this route may have done so to reference the destruction of the Jewish quarter. It was organized almost on the anniversary of the violence, July 11, 1395.[16] While rogation pro-

---

16. July 11 was a Sunday, and the riot of 1391 had also taken place on Sunday: July 9, four years earlier. AMV, A-20, 241v–242r.

cessions were still infrequent in the late fourteenth century, therefore, those
that were organized served to emphasize the Christianity of the city.

Processions and the Rise of Valencia in the 1420s

King Martí the Humane died childless in the spring of 1410, without having
resolved the matter of the succession to the throne of Aragón. The next king,
Castilian prince Fernando of Antequera, was not officially proclaimed until
June 1412. The violence of the two-year interregnum took its toll on Valencia's citizens, many of whom were killed in the Battle of Morvedre in February 1412. In 1418 a new king, Alfons the Magnanimous, altered the structure
of the municipal government. Rather than the structure of jurats and *consell*,
a new body, the *consell secret*—made up of the jurats, the *racional* (Crown-
appointed city treasurer), and a few other officials—served as the municipal
executive. The full council met less frequently, and governance increasingly
fell to the jurats and racional.[17] Throughout this unstable period, as was noted
in chapter 3, the council continued its efforts to widen the city's streets, particularly the major processional routes. By the 1420s, therefore, the city was
under new leadership and had streets better suited for urban ritual.

The 1420s saw a new interest in the rogation procession as a response to
natural disaster. In the spring of 1421 the council collaborated with Hug de
Llupia, the bishop of Valencia, to announce a series of rogation processions
celebrating the three Rogation Days leading up to the Feast of the Ascension.
Rogation Days were long-standing liturgical celebrations, but these processions
were also rogations in the other sense of the term; they would implore God
to relieve "the pestilence from which many in this [city] are dying suddenly."[18]
These were the first extraordinary rogation processions in Valencia to be organized as a series rather than as single processions. The text of the announcements was also innovative in placing the processions in a larger context of
Christian piety. They instructed faithful Christians to conduct themselves in
such a manner during the processional days that their prayers might be accept-
able to God. To that end, Bishop Hug announced indulgences and forbade
activities that might "provoke people more to crimes and sins than to spiritual things." The council, for its part, enjoined those along the processional
route to clean the streets in front of their houses, ordered that workplaces be
closed, and forbade games so that "in these days the lips of each person should

17. Narbona, "Alfonso el Magnánimo," 593–617.
18. "Pestilencia per la qual molts de aquella ciutat moren subitament." AMV, A-27, 292v.

only wag in saying prayers or sacrifices pleasing to Our Lord, and not things by which he might be provoked to anger against his people."[19] As with the Feast of Corpus Christi, a moment in the liturgical calendar was here used to emphasize the Christian identity of the city of Valencia. These Rogation Day processions were not repeated, but the following year bishop and council announced a procession for plague relief, from the cathedral to the Chapel of Santa Maria de Gràcia. Again Bishop Hug declared indulgences for participants.[20] In both of these instances municipal authority joined with ecclesiastical authority in declaring a period of time sanctified to Christian worship in order to relieve environmental crisis.

In December 1424 the council announced another rogation procession, this time for drought. The announcement set forth an unusually elaborate account of the role of penitence in preserving good weather:

> Our creator and all powerful Lord God . . . has taken from us the rain waters that at the opportune times are accustomed to fall . . . He, [as a] just Lord God, has justly sent [this misfortune] to us, because the multitude of our sins and the ugliness of our faults and iniquities have horribly offended his divine majesty and persistently provoked his anger against us. And knowing that the remedy to placate our merciful Lord God is that we, all together, with bitter contrition for the committed sins and with firm intent to amend our lives, [cry] out [and] invoke his magnanimity and mercy, his clemency and pity with works of charity and devoted prayers, we pray and supplicate him to revoke and take away his indignation and become merciful toward us.[21]

This text again links disaster relief not only to rogation but also to Christian penitential practice. As in 1421 and 1422, Bishop Hug was probably the innovator here. The council made all procession announcements on behalf of itself, the bishop, and the cathedral chapter, but these three announcements are

---

19. "Les quals plus provoquen les gents a delicis e peccats que a coses spirituals . . . come en aquests dies solament los labis de cascu deien vagar en dir oracions o sacrificis placants a nostre senyor e no coses ab les quals sia provocat a ira contra lo seu poble." AMV, A-27, 292v.

20. AMV, A-27, 385v.

21. "[N]ostre creador e tot poderos Deu e Senyor . . . ha manades tolre e levar nos les aygues pluvials qui en los temps congruents solien caure sobre la terra . . . los quals flagells e plagues ell, just Deu e Senyor nos ha trameses e tramet dignament per la multitud dels nostres peccats e per la legea de les culpes e iniquitats nostres qui han orreament offensa la sua divina maiestat e provocada importunament la sua ira contra nosaltres. E conexents quel remey a placar lo nostre misericordios Deu e Senyor es que tots ensemps ab contricio amara dels comesos peccats e ab ferm proposit de esmenar la vida clamants invoquem la sua benignitat e misericordia la sua clemencia e pietat e ab obres de caritat e devotes oracions lo prequem e suppliquem que revoch e tolga de nosaltres la sua indignacio e ira es gire misericordios vers nosaltres." AMV, A-28, 104r–v.

unusual in that they refer directly to the bishop by name. Experiments with the procession format continued after Bishop Hug's death, but stressed communal identity rather than penitential practice.

There is a gap in the surviving council records from 1425 to 1428. These years marked a shift in the city's position within the Crown of Aragon. In October 1425 the Valencian council offered King Alfons the Magnanimous 11,000 sous for every month that he and his court resided in the city. The council hoped to recoup its investment not only in the prestige and influence that came with the royal presence but also in taxes on the commerce generated by the court. Such Keynesian arrangements were by no means unheard of, and may have seemed particularly appropriate with Alfons, who had already made clear his inclination toward overseas adventures and was perpetually short of money with which to pursue them.[22] Alfons took the bait. From 1425 through the end of 1428 he was more or less continuously resident in the city of Valencia, and the city was his favored peninsular residence even thereafter. Indeed, by the later fifteenth century Valencia would surpass Barcelona not only in royal favor but in commercial wealth. Valencian industries—particularly silk and ceramics—became ever more profitable, while the Catalan civil war dealt a blow to trade in the north.[23]

The extant council records after 1428 show that the city was on the rise, but not necessarily flush with funds; the council was still paying the subsidy to Alfons, and tax revenues had probably not risen to compensate. Nonetheless, it seems to have been willing to invest in rogation processions. The elaborate spectacles of the court, particularly the tourneys held in the city marketplace, may have led Valencians to a greater appreciation of the possibilities of public ritual.[24] The city may also have felt the need to compete with these spectacles for attention and prestige. In January 1428 the city paid the Convent of Sant Domènec five lliures and ten sous to relocate a gate in the convent wall "in such a way that it serve for [rogation] processions." A recent procession to the convent to ask for protection against earthquakes had found the current gate unsatisfactory.[25]

---

22. Juan Vicente García Marsilla, "El impacto de la corte en la ciudad: Alfonso el Magnánimo en Valencia (1425–1428)," in *El alimento del estado y la salud de la "res publica": Orígenes, estructura y desarrollo del gasto público en Europa*, ed. Angel Galán Sánchez, Carretero Zamora, and Juan Manuel (Madrid: Instituto de Estudios Fiscales y Universidad de Málaga, 2013), 291–308. García Marsilla concludes that the city did not, ultimately, recoup its expenditure in tax revenue, but the loans the city made to the king during the same period did consolidate the public debt market to the advantage of the patricians on the council.

23. P. Iradiel, "L'evolució econòmica," in *Història del país Valencià*, vol. 2, *De la conquista a la federació hispánica*, ed. E. Belenguer (Barcelona: Edicions 62, 1989), 267–324.

24. García Marsilla, "El impacto de la corte," 297–298, 300–301.

25. AMV, J-47, 53v. The rogation procession for earthquake protection was almost certainly on account of seismic activity in Catalonia between February 1427 and June 1428. Antoni Riera i Melis,

In the autumn of that same year the council began another extraordinary new series of rogation processions. This series began quietly, with a procession on October 6, because "for our sins, Our Lord God is beginning to visit epidemic diseases on this city and some areas around it."[26] Two days later the council announced the annual celebration of the anniversary of the Christian conquest of the city on the Feast of Sant Dionís (Saturday, October 9). The celebration that year included a procession to the Church of Sant Jordi (who is the patron saint of Aragon and strongly associated with Christian victory over Islam). Although the feast was celebrated every year, this was the first time since 1344 that a public announcement of the anniversary appeared in the Manuals del Consells, the main series of council records. This may be coincidence, or it may suggest a renewed focus on this celebration in the later 1420s.

The Friday after the procession commemorating the conquest the council held another procession for plague relief.[27] The Friday after that it held another. The announcement for this procession explained that "the honorable cathedral chapter has decided that [on] the Friday of each week general and devoted processions be done through the city" (see table 1). Unlike the rogations during Bishop Hug's tenure, these processions stressed Christian community more than individual piety; indulgences were not mentioned. Instead the processions were integrated into existing liturgical routine. Each began with the sound of the bell that signaled the elevation of the host during the Mass.[28] Throughout the winter of 1428 and the spring of 1429, a procession was held every Friday. Until April 22, 1429, each procession went to a different church. These included all of the religious houses founded in the immediate aftermath of the Christian conquest: all twelve parish churches and the houses of mendicant and military orders.[29] On April 23 the council declared another procession in celebration of the Feast of Sant Jordi "in order to observe the laudable custom that has been continued in this city from the time of the conquest . . . in memory of the great blessing that this city received in the time when it was restored to the

---

"Catàstrofe i societat a la Catalunya medieval: Els terratrèmols de 1427–1428," *Acta historica et archaeologica mediaevalia* 20–21 (2000): 699–735.

26. "Nostre senyor deu comença a visitar per nostres demerits aquesta Ciutat e algunes parts circumvehines per malalties epidemials." AMV, A-2,9 36v–37r.

27. AMV, A-29, 37r–v.

28. AMV, A-29, 38v–39r.

29. Mendicant and military orders included Sant Joan of the Hospital, which belonged to the Hospitalers; Santa Maria del Temple, at this point controlled by the Order of Montesa; Santa Maria de Calatrava, belonging to the Order of Calatrava; and Sant Jaume d'Uclés, belonging to the Order of Santiago. Processions were also made to the confraternity churches of Nostra Dona de Santa Maria and Santa Tecla, the foundation dates of which are today uncertain. Absent from the list was the Convent of Santa Maria del Carme, which, although a popular destination before and after 1428–20, was a later foundation, dating from the reign of Pere the Great. See Hinojosa Montalvo, *Una ciutat gran i populosa*.

Table 1   Plague rogation procession series, 1428–1429

DATE[a]	DESTINATION	EXPLANATION
Wednesday, October 6, 1428	Convent of Sant Agustí (Chapel of Santa Maria de Gràcia)	Mendicant order (Augustinian friars)
Saturday, October 9, 1428 Anniversary of the Christian conquest of Valencia (Feast of Sant Dionís)	**Church of Sant Jordi**	**Patron saint of the Crown of Aragon, associated with crusading**
Friday, October 15, 1428	Convent of Sant Domènec (Chapel of Santa Maria de la Misericordia)	Mendicant order (Dominican friars)
Friday, October 22, 1428 Announcement of weekly plague processions	**Convent of Sant Francesc**	**Mendicant order (Friars Minor)**
Thursday, October 28, 1428	Monastery of Sant Vicent Martir	Patron saint of Valencia
Friday, November 12, 1428	Church of Sant Joan of the Market	Parish church
Friday, November 19, 1428	Monastery of Santa Trinitat[b]	Order for the redemption of captives (Trinitarian friars)
Friday, November 26, 1428	Church of Sant Martí	Parish church
Friday, December 3, 1428	Convent of Santa Maria de la Mercè	Order for the redemption of captives (Mercedarian friars)
Friday, December 10, 1428	Church of Santa Caterina	Parish church
Friday, December 17, 1428	Church of Sant Andreu	Parish church
Friday, December 24, 1428	Church of Sant Esteve	Parish church
Friday, December 31, 1428	Church of Sant Tomás	Parish church
Friday, January 14, 1429	Church of Sant Nicolau	Parish church
Friday, January 21, 1429	Church of Sant Salvador	Parish church
Friday, January 28, 1429	Church of Santa Creu	Parish church
Friday, February 4, 1429	Church of Sant Barthomeu	Parish church
Friday, February 11, 1429	Church of Sant Lorenç	Parish church
Friday, February 18, 1429	Church of Sant Joan of the Hospital	Military order (Hospitalers)
Friday, February 25, 1429	Church of Santa Maria of the Temple	Military order (Order of Montesa)
Friday, March 4, 1429	Church of Santa Maria de Calatrava	Military order (Order of Calatrava)
Friday, March 11, 1429	Sant Jaume d'Uclés	Military order (Order of Santiago)
Friday, March 18, 1429	Church of Santa Tecla	Confraternity church
Friday, April 1, 1429	Valencia Cathedral	Parish church
Friday, April 8, 1429	Convent of Santa Clara	Mendicant order (Poor Clares)
Friday, April 15, 1429	Convent of Santa Magdalena	Mendicant order (Dominican nuns)
Friday, April 22, 1429	Church of Santa Maria	Confraternity church
Saturday, April 23, 1429 Feast of Sant Jordi	**Church of Sant Jordi**	**Patron saint of the Crown of Aragon, associated with crusading**
Friday, April 29, 1429 Destinations begin to repeat	**Convent of Sant Agustí (Chapel of Santa Maria de Gràcia)**	**Mendicant order (Augustinian friars)**

(continued)

Table 1   Plague rogation procession series, 1428–1429 (*continued*)

DATE[a]	DESTINATION	EXPLANATION
Friday, May 6, 1429	Monastery of Sant Vicent Martir	Patron of Valencia
Friday, May 13, 1429	Church of Sant Joan of the Market	Parish church
Friday, May 20, 1429	Convent of Sant Domènec	Mendicant order (Dominican friars)
Friday, June 3, 1429	Monastery of Santa Trinitat	Order for the redemption of captives (Mercedarian friars)
Friday, June 10, 1429	Church of Sant Martí	Parish church
Friday, June 17, 1429	Convent of Sant Francesc	Mendicant order (Franciscan friars)
Tuesday, June 21, 1429 For the king's negotiations with Castile	**Convent of Sant Agustí (Chapel of Santa Maria de Gràcia)**	**Mendicant order (Augustinian friars)**
Friday, July 1, 1429	Church of Sant Salvador	Parish church
Wednesday, July 6, 1429 Celebrating the end of the Great Schism	**Convent of Santa Maria del Carme**	**Mendicant order (Carmelite friars)**

[a] Processions in boldface type were not plague rogations.
[b] Santa Trinitat was founded shortly after the Christian conquest of Valencia as a Trinitarian monastery. In 1444 it was refounded by Queen Maria as a convent of the Order of Santa Clara (commonly known as the Poor Clares).

hands of Christians through the intercession of the glorious knight and martyr Sant Jordí."[30] This procession to the Church of Sant Jordí bookended the series that had begun with the procession to the church in October.

After this the Friday plague processions began to repeat destinations, in a similar order to those of the fall of 1428. Perhaps the council felt that the ritual was producing diminishing returns, because the last procession was held in late June. A celebration of King Alfons's repudiation of the antipope Clement VII (which finally ended the Great Schism in the Crown of Aragon), tacitly marked the end of the weekly plague processions, even though the plague itself continued into the autumn of 1429.[31] This may have been an excuse to cut short an ever-mounting bill for a ritual that was, perhaps, becoming too routine. Weekly rogations were, like the much shorter series in 1421, a unique

30. "Que per observa loable costum la qual ses continuada en aquesta Ciutat del temps de la conquesta . . . en memoria del gran beneffici que aquesta Ciutat reebe en lo temps que fon restituida a mans de Cristians migançant lo glorios Cavaller e martir Sent Jordí." AMV, A-29, 81r.
31. AMV A-29, 162v. As part of a dispute with Pope Martin V over his interests in Italy, Alfons had been keeping the Great Schism alive in his territories through support for Avignon Pope Clement VIII. In June 1429 King Alfons finally gave the word for Clement to abdicate and for his group of cardinals at Peñiscola to return their support for Martin V in Rome. See Alan Ryder, *Alfonso the Magnanimous: King of Aragon, Naples, and Sicily, 1396–1458* (Oxford: Oxford University Press, 1990), 152–163. The council declared a celebratory procession on July 5, even before the cardinals had officially elected Martin. AMV, A-29, 123r–124v.

experiment in the ritual possibilities of the rogation procession. Once again, these processions may have been the brainchild of the cathedral chapter rather than the city council.[32] The canons may also have developed other rituals during the years 1425–28, of which no record now survives.

While they were never repeated, the plague rogations of 1428–29 were a turning point in Valencian natural disaster response. More processions appear in the records between October 1428 and August 1429 than in all previous records combined. They were also explicitly integrated into the annual cycle of processions celebrating the city's Christian conquest. As has been mentioned, the bookends of this rogation procession series were two processions to the Church of Sant Jordí, one on the feast day of the saint himself, and one on the anniversary of the conquest. Although both holidays had existed in the city's celebratory repertoire for some time, and were probably annual events, announcements for both appeared in the council records that year for the first time in decades. This may suggest a renewed focus on these feasts and their symbolic possibilities. As in 1372, the council in 1428 seems to have been elaborating its calendar of Christian celebrations. And, as in 1372, these rituals of triumphant Christianity included processions for the Feast of Corpus Christi. Such processions had been held in the city for some time, but the evidence suggests that the celebrations were becoming more elaborate in the 1420s. The text of the announcement for the Corpus Christi procession in June 1428 included new language exhorting those who lived along the processional route to keep the streets clear of tables and other obstructions. They were also to refrain from throwing water out of their windows during the procession so as not to damage the clothes of those marching. The council had this year provided city officials and the Friars Minor with new clothes for the procession. In July 1428 the council complained of the mounting expenses of the celebration, particularly the costs of the banners and plays (*insignies e entremeses*), which had come to exceed three hundred florins annually. In order to bring costs down, the council signed a three-year contract with a painter named Nicolau Querol, who agreed to do the scene painting at a bulk rate.[33] In 1429, after further complaints about the expense of the procession, the council ordered the construction of cupboards (*armaris*) on the balcony overlooking the council chamber to store equipment for the plays, so that this equipment no longer needed to be recreated each year.[34] This provision suggests that the

---

32. The canons were the highest authorities in the cathedral at this time; Bishop Hug had died, and the episcopal see would remain vacant until the appointment of Alfons de Borgia in 1429.

33. AMV, A-29, 18v–19v. When that contract expired in 1431, the council renewed it for another five years. AMV, A-29, 115r.

34. AMV, A-29, 9r–v, 18v–19r, 76r–v.

problem of storage was a new one, and thus that the celebration of Corpus
Christi in Valencia had only recently begun to include elaborate props and cos-
tumes. The first major series of rogation processions was organized at the
same time that civic religious rituals in general were becoming increasingly
elaborate.

The council may not have been the primary agent of these changes. The cathedral chapter helped organize all processions, and the Feast of Corpus Christi
would have involved an even wider array of participants, including guilds and
fraternal organizations. The cathedral's internal records of these events, if they
existed, do not survive. The council's records may overstate its own role in planning these rituals. We therefore do not know if the focus on ritual in the fifteenth
century began at the initiative of the council, the cathedral chapter, or indeed
of individual councilmen or canons. But since the council continued to pay for
these rituals year after year, we can be fairly certain that a majority of the executive (which by this time meant the consell secret) believed that processions fur-
thered the interests of the municipal government.

The Rise of Processions in the Mid-Fifteenth Century

In the decades after 1429, rogation processions became ever more common
in Valencia. Before the 1420s, processions had been a relatively infrequent and
sporadically applied solution to environmental crisis. A procession was not necessarily part of the response to each natural disaster, and no more than one
procession was usually organized for any given crisis. The bishop and cathedral chapter may have led the first experiments with more elaborate series of
rogation processions in the early 1420s. After 1432, the bishopric of Valencia
became an absentee position under the Borgia family, and ecclesiastical involvement in rogation processions is less visible in the records.[35] Nonetheless, processions continued to proliferate in these decades, suggesting that at least some
initiative came by this point from the council. Perhaps as a reflection of greater
lay involvement, the format of the processions became much simpler. Rather
than series of processions or penitential initiatives, councils from the 1430s on
began to declare individual rogation processions in ever-increasing numbers
(see figure 1). Before 1428, a rogation procession for natural disaster was

35. Bishop Hug's successor, Alfonso de Borgia, resided in Valencia for only three years; from 1432
to 1455, when he was elected pope, he was an absentee bishop. His nephew and successor, Roderigo
de Borgia, likewise resided in Rome from 1455 through his own election as pope in 1492, as did his
own successor (and illegitimate son), Cesare Borgia.

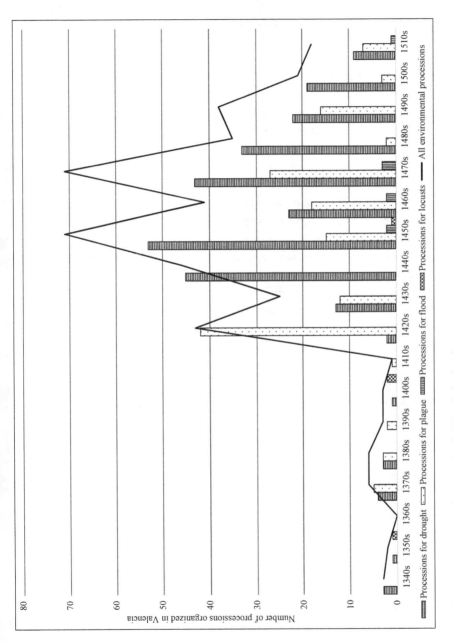

Figure 1. Rogation processions organized in Valencia, by decade

organized in Valencia once every two or three years on average. Between 1430 and 1500 the city council organized an average of nearly five processions per year. Rogation processions had become the centerpiece of municipal response to natural disaster.

The trend toward rogation processions is apparent; the council was putting on more disaster rituals after the 1420s than before. This is not due to patterns of documentary survival, nor is it primarily a function of an increasing number of natural disasters. Droughts, floods, plagues, and locust swarms were, of course, unevenly distributed across the decades, and thus the instance of processions to some extent reflects that distribution. The onset of the Little Ice Age in Iberia (see chapter 2) has been linked to variations in precipitation and temperature. Although on average this period was colder and wetter than previous centuries, it was also associated with storminess, heavy rainfall, floods, and droughts.[36] Plague likewise prospered in the colder climate of the later Middle Ages, which allowed it to establish new foci among wild rodents in Europe.[37] The evidence does not suggest a sharp increase in the number or severity of any of these disasters in the mid-fifteenth century specifically. Although processions for drought were common, tree ring proxy data suggests that the years 1420–60 were, if anything, wetter than normal.[38] Plagues occurred fairly regularly throughout this period, but outbreaks in the mid-fifteenth century were neither more frequent nor more virulent than later on.[39] There is some evidence of a peak of flood activity during the early Spörer Minimum (1431–40), a period of low solar activity associated with somewhat colder weather.[40] Yet no processions at all were organized for floods in Valencia until 1456 (see chapter 7).

---

36. Oliva et al., "The Little Ice Age."

37. See Campbell, *The Great Transition*, esp. 349–351. Ann G. Carmichael, "Plague Persistence in Western Europe: A Hypothesis," in *Pandemic Disease in the Medieval World: Rethinking the Black Death*, ed. Monica Green (York, UK: ARC Medieval Press, 2014), 157–192, has hypothesized a European plague focus. Further evidence for such a focus can be found in Maria A. Spyrou et al., "A Phylogeography of the Second Plague Pandemic Revealed through the Analysis of Historical *Y. pestis* Genomes," bioRxiv, 2018, https://doi.org/10.1101/481242.

38. These data come from the Old World Drought Atlas (OWDA); see E. R. Cook et al., "Old World Megadroughts and Pluvials during the Common Era," *Science Advances* 1, no. 10 (2015), https://doi.org/10.1126/sciadv.1500561. For more on the OWDA, see chapter 5 of the present book.

39. Later plague outbreaks have been comparatively little studied, but Ann G. Carmichael, *Plague and the Poor in Renaissance Florence* (New York: Cambridge University Press, 1986), 59–89, has suggested that fifteenth-century outbreaks tended to have lower mortality than fourteenth-century ones. For more on later plague outbreaks see chapter 6 of this book.

40. Oliva et al., "The Little Ice Age," 200; María-Carmen Llasat et al., "Floods in Catalonia (NE Spain) since the 14th Century: Climatological and Meteorological Aspects from Historical Documentary Sources and Old Instrumental Records," *Journal of Hydrology* 313, nos. 1–2 (2005): 32–47; M. J. Machado et al., "500 Years of Rainfall Variability and Extreme Hydrological Events in Southeastern Spain Drylands," *Journal of Arid Environments* 75, no. 12 (2011): 1244–1253.

Table 2 Comparison of drought rogations in 1356 and 1464

1356	1464
January 21: Procession to pray for "water, good weather, and things necessary to the realm"[a]	January 7: Procession for rain[b]
	January 26: Procession for rain[c]
	February 6: Procession of thanksgiving for rain, asking for more rain[d]
	February 8: Procession for rain[e]
	February 23: Procession for rain[f]
	March 8: Procession of thanksgiving for rain[g]
April 14: Mention of improvement in the weather (no procession)[h]	April 4: Procession of thanksgiving for rain, asking for more rain[i]

[a] AMV, A-12, 94v–95v.
[b] AMV, A-37, Mano 2 113r.
[c] AMV, A-37, Mano 2 114r–v.
[d] AMV, A-37, Mano 2 115 v.
[e] AMV, A-37, Mano 2 116 r.
[f] AMV, A-37, Mano 2 117r.
[g] AMV, A-37, Mano 2 119v.
[h] AMV, A-12, 97r–98r.
[i] AMV, A-37, Mano 2 121 v.

The rise in rogation processions was more a shift in the pattern of response than in the number of crises. More processions were being organized for each crisis, over a shorter period of time (see, for example, the comparison in table 2). Over roughly the same period of several months, the council of 1356 organized one drought procession, while the council of 1464 organized seven, responding to changing rainfall practically in real time. In the second quarter of the fifteenth century, the act of organizing a rogation procession for natural disaster moved from extraordinary to relatively routine (see the appendix). A dip in procession numbers in the first two decades of the sixteenth century, by contrast, may indicate an actual decline in perceived natural disasters; the council continued to organize processions at around the same frequency for each disaster, but disasters appear in the records less often.[41]

The councils of both the late fourteenth and the fifteenth centuries were operating in a context of relatively frequent natural disasters. In both periods the councilmen had a variety of tools with which to confront these crises. In the late fourteenth century, councils often organized material relief measures and initiated infrastructure projects (see chapters 1–2). By the 1420s, councils continued relief measures but also organized rogation processions in ever-increasing

41. For example, the council organized four processions for the drought that occurred in January–March 1502; see the appendix of the present book. There is one exception: plague processions may have been less frequent; see chapter 6 of the present book.

numbers. This was a governing choice rather than a reflection of climatic phenomena. At present it is not possible to say with certainty whether this choice was unique to the Valencian government. Published studies of municipal rogation processions almost all use data starting in 1450 or later.[42] Those that begin earlier record significantly fewer processions than appear in the Valencian documents, but this may be a problem of documentary survival.[43]

A number of paleoclimatology scholars, led by Barriendos, have used rogation processions themselves as climate proxies. Procession announcements have the advantages of being clearly dated, fairly standardized in form, and (for some municipalities) available in unbroken data series across several centuries. Since medieval municipal authorities were responsible for both calling for these processions and paying for them, it is argued, they would have had no incentive to exaggerate the number considered necessary. Thus, processions can be taken, like tree rings and speleothems, as a reliable proxy for medieval climate.[44] Like all proxies, however, processions have complications. A procession was one of a number of possible actions that could be useful to a government in a moment of stress. It would be naive to assume that such actions were politically neutral or influenced only by current climatic conditions. The perceived usefulness of ritual action was not necessarily constant over time; it changed along with a variety of political and cultural factors. While each procession almost certainly did respond to a perceived climatic reality, the eagerness of the Valencian council to use processions at all waxed markedly over time. In the second quarter of the fifteenth century, the act of organizing a rogation procession went from extraordinary to routine. If these records are to be used effectively as climate proxies, scholars need to examine and account for such large-scale shifts. This is not to say that procession records cannot be mined for climate information, but rather that such chronologies must be constructed with care. Best practices should include a holistic examination of all types of processions in order to identify trends in pro-

---

42. See, for example, Martin-Vide and Barriendos, "The Use of Rogation Ceremony Records"; Élise Hiram, "Enjeux paléoclimatiques et rôle social. Le cas de Salamanque au XVIIe siècle," *Histoire urbaine* 32 (2011): 31–52; and William A. Christian, *Local Religion in Sixteenth-Century Spain* (Princeton, NJ: Princeton University Press, 1981).

43. According to Jordi Fernández-Cuadrench, "Les processons extraordinàries a la Barcelona baix-medieval (1339–1498). Assaig tipològic," *Acta historica et archaeologica mediaevalia* 26 (2005): 403–428, only twenty-six rogation processions for natural disaster were recorded in Barcelona between 1339 and 1498. Laurent Litzenburger, "Temps de fetes, temps de prieres: Les pratiques cultuelles liées au climat à Metz," *Annales de l'Est* 1 (2014): 187–203, lists only forty-three rogations for natural disaster in Metz between 1400 and 1525.

44. For an explanation of the use of rogations as climate proxies, see Ernesto Tejedor et al., "Rogation Ceremonies: A Key to Understanding Past Drought Variability in Northeastern Spain since 1650," *Climate of the Past* 15, no. 5 (2019): 1647–1664.

cessional practice, rather than simply extracting the *pro pluvia* ceremonies from the records. For the fourteenth century and much of the fifteenth, in Valencia the practice of rogation itself was in transition, so numbers of rogation processions cannot be usefully compared across these centuries to establish the frequency or severity of droughts.

The question remains: Why did fifteenth-century councils come to consider processions so worthwhile? Whether the cathedral or the council initiated this new approach, councils from 1428 on chose repeatedly to declare processions and to pay for them. While each procession was not necessarily more expensive than other forms of piety, the multiplying numbers of processions would have represented fairly significant expenditures.[45] Changes in municipal structure in the 1410s could have eased the adoption of a new strategy of natural disaster response in the 1420s, but the specific content of the strategy does not appear to be connected to these developments. The new city leaders who emerged after the violence of the interregnum and the creation of the consell secret in 1418 might have been more open to new types of disaster response. The creation of the consell secret was also the start of a slow but steady increase in royal influence over municipal governance under the Trastámara kings. In the 1420s that influence was still fairly indirect; the king appointed the racional, who in turn chose the jurats. Royal influence on municipal policy was for the most part limited to promoting the financing of the monarch's projects (in Alfons's case, his Italian wars).[46] Late in the fifteenth century, during Ferran and Isabel's conquest of Granada, the council declared processions to celebrate the capture of each new Granadan town—rituals clearly designed to further the Catholic monarchs' political ends.[47] There is little evidence, however, that royal influence was behind the initial establishment of the processional tradition in the 1420s or that natural disaster processions would have served royal interests at this time.

The rise of Valencian rogation processions followed logically from previous councils' embrace of annual civic rituals like the Feasts of Sant Dionís and Corpus Christi. Councils had been promoting these festivals since the 1370s, alongside urban reforms that Christianized the appearance of the city. The reform efforts, particularly by the 1410s, focused particularly on widening the streets most often used in processions. The advantages of such processions would have

45. In 1456 a procession to Sant Vicent cost 496 sous and six diners. This was far less than the 2,000 sous distributed in alms during the famine of 1374–75, but not a trivial sum. AMV, q.q. 4, 125r. For more on famine and alms distribution see chapter 5 of this book.

46. Belenguer Cebrià, *Fernando el Católico*, 30–50; Narbona, "Alfonso el Magnánimo," 593–617. See also Narbona, *Valencia, municipio medieval*, 48–52.

47. See, for example, processions of thanksgiving after the Battle of Lucena in 1483, AMV, A-43, 111r–v; and after the taking of Málaga in 1487, AMV, A-45, 38v–41r.

therefore been clear to authorities by the 1420s. Civic rituals were, of course, increasingly central in late medieval urban culture, both in Spain and across Europe.[48] Rogation processions for natural disaster have largely escaped notice in the literature, but there is no doubt that they were part of the tradition of more frequent and more elaborate civic ritual. Rogation processions were organized on a highly compressed timeline, and (at least in Valencia) impressed through frequent repetition rather than elaborate spectacle. As performances they were much simpler than royal entries and Corpus Christi celebrations, and many fewer details survive about their order and composition. Nonetheless, rogation processions form a crucial element in the story of Valencian civic ritual. Particularly in 1428–29, they fit within and interacted with the regular processional calendar, itself increasingly elaborate in the early fifteenth century. By the late 1420s rogation processions would have been by far the most frequent type of civic religious rituals, organized in response to contemporary conditions that directly affected the lives of both observers and participants. In that sense, they would have shaped Valencian experience of urban ritual. As public, collective responses to environmental events, rogation processions connected the human world of urban performance to a larger, more unruly landscape. While processions for Corpus Christi or other annual festivals have been considered celebrations of the urban, built environment, rogation processions had a more complex relationship with human order and control.[49]

The particular appeal of these strings of rogation processions lay in their potential to connect the experience of natural disaster with a larger narrative of triumphant Christianity in the city of Valencia. Vicent Ferrer described a similar connection in the 1413 sermon discussed in the introduction to this book. For him, rogation processions were less about penitence than about reminding God of the privileged status of Christians. Disasters were not the just consequences of human sin, but rather the "excessive cruel[ty]" of nature, God's "slave . . . from whom we must have bread and wine and other earthly things." As God's legitimate children, Christians deserved his support, while

48. Ruiz, *A King Travels*; Devaney, *Enemies in the Plaza*; Andrew Brown, *Civic Ceremony and Ritual in Medieval Bruges, c. 1300–1520* (Cambridge: Cambridge University Press, 2011); Peter Arnade, *Realms of Ritual: Burgundian Ceremony and Civic Life in Late Medieval Ghent* (Ithaca, NY: Cornell University Press, 1996); Muir, *Civic Ritual in Renaissance Venice*; Edward Muir, "The Eye of the Procession: Ritual Ways of Seeing in the Renaissance," in *Ceremonial Culture in Pre-modern Europe*, ed. Nicholas Howe (Notre Dame, IN: University of Notre Dame Press, 2007), 129–153; Gordon Kipling, "The King's Advent Transformed: The Consecration of the City in the Sixteenth-Century Civic Triumph," in Howe, *Ceremonial Culture in Pre-modern Europe*, 89–127; Mervyn James, "Ritual, Drama and Social Body in the Late Medieval English Town," *Past and Present* 93 (1983): 3–29; Hanawalt, *Ceremony and Civility*.

49. On the meanings of Corpus Christi processions in general, see Lilley, *City and Cosmos*, esp. 158–184. On the Feast of Corpus Christi in Valencia, see chapter 3 of the present book.

his "bastards," Jews and Muslims, were owed nothing. When nature withheld the bounty of the earth from the Christians, therefore, they had to run to their father and remind him who they were. It was their "legitimacy" (that is, their Christianity) that made them worthy of help.[50] Ferrer was revered by many in Valencia at this time, including by the city council.[51] It is therefore not unreasonable to suppose that the council might have shared his outlook. For medieval Valencians, as for Ferrer, processions were an opportunity to distinguish Christian from non-Christian.

In this context, the Valencian rogation processions are remarkable for what they do not include. Rogation processions have historically been understood as ritual invocations of sacred power localized in a specific object or place. Unlike rogations in Barcelona and elsewhere in Catalonia in the fifteenth century and later, Valencian processions do not seem to have focused on the city's patron saints: Vicent Martir and (after his 1455 canonization) Vicent Ferrer. Processions to the Monastery of Sant Vicent actually declined in relative frequency as processions became more popular. According to Martin-Vide and Barriendos, later rogations in Barcelona focused on relics from the Cathedral of the Holy Cross and Santa Eulalia, the Church of Santa Madrona, and the Church of Sant Sever, starting with translation to the altar and escalating to procession, immersion in the sea, and finally pilgrimage to the sanctuary of the cathedral.[52] Although the icon at the Chapel of Santa Maria de Gràcia was a frequent destination for Valencian processions, relics were carried in the processions only very occasionally, and almost never before 1475 (see chapters 5 and 6). After the early pilgrimages to Sant Vicent Martir, Valencian procession announcements do not invoke specific saints corresponding with the destination of the procession. Nor, after Bishop Hug's death in 1427, did the procession announcements stress individual acts of penitence. Instead the focus would have been on the community of Valencian Christians, praying and with candles in their hands. As C. Clifford Flanigan observes, processions were designed to create an experience of togetherness, because each individual "must be part of the moving group and direct his or her own body in terms of the rhythms set by the group. . . . Processions thus give the impression that everyone shares the goals of the community."[53] In this case the processions must have projected the message that the city was completely, triumphantly Christian.

50. Ferrer, *Sermons*, 6:108–109. See Introduction.
51. Lindeman, "Fighting Words," 690–694.
52. Martin-Vide and Barriendos, "The Use of Rogation Ceremony Records," 212. Like most documentary series of rogation processions, however, this one only goes back to 1450.
53. C. Clifford Flanigan, "The Moving Subject: Medieval Liturgical Processions in Semiotic and Cultural Perspective," in Ashley and Hüsken, *Moving Subjects*, 39.

Most medieval sermons described rogation processions as penitential. Vicent Ferrer, however, saw them as an opportunity to insist on a Christian identity as a basis for a relationship with God and for environmental prosperity. This idea would have seemed particularly appropriate in Ferrer's native Valencia, a city whose Christian identity was both a major source of pride and an ongoing project. Valencia in the 1420s had finally achieved many of the reform goals of previous decades: the streets had been widened, the street plan rationalized, and the Jewish quarter erased from the urban landscape. It was a city on the rise: economically prosperous, and the effective capital of a warlike young king. Why would such a city mark its ascent with ever more frequent penitential processions? Because in moments of crisis (quite frequent in these years) those processions reminded the population that the city had, in a larger sense, already won. Having established its Christianity, first through conquest and then again through a long reconstruction, the city of Valencia had earned its share of "the inheritance of paradise."[54]

Councils of the late fourteenth and early fifteenth centuries used infrastructure projects to solve environmental problems and emphasize the city's Christianity (see chapters 2–3). This strategy emerged as the city council recovered from the political turmoil of the mid-fourteenth century. After another politically turbulent period, the interregnum of 1412–14, a restructured municipal government shifted strategy. Emphasis on the city's Christian identity became itself a response to environmental crises. The preoccupations of these councilmen were similar to their predecessors, but ritual performance became the focus of their efforts. This would in many ways have been an easier strategy for the council both to execute and to control. While rituals were not transformative of the surrounding environment, they were much more achievable and immediately visible to the urban population that the council sought to rule. Ambition to control the environmental narrative did not necessarily imply environmental intervention. The rise of rogation processions is visible across all types of natural disaster. These different types of disaster, however, were not interchangeable, and each had its particular dynamics.

54. Ferrer, *Sermons*, 6:108.

CHAPTER 5

Seeking the Dew of His Grace
Droughts

In a letter dated December 1424, the jurats of the city of Valencia wrote to the monks of the nearby Charterhouse of Portaceli, lamenting the drought that gripped the city: "Now in the beginning of the third year . . . we had hoped that the people would sow and the fertility of this year would repay the leanness of those past, [but] the sky is for us made of metal and does not give us the rain that it used to, and that must flow in the earth at the opportune time; the crops perish and the grasses dry, and in brief all that fecundity that the rain water used to minister to the earth is gone."[1] The Valencian council tended to respond to natural disaster with infrastructure projects in the late fourteenth and early fifteenth centuries, and then with rogation processions from the second quarter of the fifteenth century onward. By the second half of the fifteenth century, the council organized regular processions for droughts, plagues, floods, and locust swarms. Although this broad pattern held for all types of natural disaster, the council responded slightly differently to each type: there were differences in the council's

---

1. "Ara en lo començ de la tercera anyada en la qual speraven que les gents sembrarien e que la fertilitat de aquesta anyada recompensaria la flaquea de les altres passades lo cel nos es fet de metall e no dona aquelles aygues pluvials que solen e son necessaries de fluir en la terra en lo temps opportu pereixen los semeters e les erbes se sequen e que breu o digam tots aquelles fecunditats que solen ministrar les pluvials aygues irrigants la terra deffallen." AMV, g3-17, 137v–138r.

material and religious responses to droughts, plagues, floods, and locusts. In all cases, the council documents show a keen understanding of how such disasters played out on the Valencian landscape.

Drought was not only the most common natural disaster on the Valencian plain, it was the disaster around which the landscape was designed. The canals of the Valencian *horta* (the irrigated area around the city) were built to compensate for the absence of rainfall and to distribute the river flow on which agriculture depended.[2] Indeed, the social and physical structures of the horta were so resilient to drought that it might not be considered a natural disaster at all.[3] Drought did not necessarily disrupt the irrigation system or its associated agricultural practices; it merely imposed stresses on the operation of that system and triggered the imposition of emergency measures in response. Valencians were accustomed to drought and had a wide variety of measures in place with which to counteract it. Yet there can be no doubt that the council considered drought a natural disaster; it often (as in the passage above) presented drought as a disturbing interruption of the usual harmony between God, the environment, and humankind. Even before the rise of rogation processions, the council responded to droughts with collective rituals. The Valencian council possessed an array of practical tools to deal with drought, but still emphasized God's anger as its ultimate cause. Recurrent droughts were aberrations disrupting the harvests of a bountiful land.[4]

What Was a Drought?

How severe and how frequent were droughts in late medieval Valencia? The answer depends on how one defines the term *drought*. A drought is an abnormal shortage of water in the environment, but that shortage can be measured in different ways. *Meteorological drought* refers to a shortage of precipitation: the number of days without rain. *Hydrological drought* refers to a shortage of water supplies on or beneath the surface of the landscape: low levels in rivers, canals, cisterns, and springs. *Agricultural drought* refers to a shortage of mois-

---

2. Drought is also the only problem that Thomas Glick addressed in detail in his study of the irrigation system. See Glick, *Irrigation and Society*, 132–148.

3. On vulnerability, see Tim Soens, "Resilient Societies, Vulnerable People: Coping with North Sea Floods before 1800," *Past and Present* 241, no. 1 (2018): 143–177.

4. Donald Worster famously describes how plainsmen during the Dust Bowl era likewise treated drought as an aberration and rain as the natural order of things. See Donald Worster, *Dust Bowl: The Southern Plains in the 1930s* (New York: Oxford University Press, 1979), esp. 26–28.

ture in the soil of agricultural fields, threatening the crops.[5] As will become clear, the Valencian council documents made use of all three of these (and doubtless sometimes exaggerated or minimized the situation for political reasons). As this book is concerned with human perceptions of the natural world, the focus here is primarily on the council's definitions of drought, imperfect as they are; nonanthropogenic measures of drought remain useful, however, for comparison purposes.

Over the long term, the frequency of droughts is a matter of climate. As was noted in the introduction to this book, paleoclimatological research has established that, in general, conditions in Iberia were warmer, drier, and more stable during the Medieval Climate Anomaly (900–1300), and colder, wetter, and more variable during the Little Ice Age (1300–1850). The fourteenth century in Iberia seems to have been something of a transitional phase during which many of the effects of the Little Ice Age were not yet felt, particularly in the south and in the lowland areas. Research suggests that the mountains of the Sistema Ibérico from which the Guadalaviar River (today known as the Túria River) flows, experienced fairly dry (though variable) conditions between 1300 and 1400, with wetter, but also even more variable, conditions prevailing thereafter.[6]

Reconstructing historic precipitation levels in a particular area can be much trickier than identifying long-term trends. Local variations in rainfall can be considerable, so proxy data must be collected very close to the area of interest.[7] Human records of rogation processions have themselves often been used as climate proxies when reconstructing droughts in premodern Iberia (see chapter 4).[8] This practice is unreliable in a period like the fourteenth and fifteenth centuries, when rogation customs themselves were in transition. Rogation processions are therefore not used here as a proxy of drought frequency but rather to assess different drought response strategies over time. Rogations aside, a number of other proxies contain information on precipitation trends. Records of lake and fluvial sedimentary layers are relatively plentiful in eastern Iberia, but cannot be measured on an annual scale. Such records show general trends

---

5. Donald A. Wilhite, "The Enigma of Drought," in *Drought Assessment, Management, and Planning: Theory and Case Studies*, ed. Donald A. Wilhite (Boston: Kluwer Academic, 1993), 3–4.

6. Rosário Lopez Blanco and Lidia Romero Viana, "Dry and Wet Periods over the Last Millennium in Central Eastern Spain—A Paleolimnological Perspective," *Limnetica* 38, no. 1 (2019): 335–352; Charo López-Blanco et al., "Lake-Level Changes and Fire History at Lagunillo del Tejo (Spain) during the Last Millennium: Climate or Humans?," *The Holocene* 22, no. 5 (2012): 551–560.

7. Machado et al., "500 Years of Rainfall Variability," 1251.

8. See, for example, Martin-Vide and Barriendos, "The Use of Rogation Ceremony Records"; Barriendos, "Climate Change in the Iberian Peninsula," 131–159; and Tejedor et al., "Rogation Ceremonies."

over decades or centuries, but not particular years of drought or flood.[9] Tree rings, on the other hand, are annually resolved, and thus provide the most useful precipitation proxy data for historical purposes. Very old trees are rarely found on the Valencian plain, however, and the region has few tree ring series going back more than five hundred years.[10]

Although no single dendrochronological series reliably reconstructs precipitation in the late medieval city of Valencia, a reconstruction can be obtained via the Old World Drought Atlas (OWDA). This collaborative project aggregates a vast quantity of dendrochronological data to reconstruct precipitation levels throughout Europe and the Mediterranean over the last two thousand years. As is standard for such projects, these precipitation levels are expressed using the Palmer Drought Severity Index (PDSI), a measurement of relative rainfall along a spectrum above and below normal for summer in the region. The OWDA uses a PDSI spectrum from –4 to 4, where 0 is normal precipitation and –4 is extreme drought.[11] On this scale, annual precipitation in late medieval Valencia tended to hover close to the normal range; only twenty-three years between 1306 and 1519 register below –2 ("moderate drought"). Nine of those years fell between 1480 and 1500. The human impact of this string of dry years would have been offset by irrigation from the Guadalaviar, as precipitation in the river's headwaters in the late fifteenth century was much closer to normal levels.[12] The late fifteenth century aside, Valencia saw only

---

9. See Lopez Bianco and Romero Viana, "Dry and Wet Periods"; G. Sánchez-López et al., "Climate Reconstruction for the Last Two Millennia in Central Iberia: The Role of East Atlantic (EA), North Atlantic Oscillation (NAO) and Their Interplay over the Iberian Peninsula," *Quaternary Science Reviews* 149 (2016): 135–150; Fernando Barreiro-Lostres, Ana Moreno, Santiago Giralt, Margarita Caballero, and Blas Valero-Garcés, "Climate, Palaeohydrology and Land Use Change in the Central Iberian Range over the Last 1.6 kyr: The La Parra Lake Record," *The Holocene* 24, no. 10 (2014): 1177–1192; López-Blanco et al., "Lake-Level Fire Changes"; Ana Moreno, Blas Valero-Garcés, Penélope González-Sampériz, and Mayte Rico, "Flood Response to Rainfall Variability during the Last 2000 Years Inferred from the Taravilla Lake Record (Central Iberian Range, Spain)," *Journal of Paleolimnology* 40, no. 3 (2008): 943–961.

10. Oliva et al., "The Little Ice Age," table 1. For a chronology from the Iberian mountains that goes back to the seventeenth century, see Ernesto Tejedor et al., "Tree-Ring-Based Drought Reconstruction in the Iberian Range (East of Spain) since 1694," *International Journal of Biometeorology* 60, no. 3 (2016), 361–372. José Creus Novau, Ángel Fernández Cancio, and Emilio Manrique Menéndez, "Evolución de la temperatura y precipitatición anuales desde el año 1400 en el sector central de la depresión del Ebro," *Lucas Mallada* 8 (1996): 9–27, has a chronology from 1400 that shows a sharp decline in temperature and a less sharp increase in precipitation in the late fifteenth century but can tell us little about conditions before that time.

11. Cook et al., "Old World Megadroughts." For a summary of the project in laypersons' terms and a discussion of its use in a historical context, see Matt King, "The Sword and the Sun: The Old World Drought Atlas as a Source for Medieval Mediterranean History," *Al-Masāq* 29, no. 3 (2017): 221–234.

12. Precipitation reconstruction for Valencia is from the Old World Drought Atlas web application, http://drought.memphis.edu/OWDA, accessed March 20, 2020. See also Cook et al., "Old World Megadroughts."

a few years of more than moderate annual drought: six between 1351 and 1366, two in 1436 and 1437, and a few other single-year events. The famine years of the early 1370s mostly registered between normal and moderate, never dropping below −1.7 on the PDSI.

Individual droughts, however, are weather events, not annual precipitation extremes.[13] Even annually resolved climate proxies do not capture rainfall variation *during* the year, and it was this variation that created a drought for Valencian observers. Fernando Domínguez-Castro and colleagues have observed that the precipitation threshold at which towns organized drought rituals in early modern Spain varied throughout the year.[14] In Valencia, as in much of the Mediterranean, most of the rain falls in the autumn and the spring.[15] Although rain is scarcest in summer (the season captured by the PDSI), the agricultural calendar was historically adapted to that scarcity. Towns were therefore much more likely to declare drought rituals for short delays in the spring and winter rains that were vital to the grain crops than for long stretches of summer drought.[16] As the council noted, rain needed not simply to fall but to "flow in the earth at the opportune time."[17] For humans and their crops, drought was as much a matter of timing as quantity. Although neither the fourteenth nor fifteenth centuries was, by annual measures, exceptionally dry, the irregularity of weather patterns during both centuries meant that, from a human perspective, drought continued to be common.

In other words, drought, like any natural disaster, is in the eye of the beholder. A dip in water supply only becomes a drought when it has an impact on its local environment, and all of the proxies that measure drought measure these impacts in different ways. A drought for a lake, a river, or a tree is not always a drought for a city, and vice versa. Human measures of drought are a function of whether the water supply suffices (or appears as though it will suffice) for key human needs at any given moment. For the Valencian council, the most important of these needs were to irrigate the crops (with or without rationing) and to turn the mill wheels that ground the city's flour. In 1445 the city paid one En Pere Vetxo one florin for two days work "leveling," or surveying Moncada canal, where most of the city's mills were located, "to find out how much water could come there because of the milling, because

---

13. For a nuanced discussion of the relationship between climate and weather, see Degroot, *The Frigid Golden Age*, 14–17.

14. F. Domínguez-Castro et al., "A Shift in the Spatial Pattern of Iberian Droughts during the 17th Century," *Climate of the Past* 6, no. 5 (2010): 553–563.

15. A. López Gómez, *Geografia de les Terres Valencianes* (Valencia: Papers Bàsics 3i4, 1977), 29.

16. Domínguez-Castro et al., "A Shift in the Spatial Pattern," 558.

17. AMV, g3-17, 137v–138r.

of the drought."[18] The need for irrigation water varied throughout the year, but it also varied over time, depending on the intensity of cultivation in the horta. The city's milling needs were likewise a function of the need for flour, and thus of urban population. The Valencian horta was more intensively cultivated by the fourteenth and fifteenth centuries than it had been in the Andalusi period, with nearly every parcel of land irrigated and irrigation systems designed to use all the available river water (see chapter 1).[19] Despite the devastation of the Black Death, moreover, the population of the city of Valencia was growing again in the late fourteenth and fifteenth centuries as a result of immigration from the countryside.[20]

The city of Valencia in the late Middle Ages experienced few severe multi-annual dry periods, but the council perceived relatively frequent shorter-term water shortages. This book follows the council's lead and refers to these latter events as "droughts." At an annual scale, precipitation in late medieval Valencia varied relatively little from normal levels and was in many cases mitigated by the riverine water supply. Valencian systems of water distribution were also operating closer to their limits in the fourteenth and fifteenth centuries than they had been earlier, trying now to irrigate more land and feed more people. Small variations in water supply at key points in the growing season would have had significant perceived effects. This was a period when droughts were frequent enough to be noticeable but not so severe as to appear beyond all help. Municipal interventions would often have seemed capable of making a difference to human outcomes.

Material Responses

The city council defined drought primarily in terms of its effects on agriculture and milling and had a number of strategies available to address those effects. Few of the other potential impacts of a drought seem to have been an issue in Valencia. By the fourteenth century the river had silted up too much for navigation, but efforts to float timber supplies down to the city from the mountains could sometimes be fouled by low water.[21] There is no indication that the city ran short of water for drinking or household uses, though such

18. "A per saber quina aygua hi podia venir per raho del molre les farines per raho de la secada." AMV, A-33, 195v–196r.

19. Torró, "Field and Canal Building," 100.

20. Rubio Vela, "Vicisitudes demográficas," 263–264.

21. AMV, g3-11, 101r–v.

shortages may have happened elsewhere in the kingdom.[22] Most drinking water in the city probably came from private wells rather than from the irrigation network. Meanwhile, the canals of the horta needed to maintain a water level sufficient to turn a mill wheel, but the water itself was not used up by the milling.[23] If the water level was sufficient for milling, therefore, it would probably also have sufficed for domestic purposes.

As regards the council's material strategies for drought, both long-term and short-term measures were available. In the short term, the council could work to regulate the sharing of water within the irrigation network, thereby securing a larger share of that water for the city. If the shortage was thought to be too severe for such measures, the council could attempt to bypass the need for water by importing the products that required it (flour and grain). In the long term, the council could also increase the total water supply by bringing new sources of water into the horta. Since a shortage of water for milling or irrigation could cause political problems, the council would probably have been inclined to overestimate the city's future needs.

While under ordinary circumstances the users themselves governed water distribution in the horta, the city council, in its capacity as *sobrecequier*, or senior official of the horta, became involved when the water supply was seen as insufficient. The first step was to regulate sharing of the existing supply by means of a system of turns (*tanda*) that allowed each mother canal and its subsidiaries to receive water on certain days. On the days when it was another community's turn, the hydraulic structures at the head of the canal would be modified to turn water away; when it was that canal's turn, the water was allowed to flow in. In 1481 the city council appointed two *cequiers* (officers) to go down the river opening the return ditches (*almenaras*), allowing the water to return to the river so that the city would receive the full complement guaranteed in its tanda.[24]

The council's authority over the rest of the horta was clear, but securing water from outside the city boundaries was another matter entirely. The city of Valencia was located almost at the mouth of the Guadalaviar; many communities had the opportunity to use water from the river and its tributaries before it entered the city boundaries. If it was necessary to convince these communities to share that water with the city, the jurats resorted to a combination

22. Two Valencian documents describe droughts when drinking water was said to run short "in many places," but not in the city itself. For 1422, see AMV, g3-15, 195v; for 1455–57, see Melchior Miralles, in *Crònica i dietari del capellà d'Alfons el Magnànim*, ed. Mateu Rodrigo Lizondo (Valencia: Publicacions de la Universitat de València, 2011), 4:72, pp. 236–237.

23. Glick, *Irrigation and Society*, 87.

24. AMV, A-42, 177v.

of exhortation and threats. In 1335 they demanded water from the upstream villages of Benaguasil, Riba-roja, and Vilamarxant, claiming that "the crops of the horta are in peril of loss if God and good friends do not come to our aid" but also referring obliquely to the city's rights to the river, granted by royal privilege during a drought fourteen years earlier, and to the "penalty" to be exacted if these communities took the city's water.[25]

Of course, these efforts might fail to secure sufficient water for the city's needs. On March 30, 1413, for example, the jurats wrote to the officials of several upstream villages requesting water for a day and a night on account of "the shortage of water that is in the city and for the great provision of flour that we need to make for the coming of the Lord King."[26] On April 19 they reiterated the request, again asking for water for the following day and night.[27] By May 5, however, the city desired not water but the use of the mills of Riba-roja, as the city's own mills would no longer turn.[28] And, by July 13, the city informed the officials of Paterna that it was sending thirty bakers there to produce flour for the city of Valencia.[29] The next day it also sent bakers to request flour from the Lady of Manises and requested that flour be sent by pack animal from Alzira, although the water shortage had stopped mills there as well.[30] Further requests went out on July 28 "to mill for the bakers of this city, particularly for the need of water that is in the present time in our river, for which we have shortage of flour, and said bakers consequently cannot give the full complement of bread that the people of the city deserve."[31] Being more perishable than grain, flour was imported only when the water level was low enough to stop the mills of the city entirely. Drought was, of course, a matter of perceived supply and demand; in this case, the council feared a shortage partly because a visit from the royal court brought extra mouths to feed.

The relationship between famine and drought was a complex one. Famine in the Middle Ages was generally the result of agricultural crisis, but drought was not the only crisis that could cause the loss of the harvest. Nor did an un-

---

25. AMV, g3-1, 41r–v.

26. "La gran necessitat de aygues qui es en la Ciutat & per la gran provisio de farines qui hauem a fer per la venguda del Senyor Rey." AMV, g3-11, 197r.

27. AMV, g3-11, 206r–v.

28. AMV, g3-11, 210v–211r.

29. The original reads "tres deenes de flaquers [three tens of bakers]." AMV, g3-12, 14v–15r.

30. AMV, g3-12, 16r–v.

31. "Pochs dies ha scrivim a vostra noblea que plagues a aquella dar favor en molre als flaquers daquesta Ciutat specialment per la necessitat de les aygues qui son en lo present temps en nostre Riu per la qual havem fretura de farines. E los dits flaquers per conseguent no poden dar compliment de pa segon ques mereix al poble dela dita Ciutat." AMV, g3-12, 24v–25r.

favorable harvest necessarily result in famine, since grain arrived in the city from all over the western Mediterranean. The famine of 1374–76 was the result of a coincidence of different meteorological triggers over a regional trading area: drought in Catalonia and Valencia, rain in Tuscany, drought followed by rain in the Papal States, and cold and storms in southern France.[32] Medieval Mediterranean cities were rarely able to feed themselves from the produce of their own hinterlands; years of relative scarcity were common, and grain imports more or less the norm.[33] Like most medieval city governments, the Valencian council arranged regular imports of wheat (*blat* or *forment*) to supplement the local food supply and to compensate for poor harvests. Publicly purchased grain supplies were sold from the city storehouse (*almodí*) at regulated prices, serving as a check on the rest of the grain market. Just as the council had the power to secure water in times of scarcity, so too did the city's power within the region allow it to dominate the local food supply system.[34]

When local supplies were insufficient, the city bought grain from anywhere within reach: often the Crown of Aragon (most commonly Barcelona, Mallorca, or Sicily), but also Castile and sometimes even North Africa.[35] During the drought of 1473–74 the city held rogation processions to pray specifically for good weather so that the grain ships could arrive.[36] This type of exchange was mutual; Valencia in turn received grain requests from Barcelona and Mallorca. During the famine of 1374, the jurats of Valencia wrote several times to their counterparts in Mallorca claiming, "Not only do we not have wheat with which to succor you, we do not have [wheat] for ourselves."[37] In order to secure as much grain as possible in a crowded market, the council offered incentives to import wheat during times of scarcity, in the form either of guaranteed prices for the goods at the almodí or subsidies (*ajudes*) offered to importers.[38] In extreme circumstances, none of these cities were above seizing

---

32. Franklin-Lyons and Kelleher, "Framing Mediterranean Famine."

33. Peregrine Horden and Nicholas Purcell, *The Corrupting Sea: A Study of Mediterranean History* (Oxford: Blackwell, 2000), 112–115. According to Ferran Esquilache Martí, "Paisatge agrari i alimentació a l'horta de Valencia dels segles XIII–XIV: Agricultura, ramaderia i explotació del medi natural," *Torrens: Estudis i investigacions de torrent i comarca* 16 (2006), 45, in Valencia grain imports "became an obsession of municipal politics."

34. Franklin-Lyons, *Shortage and Famine*.

35. For Barcelona, see AMV, g3-17, 88r–89r; for Mallorca, see AMV, g3-25, 20r; for Castile, North Africa, and Sicily, see AMV, g3-15, 159r–160r.

36. See AMV, A-40, 44v–45v, 49r–v, 51v–52r, 85v–86r, 90v–91r, 94r–95r.

37. "Car per veritat senyors no tant solament no hauem blats per soccorrer a vosaltres ans encara non havem per a nos." AMV, g3-3, 152v.

38. AMV, A-5, 19r–20r. See also Rafael Narbona Vizcaíno, "Finanzas municipales y patriciado urbano. Valencia a finales del trescientos," *Anuario de estudios medievales* 22 (1992): 485–512.

grain ships by force.[39] Other cities of the Crown of Aragon used similar practices to ensure a sufficient grain supply for their population, but Adam
Franklin-Lyons has argued that by the end of the fourteenth century, Valencia was most often successful.[40] The council thus participated in an ongoing
resource exchange that could be urgent but never reached true crisis propor-
tions unless, as in 1374, all the regions were facing a shortage simultaneously.

Valencia, like other Mediterranean cities, had significant economic and political power over its grain supply. Both its government and its charitable institutions also faced political and moral imperatives to make bread available to
the poor. For this reason, the city's population tended to grow in times of subsistence crisis, as the destitute in the countryside sought the city's grain stores
and charitable institutions.[41] In 1374, however, perceived and actual wheat
shortages both local and regional triggered such high bread prices that government and charities struggled to provide food to the city's population.[42]
During the famine, the jurats complained about "persons of low condition and
the foreigners, who hearing of [our] good fortune of wheat have come here
in infinite number, and whom we cannot expel, despite our ordinations and
proclamations, and despite the sicknesses and general plagues that are here
by divine justice."[43] Famine in the medieval Crown of Aragon was as much
a matter of trade and charity as of environment.

During the droughts of the early 1370s the council developed its first plans
to bring new water sources into the horta (see chapter 2). Experts surveyed
the Cabriol River, in the mountains west of the city, first during the drought
of 1371–72 and then in 1376, as the city was recovering from the famine. Meanwhile, starting in 1374, the council began to explore efforts to bring water
north from the Xúquer River watershed and revived that project in different
forms with each subsequent drought through the early fifteenth century. Also
in 1376, the council first explored the idea of bringing water from the lake of
Santa Cruz de Moya in the upper reaches of the Guadalaviar. This project, like
the Xúquer canal, received renewed interest in the early fifteenth century. All
of these projects were initiated during droughts, and particularly the extended
crisis of the mid-1370s. The city council, therefore, was capable of respond-

---

39. AMV, g3-12, 22r.

40. Franklin-Lyons, *Shortage and Famine*.

41. Rubio Vela, "Vicisitudes demográficas," 263.

42. Franklin-Lyons, *Shortage and Famine*.

43. "Persons de pocha condicio e majorment estranyes qui per fama daquests benastruchs de
blats menuts sen son aci vengudes en infinit nombre les quals gitar no hic podem no contrastants
nostres ordenations e crides ne contrastants les malalties e morts generals que son aci per divinal
juhi." AMV, g3-3, 152v–153r.

ing to droughts in a variety of ways: not only with short-term measures to counteract the risk of harvest failure, mill stoppage, and famine, but also with attempts to improve the water security of the city and its horta.

The Language of Drought

Despite the many strategies that the council employed to keep city and horta running in times of low water, its documents describe drought as a divinely ordained interruption of the relationship between earth, sky, and human beings. As the passage at the start of this chapter demonstrated, the council keenly felt the connection between abundantly flowing water, productive land, and human prosperity. The environment of Valencia was described as one where rain water usually "flow[ed] in the earth at the opportune time."[44] Yet even Francesc Eiximenis, in his 1383 encomium on the city's natural riches, stopped short of suggesting that Valencia was well endowed with rain.[45] The government of a city designed to flourish in the absence of rain still described this absence as an unequivocal sign of God's displeasure.

As Domínguez-Castro and colleagues observed for early modern Spain, the timing of the rain was everything. The Valencian council was more attuned to the need for rain to water winter and spring crops than to the longer dry stretches in the summer months.[46] This is not to say that the city did not suffer from summer droughts. The Valencian horta had two growing seasons, and thus many parts of the year when drought could interrupt the agricultural cycle. As elsewhere in the Mediterranean, wheat and barley were planted in the fall and harvested in the spring so that they would not be exposed to the summer heat. Garden crops and rice were sown in the spring and harvested along with grapes in the autumn. The two harvests were not, however, equivalent in importance; wheat was far more important in both diet and imagination than any of the summer crops.[47] Even in October 1421, when a drought threatened that summer harvest, it was scarcity of wheat not yet sown that signified famine: "In this city and throughout the Kingdom of Valencia there is great penury and scarcity of wheat of which we have need, [because of] the great drought and sterility of waters that for one year have not rained, and the harvest will not be gathered in nor can the people now sow. . . . Our Lord

---

44. AMV, g3-17, 137v–138r.
45. Eiximenis, *Regiment de la cosa publica*, 61–76.
46. Domínguez-Castro et al., "A Shift in the Spatial Pattern," 558.
47. Franklin-Lyons and Kelleher, "Framing Mediterranean Famine.".

in his mercy has turned away his face, for which the people are troubled and dismayed."[48]

For the most part, the documents stressed the need for rain at key agricultural moments: usually around the winter planting or the spring harvest. The jurats did not pretend expertise in these matters; in January 1400 they asked the monks of the Charterhouse of Valldecrist to pray for rain, noting, "Because of the sterility of the weather [the earth] does not have that humor that according to expert men it should have if it is to be a good year in the land."[49] In a proclamation for a rogation procession in December 1424 the council declared that God had "taken away and removed from us the rainwaters that in better times are accustomed to fall over the earth, where they minister to his people fruits and foodstuffs for their livings."[50] In December 1463 the council again complained of scarcity: "For our sins we find ourselves deprived of rain for some days in such a way that the lands that have been sown and those still to be sown have great scarcity of water, such that those that have been sown cannot well produce their fruit and the others remain to be sown, and thus the beginning of the year will prove to be sterile and in no small need."[51]

In October 1475 the council declared a procession to ask for "rain and good, temperate weather such that [we] can sow most abundantly so that, with God's help, it may be a fertile year so that we can better sustain human life."[52] Again and again the documents reiterate that without appropriately timed rain, "the people cannot sow, nor can the earth become fruitful."[53] Later in the spring, concern shifted from the sowing to the harvest. In February 1473 the council's prayer was that God grant "clean, pure, and fitting rain over the earth

---

48. "En aquesta Ciutat e per tot lo Regne de Valent ha gran penuria e fretura de forments nes que no seria ops. E es ne causa la gran seccada e sterilitat daygues car per dun any ha que noy ha plogut e no sia collit splet ne huy les gents poden sembrar. . . . Nostre Senyor per sa merce hi gire la cara de que senyor comunament la gent ne esta tribulada e ab esmay." AMV, g3-15, 159r.

49. "La terra que per la sterilitat del temps no ha aquella humor que a veiars domes experts dauria haver si bon any deu esser en la terra." AMV, g3-6, 275r.

50. "El nostre creador e tot poderos Deu e Senyor apres altres flagells quens trames en los anys prop passats ara en aquest any ha manades tolre e levar nos les aygues pluvials qui en los temps congruents solien caure sobre la terra don al seu poble eren ministrats fruyts e aliments per lurs viures." AMV, A-27, 264v.

51. "Nos trobam privats de pluja de alguns dies atras en tanta manera que les terres sembrades e per sembrar ne passen gran fretura tant qles sembrades no poden bonament produyr llurs fruyt & les altres resten per sembrar e axi lo principa de la anyada covent se demostraria steril e en no poca falta." AMV, g3-26, 41r–v.

52. "Pluga e bon temps temprat per modo que puxen sembrar abundantissimament per que migançant lo divinal aduitori sia fertil anyada perque millor puxam sustentat la vida humana." AMV, A-40, 231r.

53. AMV, g3-26, 275r. See also AMV, g3-27, 103v–104r; and AMV, g3-25, 40v–41r.

because with the intercession of his grace the harvests that are in the care of the earth might be fruitful and give and render that which is necessary for the sustenance of human life."[54] As the rogation procession announcements became more elaborately worded over the course of the fifteenth century, the council requested not simply rain, but "fitting, clean, and pure rain" (*pluja congruent, neta i pura*).[55]

God granted the proper amount of rain at the proper time, which prompted the earth to put forth its natural abundance and thereby sustain human life. God's withdrawal of the rain was what made the earth hard and sterile. The earth was naturally fertile, but it required God's help. The council articulated this idea most clearly in the winter of 1424:

> Seeing that our creator and all-powerful Lord God, after other scourges sent to us in the last few years, now in this year has taken and removed from us the rain water that in fitting times was accustomed to fall over the earth . . . we pray . . . that he revoke and take away from us his indignation, and [his] anger turn to mercy toward us. And from this spring [*font*] of his infinite mercy that never fails us, [that] he send from heaven temperate waters that irrigate the earth, and the dew of his grace that fertilizes it abundantly so that we, his creation and the work of his hands, sustained by his grace and mercy by temporal fruits, may praise and bless, adore and glorify him as our own Lord God.[56]

Here the rain was portrayed as the physical manifestation of God's grace, which nourished the earth and humanity.

Even documents that dealt with material matters presented divine anger as the ultimate cause of drought. In April 1356 the council suspended its subsidy of wheat imports because "our Lord God in his mercy has improved the weather."[57] In July 1374 the council authorized the jurats to look into antifamine measures because "by divine justice there is a great scarcity of wheat

---

54. "Pluja congruent neda e pura sobre la terra perque mijancant la sua gracia los splets que acomanats son ala terra puixen fructificar e donar e retre lo que es mester per sustenacio de la vida humana." AMV, A-39, 195r–v.

55. AMV, A-41, 167v–168r.

56. "Veents quel nostre creador e tot poderos Deu e Senyor apres altres flagells quens trames en los anys prop passats ara en aquest any ha manades tolre e levar nos les aygues pluvials qui en los temps congruents solien caure sobre la terra . . . e suppliquem que revoch e tolga de nosaltres la sua indignacio e ira es gire misericordios vers nosaltres. E daquella font que james no defall de la sua misericordia infinida nos trameta del cel aygues temprades que irriguen la terra e los ros de la sua gracia qui abundosament la fecunde a fi que nosaltres factura sua e obres de les sues mans sustentats per la sua gracia e merce dels fruyts temporals loem e beneescam adorem e glorifiquem ell nostre propiciu Deu e Senyor." AMV, A-28, 104r–v.

57. "Nostre Senyor Deus per la sua merce haia millorat lo temps." AMV, A-12, 97r–98r.

and hunger in the land."[58] The following month the council observed that the wine harvest was poor "by reason of the great droughts and sterility of the crops and fruits of the earth, which by divine justice have been and are."[59] The council of 1420 similarly sought to organize imports of wheat, which had risen in price because "our Lord has not granted rain over the face of the earth in this season of sowing."[60] Prayers for divine aid were also in some cases connected to the functioning of the water system. The council organized imports of flour from neighboring towns in March 1473, claiming that "Our Lord God, for our sins, does not wish to give us rain."[61] As has been noted, the city held processions that same year to pray for good weather so that the grain ships could arrive.[62] None of these statements necessarily reflects the private beliefs of the councilmen. They are significant, rather, because they were public (or semipublic) statements. In both material and religious contexts, the council chose to present droughts as the will of God.

Rituals for Drought

The council also chose to present appeals to divine mercy as effective responses to drought. God was considered the ultimate cause of all natural phenomena, in the sense that nothing in the material world could happen contrary to his will (see chapter 4). Most medieval observers had a more specific chain of causation in mind; God, angered by the sins of human beings in a particular place, chastised them with environmental misfortunes. Religious responses sought to persuade this angry God to cease his punishment. This could be done in two ways: by fixing the misbehavior or by appealing to divine mercy. Either a specific set of sins and sinners was said to have triggered divine anger or the calamity was ascribed to the sins of the population in general. In the former case, the council instituted moral reforms targeting specific sins, while in the latter it organized collective rituals that demonstrated general piety. Both approaches were intended to resolve a crisis by appeasing God's anger, but with a different logic and to different effect. Naming specific sins focused blame on

---

58. "Per divinal juhi ha gran fretura de blats e fam en la terra." AMV, A-16, 209r–v.

59. "Per rao deles grans seccades e esterilitats dels esplets e fruyts dela terra les quals per lo divinal juhi son estades e son." AMV, A-16, 213r–v.

60. "Nostre senyor no ha donada pluja sobre la faç de la terra en aquest temps del sementiri lo preu dels forments se començava a encarir." AMV, A-27, 264v.

61. "Considerant que Nostre Senyor Deu per nostres peccats nons vol dar pluia per fretura de la qual los molins ja no basten a molre lo que seria necessari per sustenacio dela vida humana per lo gran poble que en la present Ciutat." AMV, A-39, 206v–207r.

62. See AMV, A-40, 44v–45v, 49r–v, 51v–52r, 85v–86r, 90v–91r, 94r–95r.

particular groups, while citing humanity's general sinfulness diffused the responsibility over the population as a whole. Attributing a disaster to God's anger at human sin, in other words, did not necessarily mean blaming any particular sinners. The Valencian council did associate plague with certain sinners (see chapter 6). For droughts, by contrast, the council tended to organize rituals that emphasized collective penitence and community unity.

Valencian councils organized a variety of rituals in response to droughts over the course of the fourteenth, fifteenth, and early sixteenth centuries. Only once, in the early fourteenth century, did these rituals associate the drought with particular sins or sinners. In May 1345, after having organized a rogation procession in April,

> the citizen jurats in the . . . council [proposed] that since many times it has been reasoned and said that the superfluity and vanity and bad use that is in the city was strongly displeasing to God and abominable to humans: that women wear long skirts and short cloaks and other apparel. For these vanities and others our Lord God gives to the people many tribulations, [such] as holding back the rain so that the wheat may not be fruitful nor improve as in other ways for our sins. How good would it be if a statute and ordination were made that women should wear skirts only to cover their honesty and not in superfluity nor vanity! And if the statute were made and said vanities and other vices provided for in the law of God by the council in the manner correct in the eyes of God, in his mercy he would give us rain and good weather and fertility and abundance of victuals and he would dispel from us many tribulations and anxieties that we deserve on account of our sins.[63]

A week later the council devised a list of statutes to eliminate "vanities and superfluities [for which] our Lord God gives us many tribulations, such as holding back the rain in times of necessity."[64] As for the upcoming Feast of Sant Joan the Baptist, it was deemed that "no woman of the city and its boundaries shall

---

63. "Fo proposat per los Jurats Ciutadans en lo dit consell que com molts vegades fos raonat & parlat que fort era desplaent a Deu & abominable als gents la sobrefluitat & vanitat & mal us que es en la Ciutat de portar les dones longues faldes en mantells cots & altres vestidurs per les quals vanitats & altres nostre Senyor Deus dona a les gents molts tribulacions axi en retenir se la pluia per que los blats no poden fructificar ne mellorar com en altres maneres per nostres peccats. Que bo serie quen fos fet statut & ordenacio que les dones portassen faldes tantsolament per cobrir lur onestat & no asobre fluitat ne vanitat. E si lo dit statut se faya & en les dites vanitats & altres vicis vedats en la ley de deu si provehir per lo consell en manera deguda Nostre Senyor Deus per la sua misericordia donaria a nos pluia & bon temps & fertilitat & abundancia de vitualles & lunyaria de nos molts tribulacions & angusties ques fona per merexament de nostres peccats." AMV, A-4, 484v.

64. "Vanitats & sobrefluitats Nostre Senyor Deu dona a nos moltes tribulationes axi en retenir se la pluia en temps de necessitat." AMV, A-4, 489v–490r.

wear or dare to wear the skirts of her mantle or cotte or other clothing beyond three *palms* of an *alna*" (approximately seventy-five centimeters—i.e., ankle length). Each time she was caught with trailing skirts, she would have to pay a fine of five morabatins, to be taken out of her dowry.[65] The same legislation also restricted mourning garb; Valencians could wear mourning only for their lord, their parents, sisters and brothers, uncles, husbands and wives, and anyone whose heir they were. The legislation also set time limits on mourning for everyone except widows, and on the price of candles burned in cemeteries on the Feast of All Saints (two diners or less). Finally, the city declared its patronage of a home for repentant prostitutes, which would induce them not to sin.[66]

The three noblemen present at the meeting that day, the jurat En Pere Roiç de Corella and the *consellers* En Jacme Castella and En Ramon Costa, objected to these measures, which they said were "contrary to the liberties of rich noble men [*richs homes cavallers*]."[67] They were not wrong. As Diane Owen Hughes has observed, sumptuary laws in the fourteenth century were intended to regulate excess rather than police class boundaries. They tended to target the aristocracy. Unlike the better-known legislation of the Renaissance, these laws were as concerned with funerals as with dress, since funeral rites showcased the dynastic pretensions of noble families.[68] The council overruled the nobles' objections and made a public proclamation of the restrictions on May 20, 1345. In drawing an association between disaster and aristocratic excess, the council sought to frame the wasting of the earth's wealth as God's response to humans' overvaluing of their own riches; vain noblewomen had preferred their material wealth to the gifts of Christ.[69] The aristocrats, however, seem to have prevailed in the end. The council of 1345 was both the first and the last in Valencia to associate drought with vanity. Indeed, this was virtually the only instance in which a Valencian council sought to connect a drought to any specific types of sins or sinners.[70]

---

65. "Stabiliren & ordenaren que alcuna dona de la ciutat & terma daquella no port o gos portar faldes en mantell o cot o altres vestidures sues ultra tres palms dalna. E si contre feytt sera pagara per pena v morabatins per aytantes vegades com atrobada sera portar les dits faldes." AMV, A-4, 490r–v.

66. AMV, A-4, 490r–491v.

67. AMV, A-4, 491v–492r.

68. Diane Owen Hughes, "Sumptuary Law and Social Relations in Renaissance Italy," in *The Italian Renaissance: The Essential Readings*, ed. Paula Findlen (Malden, MA: Blackwell, 2002), 128–129, 138, 141.

69. Gerhard Jaritz, "Outer Appearance, Late Medieval Public Space, and the Law," in *At the Edge of the Law: Socially Unacceptable and Illegal Behavior in the Middle Ages and the Early Modern Period* (Krems, Austria: Medium Aevum Quotidianum, 2012), 51–54.

70. In 1413, inspired by Vicent Ferrer's preaching, the council issued regulations against sins that "per divinal juhi se enseguesquen mortaldats guerres fams sequedats lagosta terratremol e altres diverses greus plagues e persequicions [by divine justice engender mortalities, wars, famines, droughts, locusts, earthquakes, and diverse other grave plagues and persecutions]." AMV, A-25, 141r. No such

Councils after 1345 preferred to respond to drought with collective rituals that emphasized the Christian unity of the city. In the fourteenth century these rituals included both rogation processions and public distributions of alms to the poor. By the second quarter of the fifteenth century, however, councils increasingly favored rogation processions over almsgiving rituals. Throughout the period, religious responses to drought show a closer connection between city and horta than was the case for other types of disaster.

Almsgiving as a pious act with redemptive power for the giver had deep roots in Christian tradition, but the appropriate identity of the recipient of alms underwent a number of shifts through the medieval period. Early medieval almsgiving was intended to demonstrate the giver's pious contempt for wealth rather than to alter the condition of the recipient. High medieval charitable institutions gave both to the involuntarily poor and to those who had, through adoption of religious life, entered a state of voluntary poverty. In the increasingly crisis-prone fourteenth century, donors began to perceive scarcity in their own resources and to draw finer distinctions among the poor. Beggars, particularly itinerant ones, became threats to social order, while charity was reserved for respectable dependents. These "shamefaced poor" (*pobres vergonyants*) were those in straitened circumstances; they could no longer maintain their position in society without assistance but were too decorous to go out and beg. By the end of the fourteenth century, wills and other private charity increasingly favored this group, though the older style of public almsgiving (particularly at aristocratic funerals), survived well into the following century.[71]

The Valencian council's charitable giving paralleled these private trends. In January 1343, the council announced that 3,000 sous would be given out on the coming Friday morning to relieve drought. When the cathedral bell sounded, the poor should present themselves at their parish church, and when it sounded the second time, alms would be publicly distributed to those assembled.[72] During the early 1370s, councils announced public almsgiving alongside rogation processions as twin remedies for drought. In 1372 alms were distributed at the end of the processional route, in front of the cathedral.[73] In 1371 and 1374 they were given out the following day, in the courtyard of the Friars Minor.[74] By February 1374 the announcement specified that "the

calamities, however, were taking place in the city at the time. AMV, A-18, 80r–v. Regarding moral reform legislation and natural disaster, see chapter 6 of this book.

71. James William Brodman, *Charity and Welfare: Hospitals and the Poor in Medieval Catalonia* (Philadelphia: University of Pennsylvania Press, 1998), 1–6. See also Pullan, "Plague and Perceptions of the Poor," 101–123.

72. AMV, A-4, 282r–284r.

73. AMV, A-16, 102v–103r.

74. AMV, A-16, 44r–v, 185v–186v.

shamefaced poor and . . . male and female religious" were the appropriate recipients of such charity.[75] Five months later, in July, the council ordered the
expulsion of all "strangers and vagabonds" from the city, whether male or female, Christian, Jewish, or Muslim, so that they would not continue to con-
sume the food required by the city's own citizens.[76]

Almsgiving during droughts may have been considered a practical measure,
meant to feed the poor as well as to redeem sins. Many charitable institutions
were overwhelmed during the famine years of the 1370s. In 1374 one of Valencia's main hospitals, En Clapers, reduced the weight of its loaves of bread.[77]
In February of that year the city council publicly distributed 12,000 sous in alms
to the deserving poor. In April 1375 it authorized the distribution of between
one and 2,000 florins (22,000 to 44,000 sous), to the religious and the shamefaced
poor, as well as public almsgiving to "poor mendicants" at the rate of four diners
per person.[78] According to Franklin-Lyons's estimate, an individual could eat
reasonably well for 175 sous per year, or about 5.75 diners per day, in a period of
normal grain prices.[79] The four diners given to mendicants was therefore a fairly
nominal sum during a famine. The amounts distributed to the deserving poor
were somewhat more significant. The population of Valencia in the 1370s has
been estimated at between five thousand and eight thousand households.[80] We
cannot know what percentage of these were considered "deserving poor," but
the 12,000 sous distributed in 1374 could have fed about 715 households of five
individuals—between 9 and 14 percent of the population—for one week during
a period of normal food prices. In 1374 it would not have lasted so long. The
1375 alms could have fed a much higher percentage of households, or fed them
for longer. These sums were probably enough to have made a short-term difference in the lives of the poor, but that may not have been their primary purpose.
These were public rituals of natural disaster response.

Probably due to changing sentiments toward the poor, such rituals did not
last beyond the crisis years of the early 1370s. While alms continued to be distributed through the early fifteenth century, the council turned away from public almsgiving. In 1384 the council authorized 2,000 sous in charity to end
drought, plague, the Great Schism, and the conflicts between the king and his

75. AMV, A-16, 185v–186v.
76. AMV, A-16, 210r.
77. Brodman, *Charity and Welfare*, 23. Franklin-Lyons, *Shortage and Famine*.
78. The florin of Aragon fluctuated in value relative to other Aragonese currencies but was worth twenty-two sous of Valencia in 1433. Peter Spufford, *Handbook of Medieval Exchange* (London: The Royal Historical Society, 1986), 148–149; AMV, A-16, 260r–v.
79. Franklin-Lyons, *Shortage and Famine*.
80. The city's population grew from five thousand households in 1355 to eight thousand in 1415. Narbona, "Finanza municipales," 497.

corts, alongside a procession for the same purpose. The money, however, was not to be distributed in conjunction with the procession, but rather "in celebration of masses and to the shamefaced poor and mendicants and in other pious uses at the good discretion and knowledge of these jurats."[81] Similarly, during Lent in 1386, the council sought to relieve the drought by distributing 12,000 sous to various pious places chosen by the jurats, including the poor boxes (*bacins*) for the shamefaced poor of the city's parishes.[82] In 1425 the council ordered 100 lliures (2,000 sous) be "distributed to the parishes to be given to the shamefaced poor."[83] Although the city treasury continued to distribute charity, including in response to natural disasters, the giving itself became a private affair among the respectable needy of the city's neighborhoods.

In addition to the prayers of the deserving poor, the council enlisted religious assistance against drought from all over the horta. The jurats wrote regularly to the monks of the Charterhouse of Valldecrist and other religious houses in the region, asking them to pray for rain.[84] The list of monasteries so petitioned eventually grew to about a dozen, including some of the most prominent foundations in the kingdom. Despite the ostensible efficacy of prayers, the council rarely requested such assistance during other types of natural disaster.[85] Perhaps because drought primarily affected the agricultural spaces of the horta, the council's drought responses were more likely to look beyond the city walls.

The most common type of religious response to drought was, of course, the rogation procession. As was the case with rogations generally, processions for drought were less common in the fourteenth century and multiplied from the 1420s on. More records of rogations for drought survive than for any other type of natural disaster: 280 out of a total 449 recorded processions. Drought was the most common disaster in Valencia, but it was also well suited to rogation

---

81. "En celebrato de misses & a pobres vergonyants e mendicants com en altres piadoses vuses a bona discretio & coneguda dels dits jurats." AMV, A-18, 26v–27r.

82. AMV, A-18, 132r–v; Brodman, *Charity and Welfare*, 19.

83. AMV, A-28, 123r–v.

84. These included the religious houses of Friars Minor de Morvedre, Portaceli, Sant Blay de Sogorb, Sant Espirit, Sant Jeroni de Gandia, Sant Onofres, Santa Clara de Gandia, Santa Maria de Jesús near Puçol, Santa Maria de la Murta, Santa Maria del Puig, Valldecrist, Valldigna, and Verge Maria de Xelva. The council sent requests for prayers for rain in 1400, 1438, 1455 (two), 1456, 1457, 1459, 1461, 1463, 1468, 1477, 1478 (two), 1482, 1499, 1502, and 1512; see AMV, g3-6, 275r; AMV, g3-19, 36v–37r; AMV, g3-22, 127r–v, 204r–v, 206r–207r; AMV, g3-23, 247v–248r; AMV, g3-25, 40v–41r; AMV, g3-26, 41r–v; AMV, g3-26, 275r; AMV, g3-27, 103v–104r; AMV, g3-28, 167v–168r; AMV, g3-29, 78r–81r; AMV, g3-30, 47v–49r; AMV, g3-33, 158v–159v, 285r–286r; and AMV, g3-38, 77r–78r.

85. On the council's 1424 request for prayers to stop rain, see chapter 7 of the present book. Similar requests were made in 1462; see AMV, g3-17, 82r–83r; and AMV, g3-25, 58r–58v, 74r–v. Requests for prayers against epidemics appear in 1450, 1478, 1505, and 1508; See AMV, g3-21, 86v–87r; AMV, g3-29, 2r–v; AMV, g3-34, 263v–265r; and AMV, g3-35, 276r.

processions. Droughts go on for a relatively long time (at least in comparison to floods and locust swarms), and much of their tension is in the time spent waiting. The council probably found it expedient to organize something for Valencians to do while waiting for the rain to arrive.

For the most part, the format and common destinations for these processions were the same as those for other natural disasters. This is partly because there were so many drought processions that they shape our understanding of the average rogation. It is also the case that most drought processions were fairly straightforward, with few unusual features. Announcements of drought processions almost never mention relics (with the exception of three in 1481, 1485, and 1506 that featured the head and body of Sant Lluís of Anjou, the boy bishop whose relics had been carried off during the sacking of Marseille in 1423).[86] This may be the result of documentary emphasis rather than practice. An account book entry for 1409 mentions in passing "the reliquary that was reverentially carried by the bishop in the [drought] procession."[87] Seventy-nine percent of drought processions went to the five most popular destinations: the Chapel of Santa Maria de Gràcia in the Convent of Sant Agustí, the Convent of Santa Maria del Carme, the Chapel of Santa Maria de la Misericordia in the Convent of Sant Domènec, the Monastery of Santa Trinitat across the river, and the Monastery of Sant Vicent Martir (see map 4.1 in chapter 4). Most of the others went to various convents and parish churches in and around the city.

One type of procession was organized only for drought: processions "to places outside the city." Unlike the vast majority of rogation processions, these took place mostly outside the city walls. The faithful would march from the cathedral directly to one of the city gates and then wend their way to various monasteries and holy places in the surrounding area. Unlike the usual processions, which would have taken a couple of hours, these processions lasted up to a week. On their return they were often met at the city gate by a second procession, which would accompany them the last steps to the cathedral.[88] They were thus much more like pilgrimages than rogation processions in the city of Valencia normally were. The participants seem to have been a smaller, preselected group of the faithful. In 1385 "some devout and honest persons, both . . . religious and laymen and women and children" undertook, "accord-

86. See Holly J. Grieco, "'In Some Way Even More Than Before': Approaches to Understanding St. Louis of Anjou, Franciscan Bishop of Toulouse," in *Center and Periphery: Studies on Power in the Medieval World in Honor of William Chester Jordan*, ed. Katherine L. Jansen, G. Geltner, and Anne E. Lester (Boston: Brill, 2013), 135–156. See also AMV, A-42, 103r–v; AMV, A-44, 108v; and AMV, A-52, 164r–165r.

87. "Lo Reliquari qui Reverencialment fon portat per bisbe en la processo." AMV, J-36, 39v–40r.

88. This happened, for example, in 1456; see, AMV, A-36, 57r.

ing to what has been discussed in the Council," a procession to "some holy and devout places outside the city" to ask that God send rain and good weather. Because "many needy persons" would be among them, the council contributed an extra twenty-five lliures in charity for their maintenance on the journey.[89] Similarly, in 1425 the council provided ten lliures in charity for the shamefaced poor going on a procession for rain to places outside the city, and in other cases the council paid for the provisions of such expeditions.[90] An account book entry for 1432 notes expenses for twenty-six priests and twenty-five youths on a similar procession. The council documents only rarely specify where these processions went. Most often they simply say that the processions went to the "usual places" (lochs acostumats). Some of these places lay beyond the boundaries of the Valencian horta. In 1385 the procession was to end at Santa Maria del Puig, fifteen kilometers north along the coast, before returning to the city.[91] In 1432 the youths and priests made a loop to the south through the villages of Alginet and Guadassuar to the town of Alzira and the Monastery of Santa Maria de la Murta, and then back via Cullera and the villages of Almussafes, Torrent, and Quart.[92] A similar procession in 1506 began at Sant Vicent Martir and then went on to the nearby Convent of Santa Maria de Jesús and the village of Albal just south of the horta. From there the text notes that the procession went to "the usual places" before ending up at the Monastery of Santa Maria del Puig in the north.[93] Processions to places outside the city accounted for 8 percent of the total number of drought processions: twenty-three in all. If "outside the city" is treated as a single destination, it was the fourth most popular destination for drought processions, ahead of the Monastery of Sant Vicent Martir. Whatever their destinations, these processions, or pilgrimages, wound their way through the rural places around the city: irrigated agricultural lands that felt the impact of drought.[94] In that

89. "Item com alcunes devotes & honestes persons axi ecclesiastiques & religioses com legues homes & dones & infants, segons fon raonat en lo dit consell, entenguessen & haguessen acordat de anar en processo dicmenge prop vinent en alcuns sants & devots lochs fora la dita Ciutat per demana e impetrar de la divinal ajuda pluja & bon temps que es molt necessaria la terra. E entre les sobredites anassen o anar deguessen moltes persones freturoses & lur bona intencio & obra fos meritoria & profitosa a la cosa publica per tal lo dit consell delibradament & concordant volch & tench per be que de la peccunia comuna de la dita Ciutat fossen dades per reverencia de deu & per caritat a les dites persons en ajudade lur provisio faedora per ma dalcuna honesta de les dites persones en loch del Clavari de la dita Ciutat vint & cinch libres." AMV, A-18, 80r–v.
90. AMV, A-28, 123r–v. There were two such instances in 1421; see AMV, J-42, 32r; and AMV, J-43, 11r–v.
91. AMV, I-14, 35r–v.
92. AMV, J-52, 74r–v.
93. AMV, A-52, 151r–v.
94. Councils did not organize these processions for locust swarms, even though those were also primarily agricultural disasters.

sense, like the requests for prayers from extramural monasteries, they served the purpose of connecting city and countryside.

Although it was in many ways the typical natural disaster on the Valencian plain, drought had its own particular characteristics. It was the disaster for which the hydraulic infrastructure was designed, and as such one for which the council was singularly well prepared. The council was able not only to secure greater shares of water for the city but also plan long-term projects to increase the overall supply. When the water failed, and famine threatened, it activated a number of mechanisms to bring grain and flour to supply the city's needs. And yet, alongside all of these measures, the council documents continually frame drought as an act of God and withdrawal of the rain in particular as divine judgment on human sins. The specific nature of these sins was less important than the relationship between God and the rain. Councils after 1345 did not issue moral reform legislation to fix the city's evils, but they continued to find ways to approach God. The city's rituals for drought also had a wider focus than rituals for other types of disaster. The council requested prayers from religious houses across the kingdom and organized extended processions that traveled all over the horta. The religious responses to drought thus seem to have echoed the agricultural geography of the disaster itself. The emphasis on divine causation of droughts and the focus on collective ritual may seem fairly typical of medieval disaster response generally. Yet Valencian councils had distinctly different approaches to plagues, floods, and locust swarms.

CHAPTER 6

From Purification to Protection

Plague

In July 1395 the city council of Valencia decided to take action. Plague had been in the city since March, and despite the council's best efforts, the death toll continued to rise. On July 6 it authorized funds for the removal of animal corpses from the city streets and organized a procession and charitable donations "to placate divine anger . . . for said plague." A week later the councilmen proposed a more comprehensive account of the causes of the epidemic, noting that "it was . . . reasoned by some in the present council who understood and believed that, among the other sinners [for] whom divine anger sent the plague of general mortality that is at present in the city, was the sustaining of pimps, bad women, and gamblers, from whom there have been groups of demons. And furthermore, the ugly curses that common ill-bred people make in many places [naming] the precious body of Jesus Christ and of the sacred Virgin his mother and of other saints of Paradise."[1] The council did not, as a rule, blame drought on specific sins or sinners (see chapter 5), and it was not in the habit of doing so for floods or

---

1. "E com fos proposat & raonat per alcuns en lo present Consell que entenien & crehien que entre les altres peccats per los quals la ira divinal tremetia la plaga de general mortalidat que de present es en la dita Ciutat era lo sosteniment dalcavots de avols fembres & de tafirs & jugadors dels quels hi hauia stols dels demonis. E aximateix lo letg jurar que les comuns gents mal nodrides fahien de diverses partides no nomenadores del precios cos de Jehu Xrist & de la sagrada Verge mare sua & daltres sants & santes de paradis." AMV, A-20, 244r.

locusts either (see chapter 7). The evidence suggests that the council commonly made such associations only for plague. When the council blamed an epidemic on certain sins or sinners, in other words, the logic of that blame was not generic to natural disaster but rather specific to plague. Because understandings of the causes of plague were intimately linked to human behavior and misbehavior, responses to plague mirrored social tensions in a way that responses to other disasters did not. The city government's ritual and material responses to plague formed a coherent vision of the workings of disease in the Valencian environment—one that changed dramatically over time in both its religious and material forms.[2]

Until the later fifteenth century the Valencian councilmen associated plague with sinners because they understood plague—indeed, disease in general—as the result of moral and material corruption. The sins thought to cause plague were sins of corruption that implicated and threatened the entire social body of the city. Around 1475, however, the council shifted focus; it began to treat plague as contagious, and enlisted both material and spiritual protectors to guard the city's perimeter against external threat. Not only were material and ritual responses to this disaster informed by a specific concept of what plague was and how it worked, but secular and spiritual plague responses in Valencia also evolved over time and in response to changing notions of disease.

The scholarly consensus is that *Yersinia pestis* was the primary disease responsible for the Black Death of 1348 and for most subsequent plagues in the fourteenth, fifteenth, and sixteenth centuries. Over the past decade, ancient DNA (aDNA) analysis of human remains from a number of archeological sites, including Barcelona, have confirmed the presence of *Yersinia pestis* during the Black Death.[3] Most subsequent outbreaks of plague remain to be similarly confirmed, but the presumption is that most of these were also outbreaks of bubonic plague.[4] Medieval observers may have folded outbreaks of other diseases, such as typhus, into the "plague" category. This is particularly likely to have been the case in Valencia, which, although possessed of an early medical

---

2. Naama Cohen-Hanegbi, *Caring for the Living Soul: Emotions, Medicine and Penance in the Late Medieval Mediterranean* (Leiden: Brill, 2017), 134–170, has made a similar argument about Castilian medical practitioners.

3. Maria A. Spyrou et al., "Historical *Y. pestis* Genomes Reveal the European Black Death as the Source of Ancient and Modern Plague Pandemics," *Cell Host and Microbe* 19, no. 6 (2016): 874–81. See also Kirsten I. Bos et al., "A Draft Genome of *Yersinia pestis* from Victims of the Black Death," *Nature* 478 (2011): 506–510.

4. For evidence that plague persisted in Europe after 1348, see Kirsten I. Bos et al., "Eighteenth-Century *Yersinia pestis* Genomes Reveal the Long-Term Persistence of an Historical Plague Focus," *eLife* 5 (2016), https://doi.org/10.7554/eLife.12994.001; and Lisa Seifert et al., "Genotyping *Yersinia pestis* in Historical Plague: Evidence for Long-Term Persistence of *Y. pestis* in Europe from the 14th to the 17th Century," *PLoS ONE* 11, no. 1, https://doi.org/10.1371/journal.pone.0145194.

licensing system and a network of municipal hospitals, lacked an official medical infrastructure and thus any detailed record of plague symptoms.[5] Although the Valencian council sometimes cooperated with local doctors, its notion of plague (*plaga, mortaldat,* or occasionally *glanola*) remained ill defined and cannot be equated with modern diagnoses of bubonic plague. As aDNA evidence is thus far lacking for Valencian plague outbreaks in the late fourteenth and fifteenth centuries, it cannot be asserted that *Yersinia pestis* was solely responsible for all of the plague outbreaks discussed in this chapter, but it must have played an important role in at least some of them.

Plague has not always been considered a natural disaster. The term *natural disaster* is here used narrowly, to refer to a crisis thought to emerge from the environment. That medieval plague ought to be considered a natural disaster in this sense is clear from Luis García-Ballester's definition of medieval health as "a balance between [an] individual's body and the environment." According to this understanding, a catastrophic outbreak of disease arose from the natural world and affected all living things.[6] Thus, Jacme d'Agramont averred that the Black Death had caused orange trees in Barcelona, Mallorca, and Valencia to die.[7]

Modern scholarship has similarly begun to draw connections between plague and the state of the natural world.[8] Plague is primarily a disease of rodent hosts and arthropod vectors. Climatic disruptions (including temperature and precipitation changes) can cause population surges or collapses among sylvatic rodent populations where plague is endemic (called foci or reservoirs of plague). These shifts in the rodent population can bring fleas in contact with new animal hosts, including those who live and move with human beings (commensal species). It is under such circumstances that what is normally a

---

5. On a suspected outbreak of typhus in the fifteenth century and the state medical infrastructure in Milan, see Ann G. Carmichael, "Epidemics and State Medicine in Fifteenth-Century Milan," in *Medicine from the Black Death to the French Disease,* ed. Roger French, Jon Arrizabalaga, Andrew Cunningham, and Luis García-Ballester (Aldershot, UK: Routledge, 1998), 221–247. On Valencia's medical licensing system, see Luis García-Ballester, Michael R. McVaugh, and Agustín Rubio Vela, *Medical Licensing and Learning in Fourteenth-Century Valencia* (Philadelphia: American Philosophical Society, 1989). On Valencia's hospitals, see Agustín Rubio Vela, *Pobreza, enfermedad y asistencia hospitalaria en la Valencia del siglo XIV* (Valencia: Institución Alfonso el Magnánimo, 1984).

6. Luis García-Ballester, "The Construction of a New Form of Learning and Practicing Medicine in Medieval Latin Europe," in *Galen and Galenism: Theory and Medical Practice from Antiquity to the European Renaissance,* ed. Jon Arrizabalaga, Montserrat Cabré, Lluís Cifuentes, and Fernando Salmón (Aldershot, UK: Routledge, 2002), 89.

7. Jacme d'Agramont, *Regiment de preservació de pestilència (1348),* 2nd ed., ed. Joan Veny, (Barcelona: Col·lecció Scripta, Universitat de Barcelona, 2015), 66.

8. For an overview of this scholarship for the late antique period, see Timothy P. Newfield, "Mysterious and Mortiferous Clouds: The Climate Cooling and Disease Burden of Late Antiquity," in *Environment and Society in the Long Late Antiquity,* ed. Adam Izdebski and Michael Mulryan (Leiden: Brill, 2018), 89–115.

rodent disease becomes a human epidemic.[9] On a basic level, this phenomenon is well understood, but new research avenues have emerged. First, more species were probably involved in medieval plague transmission than the black rat (*Rattus rattus*) and the rat flea (*Xenopsylla cheopis*) so beloved of historians. Many commensal and wild rodent species can host—and many fleas can transmit—*Yersinia pestis*. Cats and other domestic animals may serve as hosts, and lice and fleas may transmit the bacterium.[10] The geographic scope of inquiry is also undergoing a shift. A growing body of evidence suggests that, while the initial fourteenth-century wave of plague (the Black Death) was imported to Europe from Central Asia, subsequent outbreaks emerged from one or more plague foci within Europe itself. These European plague foci, which no longer exist today, may have emerged as a result of the cooler temperatures prevailing during the Little Ice Age. They are likely to have been sited in mountainous regions, but have yet to be definitively located, either by plague scientists or by historians.[11] Plague outbreaks in Valencia, therefore, would have been part of a complex regional or continental chain of events, involving both sylvatic and commensal host species, as well as the movement of human beings. These events would in part have been shaped by the climatic variability of the early Little Ice Age. While it is not yet possible to reconstruct exactly where Valencian plagues originated and which climates were implicated in their spread, this research shows the importance of examining plague in a broader environmental context.

As with other natural disasters, plague was for the Valencian council a matter both spiritual and material. This was not unusual for natural disasters, nor was it unusual in the realm of medicine, where the sacred and the secular were intertwined in the eyes of physicians, clergy, and the general public.[12]

---

9. Boris Schmid, Ulf Büntgen, W. Ryan Easterday, Christian Ginzler, Lars Walløe, Barbara Bramanti, and Nols Chr. Stenseth, "Climate-Driven introductions of the Black Death and Successive Plague Reintroductions into Europe," *PNAS* 112 (2015): 3020; Campbell, *The Great Transition*, 235–252.

10. See, for example, Newfield, "Mysterious and Mortiferous Clouds," 91; Monica Green, "Taking 'Pandemic' Seriously: Making the Black Death Global," in Green, *Pandemic Disease in the Medieval World*, 31–34; Michelle Ziegler, "The Black Death and the Future of the Plague," in Green, *Pandemic Disease in the Medieval World*, 265–269; and Campbell, *The Great Transition*, 230–235.

11. Spyrou et al., "Historical *Y. pestis* Genomes"; Bos et al., "Eighteenth-Century *Yersinia pestis* Genomes"; Seifert et al., "Genotyping *Yersinia pestis* in Historical Plague"; Carmichael, "Plague Persistence in Western Europe."

12. See, for example, Coomans, *Community, Urban Health and Environment*; John Henderson, *The Renaissance Hospital: Healing the Body and Healing the Soul* (New Haven, CT: Yale University Press, 2006); Cohen-Hanegbi, *Caring for the Living Soul*; Peregrine Horden, "Ritual and Public Health in the Early Medieval City," in *Body and City: Histories of Urban Public Health*, ed. Sally Sheard and Helen Power (London: Ashgate, 2000), 17–40; Rawcliffe, *Urban Bodies*, 55–115; and Justin Stearns, *Infectious Ideas: Contagion in Premodern Islamic and Christian Thought in the Western Mediterranean* (Baltimore: Johns Hopkins University Press, 2011). For more strictly religious treatments of plague response, see Hanska, *Strategies of*

Spiritual and material responses developed from a common understanding of the causes of plague and evolved with that understanding in the later fifteenth century. Plague rituals were not only matters of tradition in medieval Valencia; they shifted over time, just as other public health practices did.

Blame and Disease through the Black Death

Religious rituals for natural disaster were meant to appease divine anger (see chapter 5), but such rituals did not necessarily involve blaming any particular sinners. With one early exception, drought rituals emphasized collective responsibility, citing the sinfulness of humanity in general. Plague alone among natural disasters inspired rituals that blamed specific sins or groups of sinners. After the Black Death, the sinners that the Valencian council blamed for plague were almost always Christians. But in the first half of the fourteenth century, councils several times asserted that the sins of religious minorities, or the mixing of faiths, would lead to disaster. These assertions seem to have been rhetorical statements rather than responses to real epidemics. The council's response to the Black Death of 1348 is also, for different reasons, unclear.

In 1326 the council put forward a series of ordinations intended to maintain the sanctity of festival days that regulated commerce, the mixing of faiths, and the public presence of Jews, Muslims, and prostitutes in the city. As a prologue to this legislation it declared that the sins of the city had prompted God to "engender in the air diverse tempests of menace . . . and even cause illnesses and sudden deaths to those who do not convert themselves to good and divorce themselves from sin."[13] Although Agustín Rubio Vela considers this evidence of a plague in Valencia in 1326, the phrasing and context suggest instead that the threat of illness was a rhetorical device.[14] If there really were an epidemic in the city, it would have been quite surprising for the council to suggest that only sinners would die.

In a November 1335 letter the jurats complained to the king that Muslim men consorting with one another and with Christian prostitutes in suburban

---

Sanity and Survival; Heinrich Dormeier, "Saints as Protectors against Plague: Problems of Definition and Economic and Social Implications," in *Living with the Black Death*, ed. Lars Bisgaard and Leif Sønder-gaard (Odense: University Press of Southern Denmark, 2009), 61–186. For Spain, see Stearns, *Infectious Ideas*; and Christian, *Local Religion in Sixteenth-Century Spain*. See also Justin Stearns, "New Directions in the Study of Religious Responses to the Black Death," *History Compass* 7, no. 5 (2009): 1363–1375, which includes Islamic and Jewish responses.

13. AMV, A-1, 280v–282r.

14. Agustín Rubio Vela, *Pesta Negra, Crisis y comportamientos sociales en la España del siglo XIV: La ciudad de Valencia (1348–1401)* (Granada: Universidad de Granada, 1979), 20–21.

taverns had brought down the wrath of God in the form of drought, famine, hail, fog, illnesses, and sudden deaths.[15] If the council was referring to a real epidemic, it would have been that of the previous year (1334), which the jurats had several months earlier blamed on the runoff from the irrigation of rice fields.[16] Here again the mention of disease seems to have been meant to add weight to the main aim of the letter (a call for tavern regulation) rather than to describe a response to an ongoing crisis.

Finally, in 1351, the bishop of Valencia requested the city's help in prosecuting sins in the Muslim and Jewish quarters "so that . . . our all-powerful Lord God not send us pestilences in the earth."[17] The text of the request makes clear that there was no actual epidemic in the city, though the memory of the Black Death would in this case have been fresh.

In all three of these cases human sins, including the perceived misbehavior of Jews and Muslims, were associated with the threat of disease in the city. And in all three cases this association seems to have been rhetorical; no plagues were taking place at the times these statements were made.

About the council's response to the Black Death itself, little can be known for certain. Jews in Valencia were attacked and killed in 1348, as were other Jewish communities in the Crown of Aragon. The violence in Valencia, however, is known only from the 1994 archeological discovery of a mass grave in the city's Jewish cemetery. Alongside plague victims, this grave contained the bodies of twelve individuals bearing evidence of fatal injuries, many inflicted with swords by attackers on horseback.[18] This suggests that at least some of the attackers were wealthy; perhaps the councilmen themselves were among them.[19] The Black Death in Valencia coincided with the antiroyalist rebellion known as the Union Revolt, in which the city council played a leading role (see chapter 2). In fact, when the Black Death arrived in the city in May 1348, the rebels were holding King Pere the Ceremonious prisoner. Once Pere regained his freedom and repressed the revolt, he ordered the documents of the rebel-

15. AMV, g3-1, 51r–v.

16. AMV, g3-1, 37r–39v.

17. AMV, A-10, 25v–26r.

18. Matías Calvo Gálvez and Josep Vicent Lerma, "Peste Negra y pogromo en la ciudad de Valencia: La evidencia arqueológica," *Revista de Arqueología* 19 (1998): 50–59; Matías Calvo Gálvez, "Necrópolis judía de Valencia: Nuevos datos," in *Juderías y sinagogas de la Sefarad medieval, en memoria de José Luis Lacave Riaño*, ed. Ana María López Álvarez and Ricardo Benito Izquierdo (Cuenca, Spain: Ediciones de la Universidad de Castilla La Mancha, 2003), 599–601.

19. The city council and mayor of Tàrrega in Catalonia participated in the massacre of that town's Jews in 1348; Susan Einbinder, *After the Black Death: Plague and Commemoration among Iberian Jews* (Philadelphia: University of Pennsylvania Press, 2018), 117–147. On the Valencian council's passive collaboration with the later 1391 assault, see Agresta, "'Unfortunate Jews' and Urban Ugliness."

lious city government to be destroyed.[20] The Black Death in Valencia was thus not only a period of intense antiroyalism, but also a period of scarce surviving documentation. Both Alexandra Guerson and Mark Meyerson have argued that contemporary assaults on Jews elsewhere in the Crown of Aragon should be understood as part of the rebellion rather than as a response to the plague.[21] Although plague and antiroyalism are not mutually exclusive as motives for anti-Jewish violence, insufficient evidence survives to determine whether either was the pretext for the Valencian assault.

Religious violence associated with plague (and with natural disaster generally) seems to have stopped with the Black Death.[22] Samuel Cohn has argued that attacks on Jews ceased to be common in Europe during the plagues that followed the Black Death, though associations between Jews and plague were revived in some places in the early modern period.[23] The evidence from Valencia supports Cohn's observation. This development is somewhat surprising, as Christian hostility toward religious minorities was, if anything, increasing in the Crown of Aragon in the later fourteenth century.[24] Nonetheless, later episodes of religious violence in Valencia cannot be tied to natural disaster, and rhetorical statements blaming religious minorities for crises largely disappeared.[25] Only one case of blaming religious minorities for natural disaster appears after 1351. In March 1413 the jurats wrote the king about Judaizing among the city's New Christians. Such practices, they declared, "provoke our Lord to send us plagues and pestilences."[26]

---

20. "Introducció," in Lizondo, *Diplomatari de la Unió del Regne de València*, 13–16.

21. Alexandra Eni Paiva Guerson de Oliveira, "Coping with Crises: Christian-Jewish Relations in Catalonia and Aragon, 1380–1391" (PhD diss., University of Toronto, 2012), 28–37, https://tspace .library.utoronto.ca/bitstream/1807/32724/3/GuersondeOliveira_Alexandra_EP_201206_PhD _thesis.pdf, 28–37; Meyerson, "Victims and Players," 70–102.

22. On antiroyalist violence against Jews in Valencia, David Nirenberg, *Anti-Judaism: The Western Tradition* (New York: W. W. Norton, 2013), 183–216; and Nirenberg, *Neighboring Faiths*, 75–88.

23. Samuel Cohn, "The Black Death and the Burning of the Jews," *Past and Present* 196, no. 1 (2007): 3–36; and Samuel Cohn, *The Black Death Transformed: Disease and Culture in Early Renaissance Europe* (London: Bloomsbury, 2002), 223–252. See also the association between Jews and contagion in Udine in 1556 in Ann G. Carmichael, "The Last Past Plague: The Uses of Memory in Renaissance Epidemics," *Journal of the History of Medicine and Allied Sciences* 53, no. 2 (1998): 135–138.

24. See Agresta, "Unfortunate Jews and Urban Ugliness," 320–323. See also chapter 3 of the present book.

25. The assaults on the Jewish and Muslim quarters in 1391 and on the Muslim quarter in 1455 did not involve natural disasters. Mark D. Meyerson, *The Muslims of Valencia in the Age of Fernando and Isabel: Between Coexistence and Crusade* (Berkeley: University of California Press, 1991), 89, associates the violence in 1455 with a drought, but while there is evidence of drought in the city in March 1455, and again in November of that year, the riot took place in June, and there is no evidence of drought-related tension in the preceding weeks.

26. "Son occasio de provocar nostre Senyor a donar sobre nosaltres plagues e pestilencies sien de vostra senyoria." AMV, g3-11, 190v–191r.

There was no plague in Valencia in the spring of 1413, but the Dominican preacher Vicent Ferrer was then in the city, and Ferrer's sermons had a powerful impact on city councils wherever he went.[27] It is not, therefore, surprising that the council of 1413 expressed somewhat atypical opinions on Jews and disaster.

Writing in the late fifteenth century, the Valencian chronicler Melchior Miralles identified twelve plagues (*mortaldats*) that had affected the city from 1348 up to his own time. Rubio Vela's research brought the total to twenty-five outbreaks of plague in Valencia between 1348 and 1519.[28] The Valencian city council drew an association between a natural disaster and specific sins or sinners seven times after 1351. In all of these cases it blamed Christian sinners, and all were related to plague.[29]

Material Corruption

The sins associated with plague are best understood in the context of Valencian public health practice. Unlike drought, plague's material causes were directly linked to human misbehavior that fell under the council's purview. Well before the council of 1395 blamed that year's plague on the corruption of pimps, bad women, and gamblers, it arranged for the removal from the city streets of "dead dogs, cats, rats, and other dead things that people throw in the streets and squares, and which in these times of summer and epidemic give great corruption to the city."[30] Plague was unique among natural disasters in that its material causes—filth and corruption—had a moral flavor. Preachers do not seem to have singled out plague in this way, but the city government, ever preoccupied with urban hygiene, pursued religious plague prevention efforts similar to its material ones.

In Galenic medical theory, corruption was the most common cause of epidemic disease. Both moral and material misbehavior could result in corruption,

---

27. Lindeman, "Fighting Words," 690–720. On Ferrer's influence over the council, see Lindeman, "Fighting Words," and Daileader, *Saint Vincent Ferrer*, 88–89.

28. Miralles listed 1348, 1362, 1375, 1384, 1395, 1401–2, 1428–29, 1439, 1450, 1459–60, 1475, and 1478. Melchior Miralles, *Crònica i dietari*, 3:32, p. 150. To these Rubio Vela added plagues in 1380, 1403, 1410–11, 1414, 1420–21, 1422, 1464, 1466–67, 1489–90, and 1494. Rubio Vela, *Pesta Negra*, 27–28; and Rubio Vela, "Las epidemias de peste." Further outbreaks occurred in 1508–9, 1510, and 1519.

29. The council blamed specific sinners twice in 1395, and in 1414, 1450, 1457, 1489, and 1490.

30. "Item lo dit Consell per placar la ira divinal & obtenir daquella relevatio de la present plaga de mortaldat . . . atorga & provei que sia feta caritat & almoyna a pobres vergonyants. . . . Mes avant ordena & provehi . . . que dicmenge prop vinent sia feta general processo . . . per impetrar la divinal misericordia sobre a dita plaga . . . que en lo present temps destiu & de epidemia daven gran corrupcio a la dita Ciutat cans gats rates & semblants coses mortes que les Gents lancen per places & per carrers." AMV, A-20, 242r.

which presented a danger if left unchecked.[31] Corruption could occur in air, water, or food, but corrupt air, or miasma, was perceived as the most common.[32] Corrupt air could have many causes: the wrath of God, an unfavorable alignment of the planets (such as the "triple conjunction" of Jupiter, Mars, and Saturn that the scholars in Paris blamed for the Black Death), humid winds, rotting bodies on a battlefield, or fumes released by earthquakes. More prosaically, any decay or stagnation could corrupt the air around it and cause illness to those nearby.[33]

Scholars of medieval public health have established beyond doubt that medieval and early modern city governments used hygiene measures to limit the spread of disease.[34] The Valencian city council, like city councils across medieval Europe, focused most of its public health efforts on the regular removal of corrupt matter.[35] Although medical wisdom held that miasmas could as easily be caused by celestial as terrestrial phenomena, the Valencian council focused on the material world under its control: the world of streets and canals to be cleared of refuse. Corruption was the result of human misbehavior or neglect that introduced waste or blockage into the fragile urban system. As Carole Rawcliffe has observed, while the physical interdependence of the

31. Arrizabalaga, "Facing the Black Death," 245; Rawcliffe, *Urban Bodies*, 55–115.

32. Ann G. Carmichael, "Contagion Theory and Contagion Practice in Fifteenth-Century Milan," *Renaissance Quarterly* 44, no. 2 (1991): 229.

33. Laura A. Smoller, "Of Earthquakes, Hail, Frogs, and Geography: Plague and the Investigation of the Apocalypse in the Later Middle Ages," in *Last Things: Death and the Apocalypse in the Middle Ages*, ed. Caroline Walker Bynum and Paul Freedman (Philadelphia: University of Pennsylvania Press, 2000), 172; John Aberth, *From the Brink of the Apocalypse: Confronting Famine, War, Plague and Death in the Later Middle Ages*, 2nd ed. (London: Routledge, 2010), 99.

34. See Zlata Blažina Tomić and Vesna Blažina, *Expelling the Plague: The Health Office and the Implementation of Quarantine in Dubrovnik, 1377–1533* (Montreal: McGill-Queens University Press, 2015); Kristy Wilson Bowers, *Plague and Public Health in Early Modern Seville* (Rochester: Rochester University Press, 2013); Coomans, *Community, Urban Health and Environment*, Coomans and Guy Geltner, "On the Street and in the Bathhouse: Medieval Galenism in Action?," *Anuario de Estudios Medievales* 43, no. 1 (2013): 53–82; Jane L. Stevens Crawshaw, *Plague Hospitals: Public Health for the City in Early Modern Venice* (Farnham, UK: Ashgate, 2012); Isla Fay, *Health and the City: Disease, Environment and Government in Norwich, 1200–1575* (Woodbridge, UK: Boydell and Brewer, 2015); Guy Geltner, "The Path to Pistoia: Urban Hygiene before the Black Death," *Past and Present* 246, no. 1 (2020): 3–33; Guy Geltner, *Roads to Health: Infrastructure and Urban Wellbeing in Later Medieval Italy* (Philadelphia: University of Pennsylvania Press, 2019); Teresa Huguet-Termes, "Madrid Hospitals and Welfare in the Context of the Hapsburg Empire," *Medical History* 53, no. S29 (2009): 64–85; and Rawcliffe, *Urban Bodies*.

35. On the connection between such efforts and Galenic medical theory in the Crown of Aragon, see García-Ballester, "The Construction of a New Form of Learning," 89–91; and Guillem Roca Cabau, "Medidas municipales contra la peste en la Lleida del siglo XIV e inicios del XV," *Dynamis* 38, no. 1 (2018): 15–39. For such efforts elsewhere, see Fay, *Health and the City*; Rawcliffe, *Urban Bodies*; Coomans and Geltner, "On the Street and in the Bathhouse"; Guy Geltner, "Finding Matter out of Place: Bologna's 'Dirt' (Fango) Officials in the History of Premodern Public Health," in *The Far-Sighted Gaze of Capital Cities: Essays in Honor of Francesca Bocchi*, ed. Rosa Smurra, Houbert Houben, and Manuela Ghizzoni. Rome: Viella, 307–321, and Geltner, "The Path to Pistoia," 3–33.

urban body was often used as an analogy for social cooperation, it also meant that infection in one part posed a risk to the whole.[36]

Jacme d'Agramont, whose 1348 *Regiment de preservació de pestilència*, dedicated to the jurats of Lleida, was both the earliest plague treatise and the one most applicable to the Valencian context, noted that a dirty city was one in danger of plague. In particular, excrement and the bodies, guts, and blood of dead animals, if left in the public space, would cause "great infection in the air."[37] Excrement was not much of a problem in Valencia because of its value as fertilizer in the *horta* (the irrigated area around the city), where pasturing animals was forbidden. While English cities, as Dolly Jørgensen has shown, ran waste carts as a city service, Valencia awarded licenses to private individuals for the right to remove human and animal waste from city streets.[38] The *femeters* (manure collectors) were apparently so eager to do their work that the council in 1398 had to forbid them from making collections in the city on Sundays, feast days, or at night after matins.[39] The excrement would be left to decompose on suburban manure piles, ideally well away from public roads to avoid infecting passersby. In 1327 the council forbade such piles on the road to the Monastery of Sant Vicent out of respect for the saint.[40]

Slaughtering, butchering, and the bleeding of animals by veterinarians were also tightly regulated to keep blood, guts, and corpses off the streets.[41] The council likewise banned throwing rubbish and animal parts into the city's canals, were they could block water flow and create corrupt, stagnant pools.[42] Two years after the plague of 1395, the council created a new official, known as a *malaropa*, to walk the streets of the city daily, collecting and disposing of the corpses of dogs, cats, rats, "and other dead things that ill-mannered people are accustomed to throw in the streets and squares and which bring stench and infection to the city."[43] The position of malaropa initially only existed in

---

36. Rawcliffe, "The Concept of Health in Late Medieval Society," 318.

37. D'Agramont, *Regiment de preservació de pestilència*, 58.

38. Dolly Jørgensen, "Cooperative Sanitation: Managing Streets and Gutters in Late Medieval England and Scandinavia," *Technology and Culture* 49, no. 3 (2008): 562–563.

39. AMV, A-21, 164r. Unusually, this statute stipulates that if the offender is a servant (*macip*) or captive Muslim slave (*catiu*), the fine will be paid by his master. This suggests that the unpleasant but profitable job of femeter was understood to be one normally performed by the enslaved.

40. AMV, A-2, 9v; AMV, A-20, 96v–97r.

41. AMV, A-3, 290r–v.

42. AMV, A-1, 189r; AMV, A-2, 12r; AMV, A-6, 37v, 56v–57v; AMV, A-3, 133r.

43. AMV, I-21, 31r. "Una fadri o un prom ab son ase lo qual en los meses de juny juliol agost & setembre de cascun any vaia per les places & carrers de la Ciutat cascu jorn & lleu daqui & pose & port sobre son ase cans gats rates nodriment & altres semblants coses mortes que les Gents de mal us solen lançar per les dites places & carrers donant pudor & infecto a la Ciutat." AMV, A-21, 121r–v.

the summer months, but by 1401 it was a year-round job.[44] In 1503 the council fired the current malaropa, Pere Ripoll, who "served so badly in his office that the whole city is full of dead cats, dogs, and chickens."[45]

The council was thus engaged throughout the fourteenth and fifteenth centuries in public health efforts intended to remove or prevent corruption in the urban space. These efforts were not limited to periods of plague; they predated the Black Death, and were expanded in the decades that followed it.[46] In these years the council treated plague, like other illnesses, as the result of corruption from the surrounding environment. Corruption sprang from human misbehavior: lazy householders or greedy butchers dumped filth that threatened to infect the whole population. Until the later fifteenth century, the council's public health strategy was to keep the city on a strict regimen, regularly purging the corruption that accumulated within its boundaries.

Moral Corruption

Just as the city's best material defense against plague was cleanliness, the best religious defense was moral hygiene. For city rulers, as Rawcliffe has observed, dangerous corruption included both material and moral hazards.[47] In the fourteenth and early fifteenth centuries, a focus on this sort of corruption distinguished the Valencian council's religious responses to plague from those of other kinds of crises. As with other natural disasters, the most common religious response was the rogation procession. Like processions for drought, processions for plague were organized in increasing numbers from the 1420s onward. Before the later fifteenth century they also tended to follow the same format and go to the same churches as did the drought processions.[48] Gifts of alms, including those for the burial of poor plague victims, appear frequently during plagues through the end of the fourteenth century and less

---

44. AMV, A-22, 137v–138r.

45. "En Pere Ripoll serveix mal en lo seu offici de Malaropa com no vulla servir aquell ans tota la ciutat esta plena de gats e goses e gallines mortes per ço revoquen quell del dit offici." AMV, A-51, 128r.

46. On urban public health as a pre–Black Death phenomenon, see Geltner, "The Path to Pistoia."

47. Rawcliffe, *Urban Bodies*, 54–56, 110–115.

48. Most were directed to the Chapel of Santa Maria de Gràcia in the Convent of Sant Agustí, though the Chapel of Santa Maria de la Misericordia in the Convent of Sant Domènec, the Convent of Santa Maria del Carme, the Monastery of Sant Vicent Martir, and the Monastery of the Santa Trinitat were also popular.

often thereafter (see chapter 4).[49] The councils of 1374, 1401, and 1414 also sought papal indulgences for those who died unshriven on account of the plague.[50]

During some plagues, however, the council supplemented these collective rituals with measures targeting sins of corruption. This began in 1395. In March of that year the council observed that "in the opinion of many" the sins of bad legal representatives (*procuradors*) had provoked God to send the current plague.[51] In July it issued the statement with which this chapter began: a set of moral reform measures that blamed the plague on procuring, prostitution, gambling, and blasphemy. Gambling and blasphemy were linked, as the process of gaming was thought to encourage blasphemous utterances.[52] These sins were neither particularly uncommon nor particularly extreme; they were garden-variety corruption, not crimes against nature like treason or sodomy.[53] During the plague of 1414 the council similarly sought to investigate and punish "public sins . . . as much of carnality as of gaming, from whence follows words of blasphemy to Our Lord for which, as it is found in Holy Scripture, come pestilential plagues . . . and other public and secret punishments." In order to "mitigate [God's] wrath, that he send health of body and soul to the earth," the council appointed worthy men (*prohomes*) to investigate such infractions in each parish. It also entreated the bishop to punish those who fell under his jurisdiction.[54]

The link between plague and these two sets of sins (prostitution and procuring on the one hand, and gambling and blasphemy on the other) would persist into the sixteenth century.[55] In 1450 plague again prompted a set of moral reforms, and once again the targets were "gamblers, blasphemers, swearers, pimps, bad women and others."[56] Seven years later the council issued an almost identical set of reforms in response to the Naples earthquake of 1457. Naples had, since 1442, been part of the Crown of Aragon, and King Alfons the Magnanimous was there at the time of the earthquake. The text of the legislation makes clear that the quake was of interest to Valencians as a potential source of

49. AMV, A-16, 263v.

50. AMV, g3-3, 97v–98r; 146v; AMV, g3-3, 175r–v; AMV, g3-7, 138r–v; AMV, g3-12, 150v.

51. AMV, A-20, 215r–v.

52. A document from 1371 forbids playing cards because the blasphemies uttered in gambling houses anger God. AMV, A-16, 47v–48r.

53. These, along with counterfeiting, were the three most serious crimes prosecuted in the city of Valencia. Rafael Narbona Vizcaíno, *Malhechores, violencia y justicia ciudadana en la Valencia bajomedieval* (Valencia: Ajuntament de Valencia, 1990), 151.

54. "Per ço que sia mitigada la sua ira e trameta salut de cos e de anima en la terra." AMV, A-25, 388v–389r. Other documents show that plague was then in the city. AMV, A-25, 381r–v.

55. For a very similar set of moral reform measures during a plague in 1521, see AMV, A-59, 275r–277v.

56. AMV, A-35, 19r–v.

miasma, which, once released from the depths of the earth, might travel to infect any region.[57] After giving thanks that the king had survived unscathed, the council noted the need to "extirpate the vices, crimes, and public and most abominable sins that are committed [in Valencia] every day against divine majesty, [so that] our Lord God might be better pleased to guard and preserve this city and kingdom and all the individuals within it from a similar earthquake and from plagues and from all persecution and adversity."[58]

The measures taken in 1457 were along the lines established in 1414 and 1450, but more comprehensive: as "gaming houses [were] schools and temples of cursing God," they were forbidden in the city, as were betting and blasphemy.[59] Not only procurers but also frequenters of brothels were banished, and women who consorted with married men were to be designated prostitutes. Women were not to prostitute their daughters, nor men their wives. Notorious prostitutes were banished to the suburbs or the prostitutes' quarter (bordell) because they "corrupt[ed] good women." The city's nuns were not to leave their convents, or to speak to men, and laywomen were not to wear excessively long skirts.[60] In a letter describing the legislation, the jurats added that criminal justice officers had apprehended "four very famous madams who had long practiced procurement in their houses." The previous Monday the four had been "flogged through the city mounted on asses and with mud on their heads according to the form of the statutes of the city." God was so pleased with this action, the jurats said, that it rained immediately thereafter, ending a drought.[61] Once more during the plague of 1489 the council passed a set of restrictions on gambling and prostitution, and when the plague continued into the following year, the council forbade prostitutes from plying their trade near churches, where they bothered devout Christians and interrupted processions.[62] Until the last decade of the century, in other words, the sins associated with plague were fairly consistent in their themes.

---

57. On earthquakes as a source of plague, see d'Agramont, *Regiment de preservació de pestilència*, 56–57.

58. "Extirpar los vicis crims & peccats publichs & molt abhominables que tots jorns se cometen contra la divinal maiestat per que feta correcio de aquells nostre Senyor Deu sia mils placat en guardar & preservar aquesta Ciutat & Regne & tots los singulars daquells de semblant terratremol & de mortaldats & de tota persecucio & adversitat." AMV, A-36, 156v–160r.

59. "Com experiencia mostre que tafureries son escoles & temples de malahir Deu." AMV, A-36, 160v–161r.

60. AMV, A-36, 159r–160v.

61. "Quatre alcavotes molt affamades las quals havia gran temps usaven de offici dalcavoteria en lurs cases . . . e lo dilluns ara propassat . . . toltes son estades acotades per la dita Ciutat a cavall en sengles asens e ab allaços al cap segons forma de les ordinacions dela dita Ciutat." AMV, g3-23, 85r.

62. The text of the 1489 legislation notes that these offenses promoted divine indignation in the form of "mortaldats guerres fams sequedats terratremol e altres greus flagells plagues e persecucions" (mortalities, wars, famines, droughts, earthquake and other tribulations, plagues and persecutions).

These themes were not coincidental; both gambling and procuring constituted moral corruption. Gambling and prostitution were perennial phenomena in medieval towns, and moral discussions of both were linked to ambivalence about the role of money and economic transactions in society.[63] In Valencia both were sins of the immigrant poor. Those who made their living from gambling and prostitution in the city tended to be poor, and were almost always migrants with limited social networks. The men were often former sailors or soldiers left maimed or simply unemployed.[64] In *Regiment de la cosa publica,* Francesc Eiximenis warned the city's leaders about this group: "As a great part of [the city's population] is not native to here, and is not rich, they are very difficult to rule because they revolt very easily."[65] City governments across Europe shared these concerns, and historians Ann Carmichael and Brian Pullan have observed a growing association between plague and the poor—particularly the criminal poor—in the later fifteenth century.[66] In Valencia this association was present from the late fourteenth century on. During the same plague that saw the first moral reform legislation, in 1395, the council also issued its only major set of restrictions on begging, probably inspired by Eiximenis, for whom the "worthless" poor were "like useless limbs on the body . . . that damage the living."[67]

In Valencia, however, the plague's connection with prostitution and gambling proved much more enduring than its connection with begging, which does not appear again in the records. While all three were crimes of the immigrant poor, gambling and prostitution linked this group to the social body as a whole. Professional gamblers and prostitutes may have been marginal, but their customers fit no such profile; they may be assumed to include much of the lay male population, including members of the city's ruling families. In this sense, the preoccupation of the Valencian council with gambling and pro-

AMV, A-45, 328v. Another council document, however, shows that only plague was actually present. AMV, A-45, 352v–353v. On prostitutes near churches, see AMV, A-45, 388v–389r.

63. Giovanni Ceccarelli, "Gambling and Economic Thought in the Late Middle Ages," *Ludica: Annali di storia e civiltà del gioco* 12 (2009): 54–63.

64. Rafael Narbona Vizcaíno, *Pueblo, poder y sexo: Valencia medieval, 1306–1420* (Valencia: Diputació de Valencia, 1992), 45. On the experiences of female migrants to Valencia see also Dana Wessell Lightfoot, *Women, Dowries and Agency: Marriage in Fifteenth-Century Valencia* (Manchester: Manchester University Press, 2013), 14–21.

65. "Com que gran part de la gent que s'ha mencionat [the population of the city] no és natural d'ací i no és molt rica, result més difícil de regir perquè s'avalota més fàcilment." Eiximenis, *Regiment de la cosa publica,* 57.

66. Carmichael, *Plague and the Poor*; Pullan, "Plague and Perceptions of the Poor."

67. The antibegging legislation measure included a grant of ten florins to Eiximenis for his "many and great works" on behalf of the city. AMV, A-20, 244v, 264v–265v; Eiximenis, *Regiment de la cosa publica,* 180–181, 183.

curing was not only about the dangerous poor; these were sins that implicated society more generally.

As Michelle Laughran, Carole Rawcliffe, and others have shown, urban public health was often understood in the Middle Ages by analogy to the human
body, and sexual sins in particular linked to the physical corruption of that
body.[68] In *Regiment de la cosa publica*, Eiximenis argued that city rulers should
forbid "all the professions that corrupt or that provoke evil, like public or professional gamblers, quarrelers, and procurers."[69] In a sermon on prostitution,
Vicent Ferrer quoted Paul's letter to the Corinthians: "Do you not know that a
little leaven corrupts the entire dough? . . . Therefore, eject the prostitute into
the street, for on her account so many plagues have come upon you."[70] In other
sermons, Ferrer claimed that a single prostitute could corrupt fifty, seventy, or
even 120 good women.[71] For these authors, as for the council, both material
and spiritual corruption had health implications for those nearby.

Valencia seems to have been the first city in Iberia to regulate prostitution,
and the official bordell (or *pobla de les fembres avols*) is attested to as early as 1325.[72]
The bordell was located outside the original city walls, near the *moreria* (Muslim
quarter), in an area that had been fairly isolated from the city center (see map 3).
The construction of the new walls in 1356, however, brought both Muslims and
prostitutes within the city.[73] Both the containment of the prostitutes within the
quarter and the containment of the quarter itself were ongoing preoccupations
of the council in these years. Prostitutes were repeatedly banned from other
parts of the city, and the bordell itself was walled off in 1392.[74] The jurats proposed to inspect the walls themselves, to make sure that they were too high to

68. Michelle Anne Laughran, "The Body, Public Health and Social Control in Sixteenth-Century
Venice," (PhD diss., University of Connecticut, 1998): 9–104; Rawcliffe, *Urban Bodies*, 54–56, 110–115.

69. "Tots els oficis que corrompen o que provoquen el mal, com són els jugadors públics i else
jugadors professionals, else renyidors i els alcavots." Eiximenis, *Regiment de la cosa publica*, 190.

70. Vicent Ferrer, *Sermons*, vo. 3, ed. Gret Schib (Barcelona: Editorial Barcino, 1975), 111–113,
quoted in David Nirenberg, "Conversion, Sex, and Segregation: Jews and Christians in Medieval
Spain," *American Historical Review* 107, no. 4 (2002): 1070.

71. Daileader, *Saint Vincent Ferrer*, 89.

72. Noelia Rangel López, "Moras, jóvenes y prostitutas: Acerca de la prostitución Valencia a finales de la Edad Media," *Miscelána medieval murciana* 32 (2008): 122–123.

73. V. Graullera Sanz, "El fin del burdel de Valencia (s. XIII al s. XVIII)," in *Mujer, marginación y
violencia entre la edad media y los tiempos modernos* (Cordoba: Servicio de Publicaciones de la Universitat
de Cordoba, 2006), 357–358.

74. In 1350 the council ordered both prostitutes and madams to stay out of "honest streets" so that
they would not be a bad example to good women. AMV, A-9, 132v. In 1373, prostitutes were forbidden
from working in innsAMV, A-16, 144v. In 1394 and 1398 they were again expelled from other parts of the
city and returned to the bordell. AMV, A-20, 196v; AMV, A-21, 222r–v. Starting in 1385 they were con-
fined to a newly established "home for repentant women" (*casa de les dones de penetencia*) during holy
week, where they were lodged at the city's expense. Later funds were allotted for their dowries if they
chose to marry. AMV, A-18, 80r–v; AMV, A-19, 124v–125r.

climb.[75] Despite all of this, the council never attempted to ban prostitution itself; in Valencia, as elsewhere, prostitutes were a sewer through which inappropriate male sexuality could be safely channeled. As such, they were a noxious but necessary evil that allowed the rest of society to function smoothly.[76]

It was not prostitutes, but rather their pimps, who were offensive to God. Not only did procurers constitute a criminal underclass and prevent prostitutes from repenting their sins, the relationship between pimp and prostitute was seen as a threat to the stability of the family and thus to the social order. According to Eiximenis, this relationship was a sinful alternative to true marriage, one from which "generation could not occur, as God has ordained." Sterile and unconsecrated, it could produce neither lineage nor patrimony—the two cornerstones of a stable social order.[77] Recall that in the reforms instituted after the Naples earthquake, the distinction between concubine and prostitute was collapsed and procuring was forbidden within families. These measures were intended to separate prostitution and procurement from family relationships; blurring these boundaries threatened society as a whole.

Gambling was likewise a sin of corruption. While prostitution threatened honest women and honest marriage, gambling corrupted young men, leading them into further sin. Professional gamblers tended to come from the same marginal, immigrant class as pimps, but the council was chiefly concerned about their effect on the good citizens who frequented gambling houses.[78] Medieval theologians were divided on the extent to which gambling was sinful.[79] For the council of Valencia, it damaged the public good not only because of the "many blasphemies . . . that [were] said against God, and the Virgin Mary his mother, and other saints of paradise" but also because "many persons of diverse ages including the sons of citizens of the city . . . ruin them-

---

75. AMV, A-20, 27r–v.

76. This sentiment comes originally from Augustine, via St. Thomas Aquinas, who added the image of the sewer. Brian Pullan, *Tolerance, Regulation and Rescue: Dishonoured Women and Abandoned Children in Italy, 1300–1800* (Manchester, UK: Manchester University Press, 2016), 30. See also Roger Benito Julià, "La prostitución y la alcahuetería en la Barcelona bajomedieval (siglos XIV–XV)," *Miscelánea medieval murciana* 32 (2008): 9–21.

77. Francesc Eiximenis, *Lo crestiá*, chap. 380, quoted in Narbona, *Pueblo, poder y sexo*, 153. On marriage, see Eiximenis, *Regiment de la cosa publica*, 195–196. The sterility of prostitutes was a trope of medieval moral writing; see Ruth Mazo Karras, *Sexuality in Medieval Europe: Doing unto others* (Abingdon, 2012), 137. Pimps also competed for control of prostitutes with municipally licensed brothel keepers (*hostalers*), from whom the city collected revenue; see Eukene Lacarra Lanz, "Legal and Clandestine Prostitution in Medieval Spain," *Bulletin of Hispanic Studies* 79:3 (2002): 269; and Narbona, *Pueblo, poder y sexo*, 175.

78. Narbona, *Pueblo, poder y sexo*, 39.

79. Ceccarelli, "Gambling and Economic Thought," 54–63.

selves and lose their goods."[80] Gambling, in other words, wasted the patrimony on which the family and lineage depended.

Both prostitution and gambling, therefore, were sins practiced by marginal people that implicated the whole of society and threatened to corrupt the social fabric. Both were fairly widespread and fairly innocuous sins, which nonetheless had troubling implications when practiced on a larger scale. Although the sins that caused plague were those of the immigrant poor, the council's account of the association between plague and these particular sins involved the pillars of society as well as those on its margins. Rather than blaming the plague on a few people who had committed heinous crimes, the council described it as the result of routine corruption that, unchecked, had spread to threaten the social body. The council's account of the spiritual causes of plague, in other words, was directly analogous to its account of the material causes; gamblers, prostitutes, and procurers were for the council the equivalent of trash or filth left to corrupt in the public space. This narrative persisted through generations of councilmen and was distinct from those for other types of disaster. While droughts, floods, and locusts mainly inspired calls for collective penitence, the council consistently associated plague with sins of corruption that threatened the moral health of the city.

Contagion Control

Religious and material responses to plague were intertwined, but both also shifted over time in response to changing medical ideas. The association between plague and corruption in Valencia continued through the end of the fifteenth century. But starting in the 1450s, and accelerating in the 1470s, the council also began to treat plague as contagious: moving not on the wind but between the bodies and belongings of human beings. Concepts of contagion appear in medical texts throughout the medieval period, and from 1348 on, most plague treatises, including that of Jacme d'Agramont, cited contagion as one of many factors in the spread of plague.[81] Contagion could coexist with

---

80. "E aquelles redundar en gran offensa de la divinal majestat per moltes blasfemies que en les dites tafureries & jochs se dien contra Deu & la Verge Nostra Dona Santa Maria mare sua & altres sants de parais. Redundar encara en gran dampnatge de la cosa publica per moltes persones de diverses edats axi fills dels habitadors de la dita Ciutat com altres quis enaulien es desfahien de lurs bens es perdien per occasio daytal escola viciosa." AMV, A-16, 47v–48r.

81. Arrizabalaga, "Facing the Black Death," 259–264; Stearns, *Infectious Ideas*, 91–96. On the challenges of placing contagion within classical medical theory, see Carmichael, "Contagion Theory," 225–230; Melissa P. Chase, "Fevers, Poisons, and Apostemes: Authority and Experience in Montpellier

other types of causation; just as disease was a putrefaction within the body caused by corrupted air, this same putrefaction corrupted the breath and made each individual a miniature source of miasma.[82]

Before the mid-fifteenth century there was no trace of contagion theory in the plague prevention efforts of the Valencian city council. Although the council was aware that plague could arrive in the city from elsewhere, it was primarily concerned with corruption arising from the city itself.[83] But starting in the mid-fifteenth century and particularly from the 1470s on, the council began to treat plague as a hazard that was carried to the city in the bodies and goods of travelers. Plague was now treated first and foremost as an external threat, and plague response therefore required emergency defense rather than regular, internal cleansing. Theories of corruption and contagion were not necessarily in conflict; the council in the later fifteenth century shifted its prevention strategy, but not its whole concept of disease causation. This shift was, however, significant, as it created a sharp rupture in the council's official responses to plague.

The idea of contagion appeared first in a royal edict of 1440. Queen Maria, acting as regent during the absence of King Alfons in Naples, prohibited infected foreigners from entering the city because "experience has clearly shown all pestilential illness to be contagious, and that persons having the pestilence have been the principle and cause of the sudden appearance of great mortalities in diverse cities and towns." For this reason, "any stranger of any condition or standing who feels in himself or has the pestilence" was not to enter the city at any time, day or night. Any inhabitants of the city who harbored such a person would find all of their goods forfeited to the queen, and the infected person would be expelled. Any medical practitioner who knew of plague and did not divulge it to the jurats within one day would face a similar penalty.[84] Ten years later, in 1450, the council itself issued a similar proclamation. Again it asserted that "experience shows and has manifestly shown the pestilential sickness to be contagious, and in consequence all communion

---

Plague Treatises," *Annals of the New York Academy of Sciences* 441 (1985): 162–163; and Vivian Nutton, "The Seeds of Disease: An Explanation of Contagion and Infection from the Greeks to the Renaissance," *Medical History* 27, no. 1 (1983): 1–34.

82. Annemarie Kinzelbach, "Infection, Contagion, and Public Health Late Medieval and Early Modern German Imperial Towns," *Journal of the History of Medicine and Allied Sciences* 61, no. 3 (2006): 369–389.

83. In November 1370, for example, the council ordered a procession to be held to pray that God lift the plague currently ravaging Catalonia and that it not spread to the city or kingdom of Valencia. AMV, A-15, 143v–144r.

84. "Com experiencia assats clara haia mostrat tot mal pestilencial esser contagios e que per sobrevenir en algunes Ciutat viles e lochs personas havents mal de pestilencia han donat principi e causa en diverses Ciutat viles & lochs d grans mortalitats." AMV, A-32, 191r.

with those who are touched with this illness is to be avoided." This time the ban on strangers applied not only to the sick but also to whoever had come in the last month "from a place where they are dying of pestilence, in particular the city and kingdom of Mallorca, and the towns of Gandia, Dénia, and Xàbia."[85]

Following this edict, the council let the idea of contagion drop for more than two decades.[86] Only in 1476 did the jurats bring it up again, announcing:

> As it pertains to their office to provide for the good rule, conservation and health of the City and its inhabitants, as much as pertains to human providence, first commending all things to divine . . . providence, from which all good and grace descends to us, and knowing that experience has shown many times that the pestilence and plague is initiated and caused in the present city (our Lord God having permitted it) by the coming, taking in, and receiving in the city and in the suburbs, houses, and gardens near and around it of persons sick or infected with plague coming from some pestilent places by sea or by land, from which cause follows great and inestimable damage to the city.

For this reason no sick persons were to be received in the city, nor was anyone to harbor them within the walls. Furthermore, no one from the infected cities and towns was to be admitted, even if they showed themselves to be healthy, until they had been forty days in places free from plague. Those bringing food supplies to the city were exempt from this ban; they merely had to show themselves to not be ill. The dead, however, were not exempt; no one was to bring "corpses of men or women who died of the pestilence within the city walls to bury them, because the infection of corpses is much worse and produces greater infection than that of the sick or other living persons infected with the pestilence."[87] Such corpses were to be buried outside the walls for six months before being moved into the city. Finally, all but five of the city gates were to

---

85. "Com experiencia mostre & haia mostrat manifestament lo mal de pestilencia esser contagios e per conseguent deures squivar tota comunio de aquells qui de tal malaltia son tocats pertal los dits honorables justic jurats & consell per benefici del poble de la dita Ciutat manen intime & notifique que no sia person alguna de quantaque dignitat condicio o stament sia que vinga de loch on se muyren de pestilencia specialment de la Ciutat e Regne de Mallorqua de vila de Gandia de la vila de Denia e del loch de Xabea gos o presumesca entrar dins la Ciutat de Valentia ravals & lochs circumvehins de aquella." AMV, A-35, 39v.

86. Plague broke out in the city at least three times during this period: in 1459, 1460, and 1466–67.

87. For another possible instance of postmortem contagion, see Joëlle Rollo-Koster, "Failed Ritual? Medieval Papal Funerals and the Death of Clement VI (1352)," in *Histories of Post-mortem Contagion: Infectious Corpses and Contested Burials*, ed. Christos Lynteris and Nicholas Evans (London: Palgrave Macmillan, 2017), 27–53.

be closed, and trustworthy guards posted to observe the ordinances.[88] According to Miralles, the guards "asked those who came to Valencia under oath whether they came from places of mortality," but there is no indication that they made medical diagnoses.[89]

Restrictions similar to those of 1476 accompanied each subsequent outbreak of plague.[90] From this point onward, the city focused its public health response on keeping out the infected. This shift occurred on the city council's own initiative but was part of a broader trend toward quarantine measures elsewhere in the western Mediterranean, which accompanied a growing medical consensus on the contagious nature of plague.[91] The new focus on contagion did not constitute a new theory of disease; it was instead a layering of new priorities over old ones.[92] The fight against miasma now focused on the bodies of outsiders rather than corruption in the city. Hygienic efforts remained in the background but received significantly less attention; by 1508 the council complained that the streets of the city had become filthy and full of trash "because of the depopulation of the city on account of the pestilence."[93] By then, not only prominent citizens but the whole Valencian council routinely fled the

88. AMV, A-40, 254r–255v. This announcement is published and analyzed in Mercedes Gallent Marco and José María Barnardo Paniagua, "Comunicación en tiempo de peste. 'Les Crides' en la Valencia del xv," *Saitabi* 51–52 (2001–2): 113–136.

89. "Enterrogasen en sagrament los que venien a València si venien dels lochs de mortalitat." Miralles, in *Crònica i dietari*, 4:798, p. 444.

90. Similar regulations were enacted during subsequent outbreaks of plague. For 1477, see AMV, A-41, 9v; for 1481, see AMV, A-42, 102r–103r; for 1483, see AMV, A-43, 108v–109r, 132v–134v; for 1485, see AMV, A-44, 109r–v; for 1487, AMV, A-45, 10v–11v; for 1489, see AMV, A-45, 281v–282r; for 1491, see AMV, A-46, 87v; for 1494, see AMV, A-48, 6v–7r; for 1495, see AMV, A-48, 212r–214r; for 1501, see AMV, A-50, 509v–510r; for 1507, see AMV, A-53, 301v–302v; for 1508, see AMV, A-53, 464v; for 1509, see AMV, A-54, 14v–15r; for 1510, see AMV, A-54, 30v–31r; for 1515, see AMV, A-56, 294v; for 1518, see AMV, A-57, 862r–v; for 1519, see AMV, A-58, 343r–344v. The 1483 regulations are published and analyzed in Jaume Chiner Gimeno, "Prevención y peste en la Valencia del siglo XV: Unas ordenanzas de 1483," in *1490: En el umbral de la modernidad; El Mediterráneo europeo y las ciudades en el tránsito de los siglos XV–XVI*, ed. José Hinojosa Montalvo and Jesús Pradells Nadal (Valencia: Monografies del Consell Valencià de Cultura, 1994), 25–33.

91. Blažina Tomić and Blažina, *Expelling the Plague*; Coomans, *Community, Urban Health and Environment*, 223–231; Crawshaw "The Renaissance Invention of Quarantine," in *Society in an Age of Plague*, ed. Linda Clark and Carole Rawcliffe (Suffolk, UK: Woodbridge, 2013): 161–174; Pullan, "Plague and Perceptions of the Poor," 112–113; Carmichael, "Contagion Theory," 213, 221–232; and Brian Pullan, "Plague Legislation in the Italian Renaissance," *Bulletin of the History of Medicine* 57, no. 4 (1983): 508–525. More locally, the first trade and travel ban in Lleida was put into effect in 1457; see Roca, "Medidas municipales contra la peste," 37.

92. See Nutton, "The Seeds of Disease," 1–34; and Carmichael, "Contagion Theory."

93. "Speriencia se mostre les tantes y tan grans inmundicies, fems, draps e altres brutedats que per la dita ciutat, carrers plases, e carrerons de aquella son e aço causa de la despulacio de la dita ciutat per causa de la pestilencia." AMV, A-54, 4r. In contrast, Kristy Wilson Bowers and Sandra Cavallo both observe that health boards put in new urban filth control measures during plague. See Bowers, *Plague and Public Health*, 33–34; and Sandra Cavallo, *Charity and Power in Early Modern Italy: Benefactors and Their Motives in Turin, 1541–1789* (Cambridge: Cambridge University Press, 1995), 49.

city during plagues, a practice that seems to have begun in the later fifteenth century.[94]

Although the adoption of quarantine and related anticontagion measures was long hailed as a milestone in the history of public health, some historians of medicine have been skeptical about whether quarantines, of whole towns or of individuals, were effective at stopping the spread of plague.[95] There is some reason to doubt their effectiveness in Valencia. The 1476 quarantine was imposed at the end of an epidemic that, according to Miralles, had already been raging for ten months.[96] Food imports were entirely exempt from quarantine, though, as Aaron Shakow has noted, grain shipments would have been an excellent vehicle for infected rodents.[97]

Alongside the shift to quarantine, the council developed a new interest in isolating the city's poor. Historians of late medieval and early modern plagues have long noted an increasing focus on the poor as plague carriers in the late fifteenth and early sixteenth centuries.[98] In May 1494 the council for the first time distributed funds to deal with the poor during a plague. The money was to be used for "guards . . . nails and iron bars to close the doors of the houses of those persons who have died of plague."[99] The council later allotted funds for medical care, and by 1509 had a temporary lazaretto in a rented farmhouse on the port road. This ad hoc arrangement continued for another ten years; not until 1519 did the council purchase a plague house of its own.[100] Well into the sixteenth century, then, the council focused primarily on guarding the city's perimeter, and only secondarily on internal quarantine.

What prompted the council to shift focus to contagion? When Queen Maria imposed the first "trade and travel" ban in Valencia in 1440, King Alfons had been in Italy for several years, engaged in the conquest of Naples. Such bans

94. Although individuals were absent from the council during plagues throughout the fifteenth century, the whole council met outside the city for the first time in 1490, "because some gentlemen did not want to enter into the city" on account of the plague. AMV, A-46 7r.

95. See, for example, Crawshaw, *Plague Hospitals*, 10; and Cavallo, *Charity and Power*, 47. For a more favorable view of the effectiveness of premodern quarantine, see Blazïna Tomić and Blazïna, *Expelling the Plague*, 44–46.

96. Miralles, *Crònica i dietari* 3:32, p. 151. Rubio Vela, "Las epidemias de peste," 1212, concurs with this chronology.

97. Aaron Shakow, "Marks of Contagion: The Plague, the Bourse, the Word and the Law in the Early Modern Mediterranean, 1720–1762" (PhD diss., Harvard University, 2009), 54.

98. Both Pullan, "Plague and Perceptions of the Poor in Early Modern Italy," and Carmichael, *Plague and the Poor*, have argued that flight and quarantine were both linked to a growing association between plague and the poor.

99. "Per a claus e fferradures per tancar les portes de les cases de algunes persones que se son mortes de peste." AMV, A-48, 24v–25r.

100. Regarding medical care, see AMV, A-48, 67v–68r, 86v–87r. Regarding the rental, and then purchase, of a plague house, see AMV, A-58, 586r; and AMV, A-59, 148v.

had been commonplace in Italy since the 1420s. The first ban was therefore likely a result of Italian influence, but it took another generation before the Valencian council adopted the practice wholeheartedly. In making this shift the Valencian council was probably not running ahead of local medical consensus, which would have accepted contagion as a mechanism of plague transmission.[101] Indeed, the bans' emphasis on "experience" may refer to the shifting priorities of the city's medical community. In the late fifteenth century the academic study of medicine was beginning to flourish in Valencia; it was a process that would culminate in the founding of the university (Estudi General) at the turn of the sixteenth century.[102] In the 1470s a new medical establishment was on the rise, focused on the newly established College of Surgery (Escola de Cirurgia). In 1478 the king granted this college the right to perform dissections, so its faculty might "see, know, communicate, and prove with their own eyes those things occluded and hidden in earthly bodies." Luis García-Ballester considers this the dawn in Valencia of a new medical methodology that privileged visible reality over received wisdom, and an emphasis on quarantine as the wisdom of "experience" may have been part of that shift.[103] A central figure in this medical community, Lluís Alcanyís, later composed a treatise on plague, written in 1489 and printed in Valencia in the first months of 1490. In the treatise he warns against "communication with infected people and those who come from an infected place, for which cause, as it has been seen, many cities and towns come to great ruin, as is proved by long experience."[104]

The council's sudden enthusiasm for quarantine might also have owed something to the contemporary political climate. In 1476 the Catalan Civil War was still a recent memory, and the King of Aragon was embroiled in a border conflict

---

101. Carmichael, in "Contagion Theory," 213–256, proposed that health officials in Milan had accepted contagion before physicians did, but has since revised her opinion; see Carmichael, "Epidemics and State Medicine," 221–247. On Valencian physicians' acceptance of contagion, see Roger French and Jon Arrizabalaga, "Coping with the French Disease: University Practitioners' Strategies and Tactics in the Transition from the Fifteenth to the Sixteenth Century," in *Medicine from the Black Death to the French Disease*, ed. Roger French et al. (Aldershot, UK: Routledge, 1998), 267–273.

102. On prominent Valencians in the medical schools of Italy in the later fifteenth century, see Jon Arrizabalaga, Luis García-Ballester, and Fernando Salmón, "Intellectual Relations between the Crown of Aragon and Italy (1470–1520): Valencian Medicine Students in General Studies in Siena, Pisa, Ferrara, and Padua," *Dynamis* 9 (1989): 117–47.

103. "Poder veure, saber tractar e provehir per los propis ulls aquelles coses ocultes e amagades dins los cossos mundanals." Luis García-Ballester, *La medicina a la València medieval: Medicina i societat en un país medieval mediterrani* (Valencia: Institució Valenciana d'Estudis i Investigació, 1988): 59–60.

104. "Comunicar ab gents infectes e que vinguen de loch infecte, com se sia vist per tal occasió moltes ciutats e viles venir en gran ruyna, segons se comprova per larges experiències." Lluís Alcanyís, *Regiment preservatiu e curatiu de la pestilència*, ed. Josés M. López Piñero and Antoni Ferrando (Valencia: Publicacions de la Universitat de Valencia, 1999), 147.

with France, while Castile was still engaged its own civil strife. This may, there-fore, have been a moment when concern about the outside world would have outweighed the economic cost of disrupting trade.[105] Whatever the impetus, the council shifted decisively in 1475 from a public health strategy of eliminating cor-ruption within the city to one focused on contagion coming from outside. And just as the focus on corruption had been both material and religious, the new focus on contagion permeated all aspects of the council's response to plague.

Contagion and Piety

While the shift to anticontagion measures, and particularly the growing use of quarantine, is well documented in Italy and elsewhere, there has been little study of the effect of this shift on religious understandings of disease. In Valen-cia new rituals emerged alongside quarantine that echoed the logic of conta-gion. Just as religious responses in the fourteenth and early fifteenth centuries had addressed moral corruption within the urban body, those of the later fif-teenth and early sixteenth centuries sought to protect the city from external threat. Civic plague rituals, in other words, were not merely traditions but were also adapted to changing understandings of disaster.

During the epidemic of 1475–76, when the council adopted quarantine as its main plague prevention measure, it also experimented with the format of the rogation procession. The rogation procession was the most common form of religious response to all natural disasters, including plague, and its format varied little across decade or disaster (see chapters 4–5). After the initial ex-periments of the 1420s (see chapter 4), the council did not tend to announce processions as a formal sequence, nor did the order of destinations follow any clear pattern. They also did not usually feature relics or holy images, as was common in other cities.[106]

In 1475, however, the council declared two series of processions for plague relief. The first, announced on July 17, consisted of "four processions on four consecutive days . . . passing through the whole city." Each procession was to visit three of the city's twelve parishes, in the east, west, north, and south (see

---

105. On the cost in early modern Seville, see Kristy Wilson Bowers, "Balancing Individual and Communal Needs: Plague and Public Health in Early Modern Seville," *Bulletin of the History of Medi-cine* 81, no. 2 (2007): 335–358.

106. On customs in Barcelona, see Martin-Vide and Barriendos, "The Use of Rogation Cere-mony Records," 201–221.

map 6).[107] Two weeks later the council declared a second set of processions, which would go to each of the city's four main gates, and at each gate affix "an image and figure of the holy guardian angel of the city."[108] For the first time, processions formed a sequence that held symbolic meaning: marking off and sanctifying the boundaries of the city. The first procession traced a sacred topography across all twelve parishes, even though the majority of Valencian rogation processions were directed to larger monastic sites (see map 4).[109] In the second, the images of the guardian angel played a protective role, analogous to that of the guards who were, a few months later, stationed at the same gates to deny entry to outsiders.[110]

This same summer saw the first clearly documented uses of saints' relics in a Valencian rogation procession. On August 25 and again on September 4 the council announced that it would seek relief from the plague with the help of the "most illustrious and blessed Sant Lluís, son of the most serene King Charles of Great Sicily of immortal memory."[111] The body of the boy bishop Lluís of Anjou had been brought to the city after the Valencian sack of Marseilles in 1423, but neither his relics nor any others were used in Valencian rogation processions before 1475.[112] During the next few decades, processions with relics became more common in city.[113] The council organized another series of three (the head of Sant Lluís, the leg bone of Sant Vicent Ferrer, and a fragment of the True Cross) during the plague 1489–90, and a further three during the plague of

---

107. The first procession went to the parish church of Sant Tomás, the chapels of Sant Vicent Ferrer and Santa Maria de Misericordia in the Convent of Sant Domènec, and passed by the Church of Sant Joan of the Hospital on its way to the parish church of Sant Esteve. The second went to the parish churches of Sant Lorenç, Santa Creu, and Sant Bartomeu. The third went to the parish churches of Sant Nicolau, Sant Joan del Mercat, and Santa Caterina. The fourth went to the parish church of Sant Andreu, the Monastery of Santa Maria del Merce, and the Church of Sant Martí. AMV, A-40 216v–217r.

108. AMV, A-40 216v–218r. Miralles noted that the images were "painted solemnly on wood," and consecrated by the auxiliary bishop before being mounted on the gates: "En lo dit any .LXXV., per los senyors regidós de València feren fer quatre angels, pintats sobre fusta solempnament." Miralles, *Crònica i dietari*, 4:768, p. 434.

109. The most popular destinations for rogation processions were the Chapel of Santa Maria de Gràcia in the Convent of Sant Agustí, the Chapel of Santa Maria de la Misericordia in the Convent of Sant Domènec, and the Convent of Santa Maria del Carme.

110. Angels may have been particularly prominent in Valencian piety at this time; the famous angel frescoes on the ceiling of Valencia Cathedral were painted by Francesco Pagan y Paolo de San Leocadio between 1472 and 1478. Hinojosa Montalvo, *Una ciutat gran i populosa*, 1109.

111. "Lo illustrissim e beneventurat Sent Lois fill del Serenissim Rey Karles de la Gran Sicilia de immortal memoria." AMV, A-40, 221v–222r.

112. Grieco, "'In Some Way Even More Than Before,'" 135–156.

113. The head and body of St. Lluís of Anjou were also used in three drought processions, in 1481, 1485, and 1506. AMV, A-42, 103r–v; AMV, A-44, 108v; AMV, A-52, 164r–165r.

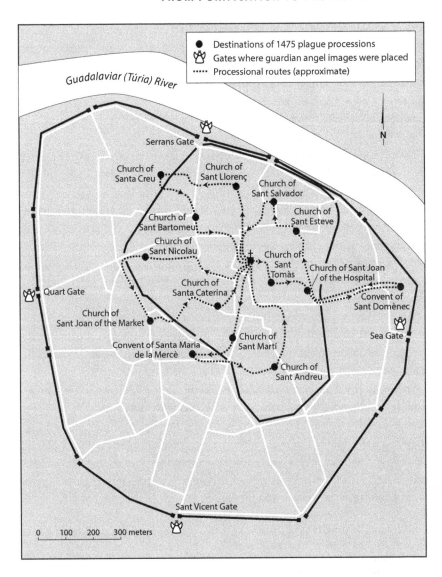

Destinations of 1475 plague processions
Gates where guardian angel images were placed
Processional routes (approximate)

Guadalaviar (Túria) River

N

Serrans Gate

Church of
Santa Creu

Church of
Sant Llorenç

Church of
Sant Salvador

Church of
Sant Bartomeu

Church of
Sant Esteve

Church of
Sant Nicolau

Church of
Sant Tomàs

Church of Sant Joan
of the Hospital

Church of
Santa Caterina

Quart Gate

Convent of
Sant Domènec

Church of
Sant Joan of the Market

Sea Gate

Convent of Santa Maria
de la Mercè

Church of
Sant Martí

Church of
Sant Andreu

Sant Vicent Gate

0   100   200   300 meters

MAP 6.   Plague processions in 1475

1494.[114] It also began to organize more processions dedicated to plague saints. In 1489 a procession was organized to the recently constructed extramural Convent of Sant Sebastià.[115] In 1494 the council declared that the Feast of Santa Anna, on July 26, would be celebrated "because at many other times it has been

114. AMV, A-45, 387v–388r; AMV, A-48, 64r–v, 68r–69r, 70r–71r.
115. AMV, A-45, 353r–v.

seen that plagues in the city were mitigated by the great merit of . . . Santa Anna."[116] In 1508, July 26 was again declared a holiday because "experience has shown [that] the plague often ceases on the feast of Santa Anna" (as indeed it had done in 1490).[117] In 1519 the council organized a procession for the health of the city to the Church of Sant Sebastià in celebration of the feast of the "glorious doctors" (*gloriosos metges*) Cosmas and Damian.[118] It further specified that this feast would be celebrated every year from then on.[119]

Such rituals, dedicated to saints who had in the past proved effective, have been documented in previous studies of Iberian civic piety, using mostly sixteenth-century records.[120] The assumption has been that while the records were recent, the practices remained unchanged from previous centuries. In Valencia the records start early enough to make it clear that evidence of the use of relics and saints for disaster relief appears rather suddenly in the later fifteenth century. The practices may have existed earlier, but not under the sponsorship of the city council. The council used them mostly for plagues rather than other disasters.

It seems reasonable, therefore, to posit an association between the protective rituals the council organized in the summer of 1475 and the protective measures it instituted at the end of the same epidemic in the spring of 1476. The adoption of quarantine practices as protection against plague, in other words, was in Valencia connected to the adoption of protective religious rituals against plague. The chronology is such that it would be difficult (and perhaps unhelpful) to say that one inspired the other; quarantine appeared first in the city, in 1440, but without lasting effect, and during the 1475–76 plague protective religious rituals were organized months before quarantine was imposed. Around 1475 all civic responses to plague, material and religious, underwent a shift from purification to protection.

---

116. "Per que en altre temps recorrent la dita gloriosa Senta Anna per sos grans merits es stat vist la peste que era en la present Ciutat esser stada mitigada & del tot extinta." AMV, A-46, 11v.

117. "Per speriencia es stat vist sobrevenint la festa de la gloriosa Senta Anna cessar la pestilencia." AMV, A-54, 4r–v. Dormeier, "Saints as Protectors," 169, notes Santa Anna's popularity as a plague saint around 1500. For the plague of 1490 ceasing on the Feast of Santa Anna, see Rubio Vela, "Las epidemias de peste," 1184.

118. On Cosmas and Damian as plague saints, see Dormeier, "Saints as Protectors," 169.

119. AMV, A-58, 539v–540r.

120. See Christian, *Local Religion in Sixteenth-Century Spain*. See also the number of studies using rogation ceremonies as environmental proxies, including Martin-Vide and Barriendos, "The Use of Rogation Ceremony Records," 201–221; Barriendos, "Climate Change in the Iberian Peninsula," 131–159; and Domínguez-Castro et al., "Reconstruction of Drought Episodes," 234. Diana Webb, *Patrons and Defenders: The Saints in the Italian City-States* (London: I. B. Tauris, 1996), 198–231, describes similar rituals, but before 1450 the crises she cites are all political rather than environmental in nature. Rawcliffe, *Urban Bodies*, 90–94, observes similarly "talismanic" uses of religious symbols in English towns in the fifteenth and sixteenth centuries.

Neither side of this shift is, in and of itself, remarkable; Valencia was by no means the first medieval city to impose quarantine or to seek saintly protection from the plague. But in the city council's medical and ritual practices both shifted at the same time. Municipal plague rituals were not static, ancient practices, but rather evolved as understandings of plague changed. Quarantine, traditionally considered the forerunner of a modern, rational approach to medicine, was in fact part of the same shift that inspired rituals of protection, long considered among the most ancient rituals in the church. Historians of medicine have been chipping away at quarantine's modernity for some years, but the primitive nature of plague rituals, like those for other natural disasters, has remained largely unchallenged.[121] In Valencia, however, protective rituals and quarantine formed part of a unified set of plague responses, just as measures against moral and material corruption had in earlier decades.

Although the Valencian city council had by the end of the fifteenth century transformed its approach to plague, the population as a whole did not necessarily share this new focus on protection over purification. Popular preachers continued to link disaster and sin. In early 1476, as the city faced not only the plague but also heavy rains, a Dominican friar named Agostí Ferrandis preached that humans would soon see a "universal sign" of God's anger at their sins. This sign might take the form of flood, fire, or earthquake, and would be "so horrible that many people will die of fright."[122] In the early 1490s a well-known mystic, Tecla Servent, recounted visions in which God threatened to send plagues and wars to destroy the world on account of the sins of the clergy—particularly sodomy.[123] In 1519 a Dominican preacher named Lluís de Castelloli blamed the plague's onset on city officials, whose laxness in prosecuting sin had angered God. As was reported in the municipal chronicle, Castelloli revealed that he had heard of "a most abominable sin": "certain persons [in the city] were practicing the sin of sodomy." He had, he said, advised municipal officials of this, but they had done nothing, "for which God was greatly offended." Hearing this indictment "the people began to murmur" and the criminal justice officers of the city soon seized and burned several accused sodomites. Among those arrested was a baker who fell under the ecclesiastical jurisdiction of the bishop of Valencia. He was not, therefore, condemned to

---

121. For critiques of quarantine, see Cavallo, *Charity and Power*, 46–48, and Carmichael, "Contagion Theory."

122. "Per los senyors regidós de València feren fer quatre angels, pintats sobre fusta solempnament." Miralles, *Crònica i dietari*, 4:786–797, pp. 440–444; Ronald E. Surtz, "Gender and Prophecy in Late Medieval Valencia," *La Corónica: A Journal of Medieval Hispanic Languages, Literatures, and Cultures* 41, no. 1 (2019): 299–302.

123. Surtz, "Gender and Prophecy," 302–315.

death, and the following Sunday Castelloli once again preached about God's anger against a city "that had not executed and burned such a public sinner." A riot ensued, and a mob seized the baker from ecclesiastical custody and burned him alive in Tossal Square.[124]

Contemporaries recorded this incident of civil unrest as the beginning of the Revolt of the Brotherhoods that was to convulse the kingdom of Valencia the following year.[125] Accounts agree that the riot in the summer of 1519 was only successful because, due to the plague, barely any municipal officials remained in the city.[126] This, the only clear instance of plague-motivated violence in Valencia after the Black Death, occurred more or less in the absence of city officials. It also occurred well after the council itself had ceased to associate plague with specific sinners. As a preacher, Castelloli's priorities would have differed from those of the city council, and these are clear in his account of the plague. Unlike the moral reforms of previous generations of councilmen, Castelloli linked plague to a much graver sin that implicated far fewer people. Sodomy was by the early sixteenth century closely associated with religious otherness in Iberian political discourse, though it had never appeared in the official civic accounts of plague.[127] Francesc Eiximenis's thoughts on the association between sodomy and disease also reached a much wider audience in the early sixteenth century, after his *Llibre de les dones* was printed in Barcelona.[128] Castelloli's account of plague was more violent and more narrowly targeted than any official government response to plague had been, perhaps because he was far less concerned about maintaining public order. For him, as for most preachers, plague was more notable as a scourge of God than for any of its particular characteristics. For generations of councilmen, however, plagues were different from floods, droughts, locusts, or earthquakes—not only in their

124. *Libre de memories de diversos sucesos e fets memorables e de coses senyalades de la ciutat e regne de Valencia (1308–1644)*, vol. 2, ed. Salvador Carreres Zacarés (Valencia: Accion Bibliografica Valenciana, 1935), 779–781.

125. On this revolt, see Ricardo García Cárcel, *Las Germanías de Valencia*, new ed. (Barcelona: Ediciones Península, 1981); and Vicent J. Vallés Borràs, *La Germanía* (Valencia: Institució Alfons el Magnànim, 2000).

126. See, for example, *El "Libre de antiquitats" de la seu de València*, ed. Joaquim Martí Mestre, (Barcelona: Publicacions de l'Abadia de Montserrat, 1994), 22r.

127. Thomas Devaney, "Virtue, Virility, and History in Fifteenth-Century Castile," *Speculum* 88, no. 3 (2013): 721–749; Barbara Weissberger, "'¡A tierra, puto!' Alfonso de Palencia's Discourse of Effeminacy," in *Queer Iberia: Sexualities, Cultures, and Crossings from the Middle Ages to the Renaissance*, ed. Josiah Blackmore and Gregory S. Hutcheson (Durham, NC: Duke University Press, 1999), 291–324.

128. Francesc Eiximenis argued that sodomy corrupted the air, and that the site of Sodom and Gomorrah "is now a lake of dead water in which no fish can live and over which no flying bird can survive." Francesc Eiximenis, quoted in Michael Solomon, "Fictions of Infection: Diseasing the Sexual Other in Francesc Eiximenis' *Lo llibre de les dones*," in Blackmore and Hutcheson, *Queer Iberia*, 277–290.

material effects but also in the religious response they demanded from the population.

Medieval Valencians did not understand all disasters in the same way, and they were not necessarily looking for someone to blame. The specific characteristics of plague, as the council understood them, shaped the council's responses to this particular disaster. The city council interpreted droughts—and, floods and swarms of locusts (see chapter 7)—as matters of collective responsibility in both religious and material terms. Because plague was understood as the result of corruption, it was linked to the sins of corruption that preoccupied the rulers of the city. These sins were the everyday sins of urban life, the moral equivalent of stagnant puddles or filth on the streets, and threatened the health of the social body only when allowed to get out of control. Successive councils' understanding of the disaster could and did change in response to new medical consensus. By the later fifteenth century the council adopted a new view of plague that located danger in the bodies of those coming into the city. As the council's medical approach to plague shifted, its religious approach changed as well, moving from a focus on purification to one of protection from threat. The introduction of quarantine was associated in Valencia with processions around the city walls, the use of relics, and special pleas to patron saints—all supposedly primitive rituals that were newly part of the city's disaster repertoire. Quarantine, therefore, ought to be understood not as a secularization of plague response but as part of a shift in focus, both medical and religious, from cleansing to protection from external threat. Of course, both internal policing and external defense remain popular governmental strategies during epidemics. And as the COVID-19 pandemic has shown, governing priorities are at least as important as medical consensus in shaping responses to disease outbreaks. Neither a focus on corruption nor a focus on contagion was more modern, more rational, or indeed more humane than the other; both combined medical knowledge with the governing preoccupations of the city council. Both corruption and contagion spread plague through natural processes compounded by human misdeeds, and both served as metaphors for imagining a society under threat.

CHAPTER 7

That for Which the King of Kings Sent the Flood?

Floods and Locusts

All types of disasters that afflicted late medieval Valencia appear somewhere in the Bible, but some have received more attention than others, both in the premodern period and in subsequent scholarship. For floods, the obvious reference point is the book of Genesis: "On that day all the springs of the great deep burst forth, and the floodgates of the heavens were opened. And rain fell on the earth forty days and forty nights."[1] And in the book of Exodus, locusts are associated with the eighth plague of Egypt: "By morning the wind had brought the locusts; they invaded all Egypt and settled down in every area of the country in great numbers. . . . They covered all the ground until it was black. They devoured all that was left after the hail—everything growing in the fields and the fruit on the trees. Nothing green remained on tree or plant in all the land of Egypt."[2]

Scholars have considered these Old Testament passages the obvious points of reference for premodern Christians faced with floods and locust swarms.[3]

---

1. Genesis 7:11–12 (New International Version).

2. Exodus 10:13–15 (New International Version).

3. Christian Rohr, "Writing a Catastrophe: Describing and Constructing Disaster Perception in Narrative Sources from the Late Middle Ages," *Historical Social Research / Historische Sozialforschung* 32, no. 3 (2007): 88–102. On floods, see Michael Kempe, "Noah's Flood: The Genesis Story and Natural Disasters in Early Modern Times," *Environment and History* 9, no. 2 (2003): 151–171. On locusts, see D. Camuffo and S. Enzi, "Locust Invasions and Climatic Factors from the Middle Ages to 1800," *Theoretical and Applied Climatology* 43, no. 1 (1991): 48; Martha Few, "Killing Locusts in Colonial Guatemala," in *Centering*

In late medieval Valencia, however, this was not the case. The Valencian council's religious responses to these particular catastrophes were more ambivalent than for any other kind of disaster. Before the later fifteenth century, the council treated floods not as religious matters but as the natural consequence of a blocked water system. And only for locusts, out of all natural disasters, did the council publicly express uncertainty on the question of natural versus divine causation.

The council's materially focused responses to these most biblical catastrophes may not be a coincidence. Conflict between experience and source material may have stymied religious comparison, as the way that these natural disasters occurred on the Valencian landscape seems not to have echoed the familiar biblical narratives. Or it may have been a matter of practicality; religious rituals did not, for various reasons, necessarily serve the aims of a municipal government responding to flood or locust swarm. Neither of these hypotheses can be conclusively proven, nor are they necessarily in conflict with one another. There is evidence that both spiritual and practical considerations were, as always, involved in the council's decision making. Whatever the thinking, the city council's apparently anomalous responses to floods and locusts reveal that the councilmen looked first to the environment and society around them in formulating their approach to natural disaster; they did not let biblical tropes shape their view of the reality at hand.[4] Although both floods and locust swarms are sudden, unpredictable, and intense events—events likely to trigger a strong emotional response—the council of Valencia did not default to terrified religiosity. Nor did it assume divine causation for all natural disasters, even if the Christian religious tradition presented obvious and colorful examples. The particularities of the local landscape shaped medieval Valencian disaster response.

Floods on the Valencian Plain

On Michaelmas Eve 1328, an autumn rainstorm beat down on the Valencian plain. The intense downpour filled the normally half empty bed of the Guadalaviar River and hurtled downstream toward the city of Valencia. The mass of water broke through the bridges near the city, which stood on the river's

Animals in Latin American History, ed. Martha Few and Zeb Tortorici (Durham, NC: Duke University Press, 2013), 62–92; and Jana Sprenger, "An Ocean of Locusts—The Perception and Control of Insect Pests in Prussian Brandenburg (1700–1850)," *Environment and History* 21, no. 4 (2015): 513–536.

4. Rohr, "Writing a Catastrophe," 92, has suggested that the opposite was true for some late medieval chroniclers.

south bank. The Guadalaviar overflowed into the upstream suburb of Rote-ros, and water ran through and down to the market square just outside the walls to the south: a low place that had, in Roman times, been a second branch of the river.[5] The bank of the river just north of the walls, in the suburb of La Xarea, was also under water (see map 3). The water filled the moats (*valls*) that ran around the city walls, into which the city sewers (*albellons*) flowed. From there the water flowed up into the sewer channels and into the city.[6]

This was one of the most severe floods of the century and the earliest of four recorded "extreme magnitude floods" of the Guadalaviar in the late me-dieval period.[7] It destroyed a number of houses in the city and its suburbs, such that the council had to pass legislation against looting in the destroyed buildings or carrying off the goods spread across the landscape. The city streets were so choked with debris from the fallen houses that the council ordered every man and woman in the city to spend the next two days clearing away "wood, brick, and tile . . . so that they might be passable."[8] Later the council complained that the river destroyed the grape, straw, rice, and other harvests, and that a storm at sea wrecked a number of vessels and their cargo.[9] Cer-tain pieces of land were so ruined that the city no longer collected tax on them; one such piece was not put back on the rolls until 1340.[10]

The clarity of the council's response was as striking as the scale of the di-saster. Three days after the flood, the council ordered,

> The moats [*valls*] of the city should be cleared of rubbish and cleaned, and likewise the mouths of the major sewers that run into them, considering the dangers and damages that could threaten the inhabitants of the city from the ruin and blockage [of the sewers and moats]; the same dangers and damages . . . that occurred on Wednesday last, Michaelmas Eve . . . the Guadalaviar River, which came at a level not seen in the memory of men . . . into one part that entered into the moats of the city, and for that reason and because the sewers of the city ran into the moats, it was

---

5. Pilar Carmona Gonzalez, "Geomorfología de la llanura de Valencia. El Río Turia y la ciudad," in *Historia de la ciudad*, vol. 2, *Territorio, sociedad y patrimonio*, ed. Sonia Dauksis Ortolá and Francesco Taberner Pastor (Valencia: Publications de la Universitat de València, 2002), 21.

6. AMV, A-2, 53r.

7. José Miguel Ruiz, Pilar Carmona, and Alejandro Pérez Cueva, "Flood Frequency and Seasonal-ity of the Jucar and Turia Mediterranean Rivers (Spain) during the 'Little Ice Age.'" *Méditerranée* 122 (2014): table 1. The other years were 1358, 1427, and 1517.

8. "Tot hom ho fembra qui age per ço et axi con fusta raiola teula per hoiy e dema tot dia agen desar o feyt desar les dits coses dels dits camins o carrers publiques a donar avisament que hom pus-cha passar per aquells." AMV, A-2, 53v.

9. AMV, A-2, 55r–56r.

10. AMV, A-4, 43v.

through these sewers that the water entered the city and the city was exposed to the peril of destruction.[11]

The flood occurred, in other words, because the city sewers had not been properly maintained. Nowhere in the council documents for this or many subsequent floods is there any indication that God caused the inundation, still less that he was moved to do so by the sins of the city. In no case before 1424 did the Valencian council describe a flood as the result of God's anger against the sins of humankind. And not until 1453 did the council begin regularly to organize religious rituals during floods, as it did with droughts and plagues from the 1420s on. Instead the councils of the fourteenth and early fifteenth centuries treated floods primarily as the natural consequence of improper hydraulic maintenance.

This down-to-earth explanation stands in sharp contrast with Florentine chronicler Giovanni Villani's account of the almost contemporary flood of the Arno River in 1333. Villani famously reported "a great debate . . . in Florence on the subject of the inundation: whether it occurred by the judgment of God or in the course of nature." This debate has been held up as a remarkable humanist questioning of the standard medieval position that floods must be the consequence of divine power.[12] Meanwhile, five years earlier in Valencia, God did not come into it at all. As Gerrit Schenk has noted, the city council of Florence also emphasized infrastructure failures (in that case, the position of weirs and mills on the Arno) as a major cause of the 1333 flood, though he suggests that the Florentine council also entertained fears of divine judgment.[13] In Valencia in 1328, as in Florence in 1333, a variety of opinions must have existed as to the cause of the flood, but the Valencian city council was unequivocal in tying the disaster to the maintenance of the water system.

---

11. "Los valls de la dita ciutat fossen escombrades & mundades & semblant les boques de les mares maiors que discorren en aquells. A esquivar perylls & dampnatges que per lenrunament & embargament daquells nos pogues enseguir als homens en la Ciutat de Valentia & a esquivar que daqui anavant semblants perylls & dampnatges nos poguessen enseguir & donar als dits habitants segons que dimecres primer passat vespra de Sent Miquel Archangel se esdevengren es donaren per occasio del Riu de Godalaviar lo qual no es memoria de homens que vengues tan gran & per la multiplicaciones daygues & gravea daquell espargi los seus raigs ço es la una partida que entra en los valls de la ciutat & per aquella occasio axi com de raho los albellons de la Ciutat degren discorrer en los valls. Per los dits albellons entra laygua del dit Riu en la Ciutat. Per la qual cosa la Ciutat fo exposada a perill de diruir & esser deserta." AMV, A-2, 54r–v.

12. On this event, see Moulinier and Redon, "L'inondation de 1333 à Florence," 91–104.

13. Gerrard Jasper Schenk, "'. . . prima ci fu la cagione de la mala provedenza de' Fiorentini . . .' Diasaster and 'Life World'—Reactions in the Commune of Florence to the Flood of November 1333," Medieval History Journal 10, nos. 1–2 (2007): 373–375. See also Marco Frati, "'Questo diluvio fece alla città e contado di Firenze infinito danno.' Danni, cause e rimedi nell'aliluvione del 1333," Città e storia 10 (2015): 1–20.

Although the Valencian plain receives very little annual rainfall, sudden and violent floods are characteristic of the area and of Mediterranean Spain more generally. Mediterranean river floods are mainly associated with intense precipitation (as opposed to other factors like snowmelt). These precipitation patterns alternate between wet and dry periods that may last decades or even centuries.[14] These variations are closely associated with the weather pattern known as the North Atlantic Oscillation (NAO); a less pronounced difference between the low-pressure atmospheric zone near Iceland and the high-pressure one near the Azores (known as a "negative NAO") correlates to rainy years and significant floods, although this correlation is subject to shifts over time.[15] In the area around Valencia, multiple proxies have shown that the period of transition to the Little Ice Age (1300–1400) was marked by variable precipitation, including several catastrophic floods.[16] The fifteenth century saw the onset of somewhat wetter conditions and more frequent floods across Mediterranean Spain. The most extreme flood conditions of the Little Ice Age, however, did not occur until the late sixteenth and early seventeenth centuries.[17] Valencia would therefore have been wetter in the fifteenth century than in the fourteenth century, but a few extreme floods occurred in both centuries. Since catastrophic floods were relatively rare events, contemporaries would probably not have observed a clear trend toward greater flood frequency.

Floods in Valencia, now as in the medieval period, are mostly likely to occur in the autumn, but a significant minority occur in the summer.[18] Torrential rains generate flash flooding in the dry gulches of the Valencian plain, and on some occasions the Guadalaviar also overflows.[19] Chronicler Melchior Miralles, who was an eyewitness to a serious flood in November 1475, reported

---

14. Gerardo Benito et al., "Holocene Flooding and Climate Change in the Mediterranean," *Catena* 130 (2015): 13–33.

15. See Gerardo Benito et al., "Palaeoflood and Floodplain Records from Spain: Evidence for Long-Term Climate Variability and Environmental Changes," *Geomorphology* 101, no. 1 (2008): 74. For a brief overview of the NAO, see Degroot, *The Frigid Golden Age*, 24–25.

16. Lopez-Blanco and Romero Viana, "Dry and Wet Periods over the Last Millennium; on the fourteenth century, see Benito et al., "Holocene Flooding and Climate Change."

17. See Benito et al., "Holocene Flooding and Climate Change," 19. Machado et al., "500 Years of Rainfall Variability," finds that 1440–90 was particularly flood prone. Ruiz, Carmona, and Pérez Cueva, "Flood Frequency and Seasonality," shows an increase in flooding on the Turia in the fifteenth century, but the real increase would not be until the late sixteenth or early seventeenth centuries. Benito et al., "Palaeoflood and Floodplain Records," 73, finds the period 1430–1660 to be a flood cluster across Spain, in both Atlantic and Mediterranean rivers.

18. These autumn rains are known locally as the *gota fría*, or cold drop. J. Javier Diez, M. Dolores Esteban, José S. López-Gutiérrez and Vicente Negro, "Meteocean Influence on Inland and Coastal Floods in the East of Spain," *Journal of Coastal Research* 29, no. 6A (2013): 72–80; Ruiz, Carmona, and Pérez Cueva, "Flood Frequency and Seasonality."

19. Carmona and Ruiz, "Historical Morphogenesis of the Turia River," 140–141, 145.

that after three days and nights of "great rain," "the rivers, gullies, torrents [were] swollen such as has never been seen nor heard of, bridges and dams broken and destroyed, lands wasted, trees destroyed, and other evils and damages done by the waters." The collapse of these structures must have further fouled the watercourses, worsening the flood. A week later, after still more rain, "the river of Valencia broke three arches of the Palace Bridge; many houses began to collapse in Valencia; fountains in the houses that had dried up ran with water, wells overflowed and ran in the streets."[20] This was an unusually extended episode; most floods lasted between one and four days.[21]

During such floods the council mustered a defense against the rising water. On October 25, 1427, "there were many rains in said city and in other parts, from which the Guadalaviar River came suddenly and escaped its limits, destroying the Temple Bridge and four arches of the Serrans Bridge and also destroying many houses on the Morvedre Road." An unusually detailed summary from the city's account books tells us that the jurats, alongside other municipal and royal officials, worked "to provide for the utility of the city on account of the great matter that was coming from the river." As the floodwater rose, these officials called for all the "masters and artisans" employed on city projects "to come immediately to the Temple Gate to give counsel to the honorable jurats to build and give [the gate] better defense, that it might be defended and the water of the river not enter into said city. Even more, because it had already begun to enter through that gate and the Sea Gate, and through all of the openings of the sewers that face the wall, and also in the Tanner's Quarter and in La Xarea [neighborhoods near the river], they were at the point of perishing." On the advice of these assembled experts, each of the city gates facing the river—from upstream to downstream: Santa Caterina, Roteros, Serrans, Trinitat, Temple, and the Sea Gate—was guarded by ten men, who were to "defend [it] by their ingenuity, so that the water of the river did not enter into the city." This they did by lowering the portcullises of the larger gates and walling up the openings, as though under siege. The jurats, meanwhile, "were continually going from one gate to another," inspecting the defense work by torchlight. By 4:00 a.m. the river had subsided by about ten *palms* (two meters), so the danger to those gates had passed. The gates to the southwest—Dyes Gate and Torrent Gate—were also

---

20. "De què vengueren los rius, baranchs, torrents, grosos, que nunqua fonch vist ni hoït dir ponts [e] açuts trenquats e deroquats, terres aramblades, arbres deroquats e alters mals e dans que les aygües avien fet. . . . E lo divenres, qui fonch primer dia de deembre, lo riu de València deroquà tres arcades del pont del Real; moltes cases comencen a caure en València; manaven e brolaven fonts en les cases, que avien asgotar, los pous venir a sobrexir e escórer en les careres." Melchior Miralles, in *Crònica i dietari*, 4:781, p. 438.

21. Ruiz, Carmona, and Pérez Cueva, "Flood Frequency and Seasonality," 123.

under threat, but from human error rather than the river itself: "Because the canal that [was] near the Torrent Gate could not collect all of the waters, some people broke it, and the water therefore entered into the city via the Torrent Gate, from which the people thought to perish, for which reason many men had to work during that night."[22] The damage from this flood was extensive; on October 13, 1428, four men and a nag were hired to clear the debris of "one wall of the first arch of the Serrans Bridge that fell . . . by reason of the great [flood]," which was still clogging the moat below the bridge nearly a year after the disaster.

Like a drought, a flood is very much in the eye of the beholder. A river over-flowing its banks is merely occupying the larger bed that is its floodplain. Valencia, like most premodern cities, stood within this larger bed.[23] In such places, as Paolo Squatriti puts it, "land and water find compromises that sometimes do not match human economic interests."[24] Although the deposition of sediment from floodwater does leave visible traces on the landscape, medieval records usually define floods in terms of their impact on human structures. This was particularly so in Valencia, where the river did not need to leave its bed to do damage. Valencia's irrigation system of dams, mills, and bridges reaching into and over the river was particularly vulnerable to high water. In April 1407 the council observed that the city was much in need of flour because of "the great deluge of waters that occurred in the month of November . . . which destroyed

---

22. "Es saber que dissapte a .xxv. del mes doctubre del any de la nativitat de Nostre Senyor .mccccxxvii. foren moltes pluges en la dita Ciutat e en altres parts per les quals vench subitament lo Riu de Guadalaviar e exint de sos limits enderroca lo pont del Temple e quatre arcades del pont dels Serrans e mes enderroca molts alberchs en lo cami de Murvedre. E los dits honrats Jurats ensemps ab los hono-rables loctinent de Governador Justicia en Criminal e altres officials de la dita Ciutat per provehir a la utilitat de la dita Ciutat per rao de la dita gran que venia per lo dit Riu e de les dites pluges provehiren e ordenaren que en moltes lochs de la dita Ciutat fossen fetes crides manants a tots los maestres e menes-trals dobra de vila que decontinent fossen al portal del Temple per donar aquella millor deffensio que fer se pogues a deffendre que laygua del dit Riu no entras en la dita Ciutat majorment com jay començas entrar per lo dit portal e per lo portal de la Mar e per tots los forats de les mares que afronten ab lo mur entant que en la Blanqueria e en la Xerea estauen en punt de perir. . . . E fon per los dits honrats Jurats provehit e ordenat que en cascu dels portals de Santa Caterina de Roteros dels Serrans de la Santa Trini-tat del Temple e de la Mar continuament estiguessen .x. homens dels dits menestral e maestres dobra de vila per deffendre per lur giny que laygua del dit Riu no entras en la dita Ciutat. . . . Encara hagueren a donar remey e ajuda als portals dels Tints e de Torrent que fossen guardats per ço com la cequia que es prop lo dit portal de Torrent no poder recullir tots les aygues algunes persones tancaren aquella e laygua ladonchs entrava en la dita Ciutat per lo dit portal de Torrent de que les gents cuydaven perir e per la dita rao molts homens hagueren a treballar en la dita nit." AMV, O-10, 207v–208v.

23. On floods that were not necessarily perceived as natural disasters, see Vera S. Candiani, *Dreaming of Dry Land: Environmental Transformation in Colonial Mexico City* (Stanford, CA: Stanford University Press, 2014); and Faisal Husain, "In the Bellies of the Marshes: Water and Power in the Countryside of Ottoman Baghdad," *Environmental History* 19, no. 4 (2014): 638–664.

24. Paolo Squatriti, "The Floods of 589 and Climate Change at the Beginning of the Middle Ages," *Speculum* 85, no. 4 (2010): 816.

and ruined all the dams of the river and among the others that of the Mestalla Canal from whence the greater part of the mills of the river take water."[25] The deluge here need not have been so very great; any damage to the city's mills set off fears of a bottleneck in the flour supply. For the council it was the possibility of a short-term subsistence crisis that made this flood a disaster.

The road network, too, was vulnerable to floods. In early 1377 a flood laid waste to the road network all around the city so that "people cannot go or pass along the roads and bridges [of the *horta* [the irrigated area around the city] without peril to themselves and their mounts and other beasts." The role of the council here was not clear. Some councilmen proposed that all the roads be repaired at the city's expense, because they were "common and public," but others argued that only the four main roads leading north, south, east, and west were a public responsibility. The repair of secondary roads, like that of the canals, should be undertaken by those whose properties fronted them.[26] The council records do not include the conclusion of this debate, but several months later the council complained of the burden of expensive road repair, suggesting that, one way or another, the cost was considerable.[27]

Floods and heavy rains often caused buildings to collapse, particularly within the city. In November 1351 the council mentioned that thirty houses had been destroyed by rains in the city in the previous month.[28] As Gregory Aldrete has noted in his study of floods in ancient Rome, the cheaper the construction materials, the greater the likelihood that water damage would lead to collapse. Wood and clay (unfired brick or wattle and daub) were extremely vulnerable to water. Fired bricks, too, could be water soluble if not heated to sufficient temperature in the kiln, as cheap bricks may not have been. The dwellings of the poor would thus have been particularly vulnerable to water, though their plight seems to have caused less concern in the council than damage to mills or roads.[29] In 1398 the council reported being bothered for days

---

25. "Per occasio del gran diluvi daygues que ere estat en lo mes de novembre prop passat lo qual derroca e gita a mal tots los açuts del Riu e entre les altres lo de la cequia de Miztalla don la maior part dels molins della lo Riu prenen aygua los quals per aquell acte cessauen molre de que la ciutat era posada en perplexitat." AMV, A-23, 169v.

26. "Cascu sabia en aquest temps e dies prop passats eren estades tantes e tan grans e continues pluges e inundacio daygues que hauien guastats los camins e diverses ponts de la orta de la dita Ciutat hoc encara partida dels ponts del Riu en tant que les gens sens perill lur e de lurs cavalcadures e daltres besties no podien anar e passar per los dits camins e ponts e majorment en aquells lochs on major perill." AMV, A-17, 134r–135r. The four main roads were the Morvedre Road (to the north), the Xátiva Road (to the south), the Sea Road (to the east), and the Quart Road (to the west).

27. This cost was cited as a reason not to commission a new clock for the city. AMV, A-17, 149v–150r.

28. AMV, A-10, 28v–29r.

29. On the unequal impact of flood disasters, see Soens, "Flood Security," 209–232.

by "a man of little and poor condition" who demanded compensation for some "little Moorish houses" that had been destroyed when part of the old city wall was taken down. The council was inclined to look favorably on his request only because of "the rains immediately after" the initial damage to the houses, which apparently put them beyond repair.[30] Even a solidly built structure, however, would not have been built to withstand the horizontal force of flood-water. Water damage could also weaken its structure and cause it to rot and crumble long after the flood had passed.[31] As most of this damage was to private property, only scattered references appear in the council records. In 1378 the council exchanged several letters with royal authorities about the jurisdiction of city officials in the *jueria* (Jewish quarter). One such letter argued that authority of the *mostaçaf*, the municipal official charged with protecting the roads, ought also to extend to the supervision of the repairs to the house of Salamo Abnaxub, which had been so damaged by the "inundation of water and of rain that occurred in the present year" that a large part of the facade had collapsed into the street.[32]

Flood Prevention: Infrastructure and Maintenance

Floods in Valencia were expected, if not predictable. As such, they were disasters for which it was possible to prepare. Extreme floods were fairly rare in Valencia. José Miguel Ruiz, Pilar Carmona, and Alejandro Pérez Cueva consider 1328, 1358, 1427, and 1517 to have been the only "extreme magnitude" floods in this period, but Miralles's account suggests that flooding in 1475 was also fairly substantial.[33] High water or heavy rain could also cause significant damage to structures, and the council records contain some dozen further mentions of such damage.[34] Efforts to prevent or ameliorate the risk of future flood damage were also fairly common. For the Valencian council, prepara-

---

30. AMV, A-21, 228r.

31. Gregory S. Aldrete, *Floods of the Tiber in Ancient Rome* (Baltimore: Johns Hopkins University Press, 2007), 112–113, 129.

32. "Salamo Abnaxub juheu de la dita Juheria enten affer per refer e tornar lo seu alberch lo qual per inundacio de aygues e de pluges que son estades en lany present sera dirruit o casi caygut en la maior partida del enfront de la carrera." AMV, g3-4, 2v–5r.

33. Ruiz, Carmona, and Pérez Cueva, "Flood Frequency and Seasonality," table 1.

34. The years were 1321(AMV A-1 178r-178v, 181r-182r); 1340 (A-4 15r-16r); 1346 (A-6 75r-75v); 1372 (A-16 116v-117r); 1377 (A-17 134r-135r, 149v-150r); 1406 (A-23 96r-96v); 1407 (A-23 169v); 1434 (A-30 154v, 156v-157r); 1453 (A-35 235r, 283v, 301r); 1462 (A-37 125r); 1487 (*Libre de Memories* vol. 1, 691) , and 1500 (*Libre de Memories* vol. 1, 718).

tion took two forms: constructing barriers to protect important areas, and opening channels to allow the water to flow freely through and out of the city. In the fourteenth century and much of the fifteenth, these material prevention measures were the center of the city's flood response. Rising water was a natural occurrence, but it was up to human infrastructure to prevent a flood.

In the aftermath of the flood of 1328, the council sought not only to rebuild but also to strengthen the infrastructure of the city. The roads and bridges that had been destroyed were to be repaired, of course, but the council also ordered repairs on the city wall (which was still the old wall that surrounded the Andalusi core of the city). The riverside suburbs of La Xarea and Roteros, which lay outside the wall, had been flooded, and so the council proposed to build an additional parapet "to prevent the river, from this point onward, having the opportunity to rise and do such damage as it has done to the suburbs of the city."[35] It was at this time that the council also ordered the "moats and the main channels of the sewers of the city" to be cleaned so that future excess water might pass more easily through the city's water system.[36] Subsequent councils likewise focused on building barriers and opening channels. Four years after this flood, in 1332, the Dominican prior Jaume Grau appealed to the city for aid in protecting his institution from future floods. The Convent of Sant Domènec stood right on the riverbank in the flood-prone La Xarea district, and the prior argued that without "immediate work . . . to block the course of the river, this monastery would be in peril of being completely destroyed and demolished." The council agreed, and granted the prior the sum of five thousand sous toward the project.[37]

The Board of Walls and Sewers (Junta de Murs i Valls) was itself established in response to the flood of 1358, with the express purpose of completing the new walls and moats that would protect the flood-prone suburbs of the city.[38] Similarly, after the flood of 1427, the council proposed that as the city had been thrown into "great worry and peril" by the severity of the October flood, "great mortar [works]" should be constructed "in such places

---

35. "Et encara a construir parets emsemblant de mur que sia fet ço es saber del alberch que fo dEn Gilabert de Cruylls en lo qual ara son construides adoberies. Lo qual mur sia continuat tro als molins dEn A. G. Catala . . . continuan damunt. Los molins en aquells lochs on sera necessari esser faedor per esquivar & tolre que daqui avant lo dit Riu no aia opportunitat de muntar & de donar semblants dampnatges que donats ha als ravals de la dita Ciutat." AMV, A-2, 55r–v.

36. "Los valls & les mares maiors dels albellons." AMV, A-2, 55r.

37. "Si ab ajuda de Deu e de bones persones din breu temps obra conuinent e per firosa no era feta aembargar lo discurs del dit Riu lo dit monestir seria en perill de diruyr & demolir del tot." AMV, A-3, 18r–19r.

38. AMV, A-13, Mano 3, 35v. Melió, La "Junta de Murs i Valls," 39–49.

and in such a manner . . . that the city be preserved from such perils and worries in the future." One of these mortar works was to be placed "below Mislata," or immediately upstream from the city.[39]

While the council proposed barrier projects after these particularly catastrophic floods, the maintenance of proper water flow was a constant feature of the city's flood preparation. In 1351, as the city stood under threat of attack from Castile, the council observed that "the moats of the city are full such that neither the sewers nor the gutters could drain before filling, for which reason the city and its houses are in great danger of falling if God gives us great rains as he has done in other times." For this reason, as well as for reasons of defense, the moats were to be cleaned.[40] Here (unusually for discussions of floods) it was God who sent the rain. It was up to humans, however, to decide whether the rain became a flood. Councils throughout this period described sewer maintenance as a flood prevention measure. In 1356 the council proclaimed that "the city of Valencia could easily be destroyed by floods because the moats are ruined," and Genoese prisoners of war then in the city would thus be put to work cleaning them.[41] Two years later the flood of 1358 so "ruined and filled" the moats that water could no longer flow through them.[42] Although this flood spurred the creations of the Board of Walls and Sewers, and thereby increased the resources available for public works projects, the councils' conception of floods did not change. In 1366 it once again ordered the moats to be cleaned because they were "very full and in ruins in such a way that if floods of water occur the buildings of the city would be in great peril."[43] The council of 1414 used similar language.[44] The moats were cleaned every five or ten years throughout this period, a process that could also be justified on public health grounds. In 1418 the council reported a "great clamor" from the city's tanners, who complained that "their houses and the whole area were in great peril when their filth and rain waters and the other runoff from

39. "La dita Ciutat fon posada en en gran congoxa e perill si noy fos estat acorregut & proveit soptosament fossen fetes grosses argamesses en certs lochs e en certa manera segons que als honrats jursts de la dita Ciutat plaura & a lur ordinacio, per tal que la Ciutat fos preservada de tals perills e congoxes en esdevenidor." AMV, A-29, 34r–v.

40. "Que les valls de la dita Ciutat eren plous enaxi que les mares ni les ayguers de les carrers de la ciutat damunt dita no podie exaguer ans essent reblertes per la qual cosa la dita ciutat & los alberchs daquella estant en gran perill de caure maiorment si deus donara grans pluges segons que hauia feit en altres temps." AMV, A-10, 28v–29r.

41. "Que la Ciutat de Valnt. per diluuis daygues porien leument esdevenir dirruinents com los valls de aquella fossen enrrunats." AMV, A-12, 54v.

42. AMV, A-13, Mano 3, 32v.

43. "Molt plens & plens e en Runats en tal guisa que si dolubis [sic] daygues se seguien los edifficis de la dita ciutat anauen a gran perill." AMV, A-14, Mano 5, 82r.

44. AMV, A-25, 402r.

their workshops could not flow in the moat, the filth of which overflowed to a great height."[45] In the case of the moat there was a clear overlap between flood risk and health hazard; both were, in a sense, forms of water damage.

On a few occasions the council went beyond clearing the existing channels for water flow and sought to create new channels entirely. The council of 1390 became concerned that erosion of the riverbanks near the Grau would lead to the destruction of the port if the river ran high. "For fear of a flood that could damage the houses of the Grau," it concluded that "it would be good and profitable to move the flow of the water of the Guadalaviar River away from the Grau . . . near En Silvestre Point."[46] This diversion was swiftly accomplished. Within two years, however, the council concurred with the Grau residents that the risk of disease from water pooling in the empty riverbed was more serious than the risk of flood, and so approved the return of the river to its original bed. Similarly, in 1439, the city government undertook the diversion of the main channel of the river away from the north bank "between the new gate of Santa Creu and that of the tannery toward the city, as it was going to converge on the hospital of En Clapers [which stood on the north bank] and there was a danger that the first flood that would come would destroy the entire Morvedre Road."[47] Once again the aim was to render a future flood less harmful by providing an appropriate channel for superfluous water.

The risk of flood damages was thus intimately connected to the city's hydraulic infrastructure. In late September 1415 the notary Francesc Scola recorded a complaint about the state of a certain sewer. This sewer, which flowed through four parishes within the old walls—Sant Bartomeu, Sant Esteve, Sant Pere, and Sant Tomás—had not, according to the complaint, been cleaned for more than twenty-five years.[48] On account of this lack of maintenance, the channel was ruined and blocked such that "rain and other water and the waste that is ordained to run in this sewer cannot flow in and through it." It was a covered sewer, meant to flow "under the earth," but in many places it had fallen

---

45. "Lurs alberchs e tota aquella partida era en gran perill quant lurs immundicies e aygues pluvials & los altres discorriments de lurs adoberies no podien decorre en lo vall les immundicies del qual sobrepugen en altitud gran." AMV, g3-14, 45r–v.

46. "Per dupte de diluvi qui poria noure als alberchs del Grau de la mar de la dita Ciutat mudar lo decorriment de laygua del Riu de Godalaviar lunyant lo del dit Grau & comencant aquest mudament prop la punta appellada dEn Silvestre." AMV, A-20, 191r–v.

47. "Girar lo riu entre lo portal nou de Santa Creu e lo de la blanqueria acostant lo vers la Ciutat com anas a ferir vers lespital dEn Clapers e estava en perill que la primera ruina que vingues no destruhis tot lo cami de Murvedre." AMV, d3-42, unnumbered folio, entry dated "Divendres a .v. del dit mes de juny [1439]," (Friday, June 5, 1439).

48. The city sewers were all cleaned in the spring of 1390, and apparently this one had not been cleaned since then. See AMV, A-19 113v. Valencia Cathedral itself served as the church for the parish of Sant Pere.

in and stood open to the sky, "and from it issues great infection and corruption, which [will] be the cause of pestilential maladies in the city, for according to the doctrine of great doctors, experts in such matters, the waste of such sewers and channels leads to corruption in the air and is a pestilential thing." This hazard was an impediment in the affairs of the neighborhood, for the street was a busy one, and people could not safely pass along it on account of the holes where the channel had fallen in. Such a situation was "indecent" in a street so public and a city so noble. And what was worse, the houses of the street were at risk because "the waters and waste . . . cannot freely run and pass through this sewer . . . [and] because of [its] ruin, the water gets in and rots the foundations and walls of the houses, and in times of rain the waters turn back and overflow, so that those who live in this street are not only in peril of the ruin of their houses but also of death if, God forbid, the houses fall." In presenting the sewer as a scandal and a public danger, the inhabitants of this street sought to have the council repair it at public expense. In this they were successful; the council did ultimately authorize its repair.[49]

This complaint frames a poorly maintained sewer as a flood risk in miniature. Because the sewer was in disrepair, the water that would normally flow easily beneath the street was spilling into it, impeding traffic and rotting the foundations of adjacent houses. At moments when the quantity of water was greater than normal, this blocked channel would overflow, to the peril of those

---

49. "La mare qui discorre sots terra per lo cami de la Freneria e engrave en lo vall vell de la Ciutat daval la casa de la Confraria de la Verge Maria per la multitut de les aygues & inmundicies qui discorren en aquella com discurreguen en la dita mare les aygues & inmundicies de la parroquia de Sent Pere & per la major part de los parroquies de Sent Bartomeu de Sent Tomas & de Sent Stheve e de altres parroquies per com gran temps ha passat almenys pus de xxv anys que no es stada refeta scurada ni mundada. Ara mester refectui & sia en bocada o enrunada entant que les dites aygues axi pluvials com altres & les inmundicies que son ordenades discorre en la dita mare no poden discorre en & per aquella. En ço es en molts lochs cayguda & sta uberta e his de aquella gran infeccio & corupcio la qual pena esser ocasio de malalties pestilencials en la dita ciutat com segons doctrina dels grans doctors en semblant stia experts per les inmundicies de semblants mares & clavegueres senseguescha corrupcio en layre & es fet pestilencial. E es gran inpediment de aquells qui per lurs afers & negocis an avenir & passar en & per lo dit carrer de la Freneria qui es hu dels prinicipals oficis de la dita ciutat & molt necessari a comun us de les gents & per co cove a moltes persones anar & passar en & per la dita carera & non poden fer bonament per lo dirruiment de la dita mare que segons dit es en lo dit carrer en molts lochs uberta la qual cosa es molt indecent que un carech asi publich & de gran trafech & passatge stigua en la manera que sta & ha stat per moltes dies en tan noble & axi insigne ciutat. E noresmenys sen spe gran & ireparable dapnatge & es ja eminent & nos pot scusir si prestament noy es provehit a aquells qui an lurs habitacions en lo dit carrer qui stan al los alberchs pigats & scalonats per ço que nos enderoque com les dites aygues & inmundicies per çolcom no podern delurament discorre & passar per la dita mare & per lo enrunament de aquella humecten & corompen los fonaments & parets dels dits alberchs & en temps de pluges reflecte. & regolfen les dites aygues & inmundicies per les dites cases & axi es stat fet en lo temporal de les pluges que pochs dies ha passats son stades per la qual raho los qui habiten en la dita carrer estan no solament en peril de diruhinament dels alberchs mas encara de mort si les dites cases cahien ço que Deus no vulla." AMV, Protocolos Francesc Scola, 3/1, 101r–101v.

nearby. Large or small, floods shared a common language of infrastructure: channels, blockage, and overflow. The whole landscape of the city of Valencia and its surroundings was designed around making water flow in the right way and to the right places. While this landscape was not designed explicitly around flood prevention, it is perhaps not surprising that the council expected it to be able to handle floods. They were, after all, natural fluctuations in the water level, not signs of God's displeasure.

Inching toward Religious Response

That the councils of the fourteenth and early fifteenth centuries treated floods primarily as natural occurrences seems the inescapable conclusion based on the surviving documents. Almost none of the council documents prior to 1424 make any mention of God's role in causing floods. Nor did any councils organize rogation processions for floods before 1453. While individual councilmen may have understood floods as divine punishment, the council as a whole seems to have had little interest in explaining them in this way until well into the fifteenth century.

The language that the council documents use to describe floods is a clear contrast to that used for droughts. Droughts were routinely described using religious language, even in documents with a secular purpose (see chapter 5). The council tended particularly to describe the absence of rain as a divinely ordained rupture in the natural relationship between the earth and humankind. Floods are also, of course, often the result of an unusual quantity of rain. Yet with the exception of the aforementioned banal remark about God sending rain, such language is entirely absent from the council documents on floods before the late fifteenth century. Phrases like "by God's judgement" (per juhi de Deu), or "it has pleased our lord to give us" (ha plagut a nostre senyor donar), which occur throughout the documents on drought, do not appear in these documents. Part of this is a question of document quantity: there were fewer floods than droughts in Valencia, and therefore fewer flood documents to examine for religious language. The types of documents also differ; droughts more often affected the grain supply, so they more often generated correspondence with other cities. In these cases it might have been conventionally appropriate to remark on God's hand in the situation. But, as we have seen, floods did occasionally affect the harvest, and there is one case of a request for supplies. In October 1413 the jurats wrote to their counterparts in the nearby town of Alzira, requesting shipments of flour, because of "the great multitude of water that came in our river and has broken all the diversion dams [açuts]," which had put the city's mills out of commission.[50] There is no word about the judgment of God. An argument of silence cannot, of course, be made very strongly, but in contrast with the material on droughts the silence is notable. These were conventional phrases. It is as though there was no conventional trope of floods as the judgment of God.

Yet we know quite well that there was. The councilmen were not highly educated, but every single one of them must have been familiar with the biblical story of Noah. The deluge in the book of Genesis was an obvious point of reference for floods for writers from the Middle Ages through the Renaissance. Christian Rohr has observed that late medieval German chroniclers even tended to use biblical phrases when describing floods in their cities.[51] Miralles used similar language in his account of the flood of 1475, noting that "the great and terrible waters began, [and] for three days and three nights the great rain did not cease, beyond measure, so that it appeared that the heavens had opened up and that the world must perish."[52] The council documents, unsurprisingly, tend to be less grandiose in their descriptions. Nonetheless, the council also made explicit reference to the biblical deluge, just not in the context of an actual flood. In February 1405 the jurats wrote to the royal governor of the kingdom of Valencia on the subject of a horrendous crime that had taken place near the city: "a Moor called Negrello . . . forcibly lay with a Christian woman [with the] agreement and conniving of the woman's husband, who used to be a Moor, and was living with his wife in Alboraia." Negrello had already been caught, and the jurats had heard that some wished the governor to show him leniency. They objected, "Your Nobility can clearly see how detestable to God this crime is, and it would be a horrible thing . . . to give a remission to *that for which the King of Kings sent the flood*, for all flesh was corrupted and the sons of men went to the daughters of the people" (my emphasis).[53] The final phrase about sons and daughters is in reference to the book of Genesis on the causes of the flood ("when the sons of God went to the daughters of humans and

50. "Per gran multitud daygua que en lo riu nostre es venguda la qual ha trencats tots los açuts daquell en tant que son a present fort destrets de farines." AMV, g3-12, 62v. Incidentally, the city also requested flour from Alzira and other cities after the flood of 1517 and did not use religious language in those letters either, though it did in its letter to the king. AMV, g3-40, 121v–126r.

51. Rohr, "Writing a Catastrophe." See also Kempe, "Noah's Flood"; and Lydia Barnett, "The Theology of Climate Change: Sin as Agency in the Enlightenment's Anthropocene," *Environmental History* 20, no. 2 (2015): 217–237.

52. "Començaren les grans e spantables aygües, que tres dies e tres nits no sesà la gran pluga, ultra mesure, que paria que los cels fosen huberts e que lo món degués perir." Miralles, *Crònica i dietari*, 4:781, p. 438.

53. "E ja pot veure vostra noblea quant es detestable a Deu aquest delicte & seria orrible cosa ab al poble fer remissio daquell lo Rey dels Senyoreiants feu lo diluvi per tal com tota carn era corrumpuda & los fills dels homens anaven a les filles de les gents." AMV, g3-8, 107v.

had children by them").[54] The city councilmen of 1405, therefore, were perfectly capable of referring to the biblical flood, and even of echoing a passage of Genesis, to refer to divine punishments of contemporary sins.

Nonetheless, neither they nor any other councilmen of the fourteenth or early fifteenth centuries took the step of applying this logic to actual floods. In November 1406 a flood broke a number of hydraulic structures on the Xúquer River, and the Valencian council received pleas for relief from the town of Alzira, but the council documents make no mention of God's role in this "great deluge of waters" (gran diluvi d'aygues).[55] Nor did the council invoke divine power the following year, when a spring flood destroyed the mills on the Mestalla Canal and threw the city into "perplexity" about where to find flour.[56]

Not until 1424 did the council finally ask for God's help with a flood. In a letter to the prior of the Charterhouse of Portaceli (from whom they often requested prayers for rain during droughts), the jurats observed,

> You have seen, most religious friars, elect servants of God and our dear friends, how our Lord God who for a very long time before now has punished and castigated our sins and delights, among the other plagues and blows, by means of droughts and scarcities of heavenly rain, now in these days we think that because we are not chastised or corrected, but rather have grown excessively, multiplying and adding sins to sins, he has changed the type and manner of punishment . . . [like a doctor changes] medicine, so that with it we may be cured of our plagues and infirmities that have been carrying us straight to eternal death. If he cured us from those with any punishment or burn of cauterization, we feel them very tenderly. And thus [we are] given and sent superfluous waters in such multitude or duration as has never been seen or heard of by those alive today, from which [we] are likewise given great damages to the people in diverse ways, which would be long to recite. . . . [Therefore] we pray, exhort, and beseech your devote, humble, and gratified prayers . . . to the Divine Majesty . . . that he give us his general grace, and especially, at present, serene weather.[57]

---

54. Genesis 6:4 (New International Version).

55. AMV, A-23, 96r–v.

56. AMV, A-23, 169v.

57. "Hauets vist molt religioses frares servidors elets de deu e nostres cars amichs com Nostre Senyor Deu qui de molt gran temps ença ha nostres peccats e delictes punits e castigats entre les altres plagues e batiments per sequetats e fretures de pluges celestials ara en aquests dies pensam que pus per aquelles nons som castigats o correguts ans hauem crescut sobergament multiplicats e afegits peccats a peccats hans mudada la spe e manera de punicio. Axi com a senyor e pare mercedios qui com

This letter is far longer than any of the many other requests for prayers that the jurats sent to the monks of Portaceli. The elaborate explanation signals that the jurats themselves were aware of the novelty of their request for prayers to *stop* rain. This in turn suggests that the absence of previous references to divine punishment is not an accident of survival; the council of 1424 did consider this a new interpretation of floods. The imagery of this particular letter is, of course, tailored to the sensibilities of an audience of the professionally religious; God is here a doctor who has given up hope of curing sin through the usual means (drought) and has therefore shifted to floods as a new medicine. The claim of novelty is somewhat disingenuous, as there had been a flood in the city as recently as 1413.[58] Nonetheless, this letter would seem to signal a new set of practices in response to floods. The 1420s were more generally a period of innovation in the Valencian council's religious responses to natural disaster (see chapter 4), so this timing is perhaps not surprising.

New religious practices around floods took some time to develop. Neither the main series of council acts (Manuals de Consells) nor the letters (Lletres Missives) survive for 1427, the year of the most severe flood of the fifteenth century. The account book (Claveria Comuna) entries for this flood, however, include a notation of expenses for constructing a stage in front of the Convent of Sant Francesc, "in which the Reverend Friar Matheu preached."[59] Complete Manuals de Consells do survive for 1434, when another "great multitude of water" broke the Mislata diversion dam, and there is no indication that the council used religious language or organized religious rituals related to this flood. The first recorded rogation procession for a rain or flood event did not occur until 1453. In January of that year the council declared a rogation procession "that God give good weather and that the waters cease."[60] It declared another in June asking for "good weather and sun, that the people may gather in their goods."[61] Another

---

nos degues tolre e delir de la faç de la terra nos muda la specie e manera de medicina ab la qual siam guarits de les plagues e infirmitats nostres les quals nos portariem prestament a la eternal mort. Si de aquelles nons curava ab alguna punicio o ardor de cautori los qual sentim molt tendrament. Ans donch ara donats e trameses perfluuis daygues en tanta multitud o duracio quanta no han vist o sentit los que huy viven dels quals a nostres vejares son donats grans dans a les gents en diverses maneres longues de recitar. . . . A vosaltres . . . pregam exortam e obsecram que ab vostres devotes humils e gratifique oracions preguets orets e suppliquets a la magestat divinal al nostre benigne salvador e redemptor Jehu Xrist al spirit sant donador de gracies que . . . donan nos la sua general gracia e spalment a present serenetat de temps." AMV, g3-17, 82r–83r.

58. AMV, g3-12, 62v.

59. "En cost e fayço de man de .i. cadafal qui fon fet denant la esgleya del Monestir de Frares Menors de la dita Ciutat en la qual preycava lo reverent Frare Matheu." AMV, O-10, 208v.

60. "Per captar gracia & misericordia de Nostre Senyor Deu migancant la dita gloriosa mare sua que us vulla dar bon temps & les aygues cessen." AMV, A-35, 235r.

61. "Per captar gracia de Nostre Senyor Deu que . . . nos vulla donar bon temps & sere en manera que les gents puxen recollir lurs bens." AMV, A-35, 283v.

procession for the cessation of rain was declared in February 1462, and three more in December 1475 and January 1476. After the flood of 1517 the council organized a procession to the Church of Sant Tomás, entreating God to give them "clear and consistent weather and take away the misfortune that, for our sins, his divine Majesty has willed and permitted to be given to this city and realm through the destruction of houses that is currently taking place."[62] This does not add up to very many processions compared to the number for drought and plague, but it is enough of a pattern to suggest that the custom had changed. By the second half of the fifteenth century, rains received a religious response from the council, but material responses did not disappear. In 1487 the council denied permission to close part of a moat because it was needed in times of rain.[63] In 1517 it busily organized imports of flour and repairs on the broken mills and dams; it paid men to clean mud, water, and trash out of the moat and other places and ordered all those who could work to assist in the effort. Those "vagabonds and idlers [who] because they do not wish to work, go secretly to . . . hostels and taverns" were to be fined and banished from the city.[64] The introduction of religious ritual alongside such measures was a significant novelty.

Why did it take the council so long to adopt the use of religious ritual for floods, and why did it finally embrace flood ritual in the latter half of the fifteenth century? The second of these questions is more easily answered than the first. By 1453 rogation processions for droughts and plagues had become regular features of the city's ritual life. The flood and rain processions, identical in form, probably emerged by analogy. In the fourteenth and early fifteenth centuries processions were not common for any type of natural disaster, and it did not occur to the council to organize them during floods. Once processions became the go-to crisis responses for droughts and plagues from the 1420s on, it would have seemed more logical to use processions for floods as well.

Even before drought and plague processions were common, however, the council still framed these other disasters in a religious context. Why did it not do so with floods in the fourteenth and early fifteenth centuries? One possible explanation is practical: floods in Valencia happen quite suddenly and end fairly quickly, and conditions in the street are perilous while they are going on. While

---

62. "Temps clar y congruent ens vulla levar lo infortuni que per nostres peccats la sua divina Magestat ha volgut e permes donar a aquesta ciutat y regne per lo derrocament de cases que sta per acaure." AMV, A-57, 858v–859r.

63. AMV, A-44, 343v–344r.

64. "Vagabunts y gallossos per no voler fer fahena se van amagadament per . . . hostals y tavernes." AMV, A-57, 550r, 856r–859r.

droughts and plagues went on for days or weeks, many floods must have begun and ended before a procession could have been organized. The jurats may have been reluctant to call citizens into the streets during a crisis situation. According to Miralles, during the first three days of rain in November 1475 "the waters . . . did not cease, the people could not go out of their houses, the provisions began to run short."[65] This is probably part of the story, but it cannot be all of it. As Miralles himself notes, the council did actually organize a rogation procession on December 9, 1475, while the rains were still ongoing.[66] It also organized two further processions of thanksgiving in January 1476, once the rain had finally lessened.[67] It was by no means impossible, therefore, for the council to organize processions for floods if it wished to do so. Even if a procession during a flood seemed inadvisable, it could have held processions of thanksgiving after the waters subsided, as the council of 1397 did on the one-year anniversary of the earthquake of 1396.[68] Nor would such practical considerations have prevented the council from using religious language to describe floods, which, as we have seen, it did not tend to do. Thus, while rogation processions might not have been an obvious fit for flood emergencies, this cannot on its own explain the material focus of fourteenth- and early fifteenth-century flood response.

Another possibility is that floods on the Valencian landscape did not, in the eyes of the councilmen, look very much like the biblical flood. In 1475 Miralles described the dry or mostly dry water channels around the city filling up: "Fountains in the houses that had dried up ran with water, wells overflowed and ran in the streets."[69] In a landscape like Valencia's, crisscrossed with water

---

65. "E, continuant no sesar les aygües e grans pluges, les gents no podien exir de lus cases, los viures començaren a man[quar]." Miralles, *Crònica i dietari*, 4:781, p. 438.

66. Miralles, *Crònica i dietari*, 4:783, p. 439.

67. One was held on January 13, the other on January 31. AMV, A-40, 245v–246r, 247r–v. The council documents describe both as processions of thanksgiving for the cessation of the rain, but Miralles's chronicle states that the rain continued until February 1. Miralles, *Crònica i dietari*, 4:785, p. 440.

68. This earthquake, which occurred on December 12, 1396, was the only earthquake recorded in the city of Valencia during the medieval period. According to the procession announcement, "by the grace of God and by the intercession of his sacred mother [the city] was preserved from damage of the earthquake . . . [which] in other places in the kingdom caused the destruction of buildings and other damages, and although in the city the earthquake was very strong but by the grace of God there were no building collapses or other damage" (Per gracia de Deu & per intercessio de la sua sagrada mare fo preservada de dan del terratremol qui en la dita festa & any terriblement fo en la dita Ciutat e mes o major en altres partides del Regne daquella en les quals per occasio del dit terratremol se seguiren derrocaments dalcuns edificis & altres dans & be que en la dita Ciutat fos lo dit terratremol fos assats fort pero per gracia de deu no sen segui tal derrocament ne altre dan). AMV, A-21, 155r. Miralles's account notes that a number of buildings did in fact collapse in the city in aftermath of this quake. Miralles, *Crònica i dietari*, 3:35, p. 153.

69. "Manaven e brolaven fonts en les cases, que avien asgotar, los pous venir a sobrexir e escórer en les careres." Miralles, *Crònica i dietari*, 4:781, p. 438.

channels both natural and constructed, perhaps floods did look like nothing so much as overflowing canals. Perhaps the relationship between floods and the city's hydraulic infrastructure was so inescapable that floods did appear to manifest as problems with that infrastructure—as blocked sewers writ large. Unpredictable and destructive as floods could be, council documents consistently stress the necessity of flood preparation. As long as the system was working properly, the damage would not be severe. In such a context, the language and rituals of divine punishment would have had very little place.

Scholars writing on flood-prone premodern societies in a variety of regions have noted that such societies did not always see floods as catastrophic aberrations.[70] While there are many instances of premodern floods being seen as signs of divine anger or the consequences of human sin, there are just as many where flooding was seen as routine, with no deeper theological significance. Roman writers interpreted floods as portents or signs of the gods' anger at human beings, but Roman infrastructure incorporated flooding as a natural feature; the Tiber River had two levels of docks to accommodate different water levels.[71] Gregory of Tours described rivers as charged with religious significance, but also spaces of "routine risk."[72] In the early modern Low Countries, private observers likewise treated coastal flooding as routine, with no deeper theological significance, while the popular press took a more apocalyptic tone.[73] Interpretations of flooding, in other words, were highly context-dependent in the premodern period, varying not only according to the objectives of the author but also according to the time and place involved.

In Valencia the councilmen looked first to the landscape, and only then to the Bible, to formulate their response to floods. As we have seen already with droughts and plagues, religious interpretations of natural disaster do not necessarily crowd out material ones. Floods in Valencia show further that the council did not necessarily require a religious element to its natural disaster response, for either spiritual or political reasons. Although, as ever, the council's voice would not have been the only one speaking on natural disasters in late medieval Valencia, it is nonetheless significant that such a powerful voice relied on a purely material interpretation of floods for so many years.

70. Petra J. E. M. van Dam, "An Amphibious Culture: Coping with Floods in the Netherlands," in *Local Places, Global Processes: Histories of Environmental Change in Britain and Beyond*, ed. Peter Coates, David Moon, and Paul Warde (Oxford: Oxbow Books, 2017), 78–93; Candiani, *Dreaming of Dry Land*; Husain, "In the Bellies of the Marshes."
71. Aldrete, *Floods of the Tiber*, 219–221; Squatriti, "The Floods of 589," 824.
72. Ellen Arnold, "Rivers of Risk and Redemption in Gregory of Tours' Writings," *Speculum* 92, no. 1 (2017): 117–143.
73. Raingard Esser, "Fear of Water and Floods in the Low Countries," in *Fear in Early Modern Society*, ed. William G. Naphy and Penny Roberts (Manchester, UK: Manchester University Press, 1997), 66.

A "Multitude of Locusts"

Like floods, locust swarms are sudden, unpredictable natural disasters vividly described in famous passages of the Old Testament. Valencian historian Agustín Rubio Vela has asserted that the association between locusts and divine punishment was clear to all medieval observers.[74] In fact, the reality in Valencia was more complicated. While the biblical associations of locust swarms were inescapable—perhaps even more so than for floods—the Valencian council documents are strikingly ambivalent about the insects' connection with divine power. Valencians seem to have been reluctant to believe that "the evil locust" was in fact an instrument of God.

In Valencia, locusts were among the rarest of natural disasters to appear in the records.[75] The first documented swarm arrived in the spring of 1358 and returned in the spring of 1359. The next swarm appeared in the first decade of the fifteenth century. Miralles records that 1407 was known as the year of the locust (any del llagosta), but Rubio Vela is skeptical given that there is no trace whatsoever in the Valencian council records.[76] Locusts definitely appeared in 1408, and again in the spring of 1409. In 1459, after the creatures were spotted elsewhere in the region, the council organized a procession asking God to spare them.[77] These prayers were answered; locusts do not appear in the records again during the period under consideration. Late medieval Valencia thus suffered two independent outbreaks of locusts, each of which produced at least one secondary outbreak the following year, and one threatened outbreak that never materialized. In comparison to other times and places, medieval Valencians were fortunate; William Christian's study of sixteenth-century Castile shows that locusts were the third most common environmental problem for which villages made religious vows, ranking ahead of drought and behind only plagues and disease of the vines.[78] In the modern period, too, locust outbreaks have been far more common in the Iberian interior (particularly the Meseta Central) than in coastal areas like Valencia.[79] This very infrequency, however, must have made the outbreaks that did occur

---

74. Agustín Rubio Vela, "Presencia de la langosta: Plagas en la Valencia," *Saitabi* 47 (1997): 275.

75. Earthquakes and fires were rarer still, with only one instance each during the late medieval period.

76. Rubio Vela, "Presencia de la langosta," 273.

77. All documents relating to locusts in fourteenth- and fifteenth- century Valencia are reproduced in Rubio Vela, "Presencia de la langosta."

78. Christian, *Local Religion*, 28.

79. P. Aragón, M. M. Coca-Abia, V. Llorente, and J. M. Lobo, "Estimation of Climatic Favourable Areas for Locust Outbreaks in Spain: Integrating Species' Presence Records and Spatial Information on Outbreaks," *Journal of Applied Entomology* 137 (2013): 616.

disturbing to observers. Unlike for floods or droughts, Valencia had little or no infrastructure in place to deal with locust swarms.

What was this "multitude of locusts"?[80] *Locust* is the term not for a species or set of species but for the swarming phase of certain types of grasshoppers. Under certain conditions these grasshoppers undergo physical and behavioral changes; the juveniles begin to aggregate in bands, while the winged adults begin to swarm. No longer requiring camouflage, they become more brightly colored. Their metabolism also speeds up; they begin to eat voraciously, and the swarm will travel long distances in search of food.[81] The conditions and processes associated with this phase change are still only partially understood. Precipitation seems to be a crucial factor, but also a complex one; both higher and lower rainfall might encourage swarming at different phases in the grasshoppers' life cycles.[82] In some cases it has been shown that human landscape disruptions—overgrazing or leaving fields fallow—can provide habitat that encourages a shift to gregarious behavior.[83]

The shift to the swarming phase can take place within several hours, and the swarm itself can last several months. The distance that the swarm travels depends on the species; some move regionally, while others cross continents. The size of the swarm also varies by species and by local conditions. The largest locust swarm ever recorded in the Old World, in Kenya in 1954, covered almost two hundred square kilometers—greater than the area of the entire Valencian horta.[84] There might be a billion individuals in such a swarm, each eating roughly its own body weight every twenty-four hours.[85] In Valencia in 1358 it was reported that the locusts "were consuming the grains (*blats*) and the vines of the horta."[86] Locusts are polyphagous, and will eat almost all

80. "Moltitut dels lagosts" AV A-13 Mano 2 58r.

81. P. A. Stevenson, "The Key to Pandora's Box," *Science* 323 (2009): 594–595.

82. Xianhui Wang and Le Kang, "Molecular Mechanisms of Phase Change in Locusts," *Annual Review of Entomology* 59 (2014): 225–244.

83. Alexandre V. Latchininsky, "Moroccan Locust Dociostaurus maroccanus (Thunberg, 1815): A Faunistic Rarity or an Important Economic Pest?," *Journal of Insect Conservation* 2, no. 3 (1998): 170–171; Arianne J. Cease, James J. Elser, Eli P. Fenichel, and Joleen C. Hadrich, "Living with Locusts: Connecting Soil Nitrogen, Locust Outbreaks, Livelihoods, and Livestock Markets," *BioScience* 65, no. 6 (2015): 551–558.

84. Jeffrey A. Lockwood, *Locust: The Devastating Rise and Mysterious Disappearance of the Insect that Shaped the American Frontier* (New York: Basic Books, 2004), 20.

85. Richard C. Hoffman, "Bugs, Beasts, and Business: Some Everyday and Long-Term Interactions between Biology and Economy in Preindustrial Europe," in *Le interazioni fra economia e ambiente biologico nell'Europa preindustriale secc. XIII–XVIII / Economic and Biological Interactions in Pre-industrial Europe from the 13th to the 18th Centuries. Atti delle "Quarantunesima Settimana di Studi," 26–30 aprile 2009,* ed. Simonetta Cavaciocchi (Florence: Firenze University Press, 2010), 145.

86. "La multitut o pestilencia dels lagosts los quals son en la orta e terma de Valencia consuma-ven los blats & vines dels dit orta." AMV, A-13, Mano 2, 65v.

cereal and garden crops cultivated by humans, including fruit and olive trees, roots, and pulses.[87] Settlers in the American West during the locust plagues of the late nineteenth century reported that Rocky Mountain locusts devoured not only crops and vegetation but also dead animals, window blinds, and the wooden handles of tools.[88]

After mating, the adults deposit pods of eggs into the ground. The next generation matures below ground during the summer, hibernates through the winter, and then erupts from the ground in the spring. The Valencian council described in 1409 how the locusts "began to break out and issue from the earth."[89] These juveniles again form bands, and, as their wings are not yet developed, march across the land, devouring whatever vegetation they encounter. Some early modern and modern authorities considered this a crucial window of opportunity for killing the creatures "before they grow the wings that they need to fly and destroy the fields."[90] After five successive molts, the locusts are mature, and the swarm takes to the air once again.

There are about twenty species of locust worldwide, unrelated to one another apart from the tendency to swarm.[91] Their ranges overlap, but their behaviors differ; identifying the species involved is both necessary for precision and almost impossible for medieval outbreaks. Richard Hoffman assumes that the locusts in medieval European records were *Schistocerca gregaria*, or the desert locust, arriving in Europe from the "steppe and semi-arid zones" on its periphery. This species of locust is known for traveling long distances, and has been responsible for several well-reported outbreaks. Migratory swarms often lay eggs that produce local swarms for one or two years following.[92] But *Schistocerca gregaria* is far from the only candidate for medieval Valencian swarms. Migratory locusts, *Locusta migratoria*, also appeared in Europe regularly during the premodern period.[93] At least eight species of locusts are currently found in Spain, the most destructive of which is the Moroccan locust,

87. Latchininsky, "Moroccan Locust," 169.

88. Lockwood, *Locust*, 12.

89. "Comencava brollar e exir de la terra." AMV, A-24, 75v–76r.

90. Archivo General de Centro América, a1.2.5-1772-25239, 1772, 3, quoted in Few, "Killing Locusts," 75. See also the practices promoted by early twentieth-century Ottoman authorities in Samuel Dolbee, "The Locust and the Starling: People, Insects, and Disease in the Late Ottoman Jazira and after, 1860–1940" (PhD diss., New York University, 2017), 63.

91. Cease et al., "Living with Locusts," 553.

92. Hoffman, "Bugs, Beasts and Business," 145. For the outbreaks of desert locusts in the late 1980s and 2004, see Sheila Rule, "Drought Easing, Africa Has New Enemy: Locusts," *New York Times*, August 7, 1986, https://www.nytimes.com/1986/08/07/world/drought-easing-africa-has-new-enemy-locusts.html; and Craig S. Smith, "Rain on Sahara's Fringe is Lovely Weather for Locusts," *New York Times*, July 21, 2004, http://www.nytimes.com/2004/07/21/international/africa/21locu.html.

93. Sprenger, "An Ocean of Locusts," 525; Cease et al., "Living with Locusts," 553.

Dociostaurus maroccanus, which despite its name lives throughout the Mediterranean region. The Moroccan locust does not travel as far as the desert locust; it is generally found in arid foothill zones, with the population swarming at irregular intervals to inhabit the nearby valley areas.[94] These swarm periods last one to three years before Moroccan locust populations revert to being ordinary grasshoppers.[95] Studies suggest that this species has been responsible for most of the outbreaks in Spain's later history.[96]

Medieval records do not allow for the identification of the species involved in the Valencian outbreaks. What hints they contain point in several directions. Records exist of swarms in in Catalonia in 1358 and in Cyprus in 1354, 1355, and 1409–12.[97] Outbreaks following so shortly on one another across distances might be a coincidence, or the insects could have been desert or migratory locusts, traveling long distances across the Mediterranean. But desert locusts are one of a number of species that lay their eggs in plowed fields—a feature that often appears in the historical records. People in a wide variety of times and places have attempted to interrupt the reproductive cycle of locusts by digging up and destroying the eggs buried in their fields.[98] In early modern Germany and in the Spanish New World, pigs and other domestic animals were let onto plowed fields to graze on locust eggs.[99] No mention of either of these practices survives in the Valencian records. The species may therefore have been the Moroccan locust, which does not lay its eggs in disturbed ground, where Valencian farmers might have discovered them. The first mention in the council records of the swarm of 1358 notes that the locusts are "in the unirrigated fields [*secans*] and other [places] in the boundaries of the city and [are] doing great damage to the crops that are in the horta."[100] That they were in the *unirrigated* fields specifically suggests that they might have come from the hills, since the dry-farmed fields tended to be located in the interior.

---

94. As Dolbee, "The Locust and the Starling," 65, has noted, it is advantageous to this species when humans cultivate edible crops in these valleys.

95. Latchininsky, "Moroccan Locust," 168.

96. Aragón et al., "Estimation of Climatic Favourable Areas," 611.

97. Ronald C. Jennings, "The Locust Problems in Cyprus," *Bulletin of the School of Oriental and African Studies* 51, no. 2 (1988): 472–473; Franklin-Lyons, *Shortage and Famine*.

98. On this practice in eighth-century China, see N. Harry Rothschild, "Sovereignty, Virtue, and Disaster Management: Chief Minister Yao Chong's Proactive Handling of the Locust Plague of 715–16," *Environmental History* 17, no. 4 (2012): 799. For the nineteenth-century United States, see Lockwood, *Locust*, 11. Ottoman officials in the nineteenth-century Jazira ordered egg-laying areas of the Moroccan locust to be plowed for the sole purpose of destroying the eggs. Dolbee, "The Locust and the Starling," 76.

99. For Brandenberg, Germany, see Sprenger, "An Ocean of Locusts," 531. For colonial Guatemala, see Few, "Killing Locusts," 81.

100. "La lagosta qui era en los secans & altres termens de la dita ciutat fahia e donaua gran dampnatge als splets que son en la orta." AMV, A-13, Mano 2, 55r–v.

In 1408 the council also noted that it was sending men "to the mountains and other places" to kill the locusts.[101] These phrases suggest a species that, like the Moroccan locust, preferred uncultivated hill country. None of these observations are conclusive; the medieval Valencian records are too limited to make a truly convincing argument as to locust species.

One further detail in the documents adds a wrinkle to the timeline of the outbreaks in Valencia. As has been mentioned, Miralles claimed that 1407 was the "year of the locust." The council records for that year contain nothing to confirm this claim, and so Rubio Vela has argued that the true year of the locust was 1408, when the council reported that locusts "came out of the earth in a great multitude."[102] Contemporary council records would ordinarily be far more trustworthy than a chronicler writing decades after the event. But why, then, did the locusts come out of the earth? In the first year of an outbreak, locusts ought to have been observed coming from the air. This observation, if correct, suggests that 1408 was the second rather than the first year of the outbreak, in which a secondary reproductive cycle had been established in the Valencian horta. The phrase may, of course, have no significance, as the councilmen were city dwellers who probably did not witness the locusts hatching. If the chronology of outbreaks recorded in the records is complete, however, then few alive in 1408 would have remembered the previous secondary outbreak in 1359. They would thus have had no reason to assume that locusts came out of the earth. This phrase suggests that one way or another, the existing record of outbreaks is incomplete; either locusts did indeed arrive in Valencia in 1407 or some unrecorded outbreak in the preceding decades led the councilmen to expect locusts to emerge from the ground.

The "Evil Locust"

As was the case with droughts, plagues, and floods, the Valencian council had both material and spiritual strategies available to fight locust swarms. Unlike with other natural disasters, the council documents sometimes blended these strategies or openly vacillated between them. On March 14, 1358, as the locusts began to eat the crops of the horta, the council's first response was to organize a procession "in honor of Our Lord God and the celestial court." As was usual at this early date, the announcement gave no details about the route

---

101. "A la muntanya e a altres parts." AMV, J-35, 45v. Rubio Vela, "Presencia de la langosta," 283.

102. "La lagosta la qual exia de la terra en gran multitut." AMV A-23 fol. 304v. This document and others relating to this outbreak are reproduced in Rubio Vela, "Presencia de la langosta," 283–286.

or destination.[103] Ten days later the council proposed that other measures be taken, as "the multitude of locusts, that were in the . . . boundaries of the city of Valencia, were doing great and intolerable damage to the grains and vineyards, so much that they have consumed nearly everything."[104] On April 18 it issued a public proclamation that men would be required in crews of fifty to "collect and destroy the locust." Those who did not wish to join these crews had to pay a fine of four diners each time they were called to serve.[105] Two days later the city reimbursed En Jacme del Mas five hundred sous that he had advanced to pay "those who had gathered in locusts."[106] As other documents indicate that those who worked these crews were paid two diners apiece, five hundred sous would have funded three thousand shifts, or sixty crews of fifty men.[107] Even if multiple crews were working at once, these efforts must have begun before the proclamation on April 18—perhaps as early as the initial notice a month before. The following year the locusts appeared again in some parts of the horta, and on April 10, 1359, the council proposed that measures be taken to stop them. No record survives in this case of what those measures may have been.

When the locusts returned in 1408, the council again took measures both sacred and secular. On March 20 it declared a procession "to pray that God lift and suppress the [locust] plague" and authorized the distribution of sixty lliures in alms to the various poor boxes of the city.[108] At the same time, it once again organized fifty-man crews to go out and kill the locusts. The accounts for April 21 show a payment of nine lliures to the weaver En Pero Loppiç for seven pairs of hemp fabric sheets, "because with said sheets is the most apt manner of killing this bad thing."[109] The crews would probably have herded

---

103. "La lagosta qui era en los secans & altres termens de la dita ciutat fahia e donaua gran dampnatge als splets que son en la orta lo consell damun dit ordena & tench per be que a honor de nostre Senyor Deu & de tota la cort celestial fos feta per la dita ciutat la qual fos celebrada en & per aquella forma & lochs que als dits honrats jurats sera ben vist fahedor & que les dits coses deguessen dir & notificar per part del dit consell al senyor Bisbe de Valencia." AMV, A-13, Mano 2, 55r.-v.

104. "Item com fos proposat en lo dit consell que la moltitut dels lagosts que eren en los termens de la Ciutat de Valencia donaven gran & importable dampnatge als blats & vinys entant que tot ho consumaven." AMV, A-13, Mano 2, 58r.

105. "Lo dit consell ordena e tench per be que tot hom com request seria anas ab son cap de .L. homes a collir e destrohir la dita lagosta e aquell qui anar noy volria que pagas quatre diners per cascuna vegada que apellats hi sera." AMV, A-13, Mano 4, 65v.

106. The original reads, "aquells qui cullissen lagosta." AMV J-3, 48v. Reproduced in Rubio Vela, "Presencia de la langosta," 281.

107. AMV J-3, 55r. Reproduced in Rubio Vela, "Presencia de la langosta," 282.

108. AMV, A-23, 304v.

109. "Pagats a'N Pero Lòppiç, brunater de la dita ciutat, VIIII lliures, moneda reals, per VII parells de lançols de cànem . . . com ab los dits lançols sie pus abta manera que altra a fer matança d'aquella cosa mala." AMV J-35, 45v. Reproduced in Rubio Vela, "Presencia de la langosta," 283.

the locusts onto the sheets, and then folded or twisted them to kill the creatures inside.[110]

The following year the locusts returned, and the council again declared a two-pronged attack: crews would be sent out to kill the locusts, while within the city the rest of the population would conduct a rogation procession to the Chapel of Santa Maria de Gràcia in the Convent of Sant Agustí.[111] Medieval Valencia's last recorded brush with locusts came in April 1459, when the council issued a proclamation saying that it had "news that in a certain part of the kingdom, toward the mountains, there abounds a great multitude of locusts, which is resulting in the destruction of food supplies." It therefore declared a procession, again to the Chapel of Santa Maria de Gràcia, to "pray to the divine majesty to guard and preserve us from such a plague."[112] Apparently this worked; locusts do not appear again in the fifteenth or early sixteenth century records.

Although locusts have long been associated with famine (and fears thereof), the evidence for this association is mixed in the medieval period. In German-speaking lands in the medieval and early modern periods, Christian Rohr and Jane Sprenger have both observed that although narratives of locust damage contain vivid descriptions of the destruction of crops, the evidence suggests that the damage was limited and did not threaten subsistence.[113] Nor, as Rubio Vela notes, is there any indication that locusts in Valencia precipitated a famine. The city did import food in 1358, but that was a fairly common occurrence, and the import records contain no reference to the locust swarm. In 1359, shortly after the locusts had reappeared in the horta, the council ceased subsidizing imports because "in the land there is, thanks be to God, a great abundance of grain."[114] During the outbreak of 1408 the council ordered the wheat sold from the *almodí* (municipal storehouse) to be offered below market price in order to stave off rumors of shortage. It achieved this with the

---

110. A similar method was used (and described in more detail) in eighteenth-century Brandenburg. Sprenger, "An Ocean of Locusts," 531–532.

111. AMV, A-23, 304v. Reproduced in Rubio Vela, "Presencia de la langosta," 283. Sant Agustí was later known as an antilocust patron, but the Chapel of Santa Maria de Gràcia was such a common destination for rogation processions that it is difficult to argue for any deeper significance here. Few, "Killing Locusts," 73.

112. "Que com haien haud noua que en certa part del Regne vers les montanyes habunda gran multitut de lagosta que redunda en destruccio dels viures. E per pregar la maiestat divina nos vulla guardar & preservar de una tal plaga han delliberat ab concordia del honorable Capitol de la Seu que dema demati faren solemne & devota processo." AMV, A-36, 158r–v.

113. Rohr, "Writing a Catastrophe," 92; Sprenger, "An Ocean of Locusts," 528.

114. "E en la terra hagues merce de Deu gran habundacia de blats." AMV, A-13, Mano 2, 28v–29v; AMV, A-13, Mano 3, 69r–v.

cooperation of merchant Lluís Menargues, who brought grain from Oriola, a town in the southwest of the kingdom.[115]

Religious and material responses to locusts were intertwined in Valencia in ways that responses to other types of disasters were not. The account books reveal that after the 1358 outbreak the council received, by order of the bishop of Valencia, five hundred sous from the funds designated for the poor of Christ, "to be distributed to those who collect locusts," at the rate of two diners per person. Five hundred sous was the amount reimbursed to En Jacme del Mas, who had paid the work crews. In other words, the material response to the 1358 locust swarm was entirely funded by the church, out of its poor box. While the council funded a procession to pray that God remove the plague, the church gave alms to those who rounded up and squashed the instruments of God's punishment. In 1408 the council ordered both the distribution of alms and the organization of killing crews in a single announcement because "the jurats [and other city officials] . . . must deal with the business of said locust by whatever remedy and whatever means appear to them appropriate."[116] This combined announcement was unusual; material and religious responses to natural disaster usually moved along separate, though parallel, paths. Although both types of responses could and did occur simultaneously, the language of the records rarely highlights this fact. The records of locust swarms, by contrast, routinely mix sacred and secular.

Other documents went further still, expressing explicit uncertainty as to whether the cause of the locust swarm was natural or divine. In the 1408 account book entry for the hemp fabric, the scribe notes that the men would take the sheets "to the mountains or other places, where[ever] is necessary to kill and suppress the locust, which is in these places and others of the kingdom, *whether by the malice of the weather or the consequences of sin*" (my emphasis).[117] This type of hedging is virtually unheard of in Valencian council records. Whatever the private musings of its officials, the city government documents tended either to make declarative statements on the causes of disaster or to elide the question of causation entirely. The records contain almost

---

115. Rubio Vela, "Presencia de la langosta," 279.

116. "E que los honorables jurats, ab los advocats de la ciutat e alcuns pròmens per ells appelladors en cambra provehissen al feyt de la dita lagosta per tot aquell remey e per totes aqueles maneres que·ls paragués ésser fahedor, en via de cinquantenes e deenes o nombre de persones que isquen de la ciutat per matar aquella mala lavor." AMV, A-23, 304v. Reproduced in Rubio Vela, "Presencia de la langosta," 283.

117. "Les cinquantenes de hòmens, los quals tots jorns van a la muntanya e a altres parts on és necessari per matar e sotsmetre la lagosta, la qual és en aquestes partides e altres del regne, faent—ho la málicia del temps o exhigents peccats." AMV J-35 45v. Reproduced in Rubio Vela, "Presencia de la langosta," 283.

no expressions of doubt when one of the possibilities is divine anger at human sin. This particular record was in an account book, not a public statement, and it thus might be possible to dismiss it as the musings of an idiosyncratic notary. When locusts reappeared in the city the following spring, however, the council made this proclamation:

> Now let all hear what the honorable justice and jurats and worthy councilors of the city Valencia would have you know. That . . . the honorable council has provided for the great damage with which the republic [cosa publica] is saddled by reason of the evil locust, which issues from the earth and wastes and devours grains, vines, fruits, and harvests, by the remedy of suppressing and killing it manually. But, as this thing might be the proverbial plague, divinely permitted by faults and sins, and it may be very necessary and profitable for us to turn to God and entreat him to mercy and pardon by masses and processions and alms and devoted prayers, said justice, jurats and worthy councilors give notice that . . . tomorrow, Saturday, before Mass, a procession will be made through the city.[118]

The council was uncertain; the locust might be a natural phenomenon, but it might also be the divine consequence of sin. As a logical analysis, this is not at all out of the ordinary in medieval devotion. But this document was not mere train of thought; it was a public statement. Why was there a display of uncertainty that was otherwise entirely absent from such proclamations? Why did the council not, as with drought responses, simply announce material and spiritual responses separately, without explaining their connection?

This document's hedging indicates that the councilmen saw a conflict between their material and spiritual responses to locusts. The only reason to highlight this conflict in a proclamation would have been if they believed that it was obvious enough to require an explanation. Perhaps the experience of fighting locusts was at odds with the experience of religious ritual. The material response to locusts was to kill them, but in a spiritual sense this meant killing the instruments

---

118. "Ara ojats què us fan saber los honrables justícia e jurats e prohòmens consellers de la ciutat de València. Que, jassia per obviar e tolre lo gran dampnatge apparellat a la cosa pública per occasió de la mala lagosta, la qual hix de la terra e guaste e devora blats, vinyes e fruyts e esplets, sie estat per l'onorable consell provehit de remey de sotsmetre e matar manualment aquella. Però, com aquesta cosa pux ésser dita plaga, permesa divinalment per demèrits e peccats, e sia molt necessari e profitós recórrer-ne a Déu e placar-lo a misericòrdia e perdó per misses e processon e almoynes e oracions devotes, per tal, los dits justícia, jurats e prohòmens notifiquen que, per lo honorable capítol de la Seu de València e per los dits justícia, jurats e prohòmens, és estat del·liberat que demà, dissapte, ans de misses, serà feta processó per la ciutat." AMV A-24, 75v-76r. Reproduced in Rubio Vela, "Presencia de la langosta," 285–286.

of divine will. While locusts could be as destructive as other natural disasters, it was also possible to do violence back to them: to kill them as one cannot kill a drought or a flood. The documents use the word *matar* ("kill") repeatedly; while one might fight other disasters metaphorically, the fight against locusts was very real indeed. If the council was conflicted about fighting a heavenly swarm, it was in good company; such concerns appear throughout the history of human interaction with locusts. N. Harry Rothschild has shown how in eighth-century China the will to take pragmatic measures against locusts was in conflict with a widespread belief that the swarm was a reflection on the character of the emperor and would resolve itself if the emperor "cultivated virtue."[119] In late nineteenth-century Bukhara, locusts were similarly "heaven-sent," while in the American West at the same time settlers were divided about whether the locusts were the punishment of God or "green imps of Satan."[120] Sprenger argues that some writers in eighteenth-century Germany resolved this contradiction with the idea that locusts represented God's challenge to human ingenuity.[121]

Beyond the experiential conflict between killing and praying, Valencians may have had difficulty imagining the locusts as divine instruments rather than as evil in and of themselves. The council's use of the term *plaga* ("plague") to describe the swarm hints at the insects' biblical connection. There are twenty-six references to locusts in the Bible, but of these the council would have been most familiar with Exodus 10:3–19 and Revelation 9:1–11. The Exodus story is also retold in the book of Psalms:

He spoke, and the locusts came
grasshoppers without number
they ate up every green thing in their land
ate up the produce of their soil.[122]

In Revelation they appear less as pests than as an avenging army: "The locusts looked like horses prepared for battle. . . . They had breastplates like breastplates of iron, and the sound of their wings was like the thundering of many horses and chariots rushing into battle."[123] Perhaps on account of this, Rohr has noted that medieval chroniclers frequently described locusts using military imagery.[124]

---

119. Rothschild, "Sovereignty, Virtue, and Disaster Management," 783–812.

120. Jeanine Elif Dağyeli, "The Fight against Heaven-Sent Insects: Dealing with Locust Plagues in the Emirate of Bukhara," *Environment and History* 26, no. 1 (2020): 94–103; Lockwood, *Locust*, 35–43.

121. Sprenger, "An Ocean of Locusts," 520–521.

122. Psalms 105:34–35 (New International Version).

123. Revelation 9:7, 9 (New International Version).

124. Rohr, "Writing A Catastrophe," 92.

While Exodus and Revelation emphasize the locusts' destructive nature, in both cases the insects act as instruments of divine power. They are fearsome but not evil. Medieval Valencian documents, by contrast, consistently describe locusts using strong negative language: "this multitude or pestilence" (*multitut o pestilència*), "this bad seed" (*aquella mala llavor*), "this evil thing" (*aquella cosa mala*), and "the evil locust" (*la mala lagosta*).[125] In her examination of locust-killing campaigns in seventeenth-century Guatemala—campaigns that, as in Valencia, combined religious processions with community killing efforts—Martha Few notes that locusts there, too, were "an ambiguous species . . . on the one hand . . . a plague, and thus . . . nonhuman; and on the other hand . . . an enemy, and thus human."[126] The swarm was a powerful, destructive force of nature, but the individual insects could be fought, could be killed and, most important, could be hated.

Even Valencia's most famous son, the Dominican preacher Vicent Ferrer, may have shared this low opinion of locusts. In 1416 Ferrer gave a sermon in the city structured on the theme of the ten Plagues of Egypt, each of which represented a modern evil that signified the coming of the end times. Locusts, he said, signified hypocritical clergy, adding,

> Why? I will tell you: the locust appears to have wings to fly, but it is a beast; and behind it has legs to snatch. This is like the hypocrite: it appears that he has wings of sanctity, and he does not have them. What is more, what does he do with his legs? Snatch what he can from people. And what does *hypocrite* mean? When the clothing that he wears does not correspond with the life that he has within, like Friars Minor, Preachers, Carmelites and Canons, who go with habits of sanctity and [are] full of stench within.[127]

Ferrer's purpose here was to equate plagues to sins, but it is perhaps telling that he chooses to describe the locust as a creature that appears to be holy but is not. Ferrer was born in Valencia in 1350, meaning that he would have been old enough to remember the locusts of 1358–59. He returned to the Crown of Aragon in 1408, so he would have heard about, though not necessarily seen, that year's swarm. In the Valencian council documents the negative epithets become more frequent and more intense during the 1408–9 outbreak ("bad seed," "evil thing," and "evil locust"). These years are also when the documents

---

125. AMV A-13 Mano 4, 65v; A-23 304v; J-35 45v; A-24 75v-76r. Reproduced in Rubio Vela, "Presencia de la langosta," 281, 283, 285–286.

126. Few, "Killing Locusts," 77.

127. Vicent Ferrer, *Sermons*, vol. 2, ed. Josep Sanchis Sivera (Barcelona: Editorial Barcino, 1934), 206–207.

show overt conflict about whether or not the locusts are divine punishment. Ferrer may have been playing on an ambiguity toward locusts that already existed among his audience.

The uncertainty that the documents show about the source of locust swarms, then, has less to do with how the council understood divine causation and more to do with how it understood locusts. Swarms of locusts are unusual among natural disasters in having a face, or rather a million identical faces, on which afflicted human beings can project their frustration. Responding materially to a natural disaster was not necessarily in conflict with a spiritual interpretation of that disaster. The act of killing locusts, however, seems to have been an experience that created its own interpretation of locusts as an enemy to be fought. The council did not reject either of these interpretations; it continued to organize religious rituals and continued to send killing crews into the mountains. Nonetheless, awareness of this contradiction permeates the surviving documents.

Given the obvious biblical parallels, responses to floods and locusts ought to have been the most straightforwardly religious of any responses to natural disaster. But, in fact, they were the least. This apparent paradox has significant implications for our understanding of premodern responses to natural disaster. In the records of the Valencian government, material responses to and explanations for floods preceded religious ones by at least a century, and religious responses only became popular at the very end of the medieval period. Only for locusts, meanwhile, out of all natural disasters, did the city government express uncertainty as to whether they were divine or natural in origin. Rohr has suggested that the Bible played such a central role in shaping medieval thinking about floods and locusts that these events "'had to' be viewed as a catastrophe, even when the actual damage was [limited]."[128] The evidence from Valencia, however, demonstrates quite the opposite. This shows the extent to which premodern interpretations of natural disaster could vary across space and time; there were many "cultural environmental histories of the Middle Ages."[129] The relationship between disaster and divine causation did not always follow the expected trajectory. Just because a biblical example of a disaster existed, that does not mean that it had to be the primary lens through which medieval people viewed their world. Just because all Christians knew that floods could be God's punishment, that does not mean that all floods were interpreted in this way. Just because locusts were a famous scourge of

---

128. Rohr, "Writing a Catastrophe," 92.
129. Arnold, *Negotiating the Landscape*.

God, that does not mean that all locusts were understood as divine in origin. The biblical connotations of these disasters had always to contend with their reality on the local landscape, which could lead to quite a different framing. The experience of killing locusts was in conflict with biblical descriptions. The look of floods on the Valencian landscape likewise had little in common with the story of Noah. The effects of a more local view were not always the same; Valencians always organized rituals for locusts, but did so only late in the fifteenth century for floods. Both sets of responses reflect the particular ways that these crises were experienced on the Valencian landscape rather than a universal Christian reference point. Despite the credentials of their biblical forebears, neither Valencian floods nor Valencian locusts fit very well into the role of divine scourge.

Conclusion

In the Square of the Virgin, next to the Valencia Cathedral, stands a fountain adorned with nine nude figures. In the center reclines a bearded man, representing the river, known since the nineteenth century not as the Arabic-derived Guadalaviar but by its classical name: Túria. Around the Túria stand eight smaller female figures, each carrying a jar of flowing water, who represent the eight canals that irrigate the Valencian *horta*. The Square of the Virgin is also the meeting place of the Water Court (Tribunal de les Aigües), advertised in guidebooks as a preconquest institution though there is little evidence of its existence before the modern period.[1] This court convenes every Thursday amid a crowd of tourists. Eight men in ceremonial garb assemble outside the Apostles' Door of the cathedral and call out the names of the eight canals in turn, inviting any user of those canals with an irrigation grievance to come forward and be heard. Most Thursdays, however, these calls are met with silence. The city of Valencia has grown to cover much of the horta so that many of the canals now run beneath urban streets, safe from meddling by greedy irrigators. Although the Water Court retains legal force, it is more a celebration of heritage than a living reality.

The same could be said for the river itself. By the time the bronze Túria and his maidens were installed in the Square of the Virgin in 1976, the river

---

1. Glick, *Irrigation and Society*, 64–68.

system they represented no longer existed. After a flood in 1589, the medieval Board of Walls and Sewers (Junta de Murs i Valls) was replaced with a body known as New River Construction (Fabrica Nova del Riu), tasked with building parapets on both banks of the river to avert future inundations.[2] New canals and other projects to contain and channel the river continued throughout the early modern and modern periods. Nevertheless, floods still troubled the city, particularly after the demolition in the nineteenth century of its protective barrier of walls. The last and greatest flood came on October 14, 1957, when two successive waves of water burst the banks of the river, submerging the city center and killing at least eighty-one people.[3] In the aftermath of this disaster, the government diverted the river to an ample concrete channel running well south of the urban core. The plan, devised by local government and officially sanctioned at the national level, was to use the old course of the river as a transportation corridor, modernizing the city's rail and highway links while reducing its vulnerability to natural disaster. By the later years of the regime of Francisco Franco, opposition from local environmental activists stalled this project. After the transition to democracy the riverbed was transformed instead into a large public park, now considered one of the crowning glories of the city.[4] The constructed landscape of medieval Valencia has thus been replaced by a new construction, from which the ambitions of the Middle Ages have been effectively erased.

Long before the disappearance of the river, the social conditions that shaped medieval Valencian environmental policy had also been transformed. By the mid-sixteenth century the Christian purity of the city had gone from aspiration to fait accompli. The Spanish Inquisition set up shop in Valencia in 1481, focusing its efforts on the city's conversos and their contacts with the Jews of neighboring Morvedre.[5] Prosecutions continued even after the expulsion of those Jews in 1492. The city's Muslim quarter had begun to empty after the assault of 1455, and rioters forcibly converted the final twenty families during the Revolt of the Brotherhoods (Germanies) in 1521.[6] By the later sixteenth century, Valencia was the base of operations for Archbishop Juan de Ribera's

2. Melió, La "Junta de Murs i Valls," 13–14.

3. C. Puertes and F. Francés, "La riada de Valencia de 1957: Reconstrucción hidrológica y sedimentológica y análisis comparativo con la situación actual," Ingeniería del agua 20, no. 4 (2016): 182.

4. Francisco Pérez Puche, Hasta aquí llegó la riada (Valencia: Ajuntament de Valencia, 2007). On Valencian environmental activism in the twentieth century, see Sarah R. Hamilton, Cultivating Nature: The Conservation of a Valencian Working Landscape (Seattle: University of Washington Press, 2018).

5. Meyerson, A Jewish Renaissance, 228–239.

6. Hinojosa Montalvo, Una ciutat gran i populosa, 169; Isabelle Poutrin, "La conversion des musulmans de Valence (1521–1525) et la doctrine de l'église sur les baptêmes forcés," Revue historique 648, no. 4 (2008): 819–855; Meyerson, The Muslims of Valencia, 89–90, 272.

efforts to fully Christianize these converts, and the port from which many of them were expelled from Spain in 1609.[7] Early modern Valencia was thus a more completely Christian city than medieval Valencia had been. It was also less autonomous and less significant. The processes of royal centralization that had begun with the Trastámara dynasty and intensified under the Catholic Monarchs continued under their successors. The urban government of early modern Valencia could only dream of the latitude afforded to its medieval predecessors; it marched increasingly in lockstep with the will of the expanding state.[8] As this state derived its wealth from its overseas empire, Mediterranean ports like Valencia lost ground to Atlantic ones—particularly Seville. In retrospect it became clear that the prosperity and political significance that Valencia enjoyed during the fifteenth century had in fact constituted its golden age.

Although few traces remain today of the landscape and society of medieval Valencia, the issues that its government faced continue to confront municipal governments around the world. In our era of accelerating climate change and global pandemics, natural disasters strike with increasing frequency. City governments are key responders to such disasters, so each such disaster forces a city government to choose how it will respond. Like the jurats and council (*consell*) of Valencia, modern city governments possess an array of possible responses, from the technological to the ritual. They may choose to focus on recovery or to initiate infrastructure to prevent future disasters. They may emphasize community unity or call out misbehavior that contributed to the crisis. As this book has shown, none of these strategies is new. The ability to respond materially to natural disaster, over both the short and long term, is by no means a modern phenomenon. A sense of collective responsibility for natural disaster long precedes awareness of anthropogenic climate change. Scapegoating marginalized groups, meanwhile, is at least as much a feature of modern plagues as medieval ones. Whatever strategies they employ, cities continue to choose their responses as Valencia did: according to their (often shifting) governing priorities for the places that they rule.

To argue that medieval people made choices with regard to their environments is thus to argue that "modern" patterns of environmental rule and response are quite old indeed. Governmental efforts to reshape landscapes do not all owe their genesis to the emergence of capitalism, modern technology, or the modern state. All of these transformed European relationships with the

---

7. Benjamin Ehler, *Between Christians and Moriscos: Juan de Ribera and Religious Reform in Valencia, 1568–1614* (Baltimore: Johns Hopkins University Press, 2006).

8. On the increasing power of the Crown over Valencian affairs in general during the reign of the Catholic monarchs, see Belenguer Cebrià, *Fernando el Católico*. On the authority of the early modern Spanish state over environmental matters, see Wing, *Roots of Empire*.

natural world in scale and degree, but not necessarily in kind. There was no premodern European Eden in which technological limits or pious terror enforced harmony with the natural world, and thus no fall to be sought in the early modern period.

It is not enough, however, to assert that medieval people used material means to reshape their landscapes and respond to natural disaster. This book has also sought to show how and why the government of Valencia did so, and how those approaches interacted with an (equally rational) deployment of religious language and rituals. The particular history of municipal environmental policy in Valencia was of course the result of particular local dynamics. The long and robust tradition of human intervention in the environment was in some respects a legacy of the Andalusi period and in others a product of colonization. The intense emphasis that the council placed on the city's Christian identity can likewise be traced to the conquest, colonization, and the city's religious makeup. These histories were not unique to Valencia, but they are in some respects characteristic of the cities of southeastern Spain. Nor are they, on their own, determinative; different local circumstances in other nearby cities may have led to a very different history of environmental intervention. The field of medieval Iberian environmental history is in its infancy; more research is required to say with certainty how Valencia was typical of late medieval Iberian cities (or indeed late medieval cities generally) and how it was not.

But the particularity of the Valencian case is part of the point. The city councilmen were not reading their landscape through either faith or fear so much as through the lens of their own local preoccupations. The decisions that the council made in the Valencian environment were the result of the aspirations of their offices, of the religious contradictions in Valencian society, and of the characteristics of the landscape itself. The first four chapters of this book showed how the council's decision making changed over time, according to the council's governing priorities. The final three showed how, despite those priorities, the councilmen were able to perceive the specific characteristics of different natural disasters and tailor their responses accordingly. On the one hand, medieval environmental history can and should be integrated into medieval social and cultural history; the shifting priorities of the Valencian council in the landscape dovetailed with the perceived exigencies of interfaith coexistence (*convivencia*) and colonization. On the other hand, the environment was not only a mirror for other concerns; the different characteristics of drought, plague, flood, and locust swarms also shaped different municipal responses. While the details here are specific to Valencia, to Iberia, and to the Middle Ages, the larger point is not: as a governing choice, a ritual is no more or less practical than a construction project. Both rituals and construction projects, moreover, can emerge from a full understanding of environmental, cultural, and social reality.

Governments have long had choices about how to shape their environments. Those choices have always been complicated, in ways that reflect the societies they rule. This book has sought to paint a nuanced picture of such choices in an age of natural disasters. Following the Dominican preacher Vicent Ferrer's lead, it has been a family portrait: divinity, environment, and government as a distant father, an enslaved woman, and a group of enterprising offspring. For the Valencian council, governance of the environment entangled the ritualistic and the practical and overlaid cultural considerations with logistical concerns. The medieval Valencian environment has vanished, but many of these entanglements remain today.

APPENDIX

Rogation Processions Held for Natural Disasters in Valencia, 1300–1519

DATE OF PROCESSION	PURPOSE	DESTINATION	SECONDARY DESTINATIONS	COMMENTS	ARCHIVE LOCATION
Friday, February 28, 1343	Drought	Monastery of Sant Vicent Martir			AMV, A-4, 179r
Saturday, January 3, 1344	Drought	Monastery of Sant Vicent Martir			AMV, A-4, 283v
Friday, April 15, 1345*	Drought	Monastery of Sant Vicent Martir			AMV, A-4, 470v
Friday, January 22, 1356 (Feast of Sant Vicent Martir)	Drought	Monastery of Sant Vicent Martir			AMV, A-12, 95r–v
Tuesday, March 14, 1357*	Locusts	None given			AMV, A-13, Mano 2, 55r–v
Friday, November 29, 1370*	Plague	None given		That the plague in Catalonia might spare Valencia	AMV, A-15, 143v–144r
Saturday, December 13, 1371 (Feast of Santa Llúcia)	Drought / plague	Monastery of Sant Vicent Martir		For relief from drought of past autumn/winter; plague in nearby places	AMV, A-16, 43v–44v
Saturday, August 14, 1372 (eve of the Feast of the Assumption)	Plague	Convent of Santa Maria del Carme			AMV, A-16, 97r; AMV, A-16, 102v–103r
Friday, February 24, 1374 (Feast of Sant Macià)	Drought	Monastery of Sant Vicent Martir			AMV, A-16, 185v–186v
Saturday, October 28, 1374	Drought / plague / famine	Monastery of Sant Vicent Martir			AMV, A-16, 230v–231r
Friday, April 6, 1375	Drought / plague	Convent of Sant Agustí (Chapel of Santa Maria de Gràcia)			AMV, A-16, 260r–v
Saturday, June 9, 1380	Unspecified adversities	Monastery of Sant Vicent Martir			AMV, A-17, 226r–v
Friday, August 24, 1380 (Feast of Sant Bartomeu)	Plague	None given			AMV, A-17, 232r
Saturday, March 8, 1382*	Drought	None given		For relief from drought of past winter / early spring	AMV, A-17, 274v

Date	Reason	Location	Notes	Reference
Saturday, November 21, 1383	Plague	Monastery of Sant Vicent Màrtir		AMV, A-18, 33r–v
Friday, March 4, 1384*	Drought / plague	None given	For the Great Schism, discord between king and corts, harvest in peril from drought, and general plague (mortaldat)	AMV, A-18, 26v–27r
Sunday, March 18, 1385	Drought	Places outside the city		AMV, A-18, 80r–v
Tuesday, June 1, 1395	Plague	Convent of Sant Agustí (Chapel of Santa Maria de Gràcia)		AMV, A-20, 230v
Sunday, July 11, 1395	Plague	Convent of Sant Domènec (Chapel of Santa Maria de la Misericordia)		AMV, A-20, 241v–242r
Tuesday, December 18, 1397 (Feast of the Expectation of the Virgin)	Earthquake	Convent of Sant Agustí (Chapel of Santa Maria de Gràcia)	One year after earthquake	AMV, A-21, 155r
Sunday, July 30, 1402	Drought	Convent of Sant Agustí (Chapel of Santa Maria de Gràcia)		AMV, A-22, 204r–v
Tuesday, March 20, 1408*	Locusts	None given		AMV, A-23, 304v
Saturday, March 9, 1409	Locusts	Convent of Sant Agustí (Chapel of Santa Maria de Gràcia)		AMV, A-24, 75v–76r
Friday, June 22, 1414	Plague	Convent of Sant Agustí (Chapel of Santa Maria de Gràcia)		AMV, A-25, 381r–v
Wednesday, December 11, 1420	Plague	Convent of Sant Domènec (Chapel of Santa Maria de la Misericordia)		AMV, A-27, 267v
Monday, April 28, 1421 (Rogation Days)	Plague	None given	One of three	AMV, A-27, 292r–v
Tuesday, April 29, 1421 (Rogation Days)	Plague	None given	Two of three	AMV, A-27, 292r–v

(continued)

DATE OF PROCESSION	PURPOSE	DESTINATION	SECONDARY DESTINATIONS	COMMENTS	ARCHIVE LOCATION
Wednesday, April 30, 1421 (Rogation Days)	Plague	None given		Three of three	AMV, A-27, 292r–v
Wednesday, August 20, 1421	Drought / plague / thanksgiving	Monastery of Sant Vicent Martir			AMV, A-27, 327r–v
Sunday, June 21, 1422	Plague	Convent of Sant Agustí (Chapel of Santa Maria de Gràcia)			AMV, A-27, 385v
Thursday, December 21, 1424 (Feast of Sant Tomàs)	Drought	Convent of Santa Maria del Carme			AMV, A-28, 104r–104v
Wednesday, October 6, 1428	Plague	Convent of Sant Agustí (Chapel of Santa Maria de Gràcia)			AMV, A-29, Mano 1 36v–37r
Friday, October 15, 1428	Plague	Convent of Sant Domènec (Chapel of Santa Maria de la Misericòrdia)			AMV, A-29, Mano 1 37r–38v
Friday, October 22, 1428	Plague	Convent of Sant Francesc		Weekly processions for plague	AMV, A-29, Mano 1 38v–39r
Thursday, October 28, 1428 (Feast of Sants Simó and Judes)	Plague	Monastery of Sant Vicent Martir		Weekly processions for plague	AMV, A-29, Mano 1 43r–v
Friday, November 12, 1428	Plague	Church of Sant Joan of the Market		Weekly processions for plague	AMV, A-29, Mano 1 41v
Friday, November 19, 1428	Plague	Monastery of Santa Trinitat		Weekly processions for plague	AMV, A-29, Mano 1 42v
Friday, November 26, 1428	Plague	Church of Sant Martí		Weekly processions for plague	AMV, A-29, Mano 1 43v–44r
Friday, December 3, 1428	Plague	Convent of Santa Maria de la Mercè		Weekly processions for plague	AMV, A-29, Mano 1 44r–v

Friday, December 10, 1428	Plague	Church of Santa Caterina	Weekly processions for plague	AMV, A-29, Mano 1 45r
Friday, December 17, 1428	Plague	Church of Sant Andreu	Weekly processions for plague	AMV, A-29, Mano 1 49v–50r
Friday, December 24, 1428	Plague	Church of Sant Esteve	Weekly processions for plague	AMV, A-29, Mano 1 60v–61r
Friday, December 31, 1428	Plague	Church of Sant Tomàs	Weekly processions for plague	AMV, A-29, Mano 1 61r
Friday, January 14, 1429	Plague	Church of Sant Nicolau	Weekly processions for plague	AMV, A-29, Mano 1 61r
Friday, January 21, 1429	Plague	Church of Sant Salvador	Weekly processions for plague	AMV, A-29, Mano 1 65r–v
Friday, January 28, 1429	Plague	Church of Santa Creu	Weekly processions for plague	AMV, A-29, Mano 1 66r
Friday, February 4, 1429	Plague	Church of Sant Bartomeu	Weekly processions for plague	AMV, A-29, Mano 1 66r
Friday, February 11, 1429	Plague	Church of Sant Lorenç	Weekly processions for plague	AMV, A-29, Mano 1 66r
Friday, February 18, 1429	Plague	Church of Sant Joan of the Hospital	Weekly processions for plague	AMV, A-29, Mano 1 66v
Friday, Feburary 25, 1429	Plague	Church of Santa Maria of the Temple	Weekly processions for plague	AMV, A-29, Mano 1 66v
Friday, March 4, 1429	Plague	Church of Santa Maria de Calatrava	Weekly processions for plague	AMV, A-29, Mano 1 67r
Friday, March 11, 1429	Plague	Confraternity Church of Sant Jaume d'Uclés	Weekly processions for plague	AMV, A-29, Mano 1 67r
Friday, March 18, 1429	Plague	Confraternity Church of Santa Tecla	Weekly processions for plague	AMV, A-29, Mano 1 69v
Friday, April 1, 1429	Plague	Valencia Cathedral	Weekly processions for plague	AMV, A-29, Mano 1 70r
				AMV, A-29, Mano 1 70v

(continued)

DATE OF PROCESSION	PURPOSE	DESTINATION	SECONDARY DESTINATIONS	COMMENTS	ARCHIVE LOCATION
Friday, April 8, 1429	Plague	Convent of Santa Clara		Weekly processions for plague	AMV, A-29, Mano 1 78r
Friday, April 15, 1429	Plague	Convent of Santa Magdalena		Weekly processions for plague	AMV, A-29, Mano 1 78r
Friday, April 22, 1429	Plague	Confraternity Church of Nostra Dona de Santa Maria		Weekly processions for plague	AMV, A-29, Mano 1 80v
Friday, April 29, 1429	Plague	Convent of Sant Agustí (Chapel of Santa Maria de Gràcia)		Weekly processions for plague	AMV, A-29, Mano 1 81r
Friday, May 6, 1429	Plague	Monastery of Sant Vicent Martir		Weekly processions for plague	AMV, A-29, Mano 1 81v
Friday, May 13, 1429	Plague	Church of Sant Joan of the Market		Weekly processions for plague	AMV, A-29, Mano 1 81v
Friday, May 20, 1429	Plague	Convent of Sant Domènec		Weekly processions for plague	AMV, A-29, Mano 1 103r
Friday, June 3, 1429	Plague	Monastery of Santa Trinitat		Weekly processions for plague	AMV, A-29, Mano 1 110v
Friday, June 10, 1429	Plague	Church of Sant Martí		Weekly processions for plague	AMV, A-29, Mano 1 110v–111r
Friday, June 17, 1429	Plague	Convent of Sant Francesc		Weekly processions for plague	AMV, A-29, Mano 1 116v
Friday, July 1, 1429	Plague	Church of Sant Salvador		Weekly processions for plague	AMV, A-29, Mano 1 121v
Thursday, August 25, 1429*	Plague	Convent of Sant Domènec (Chapel of Santa Maria de la Misericordia)			AMV, A-29, Mano 1 138r
Friday, December 9, 1429*	Plague / thanksgiving	Convent of Sant Agustí (Chapel of Santa Maria de Gràcia)			AMV, A-29, Mano 1 162v

Date	Event	Location		Reference
Friday, March 2, 1431	Drought	Convent of Sant Agustí (Chapel of Santa Maria de Gràcia)		AMV, A-29, Mano 2, 101r
Wednesday, October 31, 1431	Drought	Convent of Sant Agustí (Chapel of Santa Maria de Gràcia)		AMV, A-29, Mano 2, 158r
Wednesday, November 28, 1431	Drought	Church of Sant Esteve		AMV, A-29, Mano 2, 162v
Wednesday, December 5, 1431	Drought	Convent of Santa Maria del Carme		AMV, A-29, Mano 2, 164r–v
Monday, March 17, 1432	Drought	Convent of Sant Agustí (Chapel of Santa Maria de Gràcia)		AMV, A-29, Mano 2, 186r–v
Wednesday, April 9, 1432	Drought	Church of Sant Esteve		AMV, A-29, Mano 2, 188v–189r
Monday, April 14, 1432	Drought	Convent of Santa Maria del Carme		AMV, A-29, Mano 2, 193v
Tuesday, August 26, 1432	Drought	Convent of Santa Maria del Carme		AMV, A-30, 22r
Friday, September 5, 1432	Drought / thanksgiving	Convent of Sant Agustí (Chapel of Santa Maria de Gràcia)		AMV, A-30, 23v–24r
Saturday, March 12, 1435 (Feast of Sant Gregori)	Drought	Convent of Santa Magdalena	Church of Sant Joan of the Market	AMV, A-30, 246v–247r
Wednesday, April 6, 1435	Drought	Convent of Santa Maria del Carme		AMV, A-30, 254v
Friday, November 28, 1438	Drought	Convent of Sant Agustí (Chapel of Santa Maria de Gràcia)	Convent of Santa Maria de la Mercè	AMV, A-32, Mano 1, 30v–31r
Saturday, March 21, 1439	Drought	Convent of Sant Agustí (Chapel of Santa Maria de Gràcia)	Convent of Santa Maria de la Mercè	AMV, A-32, Mano 1, 52r–v
Friday, May 22, 1439	Plague	Convent of Sant Agustí (Chapel of Santa Maria de Gràcia)		AMV, A-32, Mano 1, 65v–66r
Friday, May 29, 1439	Plague	Convent of Sant Agustí (Chapel of Santa Maria de Gràcia)		AMV, A-32, Mano 1, 74r–v

(continued)

DATE OF PROCESSION	PURPOSE	DESTINATION	SECONDARY DESTINATIONS	COMMENTS	ARCHIVE LOCATION
Thursday, June 11, 1439 (Feast of Sant Bernabeu)	Plague	Monastery of Sant Vicent Martir	Chapel of Santa Maria de Gràcia		AMV, A-32, Mano 1 79r–v
Saturday, June 20, 1439	Plague	Monastery of Santa Trinitat			AMV, A-32, Mano 1 83v
Sunday, June 28, 1439	Plague	Church of Sant Joan of the Market			AMV, A-32, Mano 1 87r–v
Sunday, July 5, 1439	Plague	Convent of Santa Maria del Carme			AMV, A-32, Mano 1 91r–v
Sunday, August 2, 1439	Plague	Convent of Sant Domènec (Chapel of Santa Maria de la Misericordia)			AMV, A-32, Mano 1 92r–v
Wednesday, August 12, 1439	Plague	Convent of Sant Francesc			AMV, A-32, Mano 1 97r–v
Monday, August 17, 1439	Plague	Church of Sant Llorenç			AMV, A-32, Mano 1 97r–v
Sunday, August 23, 1439	Plague	Convent of Sant Agustí (Chapel of Santa Maria de Gràcia)			AMV, A-32, Mano 1 101r
Sunday, September 6, 1439	Plague	Convent of Sant Agustí (Chapel of Santa Maria de Gràcia)			AMV, A-32, Mano 1 106r
Sunday, September 27, 1439	Plague / thanksgiving	Convent of Sant Agustí (Chapel of Santa Maria de Gràcia)			AMV, A-32, Mano 1 110r–110v
Thursday, August 4, 1440	Drought	Convent of Sant Agustí (Chapel of Santa Maria de Gràcia)			AMV, A-32, Mano 1 190v–191r
Saturday, May 6, 1441	Drought	Convent of Sant Domènec (Chapel of Santa Maria de la Misericordia)	Church of Sant Esteve		AMV, A-32, Mano 1 248v

Date		Location		Reference
Saturday, March 17, 1442	Drought	Convent of Sant Agustí (Chapel of Santa Maria de Gràcia)		AMV, A-32, Mano 2 45r–v
Tuesday, March 20, 1442	Drought	Convent of Sant Domènec (Chapel of Santa Maria de la Misericordia)		AMV, A-32, Mano 2 45v–46r
Friday, March 23, 1442	Drought	Convent of Santa Maria del Carme		AMV, A-32, Mano 2 46r–v
Thursday, April 5, 1442	Drought	Monastery of Sant Vicent Màrtir		AMV, A-32, Mano 2 46v–47r
Saturday, April 7, 1442	Drought	Church of Sant Joan of the Market		AMV, A-32, Mano 2 47r–v
Tuesday, April 17, 1442	Drought / thanksgiving	Convent of Sant Agustí (Chapel of Santa Maria de Gràcia)		AMV, A-32, Mano 2 49v; AMV, A-32, Mano 2 124r–v
Wednesday, May 1, 1443 (Feast of Sants Felip and Jaume)	Drought	Monastery of Sant Vicent Màrtir		AMV, A-32, Mano 2 124v–125r
Saturday, August 3, 1443	Drought	Convent of Sant Agustí (Chapel of Santa Maria de Gràcia)		AMV, A-32, Mano 2 152r
Saturday, August 10, 1443	Drought	Convent of Sant Domènec (Chapel of Santa Maria de la Misericordia)		AMV, A-32, Mano 2 152v
Saturday, April 25, 1444 (Feast of Sant Marc)	Drought	Convent of Sant Agustí (Chapel of Santa Maria de Gràcia)		AMV, A-32, Mano 2 198v
Wednesday, April 29, 1444	Drought	Church of Sant Nicolau	Church of Sant Bartomeu	AMV, A-32, Mano 2 200r–v
Friday May 1, 1444	Drought	Monastery of Sant Vicent Màrtir		AMV, A-32, Mano 2 200r–v; 201r–v
Friday, July 10, 1444 (Feast of Sant Cristòfol)	Drought	Convent of Santa Maria del Carme		AMV, A-33, 16r–v

(continued)

DATE OF PROCESSION	PURPOSE	DESTINATION	SECONDARY DESTINATIONS	COMMENTS	ARCHIVE LOCATION
Saturday, July 18, 1444	Drought	Convent of Sant Agustí (Chapel of Santa Maria de Gràcia)			AMV, A-33, 17r–v
Tuesday, July 28, 1444	Drought	Convent of Sant Domènec (Chapel of Santa Maria de la Misericòrdia)			AMV, A-33, 18r–v
Friday, July 31, 1444	Drought	Church of Sant Joan of the Market			AMV, A-33, 19r–v
Saturday, March 6, 1445	Drought	Convent of Sant Domènec (Chapel of Santa Maria de la Misericòrdia)			AMV, A-33, 81v–82r
Monday, March 22, 1445	Drought	Convent of Sant Agustí (Chapel of Santa Maria de Gràcia)			AMV, A-33, 83v–84r
Tuesday, March 30, 1445	Drought	Monastery of Sant Vicent Màrtir			AMV, A-33, 84r–v
Friday, April 2, 1445	Drought	Convent of Santa Maria del Carme			AMV, A-33, 85r
Friday, August 20, 1445	Drought	Convent of Sant Agustí (Chapel of Santa Maria de Gràcia)			AMV, A-33, 133v–134r
Wednesday, February 16, 1446	Drought	Convent of Sant Agustí (Chapel of Santa Maria de Gràcia)			AMV, A-33, 172v–173r
Monday, March 7, 1446	Drought	Convent of Sant Domènec (Chapel of Santa Maria de la Misericòrdia)			AMV, A-33, 175v–176r
Friday, March 11, 1446	Drought	Monastery of Sant Vicent Màrtir			AMV, A-33, 178v–179r
Wednesday, March 16, 1446	Drought	Convent of Santa Maria del Carme			AMV, A-33, 180r
Monday, January 9, 1447	Drought	Convent of Sant Agustí (Chapel of Santa Maria de Gràcia)			AMV, A-33, 260r–v

Date	Reason	Location	Notes	Reference
Tuesday, March 28, 1447	Fire / thanksgiving	Convent of Sant Agustí (Chapel of Santa Maria de Gràcia)		AMV, A-33, 277r–v
Tuesday, August 8, 1447	Drought	Monastery of Sant Vicent Martir		AMV, A-34, 17r–v
Saturday, December 2, 1447	Drought	Convent of Sant Agustí (Chapel of Santa Maria de Gràcia)	Convent of Santa Maria de la Mercè	AMV, A-34, 37v–38r
Friday, October 18, 1448	Drought	Convent of Sant Agustí (Chapel of Santa Maria de Gràcia)		AMV, A-34, 139r–v
Wednesday, October 30, 1448	Drought	Convent of Sant Domènec (Chapel of Santa Maria de la Misericordia)		AMV, A-34, 140r–v
Sunday, November 3, 1448	Drought	Convent of Santa Maria del Carme		AMV, A-34, 141v–142r
Monday, November 18, 1448	Drought	Places outside the city		AMV, A-34, 144v–145r
Sunday, November 24, 1448	Drought	Monastery of Santa Trinitat		AMV, A-34, 145r–v
Wednesday, March 5, 1449	Drought	Convent of Sant Agustí (Chapel of Santa Maria de Gràcia)		AMV, A-34, 169v
Friday, March 7, 1449	Drought	Convent of Sant Domènec (Chapel of Santa Maria de la Misericordia)		AMV, A-34, 170r–v
Wednesday, March 12, 1449	Drought	Monastery of Santa Trinitat		AMV, A-34, 173r–v
Friday, March 14, 1449	Drought	Convent of Santa Maria del Carme		AMV, A-34, 174r–v
Saturday, March 15 1449*	Drought	Places outside the city	Second procession to accompany this one to the city gate	AMV, A-34, 175r–v
Saturday, March 15, 1449	Drought	Monastery of Sant Vicent Martir		AMV, A-34, 175r–v
Monday, March 31, 1449	Drought	Convent of Sant Agustí (Chapel of Santa Maria de Gràcia)		AMV, A-34, 178v–179r

(continued)

DATE OF PROCESSION	PURPOSE	DESTINATION	SECONDARY DESTINATIONS	COMMENTS	ARCHIVE LOCATION
Saturday, April 5, 1449	Drought	Convent of Sant Domènec (Chapel of Santa Maria de la Misericòrdia)			AMV, A-34, 179v–180r
Monday, April 7, 1449	Drought	Church of Sant Joan of the Market			AMV, A-34, 180v
Tuesday, April 15, 1449	Drought	Monastery of Santa Trinitat			AMV, A-34, 181r
Saturday, May 16, 1450	Plague	Convent of Sant Agustí (Chapel of Santa Maria de Gràcia)			AMV, A-34, 295r–v
Monday, May 25, 1450	Plague	Convent of Sant Agustí (Chapel of Santa Maria de Gràcia)			AMV, A-35, 5r–v
Saturday, June 20, 1450	Plague	Monastery of Santa Trinitat			AMV, A-35, 16v–17r
Saturday, June 27, 1450	Plague	Church of Sant Joan of the Market			AMV, A-35, 21v–22r
Sunday, July 5, 1450	Plague	Convent of Sant Agustí (Chapel of Santa Maria de Gràcia)			AMV, A-35, 22v–23r
Sunday, July 19, 1450	Plague	Monastery of Santa Trinitat			AMV, A-35, 24r–v
Wednesday, July 22, 1450	Plague	Convent of Santa Magdalena			AMV, A-35, 25r–v
Sunday, July 26, 1450	Plague	Convent of Sant Domènec (Chapel of Santa Maria de la Misericòrdia)			AMV, A-35, 25v–26r
Sunday, August 9, 1450	Plague	Church of Sant Lorenç			AMV, A-35, 30r
Sunday, August 30, 1450	Plague	Church of Sant Andreu			AMV, A-35, 34v–35r
Sunday, September 6, 1450	Plague	Church of Santa Caterina			AMV, A-35, 37r–v
Sunday, September 13, 1450	Plague	Monastery of Santa Trinitat			AMV, A-35, 38v
Sunday, September 27, 1450	Plague / thanksgiving	Convent of Sant Agustí (Chapel of Santa Maria de Gràcia)			AMV, A-35, 40r

Date	Reason	Location	Reference
Sunday, November 15, 1450	Plague / thanksgiving	Convent of Sant Agustí (Chapel of Santa Maria de Gràcia)	AMV, A-35, 53r-v
Sunday, November 22, 1450	Plague / thanksgiving	Convent of Sant Agustí (Chapel of Santa Maria de Gràcia)	AMV, A-35, 55r-v
Monday, October 18, 1451	Drought	Convent of Sant Agustí (Chapel of Santa Maria de Gràcia)	AMV, A-35, 134v–135r
Thursday, October 28, 1451	Drought	Convent of Sant Francesc	AMV, A-35, 135r-v
Sunday, December 12, 1451	Drought	Convent of Sant Agustí (Chapel of Santa Maria de Gràcia)	AMV, A-35, 138r
Thursday, March 30, 1452	Drought	Convent of Sant Agustí (Chapel of Santa Maria de Gràcia)	AMV, A-35, 161r-v
Friday, April 14, 1452	Drought	Convent of Sant Francesc	AMV, A-35, 163r-v
Thursday, January 18, 1453	Flood	Convent of Sant Agustí (Chapel of Santa Maria de Gràcia)	AMV, A-35, 235r
Tuesday, July 10, 1453	Flood	Convent of Sant Agustí (Chapel of Santa Maria de Gràcia)	AMV, A-35, 283v–284r
Friday, February 1, 1454	Drought	Convent of Sant Domènec (Chapel of Santa Maria de la Misericordia)	AMV, A-35, 350v–351r
Friday, February 8, 1454	Drought	Convent of Santa Maria del Carme	AMV, A-35, 351r-v
Friday, February 15, 1454	Drought	Convent of Sant Agustí (Chapel of Santa Maria de Gràcia)	AMV, A-35, 353r
Saturday, February 23, 1454	Drought	Convent of Sant Agustí (Chapel of Santa Maria de Gràcia)	AMV, A-35, 357v–358r
Saturday, March 9, 1454	Drought / thanksgiving	Convent of Sant Agustí (Chapel of Santa Maria de Gràcia)	AMV, A-35, 363v
Saturday, March 8, 1455	Drought	Convent of Sant Agustí (Chapel of Santa Maria de Gràcia)	AMV, A-35, 451r-v

(continued)

DATE OF PROCESSION	PURPOSE	DESTINATION	SECONDARY DESTINATIONS	COMMENTS	ARCHIVE LOCATION
Wednesday, March 12, 1455	Drought	Convent of Sant Domènec (Chapel of Santa Maria de la Misericòrdia)			AMV, A-35, 451v–452r
Wednesday, March 19, 1455	Drought	Convent of Santa Maria del Carme			AMV, A-35, 452v–453r
Thursday, March 27, 1455	Drought	Convent of Santa Maria del Carme			AMV, A-35, 453r–v
Friday, October 31, 1455	Drought	Convent of Sant Agustí (Chapel of Santa Maria de Gràcia)			AMV, A-36, Mano 2 40r–v
Friday, December 12, 1455	Drought	Convent of Sant Agustí (Chapel of Santa Maria de Gràcia)			AMV, A-36, Mano 2 42r–v
Saturday, January 3, 1456	Drought	Convent of Santa Maria del Carme			AMV, A-36, Mano 2 52v–53r
Wednesday, January 14, 1456	Drought	Convent of Sant Domènec (Chapel of Santa Maria de la Misericòrdia)			AMV, A-36, Mano 2 54v–55r
Sunday, January 18, 1456	Drought	Places outside the city		Second procession to accompany this one to the city gate	AMV, A-36, Mano 2 56r–v
Sunday, January 25, 1456	Drought	Return of procession to places outside the city		Procession to meet returning one at city gate	AMV, A-36, Mano 2 57r
Tuesday, January 27, 1456[a]	Drought	Monastery of Santa Trinitat			AMV, A-36, Mano 2 57v–58r
Saturday, February 7, 1456	Drought	Monastery of Sant Vicent Martir			AMV, A-36, Mano 2 60r
Wednesday, February 18, 1456	Drought	Convent of Sant Francesc			AMV, A-36, Mano 2 62v–63r

Date	Reason	Location		Notes	Reference
Wednesday, March 17, 1456	Drought	Convent of Santa Maria del Carme			AMV, A-36, Mano 2 65r–v
Saturday, April 3, 1456	Drought / thanksgiving	Convent of Sant Agustí (Chapel of Santa Maria de Gràcia)			AMV, A-36, Mano 2 66r–v
Tuesday, July 20, 1456	Drought	Convent of Sant Agustí (Chapel of Santa Maria de Gràcia)			AMV, A-36, Mano 2 106v–107r
Monday, July 26, 1456	Drought	Convent of Santa Maria del Carme	Church of Sant Bartomeu, Church of Santa Creu		AMV, A-36, Mano 2 108r–v
Saturday, July 31, 1456	Drought	Convent of Sant Domènec (Chapel of Santa Maria de la Misericòrdia)			AMV, A-36, Mano 2 109r–v
Saturday, August 7, 1456	Drought	Convent of Sant Francesc			AMV, A-36, Mano 2 120v–121r
Tuesday, August 17, 1456	Drought	Monastery of Santa Trinitat			AMV, A-36, Mano 2 126r–v
Saturday, August 27, 1456	Drought	Monastery of Sant Vicent Martir			AMV, A-36, Mano 2 126v–127r
Wednesday, August 25, 1456	Drought	Church of Sant Esteve			AMV, A-36, Mano 2 128r–v
Sunday, August 29, 1456	Drought	Places outside the city	Monastery of Santa Maria de la Murta	Second procession to accompany this one to the city gate	AMV, A-36, Mano 2 128v; 129r–v
Sunday, September 5, 1456	Drought	Return of procession to places outside the city		Procession to meet returning one at city gate	AMV, A-36, Mano 2 130r–v
Thursday, October 14, 1456	Drought	Convent of Sant Agustí (Chapel of Santa Maria de Gràcia)			AMV, A-36, Mano 2 137r–v
Saturday, November 13, 1456	Drought	Convent of Santa Maria del Carme			AMV, A-36, Mano 2 142r
Monday, November 29, 1456	Drought / thanksgiving	Convent of Sant Agustí (Chapel of Santa Maria de Gràcia)		Thanks and request for more rain	AMV, A-36, Mano 2 143v

(continued)

DATE OF PROCESSION	PURPOSE	DESTINATION	SECONDARY DESTINATIONS	COMMENTS	ARCHIVE LOCATION
Saturday, December 4, 1456	Drought	Convent of Sant Domènec (Chapel of Santa Maria de la Misericordia)			AMV, A-36, Mano 2 145r–v
Sunday, January 16, 1457	Earthquake	Convent of Sant Agustí (Chapel of Santa Maria de Gràcia)		Earthquake in Naples	AMV, A-36, Mano 2 157r
Sunday, February 6, 1457	Drought	Convent of Santa Maria del Carme			AMV, A-36, Mano 2 165v
Sunday, February 20, 1457	Drought	Convent of Sant Domènec (Chapel of Santa Maria de la Misericordia)			AMV, A-36, Mano 2 169v–170r
Saturday, March 5, 1457	Drought / thanksgiving	Convent of Sant Agustí (Chapel of Santa Maria de Gràcia)		Thanks and request for more rain	AMV, A-36, Mano 2 172r–v
Saturday, May 7, 1457	Drought	Convent of Sant Agustí (Chapel of Santa Maria de Gràcia)			AMV, A-36, Mano 2 178v–179r
Thursday, June 30, 1457	Drought	Convent of Sant Agustí (Chapel of Santa Maria de Gràcia)			AMV, A-36, Mano 3 14r–v
Friday, August 26, 1457	Drought	Monastery of Santa Trinitat			AMV, A-36, Mano 3 21r–v
Saturday, November 5, 1457	Drought	Convent of Sant Agustí (Chapel of Santa Maria de Gràcia)			AMV, A-36, Mano 3 30v–31r
Wednesday, November 9, 1457	Drought	Convent of Sant Agustí (Chapel of Santa Maria de Gràcia)			AMV, A-36, Mano 3 31r–v
Saturday, December 3, 1457	Drought / thanksgiving	Convent of Sant Agustí (Chapel of Santa Maria de Gràcia)			AMV, A-36, Mano 3 35r–v
Friday, March 17, 1458	Drought	Convent of Sant Agustí (Chapel of Santa Maria de Gràcia)			AMV, A-36, Mano 3 65v–66r

Date	Reason	Location	Notes	Reference
Saturday, April 15, 1458	Drought / thanksgiving	Convent of Sant Domènec (Chapel of Santa Maria de la Misericordia)	Thanks and request for more rain	AMV, A-36, Mano 3, 66v–67r
Sunday, September 10, 1458	Drought	None given		AMV, A-36, Mano 3, 114v
Saturday, April 7, 1459	Locusts	Convent of Sant Agustí (Chapel of Santa Maria de Gràcia)	Locusts elsewhere in the kingdom	AMV, A-36, Mano 3, 158r–v
Friday, June 22, 1459	Plague	Convent of Sant Agustí (Chapel of Santa Maria de Gràcia)		AMV, A-36, Mano 3, 183r–v
Wednesday, October 31, 1459	Drought	Convent of Sant Agustí (Chapel of Santa Maria de Gràcia)		AMV, A-36, Mano 3, 196v
Wednesday, November 21, 1459	Drought / thanksgiving	Convent of Sant Agustí (Chapel of Santa Maria de Gràcia)	Thanks and request for more rain	AMV, A-36, Mano 3, 197v
Friday, April 25, 1460	Drought / thanksgiving / plague	Convent of Sant Agustí (Chapel of Santa Maria de Gràcia)	Thanks and request for more rain and end of plague	AMV, A-36, Mano 3, 209r–v
Saturday, July 12, 1460	Plague	Convent of Sant Agustí (Chapel of Santa Maria de Gràcia)		AMV, A-37, Mano 1, 14r–v
Wednesday, December 3, 1460	Plague / thanksgiving	Convent of Sant Agustí (Chapel of Santa Maria de Gràcia)		AMV, A-37, Mano 1, 33v–34r
Friday, December 12, 1460	Drought	Convent of Sant Domènec (Chapel of Santa Maria de la Misericordia)	Church of Sant Esteve	AMV, A-37, Mano 1, 34r
Saturday, January 31, 1461	Plague / thanksgiving	Convent of Santa Maria del Carme		AMV, A-37, Mano 1, 53v–54r
Sunday, February 10, 1461	Plague / thanksgiving	Convent of Sant Agustí (Chapel of Santa Maria de Gràcia)		AMV, A-37, Mano 1, 54v–55r
Saturday, November 21, 1461	Drought	Convent of Sant Agustí (Chapel of Santa Maria de Gràcia)		AMV, A-37, Mano 1, 115r
Saturday, January 30, 1462	Flood	Convent of Santa Maria del Carme		AMV, A-37, Mano 1, 125r

(continued)

DATE OF PROCESSION	PURPOSE	DESTINATION	SECONDARY DESTINATIONS	COMMENTS	ARCHIVE LOCATION
Wednesday, February 10, 1462	Flood / thanksgiving	Convent of Sant Agustí (Chapel of Santa Maria de Gràcia)			AMV, A-37, Mano 1 125v–126r
Thursday, February 24, 1463	Drought	Convent of Sant Agustí (Chapel of Santa Maria de Gràcia)		For peace, rain, and thanks for wheat supply	AMV, A-37, Mano 2 49v–50r
Saturday, March 26, 1463	Drought / thanksgiving	Convent of Sant Agustí (Chapel of Santa Maria de Gràcia)			AMV, A-37, Mano 2 52v
Saturday, April 16, 1463	Drought	Convent of Sant Domènec (Chapels of Santa Maria de la Misericordia and Sant Vicent Ferrer)			AMV, A-37, Mano 2 58v
Wednesday, April 20, 1463	Drought / thanksgiving	Monastery of Santa Trinitat			AMV, A-37, Mano 2 60v–61r
Tuesday, January 10, 1464	Drought	Convent of Sant Agustí (Chapel of Santa Maria de Gràcia)			AMV, A-37, Mano 2 113r
Saturday, January 28, 1464	Drought	Convent of Santa Maria del Carme			AMV, A-37, Mano 2 114r–v
Wednesday, February 8, 1464	Drought / thanksgiving	Convent of Sant Domènec (Chapels of Santa Maria de la Misericordia and Sant Vicent Ferrer)		Thanks and request for more rain	AMV, A-37, Mano 2 115v
Sunday, February 12, 1464	Drought	Monastery of Santa Trinitat			AMV, A-37, Mano 2 116r
Wednesday, February 29, 1464	Drought	Church of Sant Esteve			AMV, A-37, Mano 2 117r–v
Friday, March 9, 1464	Drought	Convent of Sant Agustí (Chapel of Santa Maria de Gràcia)			AMV, A-37, Mano 2 119v

Date	Cause	Location		Notes	Reference
Sunday, April 8, 1464	Drought / thanksgiving	Convent of Sant Agustí (Chapel of Santa Maria de Gràcia)		Thanks and request for more rain	AMV, A-37, Mano 2 121v
Saturday, October 18, 1466	Plague	Convent of Sant Agustí (Chapel of Santa Maria de Gràcia)			AMV, A-38, Mano 1 100v
Saturday, October 25, 1466	Plague	Convent of Sant Domènec (Chapels of Santa Maria de la Misericordia and Sant Vicent Ferrer)			AMV, A-38, Mano 1 101r–v
Saturday, November 8, 1466	Plague	Convent of Santa Maria del Carme	Church of Sant Bartomeu		AMV, A-38, Mano 1 101v–102r
Saturday, November 22, 1466	Plague	Convent of Sant Agustí (Chapel of Santa Maria de Gràcia)			AMV, A-38, Mano 1 102v–103r
Wednesday, December 3, 1466	Plague	Monastery of Santa Trinitat		One of three	AMV, A-38, Mano 1 103r–v
Thursday, December 4, 1466	Plague	Monastery of Santa Trinitat		Two of three	AMV, A-38, Mano 1 103r–v
Friday, December 5, 1466	Plague	Monastery of Santa Trinitat		Three of three	AMV, A-38, Mano 1 103r–v
Wednesday, December 10, 1466	Plague	Convent of Santa Maria de la Mercè		Prayer to "glorious doctors"	AMV, A-38, Mano 1 104r–v
Friday, December 12, 1466	Plague	Monastery of Santa Trinitat			AMV, A-38, Mano 1 105r
Tuesday, December 16, 1466	Plague	Convent of Sant Domènec (Chapels of Santa Maria de la Misericordia and Sant Vicent Ferrer)			AMV, A-38, Mano 1 105v
Saturday, February 7, 1467	Drought / plague / thanksgiving	Convent of Sant Agustí (Chapel of Santa Maria de Gràcia)			AMV, A-38, Mano 1 104v–105r
Friday, February 27, 1467	Plague	Monastery of Santa Trinitat			AMV, A-38, Mano 1 115v–116v

(continued)

DATE OF PROCESSION	PURPOSE	DESTINATION	SECONDARY DESTINATIONS	COMMENTS	ARCHIVE LOCATION
Thursday, June 11, 1467	Plague	Convent of Sant Agustí (Chapel of Santa Maria de Gràcia)			AMV, A-38, Mano 1 129v–130r
Friday, November 20, 1467	Drought	Convent of Sant Agustí (Chapel of Santa Maria de Gràcia)			AMV, A-38, Mano 1 152v
Tuesday, February 9, 1468	Drought	Convent of Sant Agustí (Chapel of Santa Maria de Gràcia)			AMV, A-38, Mano 1 167v
Tuesday, January 31, 1469	Drought	Convent of Sant Domènec (Chapels of Santa Maria de la Misericordia and Sant Vicent Ferrer)			AMV, A-38, Mano 2 41r–v
Tuesday, February 21, 1469	Drought	Convent of Sant Agustí (Chapel of Santa Maria de Gràcia)			AMV, A-38, Mano 2 43r–v
Friday, March 10, 1469	Drought	Monastery of Santa Trinitat			AMV, A-38, Mano 2 47r–v
Monday, March 13, 1469	Drought	Places outside the city		Second procession to accompany this one to the city gate	AMV, A-38, Mano 2 47v–48r
Monday, March 20, 1469	Drought	Return of procession to places outside the city		Procession to meet returning one at city gate	AMV, A-38, Mano 2 48r
Saturday, November 18, 1469	Drought	Convent of Sant Domènec (Chapels of Santa Maria de la Misericordia and Sant Vicent Ferrer)			AMV, A-38, Mano 2 89v–90r
Saturday, October 27, 1470	Drought	Convent of Sant Domènec (Chapels of Santa Maria de la Misericordia and Sant Vicent Ferrer)			AMV, A-38, Mano 2 147r

Date	Occasion	Place	Places outside the city		Reference
Monday, November 5, 1470	Drought			Second procession to accompany this one to the city gate	AMV, A-38, Mano 2 147v–148r
Saturday, December 15, 1470	Drought / thanksgiving	Convent of Sant Agustí (Chapel of Santa Maria de Gràcia)			AMV, A-38, Mano 2 154v–155r
Wednesday, May 29, 1471	Food supply / thanksgiving	Convent of Sant Agustí (Chapel of Santa Maria de Gràcia)		Thanksgiving for grain supply	AMV, A-38, Mano 2 192r–v
Saturday, October 12, 1471	Drought	Convent of Sant Agustí (Chapel of Santa Maria de Gràcia)			AMV, A-39, 25r–v
Thursday, January 9, 1472	Drought	Convent of Sant Agustí (Chapel of Santa Maria de Gràcia)			AMV, A-39, 50r–v
Saturday, February 15, 1472	Drought	Convent of Sant Domènec (Chapels of Santa Maria de la Misericòrdia and Sant Vicent Ferrer)		For peace, rain, preservation from illness	AMV, A-39, 55r–v
Saturday, April 25, 1472	Drought	Convent of Sant Agustí (Chapel of Santa Maria de Gràcia)			AMV, A-39, 93v–94r
Wednesday, November 18, 1472	Drought	Convent of Sant Domènec (Chapels of Santa Maria de la Misericòrdia and Sant Vicent Ferrer)		For peace, rain, preservation from illness	AMV, A-39, 173v–174r
Saturday, November 21, 1472	Drought	Monastery of Santa Trinitat		For peace, rain, preservation from illness	AMV, A-39, 174r–v
Monday, February 1, 1473	Drought	Convent of Sant Agustí (Chapel of Santa Maria de Gràcia)		For peace, rain, preservation from illness	AMV, A-39, 192r
Saturday, February 6, 1473	Drought	Convent of Sant Domènec (Chapels of Santa Maria de la Misericòrdia and Sant Vicent Ferrer)	Church of Sant Esteve	For peace, rain, preservation from illness	AMV, A-39, 192v–193r
Tuesday, February 9, 1473	Drought	Convent of Santa Maria del Carme		For peace, rain, preservation from illness	AMV, A-39, 193r–v

(continued)

DATE OF PROCESSION	PURPOSE	DESTINATION	SECONDARY DESTINATIONS	COMMENTS	ARCHIVE LOCATION
Sunday, February 14, 1473	Drought	Places outside the city		Second procession to accompany this one to the city gate	AMV, A-39, 195r–v
Sunday, February 21, 1473	Drought	Return of procession to places outside the city		Procession to meet returning one at city gate	AMV, A-39, 196r–v
Wednesday, Feburary 24, 1473 (Feast of Sant Macià)	Drought	Monastery of Santa Trinitat		For peace, rain, preservation from illness	AMV, A-39, 196v–197r
Saturday, March 6, 1473	Drought	Convent of Sant Domènec (Chapels of Santa Maria de la Misericordia and Sant Vicent Ferrer)	Church of Sant Esteve	For peace, rain, preservation from illness	AMV, A-39, 199r–199v
Saturday, March 13, 1473	Drought	Convent of Sant Domènec (Chapels of Santa Maria de la Misericordia and Sant Vicent Ferrer)		For peace, rain, preservation from illness	AMV, A-39, 204v–205r
Saturday, March 20, 1473	Drought	Church of Santa Caterina	Convent of Santa Magdalena, Confraternity Church of Santa Maria dels Ignoscents, Church of Sant Nicolau	For peace, rain, preservation from illness	AMV, A-39, 205v–206r
Monday, April 5, 1473	Drought	Convent of Sant Domènec (Sant Vicent Ferrer)		For peace, rain, preservation from illness	AMV, A-39, 207r–208r
Saturday, April 10, 1473	Drought	Monastery of Sant Vicent Martir	Chapel of Santa Maria de Gràcia	For peace, rain, preservation from illness	AMV, A-39, 209r–210r
Monday, April 26, 1473	Drought / thanksgiving	Convent of Sant Agustí (Chapel of Santa Maria de Gràcia)			AMV, A-39, 214r–v

Date	Weather	Location		Description	Source
Friday, November 5, 1473	Good weather	Convent of Sant Domènec (Chapels of Santa Maria de la Misericordia and Sant Vicent Ferrer)	Church of Sant Esteve	Good weather so that grain ships arrive safely	AMV, A-40, 44v–45v
Saturday, November 20, 1473	Good weather / thanksgiving	Monastery of Santa Trinitat		Thanksgiving for good weather for grain ships	AMV, A-40, 49r–49v
Friday, November 26, 1473	Good weather	Convent of Sant Agustí (Chapel of Santa Maria de Gràcia)		Good weather so that grain ships arrive safely	AMV, A-40, 51v–52r
Tuesday, February 8, 1474	Drought / good weather / thanksgiving	Convent of Sant Domènec (Chapels of Santa Maria de la Misericordia and Sant Vicent Ferrer)	Church of Sant Esteve	For rain and thanksgiving for arrival of ships	AMV, A-40, 72r–72v
Tuesday, February 15, 1474	Drought / good weather	Monastery of Santa Trinitat		For rain and good weather for ships	AMV, A-40, 72r–72v
Saturday, February 19, 1474	Drought / thanksgiving / good weather	Convent of Sant Agustí (Chapel of Santa Maria de Gràcia)		Thanks and request for rain, and good weather for ships	AMV, A-40, 74r–74v
Tuesday, March 1, 1474	Drought / good weather	Convent of Santa Maria del Carme		For rain and good weather for ships	AMV, A-40, 75v–76v
Saturday, March 12, 1474	Drought / good weather	Convent of Sant Agustí (Chapel of Santa Maria de Gràcia)		For rain and good weather for ships	AMV, A-40, 85v–86r
Thursday, March 17, 1474	Drought / good weather	Monastery of Santa Trinitat		For rain and good weather for ships	AMV, A-40, 90v–91r
Monday, April 4, 1474	Drought / thanksgiving / good weather	Convent of Sant Agustí (Chapel of Santa Maria de Gràcia)		Thanks and request for rain, good weather for ships	AMV, A-40, 94v–95r
Tuesday, November 29, 1474	Drought	Convent of Sant Agustí (Chapel of Santa Maria de Gràcia)			AMV, A-40, 159r–v
Wednesday, April 18, 1475	Drought / thanksgiving	Convent of Sant Agustí (Chapel of Santa Maria de Gràcia)			AMV, A-40, 191r–v

(continued)

DATE OF PROCESSION	PURPOSE	DESTINATION	SECONDARY DESTINATIONS	COMMENTS	ARCHIVE LOCATION
Monday, May 8, 1475	Good weather	Monastery of Santa Trinitat		For health, peace, and good weather for crops	AMV, A-40, 194v–195r
Tuesday, July 18, 1475	Plague	Convent of Sant Domènec (Chapels of Santa Maria de la Misericordia and Sant Vicent Ferrer)	Church of Sant Esteve, Sant Joan of the Hospital, Sant Tomàs	One of four (northeast)	AMV, A-40, 216v–217r
Wednesday, July 19, 1475	Plague	Church of Sant Llorenç	Church of Santa Creu, Church of Sant Bartomeu	Two of four (northwest)	AMV, A-40, 216v–217r
Thursday, July 20, 1475	Plague	Church of Sant Nicolau	Church of Santa Caterina, Church of Sant Joan of the Market	Three of four (southwest)	AMV, A-40, 216v–217r
Friday, July 21, 1475	Plague	Convent of Santa Maria de la Mercè	Church of Sant Martí, Church of Sant Andreu	Four of four (southeast)	AMV, A-40, 216v–217r
Monday, July 31, 1475	Plague	Serrans Gate, Quart Gate,		One of two, affixing images of angel to gates	AMV, A-40, 217v–218r
Tuesday, August 1, 1475	Plague	Sant Vicent Gate, Sea Gate		Two of two, affixing images of angel to gates	AMV, A-40, 217v–218r
Friday, August 25, 1475	Plague	Convent of Sant Francesc		With body of Sant Lluís de Toulouse	AMV, A-40, 221v–222r
Monday, September 4, 1475	Plague	Monastery of Santa Trinitat		With body of Sant Lluís de Toulouse	AMV, A-40, 222v–223r
Saturday, September 16, 1475	Plague	Monastery of Sant Vicent Martir			AMV, A-40, 223v–224r
Tuesday, October 3, 1475	Plague	Convent of Santa Maria del Carme			AMV, A-40, 228v

Date	Event	Location	Note	Reference
Friday, October 27, 1475	Drought / plague / thanksgiving	Convent of Sant Agustí (Chapel of Santa Maria de Gràcia)		AMV, A-40, 231r–v
Monday, December 11, 1475	Flood	Convent of Sant Agustí (Chapel of Santa Maria de Gràcia)		AMV, A-40, 232v
Saturday, January 13, 1476	Flood / thanksgiving / plague	Convent of Sant Agustí (Chapel of Santa Maria de Gràcia)		AMV, A-40, 245v–246r
Wednesday, January 31, 1476	Flood Thanksgiving/ Plague	Monastery of Sant Vicent Martir	Chapel of Santa Maria de Gràcia	AMV, A-40, 247r–v
Sunday, September 8, 1476	Plague	Convent of Sant Agustí (Chapel of Santa Maria de Gràcia)		AMV, A-40, 286r–v
Saturday, November 9, 1476	Plague	Church of Sant Martí	For relief from fevers	AMV, A-40, 300r–v
Saturday, January 25, 1477	Plague	Convent of Sant Agustí (Chapel of Santa Maria de Gràcia)	For preservation from plague	AMV, A-40, 325v–326r
Saturday, March 10, 1477	Plague	Convent of Sant Agustí (Chapel of Santa Maria de Gràcia)	For preservation from plague	AMV, A-40, 330v–331r
Saturday, October 11, 1477	Drought	Convent of Sant Agustí (Chapel of Santa Maria de Gràcia)		AMV, A-41, 60r
Friday, November 28, 1477	Drought / thanksgiving / Plague	Convent of Sant Agustí (Chapel of Santa Maria de Gràcia)		AMV, A-41, 63v
Saturday, January 31, 1478	Drought	Convent of Sant Agustí (Chapel of Santa Maria de Gràcia)		AMV, A-41, 84v
Tuesday, February 17, 1478	Drought	Monastery of Santa Trinitat		AMV, A-41, 88r–v
Saturday, April 4, 1478	Drought	Convent of Sant Agustí (Chapel of Santa Maria de Gràcia)		AMV, A-41, 94v–95r
Tuesday, June 2, 1478	Plague	Convent of Sant Agustí (Chapel of Santa Maria de Gràcia)		AMV, A-41, 120r
Friday, June 5, 1478	Plague	Monastery of Santa Trinitat		AMV, A-41, 122v–123r

(continued)

DATE OF PROCESSION	PURPOSE	DESTINATION	SECONDARY DESTINATIONS	COMMENTS	ARCHIVE LOCATION
Thursday, June 11, 1478	Plague	Convent of Sant Domènec (Chapels of Santa Maria de la Misericòrdia and Sant Vicent Ferrer)	Church of Sant Esteve		AMV, A-41, 123v–124r
Wednesday, June 17, 1478	Plague	Church of Sant Martí			AMV, A-41, 126r
Sunday, June 21, 1478	Plague	Convent of Santa Maria del Carme			AMV, A-41, 130r
Wednesday, June 24, 1478 (Feast of Sant Joan the Baptist)	Plague	Monastery of Santa Trinitat			AMV, A-41, 130v
Friday, June 26, 1478	Plague	Convent of Sant Francesc			AMV, A-41, 131v–132r
Saturday, August 8, 1478	Drought / plague	Convent of Sant Agustí (Chapel of Santa Maria de Gràcia)			AMV, A-41, 137r–v
Saturday, October 3, 1478	Plague / thanksgiving	Convent of Sant Agustí (Chapel of Santa Maria de Gràcia)		Mitigation of plague and "fevers"	AMV, A-41, 157v–158r
Wednesday, December 2, 1478	Drought	Monastery of Santa Trinitat			AMV, A-41, 166r–v
Monday, December 7, 1478	Drought	Monastery of Santa Trinitat			AMV, A-41, 166v–167r
Friday, December 11, 1478	Drought	Convent of Santa Maria del Carme			AMV, A-41, 167r–v
Sunday, December 13, 1478	Drought / good weather	Places outside the city	Monastery of Sant Vicent Martir	For rain and good weather for ships; second procession to accompany this one to Monastery of Sant Vicent Martir	AMV, A-41, 167v–168r
Sunday, December 20, 1478	Drought	Return of procession to places outside the city		Procession to meet returning one at city gate	AMV, A-41, 168v–169r

Date	Reason	Place	Notes	Reference
Saturday, March 3, 1481	Drought	Convent of Sant Agustí (Chapel of Santa Maria de Gràcia)		AMV, A-42, 93v–94r
Saturday, March 10, 1481	Drought	Monastery of Santa Trinitat		AMV, A-42, 97v–98r
Saturday, March 17, 1481	Drought	Convent of Sant Domènec (Chapels of Santa Maria de la Misericòrdia and Sant Vicent Ferrer)	Church of Sant Esteve	AMV, A-42, 98v–99r
Tuesday, April 3, 1481	Drought	Convent of Santa Maria del Carme	Church of Sant Nicolau	AMV, A-42, 100r–v
Thursday, April 5, 1481	Drought	Convent of Sant Domènec (Sant Vicent Ferrer)	Annual procession of Sant Vicent Ferrer; also for rain	AMV, A-42, 101r–v
Saturday, April 7, 1481	Drought	Church of Sant Esteve		AMV, A-42, 101v–102r
Tuesday, April 10, 1481	Drought	Church of Sant Jordi	With head of Sant Lluís de Toulouse	AMV, A-42, 103r–v
Tuesday, September 4, 1481	Drought	Convent of Sant Agustí (Chapel of Santa Maria de Gràcia)		AMV, A-42, 154v–155r
Saturday, September 15, 1481	Drought	Monastery of Santa Trinitat		AMV, A-42, 159v–160r
Thursday, October 18, 1481	Drought	Convent of Santa Maria del Carme		AMV, A-42, 177v–178r
Saturday, October 20, 1481	Drought	Convent of Sant Agustí (Chapel of Santa Maria de Gràcia)		AMV, A-42, 178r–v
Wednesday, November 7, 1481	Drought	Church of Sant Esteve		AMV, A-42, 182v–183r
Sunday, November 11, 1481	Drought	Places outside the city	Second procession to accompany this one to city gate	AMV, A-42, 183v–184r
Sunday, November 18, 1481	Drought	Return of procession to places outside city	Procession to meet returning one at city gate	AMV, A-42, 187r–v

(continued)

DATE OF PROCESSION	PURPOSE	DESTINATION	SECONDARY DESTINATIONS	COMMENTS	ARCHIVE LOCATION
Tuesday, January 21, 1483 (eve of Feast of Sant Vicent Martir)	Drought / thanksgiving	Convent of Sant Agustí (Chapel of Santa Maria de Gràcia)			AMV, A-43, 83r–v
Wednesday, November 5, 1483	Drought	Monastery of Santa Trinitat			AMV, A-43, 177v–178r
Saturday, November 15, 1483	Drought	Convent of Sant Domènec (Chapels of Santa Maria de la Misericordia and Sant Vicent Ferrer)			AMV, A-43, 180r–v
Saturday, January 3, 1484	Drought	Convent of Santa Maria del Carme			AMV, A-43, 195r–v
Sunday, January 4, 1484	Drought	Monastery of Sant Vicent Martir	Santa Maria de Gràcia		AMV, A-43, 195v–196r
Sunday, January 11, 1484	Drought	Places outside the city		Second procession to accompany this one to city gate	AMV, A-43, 205v–206r
Sunday, January 18, 1484	Drought	Return of procession to places outside the city		Procession to meet returning one at city gate	AMV, A-43, 206r–v
Sunday, January 25, 1484	Drought	Monastery of Santa Trinitat			AMV, A-43, 208r–v
Saturday, June 26, 1484	Drought	Monastery of Santa Trinitat			AMV, A-44, 15v–16r
Tuesday, July 13, 1484	Drought	Monastery of Santa Trinitat			AMV, A-44, 26v–27r
Saturday, August 21, 1484	Drought	Church of Sant Esteve			AMV, A-44, 38v–39r
Thursday, February 10, 1485	Drought	Monastery of Santa Trinitat			AMV, A-44, 102v–103r
Saturday, February 19, 1485	Drought	Convent of Sant Agustí (Chapel of Santa Maria de Gràcia)			AMV, A-44, 103v
Saturday, February 26, 1485	Drought	Convent of Santa Maria del Carme			AMV, A-44, 104r–v

Date	Type	Location		Notes	Source
Thursday, March 3, 1485	Drought	Monastery of Sant Vicent Màrtir			AMV, A-44, 104v–105r
Saturday, March 12, 1485	Drought	Convent of Sant Francesc		With body of Sant Lluís de Toulouse	AMV, A-44, 108v
Saturday, April 9, 1485	Drought / thanksgiving	Convent of Sant Agustí (Chapel of Santa Maria de Gràcia)			AMV, A-44, 117r
Saturday, February 4, 1486	Drought	Convent of Sant Agustí (Chapel of Santa Maria de Gràcia)			AMV, A-44, 231v–232r
Saturday, February 11, 1486	Drought	Monastery of Santa Trinitat			AMV, A-44, 236v–237r
Saturday, December 26, 1489	Plague	Convent of Sant Domènec (Chapel of Santa Maria del Roser)			AMV, A-45, 352v–353r
Monday, December 28, 1489	Plague	Sant Sebastià			AMV, A-45, 353r–v
Sunday, January 10, 1490	Plague	Convent of Sant Agustí (Chapel of Santa Maria de Gràcia)			AMV, A-45, 366r–v
Sunday, April 18, 1490	Plague	Convent of Sant Domènec (Sant Vicent Ferrer)			AMV, A-45, 383v–384r
Saturday, May 1, 1490	Plague	Convent of Sant Francesc (Chapel of Santa Maria de la Neu)		One of three; with head of Sant Lluís of Toulouse	AMV, A-45, 387v–388r
Sunday, May 2, 1490	Plague	Convent of Sant Domènec (Chapels of Santa Maria del Roser and Sant Vicent Ferrer)		Two of three; with relics of Sant Vicent Ferrer	AMV, A-45, 387v–388r
Monday, May 3, 1490	Plague	Church of Santa Creu	Convent of Santa Maria del Carme	Three of three; with Lignum Crucis	AMV, A-45, 387v–388r
Wednesday, May 19, 1490	Plague	Convent of Santa Maria del Carme			AMV, A-45, 391r–v
Friday, May 21, 1490	Plague	None given; circuit through city		One of three	AMV, A-45, 390r–v
Saturday, May 22, 1490	Plague	Confraternity Church of Santa Tecla		Two of three	AMV, A-45, 390r–v

(continued)

DATE OF PROCESSION	PURPOSE	DESTINATION	SECONDARY DESTINATIONS	COMMENTS	ARCHIVE LOCATION
Sunday, May 23, 1490	Plague	Monastery of Santa Trinitat		Three of three	AMV, A-45, 390r–v
Sunday, May 23, 1490	Plague	None given; circuit through city		One of two	AMV, A-45, 391v–392r
Monday, May 24, 1490	Plague	Monastery of Santa Trinitat		Two of two	AMV, A-45, 391v–392r
Friday, May 28, 1490	Plague	Monastery of Sant Vicent Martir			AMV, A-45, 393r–v
Saturday, July 12, 1494	Plague	None given		With body of Sant Lluís of Toulouse; masses in all parish churches	AMV, A-48, 64r–65v
Sunday, July 20, 1494	Plague	None given		With relics of Sant Vicent Martir and others	AMV, A-48, 68r–69r
Sunday, July 27, 1494	Plague	None given		With relics of Sant Vicent Ferrer	AMV, A-48, 70r–71r
Wednesday, August 6, 1494 (Feast of the Transfiguration)	Plague / thanksgiving	Convent of Sant Agustí (Chapel of Santa Maria de Gràcia)			AMV, A-48, 72r–v
Thursday, January 8, 1495	Drought / thanksgiving	Convent of Sant Agustí (Chapel of Santa Maria de Gràcia)			AMV, A-48, 157r–158r
Saturday, January 2, 1496	Drought / thanksgiving	Convent of Sant Agustí (Chapel of Santa Maria de Gràcia)			AMV, A-48, 333v–334r
Monday, March 21, 1496	Drought	Convent of Sant Agustí (Chapel of Santa Maria de Gràcia)	Santa Maria de la Neu		AMV, A-48, 350r–v
Wednesday, January 4, 1497	Drought	Monastery of Santa Trinitat			AMV, A-48, 526v–528v
Saturday, January 14, 1497	Drought	Church of Santa Caterina de Siena			AMV, A-48, 530v–531r
Monday, Feburary 6, 1497	Drought	Convent of Sant Agustí (Chapel of Santa Maria de Gràcia)			AMV, A-48, 533v–534r
Saturday, March 18, 1497	Drought / thanksgiving	Convent of Sant Agustí (Chapel of Santa Maria de Gràcia)			AMV, A-48, 575r–v

Date		Location	Notes	Source
Friday, March 16, 1498	Drought	Monastery of Santa Trinitat		AMV, A-49, 15r–v
Saturday, March 24, 1498	Drought	Convent of Sant Agustí (Chapel of Santa Maria de Gràcia)		AMV, A-49, 15v–16v
Thursday, March 29, 1498	Drought	Church of Sant Esteve		AMV, A-49, 16v–17r
Saturday, March 31, 1498	Drought	Church of Santa Caterina		AMV, A-49, 17v–18r
Wednesday, April 4, 1498	Drought	Convent of Sant Domènec (Sant Vicent Ferrer)		AMV, A-49, 18r–v
Sunday, April 22, 1498	Drought	Places outside the city	Second procession to accompany this one to city gate	AMV, A-49, 19r–v
Sunday, April 29, 1498	Drought	Return of procession to places outside the city	Procession to meet returning one at city gate	AMV, A-49, 20v–21r
Sunday, May 13, 1498	Drought	Convent of Sant Agustí (Chapel of Santa Maria de Gràcia)		AMV, A-49, 21v–22r
Friday, January 11, 1499	Drought	Monastery of Santa Trinitat		AMV, A-49, 37r–v
Friday, January 25, 1499	Drought	Convent of Sant Agustí (Chapel of Santa Maria de Gràcia)	One of three	AMV, A-49, 37v–39r
Wednesday, January 30, 1499	Drought	Church of Santa Caterina de Siena	Two of three	AMV, A-49, 37v–39r
Saturday, February 2, 1499	Drought	Convent of Santa Maria del Carme	Three of three	AMV, A-49, 37v–39r
Friday, February 8, 1499	Drought	Church of Sant Esteve		AMV, A-49, 39r–v
Saturday, March 2, 1499	Drought	Convent of Sant Agustí (Chapel of Santa Maria de Gràcia)		AMV, A-49, 43r–44r
Friday, September 20, 1499	Drought	Monastery of Santa Trinitat		AMV, A-50, 479r–480r
Saturday, August 1, 1500	Drought	Monastery of Santa Trinitat		AMV, A-50, 492v–493r
Saturday, January 15, 1502	Drought	Monastery of Santa Trinitat		AMV, A-50, 522r–523r
Saturday, January 15, 1502	Drought	Church of Sant Esteve		AMV, A-50, 523r–v
Wednesday, January 24, 1502	Drought	Convent of Sant Agustí (Chapel of Santa Maria de Gràcia)		AMV, A-50, 523v–524v

(continued)

DATE OF PROCESSION	PURPOSE	DESTINATION	SECONDARY DESTINATIONS	COMMENTS	ARCHIVE LOCATION
Friday, March 18, 1502	Drought	Convent of Sant Domènec	Church of Santa Caterina		AMV, A-50, 524v–525r
Saturday, November 5, 1502	Drought / good weather / thanksgiving	Convent of Sant Agustí (Chapel of Santa Maria de Gràcia)		For peace, good weather for grain ships, thanksgiving for rain	AMV, A-50, 538v–539r
Saturday, December 10, 1502	Drought	Monastery of Santa Trinitat			AMV, A-50, 542r–v
Saturday, November 15, 1505	Drought	Monastery of Santa Trinitat			AMV, A-52, 117v–117 bis r
Friday, November 28, 1505	Drought	Church of Sant Esteve			AMV, A-52, 125v–126r
Friday, December 19, 1505	Drought	Church of Santa Caterina			AMV, A-52, 132v–133r
Sunday, January 4, 1506	Drought	Places outside the city		Second procession to accompany this one to city gate	AMV, A-52, 151r–v
Sunday, January 11, 1506	Drought	Return of procession to places outside the city		Procession to meet returning one at city gate	AMV, A-52, 157v–158r
Friday, January 16, 1506	Drought / good weather	Church of Santa Caterina	Church of Sant Nicolau, Convent of Santa Clara, Church of Sant Joan of the Market	For rain for planting and good weather for grain ships	AMV, A-52, 163r–164r
Sunday, January 18, 1506	Drought / good weather	Monastery of Sant Vicent Martir	Church of Sant Jerònim, Monastery of Jerusalem	With relic of Sant Lluís de Toulouse; for rain for planting and good weather for grain ships	AMV, A-52, 164r–165r
Saturday, January 25, 1506	Drought / good weather	Monastery of Santa Trinitat		For rain for planting and good weather for grain ships	AMV, A-52, 166r–166v

Date	Type	Location	Confraternity/Church	Description	Reference
Saturday, January 31, 1506	Drought / good weather	Convent of Sant Domènec (Chapels of Sant Vicent Ferrer, Santa Maria de la Misericordia, Convent of Sant Domènec, Santa Maria del Roser)	Confraternity of Santa Maria	For rain for planting and good weather for grain ships	AMV, A-52, 171r–172r
Wednesday, February 26, 1506	Drought / good weather / thanksgiving/	Convent of Sant Agustí (Chapel of Santa Maria de Gràcia)		Thanks for arrival of grain ships from Sicily; request for rain	AMV, A-52, 175r
Sunday, April 5, 1506	Drought	Convent of Sant Domènec (Chapel of Sant Vicent Ferrer)		Feast of Sant Vicent; also for drought	AMV, A-52, 203v–204r
Thursday, July 27, 1508	Plague / thanksgiving	Convent of Sant Agustí (Chapel of Santa Maria de Gràcia)	Church of Santa Caterina, Santa Maria de la Mercè		AMV, A-54, 5r–5v
Saturday, February 3, 1509	Drought / plague / thanksgiving	Convent of Sant Agustí (Chapel of Santa Maria de Gràcia)	Church of Santa Caterina, Santa Maria de la Mercè	Plague in other parts of the kingdom	AMV, A-54, 13v–14r
Sunday, April 22, 1509	Plague	Convent of Sant Domènec (Chapel of Sant Vicent Ferrer)		For Feast of Sant Vicent; also for plague	AMV, A-54, 15r–v
Sunday, April 14, 1510	Drought	Convent of Sant Domènec (Chapel of Sant Vicent Ferrer)		Feast of Sant Vicent; also for drought	AMV, A-54, 22v–23r
Saturday, July 6, 1510	Plague	Convent of Sant Agustí (Chapel of Santa Maria de Gràcia)		Because quarantine has been breached	AMV, A-54, 27r–v
Sunday, August 4, 1510	Plague / thanksgiving	Convent of Sant Agustí (Chapel of Santa Maria de Gràcia)			AMV, A-54, 27v–28r
Saturday, April 5, 1511	Drought	Convent of Sant Domènec (Chapel of Sant Vicent Ferrer)		Feast of Sant Vicent; also for drought	AMV, A-54, 38v–39r
Saturday, February 3, 1515	Drought / thanksgiving	Convent of Sant Agustí (Chapel of Santa Maria de Gràcia)		Thanks for a little rain; request for more	AMV, A-56, 9r–10r
Saturday, February 17, 1515	Drought	Monastery of Santa Trinitat			AMV, A-56, 10r–11r
Wednesday, October 3, 1515	Drought	Monastery of Santa Trinitat			AMV, A-56, 19v–20r

(continued)

DATE OF PROCESSION	PURPOSE	DESTINATION	SECONDARY DESTINATIONS	COMMENTS	ARCHIVE LOCATION
Monday, November 5, 1515	Drought	Convent of Nostra Dona de Socors			AMV, A-56, 21v–22r
Friday, November 23, 1515	Drought	Convent of Sant Domènec (Sant Vicent Ferrer)			AMV, A-56, 22r–23r
Sunday, December 9, 1515	Drought	Places outside the city			AMV, A-56, 23r–24r
Sunday, December 16, 1515	Drought	Return of procession to places outside the city		Procession to meet returning one at city gate	AMV, A-56, 24r–v
Sunday, March 15, 1517	Good weather / Thanksgiving	Convent of Sant Agustí (Chapel of Santa Maria de Gràcia)			AMV, A-57, 839v–840r
Friday, October 11, 1517	Flood / thanksgiving	Church of Sant Tomàs		Thanks for good weather, and to stop collapse of houses	AMV, A-57, 858v–859r
Wednesday, July 13, 1519	Plague / thanksgiving	Convent of Sant Agustí (Chapel of Santa Maria de Gràcia)			AMV, A-58, 503v–504r
Friday, July 15, 1519	Plague / thanksgiving	Convent of Sant Domènec (Chapel of Sant Vicent Ferrer)			AMV, A-58, 507v–508r
Friday, August 19, 1519	Plague	Convent of Santa Maria del Carme		Request for intercession of Sant Roc	AMV, A-58, 526v–527v
Sunday, September 4, 1519	Plague / thanksgiving	Convent of Sant Agustí (Chapel of Santa Maria de Gràcia)			AMV, A-58, 530r–v
Tues., 27 September 1519 (Feast of Sants Cosme I Damià)	Plague	Convent of Sant Sebastià			AMV, A-58, 540v–541r

Note: Entries marked with * indicate the date of procession is not specified, and the date shown is the date of the document.

ᵃ Date given as "Tues., 28 January 1456," but 28 January 1456 was a Wednesday.

SELECTED BIBLIOGRAPHY

Archival Sources

Archivo de la Catedral de Valencia [ACV]
    Libros
    Pergamins
Archivo Municipal de Valencia [AMV]
    Claveria Comuna. Manuals de Albarans [I and J]
    Claveria Comuna. Libros de Cuentas [O]
    Libros de Certificaciones del Racional [q.q]
    Libros de Sotsobreria de Muros y Valladares [d³]
    Lletres Missives [g³]
    Manuals de Consells [A]
Arxiu de la Corona d'Aragó [ACA]
    Real Cancilleria

Printed Primary Sources

Alcanyís, Lluís. *Regiment preservatiu e curatiu de la pestilència*. Edited by José M.
    López Piñero and Antoni Ferrando. Valencia: Publicacions de la Universitat de
    València, 1999.
Burns, Robert I., ed. *Diplomatarium of the Crusader Kingdom of Valencia, The Registered
    Charters of Its Conqueror Jaume I, 1257–1276*, vol. 1, *Society and Documentation in
    Crusader Valencia*. Princeton, NJ: Princeton University Press, 1985.
———, ed. *Diplomatarium of the Crusader Kingdom of Valencia, The Registered Charters
    of Its Conqueror Jaume I, 1257–1276*, vol. 2, *Foundations of Crusader Valencia:
    Revolt and Recovery, 1257–1263*. Princeton, NJ: Princeton University Press,
    1991.
———, ed. *Diplomatarium of the Crusader Kingdom of Valencia, The Registered Charters of
    Its Conqueror Jaume I, 1257–1276*, vol. 3, *Transition in Crusader Valencia: Years of
    Triumph, Years of War, 1264–1270*. Princeton, NJ: Princeton University Press,
    2001.
———, ed. *Diplomatarium of the Crusader Kingdom of Valencia, The Registered Charters of
    Its Conqueror Jaume I, 1257–1276*, vol. 4, *Unifying Crusader Valencia: The Central
    Years of Jaume the Conqueror, 1270–1273*. Princeton, NJ: Princeton University
    Press, 2007.

Constable, Olivia Remie, ed. *Medieval Iberia: Readings from Christian, Muslim, and Jewish Sources.* 2nd ed. Philadelphia: University of Pennsylvania Press, 2012.
D'Agramont, Jacme. *Regiment de preservacío de la pestilencia (1348).* 2nd edition. Edited by Joan Veny. Barcelona: Col·lecció Scripta, Universitat de Barcelona, 2015.
Eiximenis, Francesc. *Regiment de la cosa publica*, ed. Lluís Blanes and Josep Palomero. Alzira, Spain: Editions Bromera, 2009.
El Primer Manual de Consells de la Ciutat de València (1306–1326). Edited and transcribed by Vicent Anyó Garcia. Valencia: Oficina de Publicaciones de l'Ajuntament de Valencia, 2001.
Epistolari de la València medieval. Edited by Agustín Rubio Vela and Antoni Ferrando. Valencia: Insitut de Filologia Valenciana / Publicaciones de l'Abadia de Montserrat, 1998.
Ferrer, Vicent. *Sermons.* Vols. 1–6. Edited by Josep Sanchis Sivera and Gret Schib. Barcelona: Editorial Barcino, 1932–1988.
Jaume I of Aragon. *The Book of Deeds of James I of Aragon: A Translation of the Medieval Catalan "Llibre dels Fets."* Translated by Damian Smith and Helena Buffery. Aldershot, UK: Ashgate, 2003.
——. *Llibre dels fets del rei En Jaume*, vols. 1–2. Edited by Jordi Bruguera. Barcelona: Editorial Barcino, 1991.
Libre de memories de diversos sucesos e fets memorables e de coses senyalades de la ciutat e regne de Valencia (1308–1644). 2 vols. Edited by Salvador Carreres Zacarés. Valencia: Accion Bibliografica Valenciana, 1930.
Miralles, Melchior. *Crònica i dietari del capellà d'Alfons el Magnànim.* Edited by Mateu Rodrigo Lizondo. Valencia: Publicacions de la Universitat de València, 2011.
Pere III el Cerimoniós. *Crònica.* Edited by Anna Cortadellas. Barcelona: Edicions 62, 1995.
Rodrigo Lizondo, Mateu, ed. *Diplomatari de la Unió del Regne de València (1347–1349).* Valencia: Fonts Historiques Valencianes, 2013.
Sainz de la Maza Lasoli, Regina. "Noticias documentadas sobre la Albufera 1283–1350." *Annals de l'Institut d'Estudis Comarcals* 2 (1983): 135–155.
Vallés Borràs, Vicent J. *La Germania.* Valencia: Institució Alfons el Magnànim, 2000.

Secondary Sources

Aberth, John. *An Environmental History of the Middle Ages: The Crucible of Nature.* London: Routledge, 2013.
Agresta, Abigail. "'Unfortunate Jews' and Urban Ugliness: Crafting a Narrative of the 1391 Assault on the Jueria of Valencia." *Journal of Medieval History* 43, no. 3 (2017): 1–22.
Aldrete, Gregory S. *Floods of the Tiber in Ancient Rome.* Baltimore: Johns Hopkins University Press, 2007.
Almela y Vives, Francisco. *Las riadas del Turia (1321–1949).* Valencia: Ayuntamiento de Valencia, 1957.
Appuhn, Karl. *A Forest on the Sea: Environmental Expertise in Renaissance Venice.* Baltimore: Johns Hopkins University Press, 2009.

Aragón, P., M. M. Coca-Abia, V. Llorente, and J. M. Lobo. "Estimation of Climatic Favourable Areas for Locust Outbreaks in Spain: Integrating Species' Presence Records and Spatial Information on Outbreaks." *Journal of Applied Entomology* 137 (2013): 610–623.

Arnold, Ellen. "An Introduction to Medieval Environmental History." *History Compass* 6, no. 3 (2008): 898–916.

———. *Negotiating the Landscape: Environment and Monastic Identity in the Medieval Ardennes*. Philadelphia: University of Pennsylvania Press, 2013.

———. "Rivers of Risk and Redemption in Gregory of Tours' Writings." *Speculum* 92, no. 1 (2017): 117–143.

Arrizabalaga, Jon. "Facing the Black Death: Perceptions and Reactions of University Medical Practitioners." In *Practical Medicine from Salerno to the Black Death*, ed. Luis García-Ballester, Roger French, Jon Arrizabalaga, and Andrew Cunningham, 237–288. Cambridge: Cambridge University Press, 1994.

Ash, Eric H. *The Draining of the Fens: Projectors, Popular Politics, and State Building in Early Modern England*. Baltimore: Johns Hopkins University Press, 2017.

Ashley, Kathleen, and Wim Hüsken. *Moving Subjects: Processional Performance in the Middle Ages and the Renaissance*. Leiden: Brill, 2001.

Assis, Yom Tov. *Jewish Economy in the Medieval Crown of Aragon, 1213–1327*. Leiden: Brill, 1997.

Azulay, Marilda, and Estrella Israel. *La Valencia judía: Espacios, límites y vivencias hasta la expulsion*. Valencia: Consell Valencià de Cultura, 2009.

Baer, Yitzhak. *A History of the Jews in Christian Spain*. Vol. 2. Philadelphia: Jewish Publication Society of America, 1961.

Balbo, Andrea, Arnald Puy, Jaime Frigola, Félix Retamero, Isabel Cacho, and Helena Kirchner. "Amplified Environmental Change from Land-Use and Climate Change in Medieval Minorca." *Land Degradation and Development* 29, no. 4 (2018): 1262–1269.

Barceló, Miquel, Helena Kirchner, and Carmen Navarro. *El agua que no duerme: Fundamentos de la arquología hidráulica andalusí*. Granada: Sierra Nevada, 1996.

Barnett, Lydia. "The Theology of Climate Change: Sin as Agency in the Enlightenment's Anthropocene." *Environmental History* 20, no. 2 (2015): 217–237.

Barriendos, Mariano. "Climate Change in the Iberian Peninsula: Indicator of Rogation Ceremonies (16th–19th Centuries)." *Revue d'histoire moderne et contemporaine* 57 (2010): 131–159.

Barriendos Vallvé, Mariano. "Climatic Variations in the Iberian Peninsula during the Late Maunder Minimum (AD 1675–1715): An Analysis of Data from Rogation Ceremonies." *The Holocene* 7, no. 1 (1997): 105–111.

Barton, Thomas W. *Contested Treasure: Jews and Authority in the Crown of Aragon*. University Park: Pennsylvania State University Press, 2015.

———. *Victory's Shadow: Conquest and Governance in Medieval Catalonia*. Ithaca, NY: Cornell University Press, 2019.

Behringer, Wolfgang. "Climatic Change and Witch-Hunting: The Impact of the Little Ice Age on Mentalities." *Climatic Change* 43, no. 1 (1999): 335–351.

Belenguer Cebrià, Ernest. *Fernando el Catolico y la ciudad de Valencia*. Valencia: Publicacions de la Universitat de València, 2012.

Benito, Gerardo, Mark G. Macklin, Christoph Zielhofer, Anna F. Jones, and Maria J. Machado. "Holocene Flooding and Climate Change in the Mediterranean." *Catena* 130 (2015): 13–33.

Benito, Gerardo, V. R. Thorndycraft, María Teresa Rico, Yolanda Sánchez-Moya, and Alfonso Sopeña. "Palaeoflood and Floodplain Records from Spain: Evidence for Long-Term Climate Variability and Environmental Changes." *Geomorphology* 101, no. 1 (2008): 68–77.

Berlioz, Jacques. *Catastrophes naturelles et calamités au Moyen Age*. Florence: SISMEL / Edizioni del Galluzzo, 1998.

Blackmore, Josiah, and Gregory S. Hutcheson, eds. *Queer Iberia: Sexualities, Cultures, and Crossings from the Middle Ages to the Renaissance*. Durham, NC: Duke University Press, 1999.

Blazĭna Tomić, Zlata, and Vesna Blazĭna. *Expelling the Plague: the Health Office and the Implementation of Quarantine in Dubrovnik, 1377–1533*. Montreal: McGill-Queens University Press, 2015.

Bocchi, Francesca. "Shaping the City: Urban Planning and Physical Structures." In *A Companion to Medieval and Renaissance Bologna*, edited by Sarah Rubin Blanshei, 56–102. Leiden: Brill 2018.

Boerefijn, Wim. "About the Ideal Layout of the City Street in the Twelfth to Sixteenth Centuries: The Myth of the Renaissance in Town Building." *Journal of Urban History* 42, no. 5 (2016): 938–952.

Bos, Kirsten I., Alexander Herbig, Jason Sahl, Nicholas Waglechner, Mattieu Fourment, Stephen A. Forrest, Jennifer Klunk, et al. "Eighteenth-Century *Yersinia pestis* Genomes Reveal the Long-Term Persistence of an Historical Plague Focus," *eLife* 5 (2016). https://doi.org/10.7554/eLife.12994.001.

Bos, Kirsten I., Verena J. Schuenemann, G. Brian Golding, Hernán A. Burbano, Nicholas Waglechner, Biran K. Coombes, Joseph B. McPhee, et al. "A Draft Genome of *Yersinia pestis* from Victims of the Black Death," *Nature* 478 (2011): 506–510.

Bowers, Kristy Wilson. *Plague and Public Health in Early Modern Seville*. Rochester, NY: Rochester University Press, 2013.

Brodman, James William. *Charity and Welfare: Hospitals and the Poor in Medieval Catalonia*. Philadelphia: University of Pennsylvania Press, 1998.

Brown, Andrew. *Civic Ceremony and Religion in Medieval Bruges, c. 1300–1520*. Cambridge: Cambridge University Press, 2011.

Bulliet, Richard W. *The Camel and the Wheel*. 2nd ed. New York: Columbia University Press, 1990.

Burns, Robert I. *Islam under the Crusaders: Colonial Survival in the Thirteenth-Century Kingdom of Valencia*. Princeton, NJ: Princeton University Press, 1973.

——. *Muslims, Christians, and Jews in the Crusader Kingdom of Valencia: Societies in Symbiosis*. Cambridge: Cambridge University Press, 1984.

Burns, Robert I., and Paul E. Chevedden. *Negotiating Cultures: Bilingual Surrender Treaties in Muslim-Crusader Spain under James the Conqueror*. Leiden: Brill, 1999.

Cabanes Pecourt, Maria de los Desamparados. "Parroquias y órdenes militares en la geografía urbana de Valencia (siglo XIII)." *Memoria ecclesiae* 27 (2005): 463–474.

Calvo Gálvez, Matías, and Josep Vicent Lerma. "Peste Negra y pogromo en la ciudad de Valencia: La evidencia arqueológica." *Revista de Arqueología* 19 (1998): 50–59.

Camenisch, Christian, and Christian Rohr. "When the Weather Turned Bad: The Research of Climate Impacts on Society and Economy during the Little Ice Age in Europe; An Overview." *Geographical Research Letters* 44, no. 1 (2018): 99–114.

Campbell, Bruce. *The Great Transition: Climate, Disease and Society in the Late-Medieval World.* Cambridge: Cambridge University Press, 2016.

Campopiano, Michele. "Rural Communities, Land Clearance and Water Management in the Po Valley in the Central and Late Middle Ages." *Journal of Medieval History*, 39, no. 4 (2013): 377–393.

Candiani, Vera S. *Dreaming of Dry Land: Environmental Transformation in Colonial Mexico City.* Stanford, CA: Stanford University Press, 2014.

Carmichael, Ann G. "Contagion Theory and Contagion Practice in Fifteenth-Century Milan." *Renaissance Quarterly* 44, no. 2 (1991): 213–256.

——. "Epidemics and State Medicine in Fifteenth-Century Milan." In *Medicine from the Black Death to the French Disease*, edited by Roger French, Jon Arrizabalaga, Andrew Cunningham, and Luis García-Ballester, 221–47. Aldershot, UK: Routledge, 1998.

——. *Plague and the Poor in Renaissance Florence.* New York: Cambridge University Press, 1986.

Carmona Gonzalez, Pilar. "Geomorfología de la llanura de Valencia. El Río Turia y la ciudad." In *Historia de la ciudad*, vol. 2, *Territorio, sociedad y patrimonio.* Edited by Sonia Dauksis Ortolá and Francesco Taberner Pastor. Valencia: Publications de la Universitat de València, 2002: 17–27.

Carmona, P., and J. M. Ruiz. "Historical Morphogenesis of the Turia River Coastal Flood Plain in the Mediterranean Littoral of Spain." *Catena* 86, no. 3 (2011): 139–149.

Carmona, Pilar, Ana-Maria Blázquez, María López-Belzunce, Santiago Riera, and Héctor Orengo. "Environmental Evolution and Mid–Late Holocene Climate Events in the Valencia Lagoon (Mediterranean Coast of Spain)," *The Holocene* 26, no. 11 (2016): 1750–1765.

Catlos, Brian. "Contexto social y 'conveniencia' en la Corona de Aragón. Propuesta de un modelo de interacción entre grupos etno-religiosos minoritarios y mayoritarios." *Revista d'història medieval* 12 (2002): 220–235.

Cease, Arianne J., James J. Elser, Eli P. Fenichel, and Joleen C. Hadrich. "Living with Locusts: Connecting Soil Nitrogen, Locust Outbreaks, Livelihoods, and Livestock Markets." *BioScience* 65, no. 6 (2015): 551–558.

Ceccarelli, Giovanni. "Gambling and Economic Thought in the Late Middle Ages." *Ludica: Annali di storia e civiltà del gioco* 12 (2009): 54–63.

Chase, Melissa P. "Fevers, Poisons, and Apostemes: Authority and Experience in Montpellier Plague Treatises." *Annals of the New York Academy of Sciences* 441 (1985): 153–170.

Chiner Gimeno, Jaume Josep. "Prevención y peste en la Valencia del siglo XV: Unas ordenanzas de 1483." In *1490. En el umbral de la modernidad. El Mediterráneo europeo y las ciudades en el tránsito de los siglos XV–XVI*, edited by José Hinojosa Montalvo and Jesús Pradells Nadal, 25–33. Valencia: Monografies del Consell Valencià de Cultura, 1994.

Christian, William A. *Local Religion in Sixteenth-Century Spain*. Princeton, NJ: Princeton University Press, 1981.

Cipolla, Carlo M. *Miasmas and Disease: Public Health and the Environment in the Pre-industrial Age*. Translated by Elizabeth Potter. New Haven, CT: Yale University Press, 1992.

Cohen-Hanegbi, Naama. *Caring for the Living Soul: Emotions, Medicine and Penance in the Late Medieval Mediterranean*. Leiden: Brill, 2017.

Cohn, Samuel. *The Black Death Transformed: Disease and Culture in Early Renaissance Europe*. London: Bloomsbury, 2002.

Coleman, David. *Creating Christian Granada: Society and Religious Culture in an Old-World Frontier City, 1492–1600*. Ithaca, NY: Cornell University Press, 2003.

Constable, Olivia Remie. *To Live Like a Moor: Christian Perceptions of Muslim Identity in Medieval and Early Modern Spain*. Edited by Robin Vose. Philadelphia: University of Pennsylvania Press, 2018.

Cook, E. R., R. Seager, Y. Kushnir, K. R. Briffa, U. Buntgen, D. Frank, P. J. Krusic, et al., "Old World Megadroughts and Pluvials during the Common Era." *Science Advances* 1, no. 10 (2015). https://doi.org/10.1126/sciadv.1500561.

Coomans, Janna. *Community, Urban Health and Environment in the Late Medieval Low Countries*. Cambridge: Cambridge University Press, 2021.

Coomans, Janna, and Guy Geltner. "On the Street and in the Bathhouse: Medieval Galenism in Action?" *Anuario de Estudios Medievales* 43, no. 1 (2013): 53–82.

Cronon, William. *Nature's Metropolis: Chicago and the Great West*. New York: W. W. Norton, 1991.

Cruselles Gómez, Enrique. "La población de la ciudad de Valencian en los siglos XIV y XV." *Revista de Historia Medieval* 10 (1999): 45–84.

Daileader, Philip. *Saint Vincent Ferrer, His World and Life: Religion and Society in Late Medieval Europe*. New York: Palgrave Macmillan, 2016.

Dauksis Ortolá, Sonia, and Francesco Taberner Pastor, eds. *Historia de la Ciudad*, vol. 2, *Territorio, sociedad y patrimonio*. Valencia: Publicacions de la Universitat de València, 2002.

Degroot, Dagomar. *The Frigid Golden Age: Climate Change, the Little Ice Age, and the Dutch Republic, 1560–1720*. Cambridge: Cambridge University Press, 2018.

Devaney, Thomas. *Enemies in the Plaza: Urban Spectacle and the End of Spanish Frontier Culture, 1460–1492*. Philadelphia: University of Pennsylvania Press, 2015.

Dolbee, Samuel. "The Locust and the Starling: People, Insects, and Disease in the Late Ottoman Jazira and after, 1860–1940." PhD diss., New York University, 2017.

Domínguez-Castro, F., R. García-Herrera, P. Ribera, and M. Barriendos, "A Shift in the Spatial Pattern of Iberian Droughts during the 17th Century." *Climate of the Past* 6, no. 5 (2010): 553–563.

Domínguez-Castro, Fernando, Juan Ignacio Santisteban Navarro, Mariano Barrien-dos, and Rosa María Mediavilla López. "Reconstruction of Drought Episodes for Central Spain from Rogation Ceremonies Recorded at the Toledo Cathedral from 1506 to 1900: A Methodological Approach." *Global and Planetary Change* 63, no. 2 (2008): 230–242.

Domínguez-Delmas, M., R. Alejano-Monge, S. Van Daalen, E. Rodríguez-Trobajo, I. García-González, J. Susperregi, T. Wazny, and E. Jansma, "Tree-Rings, Forest History and Cultural Heritage: Current State and Future Prospects of Dendro-archaeology in the Iberian Peninsula." *Journal of Archaeological Science* 57 (2015): 370–379.

Dormeier, Heinrich. "Saints as Protectors against Plague: Problems of Definition and Economic and Social Implications." In *Living with the Black Death*, edited by Lars Bisgaard and Leif Søndergaard, 61–186. Odense: University Press of Southern Denmark, 2009.

Ehler, Benjamin. *Between Christians and Moriscos: Juan de Ribera and Religious Reform in Valencia, 1568–1614*. Baltimore: Johns Hopkins University Press, 2006.

Einbinder, Susan. *After the Black Death: Plague and Commemoration among Iberian Jews*. Philadelphia: University of Pennsylvania Press, 2018.

Elif Dağyeli, Jeanine. "The Fight against Heaven-Sent Insects: Dealing with Locust Plagues in the Emirate of Bukhara." *Environment and History* 26, no. 1 (2020): 94–103.

Esquilache Martí, Ferran. "Paisatge agrari i alimentació a l'horta de Valencia dels segles XIII–XIV: Agricultura, ramaderia i explotació del medi natural." *Torrens: Estudis i investigacions de torrent i comarca* 16 (2006): 41–47.

Fay, Isla. *Health and the City: Disease, Environment and Government in Norwich, 1200–1575*. Woodbridge, UK: Boydell and Brewer, 2015.

Fernández-Armesto, Felipe. *Before Columbus: Exploration and Colonization from the Mediterranean to the Atlantic 1229–1492*. Philadelphia: University of Pennsylvania Press, 1987.

Ferragud, Carmel, and Juan Vicente García Marsilla. "The Great Fire of Medieval Valencia (1447)." *Urban History* 43, no. 4 (2015): 500–516.

Ferrer i Mallol, Maria Teresa. *Els sarraïns de la Corona Catalano-Aragonesa en el segle xiv: segregació i discriminació*. Barcelona: Consell Superior d'Investigacions Científiques, 1987.

Few, Martha. "Killing Locusts in Colonial Guatemala." In *Centering Animals in Latin American History*, edited by Martha Few and Zeb Tortorici, 62–92. Durham, NC: Duke University Press, 2013.

Franklin-Lyons, Adam. *Shortage and Famine in the Late Medieval Crown of Aragon*. State College: Pennsylvania State University Press, 2022.

Franklin-Lyons, Adam, and Marie A. Kelleher. "Framing Mediterranean Famine: Food Crisis in Fourteenth-Century Barcelona. *Speculum* 97:1 (2022).

Fumagalli, Vito. *Landscapes of Fear: Perceptions of Nature and the City in the Middle Ages*. Translated by Shayne Mitchell. Cambridge: Polity, 1994.

Furió, Antoni. "La domesticación del medio natural. Agricultura, ecología y economía en el País Valenciano en la baja Edad Media." in *El medio natural en la España medieval: Actas del I Congreso sobre Ecohistoria e Historia Medieval,* edited by Julián Clemente Ramos, 57–103. Badajoz, Spain: Universidad de Extremadura, 2001.

Furió, Antoni, and Juan Vicente García Marsilla. "La ville entre deux cultures: Valence et son urbanisme entre Islam et féodalité." In *La forme de la ville de l'Antiquité à la Renaissance*, edited by Stéphane Bourdin, Michel Paoli, and Anne Reltgen-Tallon, 37–55. Rennes, France: Presses Universitaires de Rennes, 2015.

Galloway, James A. "Storm Flooding, Coastal Defence and Land Use around the Thames Estuary and Tidal River c. 1250–1450." *Journal of Medieval History 35*, no. 2 (2009): 171–188.

Gampel, Benjamin. *Anti-Jewish Riots in the Crown of Aragon and the Royal Response, 1391–1392*. Cambridge: Cambridge University Press, 2016.

García-Ballester, Luis. "The Construction of a New Form of Learning and Practicing Medicine in Medieval Latin Europe." In *Galen and Galenism: Theory and Medical Practice from Antiquity to the European Renaissance*, edited by Jon Arrizabalaga, Montserrat Cabré, Lluís Cifuentes, and Fernando Salmón, 75–102. Aldershot, UK: Routledge, 2002.

García-Ballester, Luis, Michael R. McVaugh, and Agustín Rubio-Vela. *Medical Licensing and Learning in Fourteenth-Century Valencia*. Philadelphia: American Philosophical Society, 1989.

García Cárcel, Ricardo. *Las Germanías de Valencia*. New ed. Barcelona: Ediciones Península, 1981.

García Marsilla, Juan Vicente. "El impacto de la corte en la ciudad: Alfonso el Magnánimo en Valencia (1425–1428)." In *El alimento del estado y la salud de la 'res publica': Orígenes, estructura y desarrollo del gasto público en Europa*, edited by Angel Galán Sánchez, Carretero Zamora, and Juan Manuel, 291–308. Madrid: Instituto de Estudios Fiscales y Universidad de Málaga, 2013.

García-Oliver, Ferran. "L'espai transformat. El país Valencià de la colonització feudal." In *Jaume I: Commemoració del VIII centenari del naixement de Jaume I*, vol. 1, edited by María Teresa Ferrer i Mallol, 537–552. Barcelona: Institut d'Estudis Catalans, 2013.

——. "Quan la justícia és venjança, contra un jueu." *Anuario de estudios medievales 43*, no. 2 (2013): 577–608.

——. *The Valley of the Six Mosques: Work and Life in Medieval Valldigna*. Turnhout, Belgium: Brepols, 2011.

Geltner, Guy. "The Path to Pistoia: Urban Hygiene before the Black Death." *Past and Present 246*, no. 1 (2020): 3–33.

——. *Roads to Health: Infrastructure and Urban Wellbeing in Later Medieval Italy*. Philadelphia: University of Pennsylvania Press, 2019.

Gerrard, Christopher M. "Contest and Co-operation: Strategies for Medieval and Later Irrigation along the Upper Huecha Valley, Aragón, North-East Spain." *Water History 3*, no. 1 (2011): 3–28.

Gerrard, Christopher M., and David N. Petley. "A Risk Society? Environmental Hazards, Risk and Resilience in the Later Middle Ages in Europe." *Natural Hazards 69*, no. 1 (2013): 1051–1079.

Glick, Thomas F. *From Muslim Fortress to Christian Castle: Social and Cultural Change in Medieval Spain*. Manchester, UK: Manchester University Press, 1995.

———. *Irrigation and Society in Medieval Valencia*. Cambridge, MA: Belknap Press of Harvard University Press, 1970.

———. "Levels and Levelers: Surveying Irrigation Canals in Medieval Valencia." *Technology and Culture* 9, no. 2 (1968): 165–180.

Glick, Thomas F., Enric Guinot Rodríguez, and Luis Pablo Martínez, eds. *Els molins hidràulics valencians: Tecnologia, història i context social*. Valencia: Institució Alfons el Magnànim, 2000.Glick, Thomas F., and Helena Kirchner. "Hydraulic Systems and Technologies of Islamic Spain: History and Archaeology." In *Working with Water in Medieval Europe: Technology and Resource Use*, edited by Paolo Squatriti, 267–330. Leiden: Brill, 2000.

Green, Monica, ed. *Pandemic Disease in the Medieval World: Rethinking the Black Death*. York, UK: ARC Medieval Press, 2014.

Guidoboni, Emanuela. "Human Factors, Extreme Events and Floods in the Lower Po Plain (Northern Italy) in the 16th Century." *Environment and History* 4, no. 3 (1998): 279–308.

Guillerme, André. *The Age of Water: The Urban Environment in the North of France, A.D. 300–1800*. College Station: Texas A&M University Press, 1988.

Guinot Rodriguez, Enric. "Arpenteurs en terres de conquête. La pratique de la mesure de la terre en pays valencien pendant le XIIIe siècle." In *Expertise et valeur des choses au Moyen Age*, vol. 2, *Savoirs, écritures, pratiques*, edited by Laurent Feller and Ana Rodriguez, 275–294. Madrid: Casa de Velázquez, 2016.

———. "El gobierno del agua en las huertas medievales mediterráneas." In *Espacios de poder y formas socials en la edad media: Estudios dedicados a Ángel Barrios*, 99–118. Salamanca: Ediciones Universidad de Salamanca, 2007.

———. "La conquesta i colonització del regne de València per Jaume I. Balanç i noves perspectives." In *Jaume I: Commemoració del VIII centenari del naixement de Jaume I*, vol. 2, edited by Maria Teresa Ferrer i Mallol, 521–532. Barcelona: Institut d'Estudis Catalans, 2013.

———. "L'horta de València a la baixa Edat Mitjana. De sistema hidràulic andalusí a feudal." *Afers* 51 (2005): 271–301.

———. "Una Historia de la Huerta de Valencia." In *El patrimonio hidráulico del bajo Turia: L'horta de València*, edited by Jorge Hermosilla Pla, 60–98. Valencia: Generalitat Valenciana, Direcció General de Patrimoni Cultural, 2007.

———. "Usos i conflictes de l'aigua." *Afers* 51 (2005): 265–270.

Guinot Rodriguez, Enric, and Sergi Selma Castell. *Les séquies de l'horta nord de València: Mestall, Rascanya i Tormos*. Valencia: Generalitat Valenciana, Conselleria d'Agricultura, Pesca i Alimentació, 2005.

Guinot Rodriguez, Enric, and Josep Torró, eds. *Hidráulica agraria y sociedad feudal: Prácticas, técnicas, espacio*. Valencia: Publicacions de la Universitat de València, 2012.Guixeras, David. "L'urbanisme al *Dotzè del Crestià*," *Mot so razo* 8 (2009): 68–87.

Gunzberg i Moll, Jordí. "Epidemias i mortalidad en la Cataluña medieval, 1300–1500." In *Interazioni fra economia e ambiente biologico nell'Europa preindustriale, secc. XIII–XVIII*, edited by Simonetta Cavaciocchi, 57–81. Florence: Firenze University Press, 2010.

Haldon, John, Arlen F. Chase, Warren Eastwood, Martin Medina-Elizalde, Adam Izdebski, Francis Ludlow, Guy Middleton, Lee Mordechai, Jason Nesbit, and B. L. Turner II. "Demystifying Collapse: Climate, Environment, and Social Agency in Pre-modern Societies." *Millennium: Yearbook on the Culture and History of the First Millennium C.E.* 17, no. 1 (2020): 1–33.

Hamilton, Sarah R. *Cultivating Nature: The Conservation of a Valencian Working Landscape.* Seattle: University of Washington Press, 2018.

Hanawalt, Barbara A. *Ceremony and Civility: Civic Culture in Late Medieval London.* Oxford: Oxford University Press, 2017.

Hanska, Jussi. "Cessante causa cessat et effectus: Sin and Natural Disasters in Medieval Sermons." In *Roma, magistra mundi: Itineraria culturae medievalis. Mélanges offerts à Père L. E. Boyle à l'occasion de son 75e anniversaire*, part 3, edited by Jacqueline Hamesse, 141–153. Louvain-la-Neuve, Belgium: Fédération Internationale des Instituts d'Etudes Médiévales, 1998.

——. *Strategies of Sanity and Survival: Responses to Natural Disasters in the Middle Ages.* Helsinki: Finnish Literature Society, 2002.

Harris, A. Katie. *From Muslim to Christian Granada: Inventing a City's Past in Early Modern Spain.* Baltimore: Johns Hopkins University Press, 2007.

Henderson, John. *The Renaissance Hospital: Healing the Body and Healing the Soul.* New Haven, CT: Yale University Press, 2006.

Hinojosa Montalvo, José. *En el nombre de Yahveh. La judería de Valencia en la Edad Media.* Valencia: Ajuntament de Valencia, 2007.

——. "La intervención comunal en torno al agua: Fuentes, pozos y abrevaderos en el reino de Valencia en la baja Edad Media." *En la España medieval* 23 (2000): 367–385.

——. *Una ciutat gran i populosa: Toponimia y urbanismo en la Valencia medieval.* Vols. 1–2. Valencia: Ajuntament de Valencia, 2014.

Hoffman, Richard C. "Bugs, Beasts, and Business: Some Everyday and Long-Term Interactions between Biology and Economy in Preindustrial Europe." In *Le interazioni fra economia e ambiente biologico nell'Europa preindustriale secc. XIII– XVIII / Economic and Biological Interactions in Pre-industrial Europe from the 13th to the 18th Centuries. Atti delle "Quarantunesima Settimana di Studi," 26–30 aprile 2009*, edited by Simonetta Cavaciocchi, 137–164. Florence: Firenze University Press.

——. *An Environmental History of Medieval Europe.* Cambridge: Cambridge University Press, 2014.

Horden, Peregrine. "Ritual and Public Health in the Early Medieval City." In *Body and City: Histories of Urban Public Health*, edited by Sally Sheard and Helen Power, 17–40. London: Ashgate, 2000.

Horden, Peregrine, and Nicholas Purcell. *The Corrupting Sea: A Study of Mediterranean History.* Oxford: Blackwell, 2000.

Howe, John, and Michael Wolfe, eds. *Inventing Medieval Landscapes: Senses of Place in Western Europe.* Gainesville: University Press of Florida, 2002.

Howe, Nicholas, ed. *Ceremonial Culture in Pre-modern Europe.* Notre Dame, IN: University of Notre Dame Press, 2007.

Hughes, Diane Owen. "Sumptuary Law and Social Relations in Renaissance Italy." In *The Italian Renaissance: The Essential Readings*, edited by Paula Findlen, 124–150. Malden, MA: Blackwell, 2002.

Huguet-Termes, Teresa. "Madrid Hospitals and Welfare in the Context of the Hapsburg Empire." *Medical History* 53, no. S29 (2009): 64–85.

Hulme, Mike. "Climate Change and Memory." In *Memory in the Twenty-First Century: New Critical Perspectives from the Arts, Humanities, and Sciences*, edited by Sebastian Groes, 159–162. London: Palgrave Macmillan, 2016.

Husain, Faisal. "In the Bellies of the Marshes: Water and Power in the Countryside of Ottoman Baghdad." *Environmental History* 19, no. 4 (2014): 638–664.

James, Mervyn. "Ritual, Drama and Social Body in the Late Medieval English Town." *Past and Present* 98 (1983): 3–29.

Jordan, William Chester. *The French Monarchy and the Jews: From Philip Augustus to the Last Capetians*. Philadelphia: University of Pennsylvania Press, 1989.

Jørgensen, Dolly. "Cooperative Sanitation: Managing Streets and Gutters in Late Medieval England and Scandinavia," *Technology and Culture* 49, no. 3 (2008): 562–563.

Juneha, Monica, and Franz Mauelshagen. "Disasters and Pre-industrial Societies: Historiographic Trends and Comparative Perspectives." *Medieval History Journal* 10, nos. 1–2 (2007): 1–31.

Justice, Steven. "Did the Middle Ages Believe in Their Miracles?" *Representations* 103, no. 1 (2008): 1–29.

Karras, Ruth Mazo. *Sexuality in Medieval Europe: Doing unto Others*. Abingdon, UK: Routledge, 2012.

Kempe, Michael. "Noah's Flood: The Genesis Story and Natural Disasters in Early Modern Times," *Environment and History* 9, no. 2 (2003): 151–171.

Kennedy, Hugh. "From Polis to Madina: Urban Change in Late Antique and Early Islamic Syria." *Past and Present* 106 (1985): 3–27.

Kinzelbach, Annemarie. "Infection, Contagion, and Public Health Late Medieval and Early Modern German Imperial Towns." *Journal of the History of Medicine and Allied Sciences* 61, no. 3 (2006): 369–389.

Kirchner, Helena. "Original Design, Tribal Management and Modifications in Medieval Hydraulic Systems in the Balearic Islands (Spain)." *World Archaeology* 41, no. 1 (2009): 151–168.

Lilley, Keith D. *City and Cosmos: The Medieval World in Urban Form*. London: Reaktion Books, 2009.

Lindeman, Katherine. "Fighting Words: Vengeance, Jews, and Saint Vicent Ferrer in Late-Medieval Valencia." *Speculum* 91, no. 3 (2016): 690–723.

Llasat, María-Carmen, Mariano Barriendos, Antonio Barrera, and Tomeu Rigo. "Floods in Catalonia (NE Spain) since the 14th Century: Climatological and Meteorological Aspects from Historical Documentary Sources and Old Instrumental Records." *Journal of Hydrology* 313, nos. 1–2 (2005): 32–47.

Lockwood, Jeffrey A. *Locust: The Devastating Rise and Mysterious Disappearance of the Insect That Shaped the American Frontier*. New York: Basic Books, 2004.

López-Blanco, Charo, Marie-José Gaillard, María Rosa Miracle, and Eduardo Vicente. "Lake-Level Changes and Fire History at Lagunillo del Tejo (Spain) during the Last Millennium: Climate or Humans?" *The Holocene* 22, no. 5 (2012): 551–560.

Lopez Blanco, Rosário, and Lidia Romero Viana. "Dry and Wet Periods over the Last Millennium in Central Eastern Spain—A Paleolimnological Perspective." *Limnetica* 38, no. 1 (2019): 335–352.

López Gómez, A. *Geografia de les Terres Valencianes*. Valencia: Papers Bàsics 3i4, 1977.

Luterbacher, Jürg, Ricardo García-Herrera, Sena Akcer-On, Rob Allan, Maria-Carmen Alvarez-Castro, Gerardo Benito, et al. "A Review of 2000 Years of Paleoclimatic Evidence in the Mediterranean." In *The Climate of the Mediterranean Region: From the Past to the Future*, edited by Piero Lionello, 87–186. Amsterdam: Elsevier, 2012.

Machado, M. J., G. Benito, M. Barriendos, and F. S. Rodrigo, "500 Years of Rainfall Variability and Extreme Hydrological Events in Southeastern Spain Drylands." *Journal of Arid Environments* 75, no. 12 (2011): 1244–1253.

Magnusson, Roberta. "Medieval Urban Environmental History." *History Compass* 11, no. 3 (2013): 189–200.

Magnusson, Roberta, and Paolo Squatriti. "The Technologies of Water in Medieval Italy." In *Working with Water in Medieval Europe: Technology and Resource Use*, edited by Paolo Squatriti, 217–266. Leiden: Brill, 2000.

Manrique, Emilio, and Angel Fernandez-Cancio. "Extreme Climatic Events in Dendoclimatic Reconstructions from Spain." *Climatic Change* 44, no. 1 (2000): 123–138.

Marina, Areli. *The Italian Piazza Transformed: Parma in the Communal Age*. University Park: Pennsylvania State University Press, 2012.

Martinez, Luis Pablo. "Els molins com a clau de l'articulació de l'horta medieval de València. La sentència de 1240 entre els moliners d'Alaxar i la comunitat de Rascanya." *Afers* 51 (2005): 369–396.

Martín-Puertas, Celia, Blas L. Valero-Garcés, M. Pilar Mata, Penélope González-Sampériz, Roberto Bao, Ana Moreno, and Vania Stefanova. "Arid and Humid Phases in Southern Spain during the Last 4000 Years: The Zoñar Lake Record, Córdoba." *The Holocene* (2008) vol. 18 no. 6: 907–921.

Martin-Vide, Javier, and Mariano Barriendos Vallvé. "The Use of Rogation Ceremony Records in Climatic Reconstruction: A Case Study from Catalonia (Spain)." *Climatic Change* 30, no. 2 (1995): 201–221.

McVaugh, Michael. *Medicine before the Plague: Practitioners and the Patients in the Crown of Aragon, 1285–1345*. Cambridge: Cambridge University Press, 1993.

Melió, Vicente. *La "Junta de Murs i Valls": Historia de las obras publicas en la Valencia del antiguo régimen, siglos XIV–XVIII*. Valencia: Consell Valencià de Cultura, 1991.

Meyerson, Mark D. *A Jewish Renaissance In Fifteenth-Century Spain*. Princeton, NJ: Princeton University Press, 2004.

——. *Jews in an Iberian Frontier Kingdom: Society, Economy, and Politics in Morvedre, 1248–1391*. Leiden: Brill, 2004.

——. *The Muslims of Valencia in the Age of Fernando and Isabel: Between Coexistence and Crusade*. Berkeley: University of California Press, 1991.

——. "Victims and Players: The Attack of the Union of Valencia on the Jews of Morvedre." In *Religion, Text and Society in Medieval Spain and Northern Europe: Essays in Honor of J. N. Hillgarth*, edited by Thomas E. Burman, Mark D. Meyerson, and Leah Shopkow, 70–102. Toronto: Pontifical Institute of Medieval Studies, 2002.

Moreno, Ana, Blas L. Valero-Garcés, Penélope González-Sampériz, and Mayte Rico. "Flood Response to Rainfall Variability during the Last 2000 Years Inferred from the Taravilla Lake Record (Central Iberian Range, Spain)." *Journal of Paleolimnology* 40, no. 3 (2008): 943–961.

Morris, A. E. J. *History of Urban Form before the Industrial Revolution.* 3rd ed. Harlow, UK: Season Education, 1994.

Moulinier, Laurence, and Odile Redon. "L'inondation de 1333 à Florence. Récit et hypothèses de Giovanni Villani." *Médiévales* 36 (1999): 91–104.

Muir, Edward. *Civic Ritual in Renaissance Venice.* Princeton, NJ: Princeton University Press, 1981.

Narbona Vizcaíno, Rafael. "Alfonso el Magnánimo, Valencia y el oficio de racional." In *La Corona d'Aragona ai tempi di Alfonso II el Magnanimo: I modelli politico-istituzionali, la circolazione degli uomini, delle idee, delle merci, gli influssi sulla società e sul costume*, vol. 1, *Modelli politico-istituzionali*, edited by Guido D'Agostino and Giulia Buffardi, 593–617. Naples: Paparo, 2000.

———. "Cultura política y comunidad urbana: Valencia, siglos XIV–XV." *Edad Media: Revista de historia* 14 (2013): 171–211.

———. "El trienio negro: Valencia, 1389–1390. Turbulencias cohetáneas al asalto de la judería." *En la España medieval* 35 (2012): 177–210.

———. "Finanzas municipales y patriciado urbano. Valencia a finales del trescientos." *Anuario de estudios medievales* 22 (1992): 485–512.

———. *Pueblo, poder y sexo: Valencia medieval, 1306–1420.* Valencia: Diputació de Valencia, 1992.

———. *Valencia, municipio medieval: Poder político y luchas ciudadanas, 1239–1418.* Valencia: Ajuntament de Valencia, 1995.

Nevola, Fabrizio. *Siena: Constructing the Renaissance City.* New Haven, CT: Yale University Press, 2007.

Newfield, Timothy P. "Mysterious and Mortiferous Clouds: The Climate Cooling and Disease Burden of Late Antiquity." In *Environment and Society in the Long Late Antiquity*, edited by Adam Izdebski and Michael Mulryan, 89–115. Leiden: Brill, 2018.

Nirenberg, David. *Anti-Judaism: The Western Tradition.* New York: W. W. Norton, 2013.

———. *Communities of Violence: Persecution of Minorities in the Middle Ages.* Princeton, NJ: Princeton University Press, 1996.

———. *Neighboring Faiths: Christianity, Islam, and Judaism in the Middle Ages and Today.* Chicago: University of Chicago Press, 2015.

Nutton, Vivian. "The Seeds of Disease: An Explanation of Contagion and Infection from the Greeks to the Renaissance." *Medical History* 27, no. 1 (1983): 1–34.

Oberholzner, Frank. "From an Act of God to an Insurable Risk: The Change in the Perception of Hailstorms and Thunderstorms since the Early Modern Period." *Environment and History* 17, no. 1 (2011): 133–152.

Oliva, M., J. Ruiz-Fernández, M. Barriendos, G. Benito, J. M. Cuadrat, F. Domínguez-Castro, J. M. García-Ruiz, et al. "The Little Ice Age in Iberian Mountains." *Earth-Science Reviews* 177 (2018): 175–208.

Parker, Geoffrey. *Global Crisis: War Climate Change and Catastrophe in the Seventeenth Century.* New Haven, CT: Yale University Press, 2013.

Pérez Puche, Francisco. *Hasta Aquí Llegó la Riada*. Valencia: Ajuntament de Valencia, 2007.

Pullan, Brian. "Plague and Perceptions of the Poor in Early Modern Italy." In *Epidemics and Ideas: Essays on the Historical Perception of Pestilence*, edited by Terence Ranger and Paul Slack, 101–123. Cambridge: Cambridge University Press, 1992.

——. *Tolerance, Regulation and Rescue: Dishonoured Women and Abandoned Children in Italy, 1300–1800*. Manchester, UK: Manchester University Press, 2016.

Puy, Arnald. "Land Selection for Irrigation in al-Andalus, Spain (8th century A.D.)." *Journal of Field Archaeology* 39, no. 1 (2014): 84–100.

Rangel López, Noelia. "Moras, jóvenes y prostitutas: Acerca de la prostitución Valencia a finales de la Edad Media." *Miscelána medieval murciana* 32 (2008): 119–130.

Rawcliffe, Carole. "The Concept of Health in Late Medieval Society." In *Interazioni fra economia e ambiente biologico nell'Europa preindustriale, secc. XIII–XVIII*, edited by Simonetta Cavaciocchi, Florence: Firenze University Press, 2010.

——. *Urban Bodies: Communal Health in Late Medieval English Towns and Cities*. Woodbridge, UK: Boydell and Brewer, 2013.

Ray, Jonathan. "Beyond Tolerance and Persecution: Reassessing Our Approach to Medieval Convivencia." *Jewish Social Studies* 11, no. 2 (2005): 1–18.

Retamero, Félix. "Irrigated Agriculture, Risk and Population: The Andalusi Hydraulic Systems of the Balearic Islands as a Case Study (Xth–XIIIth Century)." In *Marqueurs des paysages et systems socio-économiques: Actes du colloque COST du Mans (7–9 décembre 2006)*, edited by Rita Compatangelo-Soussignan, Jean-René Bertrand, John Chapman, and Yves-Pierre Laffont, 135–148. Rennes, France: Presses Universitaires du Rennes, 2008.

Retamero, Félix, and Helena Kirchner. "Becoming Islanders: Migration and Settlement in the Balearic Islands (10th–13th Centuries)." In *Agricultural and Pastoral Landscapes in Pre-industrial Society: Choices, Stability, Change*, edited by Félix Retamero, Inge Schjellerup, and Althea Davies, 57–78. Oxford: Oxbow Books, 2016.

Riera, David. "Sant Vicent Ferrer, Francesc Eiximenis i el Pogrom de 1391." In *Actes del Sisè Colloqui d'Estudis Catalans a Nord-America, Vancouver 1990*, edited by K. I. Kobbervig, A. Pacheco, and M. J. Massot, 250–254. Barcelona: Publicaciones de l'Abbadia de Montserrat, 1992.

Riera i Melis, Antoni. "Catàstrofe i societat a la Catalunya medieval: Els terratrèmols de 1427–1428." *Acta historica et archaelogica medieaevalia* 20–21 (1998): 699–735.

Riera i Sans, Jaume. "Los tumultos contra las juderias de la Corona de Aragón en 1391," *Cuadernos de la historia* 8 (1977): 213–225.

Ristuccia, Nathan J. *Christianization and Commonwealth in Early Medieval Europe: A Ritual Interpretation*. Oxford: Oxford University Press, 2018.

Roca Traver, Francisco A. "Cuestiones de demografía medieval." *Hispania: Revista española de historia* 50 (1953): 3–36.

Rohr, Christian. "Man and Natural Disaster in the late Middle Ages: The Earthquake in Carinthia and Northern Italy on 25 January 1348 and Its Perception." *Environment and History* 9, no. 2 (2003): 127–149.

——. "Writing a Catastrophe: Describing and Constructing Disaster Perception in Narrative Sources from the Late Middle Ages." *Historical Social Research / Historische Sozialforschung* 32, no. 3 (2007): 88–102.

Rothschild, N. Harry. "Sovereignty, Virtue, and Disaster Management: Chief Minister Yao Chong's Proactive Handling of the Locust Plague of 715–16." *Environmental History* 17, no. 4 (2012): 783–812.

Rubio Vela, Agustín. "Jaume I. La imagen del monarca en la Valencia de los siglos XIV y XV," in *El rei Jaume I: Fets, actes i paraules*, edited by Germà Colón Domènech and Tomàs Martínez Romero, 129–155. Barcelona: Fundacio Germà Colón Domènech / Publicaions de l'Abadia de Montserrat, 2008.

——. "Las epidemias de peste en la ciudad de Valencia durante el siglo XV. Nuevas aportaciones," *Estudis castellonencs* 6 (1994–95): 1179–1222.

——. *Peste Negra, crisis y comportamientos sociales en la España del siglo XIV: La ciudad de Valencia (1348–1401)*. Granada: Universidad de Granada, 1979.

——. *Pobreza, enfermedad y asistencia hospitalaria en la Valencia del siglo XIV*. Valencia: Institución Alfonso el Magnánimo, 1984.

——. "Presencia de la langosta: Plagas en la Valencia." *Saitabi* 47 (1997): 269–288.

——. "Vicisitudes demográficas y área cultivada en la baja Edad Media. Consideraciónes sobre el caso valenciano." *Acta historica et archaelogica mediaevalia* 11–12 (1991): 259–297.

Ruiz, José Miguel, Pilar Carmona, and Alejandro Pérez Cueva, "Flood Frequency and Seasonality of the Jucar and Turia Mediterranean Rivers (Spain) during the 'Little Ice Age.'" *Méditerranée* 122 (2014): 121–130.

Ruiz, Teofilo F. *A King Travels: Festive Traditions in Late Medieval and Early Modern Spain*. Princeton, NJ: Princeton University Press, 2012.

Ruzafa García, Manuel. "Façen-se cristians los moros o muyren." In *Violència i marginació en la societat medieval*, edited by Paulino Iriadiel, 87–110. Valencia: Publicacions de la Universitat de València, 1990.

Ryder, Alan. *The Wreck of Catalonia*. Oxford: Oxford University Press, 2007.

Sánchez-López, G., A. Hernández, S. Pla-Rabes, R. M. Trigo, M. Toro, I. Granados, A. Sáez, et al. "Climate Reconstruction for the Last Two Millennia in Central Iberia: The Role of East Atlantic (EA), North Atlantic Oscillation (NAO) and Their Interplay over the Iberian Peninsula." *Quaternary Science Reviews* 149 (2016): 135–150.

Sanchis Ibor, Carles. *Regadiu i canvi ambiental a l'Albufera de València*. València: Publicacions de la Universitat de València, 2001.

Serra Desfilis, Amadeo. "El 'consell' de Valencia y el 'embelliment de la ciutat,' 1412–1460." In *Primer Congreso de Historia del Arte Valenciano: Actas, mayo 1992*, 75–79. Valencia: Conselleria de Cultura, Educació i Ciència, 1993.

Schenk, Gerrard Jasper. "'. . . prima ci fu la cagione de la mala provedenza de' Fiorentini . . .' Disaster and 'Life World'—Reactions in the Commune of Florence to the Flood of November 1333." *Medieval History Journal* 10, nos. 1–2 (2007): 355–386.

Scott, James C. *Seeing Like a State: How Certain Schemes to Improve the Human Condition Have Failed*. New Haven, CT: Yale University Press, 1999.

Selma Castell, Sergi. "Aigua i terra a la plana del Millars. La sentència arbitral de 1347." *Afers* 51 (2005): 397–406.

Shyovitz, David. *A Remembrance of His Wonders: Nature and the Supernatural in Medieval Ashkenaz*. Philadelphia: University of Pennsylvania Press, 2017.

Seifert, Lisa, Ingrid Wiechmann, Michaela Harbeck, Astrid Thomas, Gisela Grupe, Michaela Projahn, Holger C. Scholz, and Julia M. Riehm. "Genotyping *Yersinia pestis* in Historical Plague: Evidence for Long-Term Persistence of *Y. pestis* in Europe from the 14th to the 17th Century." PLoS ONE 11, no. 1 (2016). https://doi.org/10.1371/journal.pone.0145194.

Simms, Anngret, and Howard B. Clarke, eds. *Lords and Towns in Medieval Europe: The European Historic Towns Atlas Project.* Farnham, UK: Ashgate, 2015.

Smail, Daniel Lord. *Imaginary Cartographies: Possession and Identity in Late Medieval Marseille.* Ithaca, NY: Cornell University Press, 1999.

Soens, Tim. "Flood Security in the Medieval and Early Modern North Sea Area: A Question of Entitlement?," *Environment and History* 19 (2013): 209–232.

——. "Floods and Money: Funding Drainage and Flood Control in Coastal Flanders from the Thirteenth to the Sixteenth Centuries." *Continuity and Change* 26, no. 3 (2011): 333–365.

——. "Resilient Societies, Vulnerable People: Coping with North Sea Floods before 1800," *Past and Present* 241, no. 1 (2018): 143–177.

Soifer Irish, Maya. "Beyond Convivencia: Critical Reflections on the Historiography of Interfaith Relations in Christian Spain." *Journal of Medieval Iberian Studies* 1, no. 1 (2009): 19–35.

Sprenger, Jana. "An Ocean of Locusts—The Perception and Control of Insect Pests in Prussian Brandenburg (1700–1850)." *Environment and History* 21, no. 4 (2015): 513–536.

Spyrou, Maria A., Marcel Keller, Rezeda I. Tukhbatova, Elizabeth A. Nelson, Aida Andrades Valtueña, Don Walker, Amelie Alterauge, et al. "A Phylogeography of the Second Plague Pandemic Revealed through the Analysis of Historical *Y. pestis* Genomes." bioRxiv, 2018. https://doi.org/10.1101/481242.

Spyrou, Maria A., Rezeda I. Tukhbatova, Michal Feldman, Joanna Drath, Sacha Kacki, Julia Beltréan de Heredia, Susanne Arnold, et al. "Historical *Y. pestis* Genomes Reveal the European Black Death as the Source of Ancient and Modern Plague Pandemics." *Cell Host and Microbe* 19, no. 6 (2016): 874–81.

Squatriti, Paolo. "The Floods of 589 and Climate Change at the Beginning of the Middle Ages: An Italian Microhistory." *Speculum* 85, no. 4 (2010): 799–826.

——. *Water and Society in Early Medieval Italy, AD 400–1000.* Cambridge: Cambridge University Press, 1998.

Stearns, Justin. *Infectious Ideas: Contagion in Premodern Islamic and Christian Thought in the Western Mediterranean.* Baltimore: Johns Hopkins University Press, 2011.

——. "New Directions in the Study of Religious Responses to the Black Death." *History Compass* 7, no. 5 (2009): 1363–1375.

Steinberg, Ted. *Acts of God: The Unnatural History of Disaster in America.* Oxford: Oxford University Press, 2000.

Stevens Crawshaw, Jane L. *Plague Hospitals: Public Health for the City in Early Modern Venice.* Farnham, UK: Ashgate, 2012.

Tartakoff, Paola. *Between Christian and Jew Conversion and Inquisition in the Crown of Aragon, 1250–1391.* Philadelphia: University of Pennsylvania Press, 2012.

Teixidor, Josef. *Monumentos históricos de Valencia y su reino: Colección de monografías sobre la historia, geografía, cronología, epigrafía y bibliografía de esta región.* Vols. 1–2. Valencia: 1895.

Tejedor, Ernesto, Martin de Luis, Mariano Barriendos, José María Cuadrat, Jürg Leterbacher, and Miguel Ángel Saz. "Rogation Ceremonies: A Key to Understand Past Drought Variability in Northeastern Spain since 1650." *Climate of the Past* 15, no. 5 (2019): 1647–1664.

Torras i Serra, Marc. "El conflicte entre una cuitat i un bisbe. La sèquia de Manresa." *Afers* 51 (2005): 407–416.

Torró, Josep. "Arqueologia de la conquesta. Registre material, substitució de poblacions i transformació de l'espai rural valencià (segles XIII–XIV)." In *El feudalisme comptat i debatut: Formació i expansió del feudalisme català,* edited by M. Barceló, G. Feliu, A. Furió, M. Miquel, J. Sobrequés, 153–200. Valencia: Publicacions de la Universitat de València, 2003.

———. "Els camperols musulmans del regne de València. De la conquesta a la conversió," *La rella* 23 (2010): 201–212.

———. "Després dels musulmans: les primeres operacions colonitzadores al regne de València i la qüestió de les tècniques hidràuliques." In *Arqueologia medieval: La transformació de la frontera medieval musulmana,* edited by Flocel Sabaté Curull and Jesús Sucarrat. Lleida: Pagès, 2009.

———. "Field and Canal Building after the Conquest: Modifications to the Cultivated Ecosystem in the Kingdom of Valencia, ca. 1250–ca. 1350." In *Worlds of History and Economics: Essays in Honour of Andrew M. Watson,* edited by Brian Catlos, 77–108. Valencia: Publicacions de la Universitat de València, 2009.

———. "Terrasses irrigades a les muntanyes valencianes. Les transformacions de la colonització cristiana." *Afers* 51 (2005): 301–356.

———. "Tierras ganadas: Aterrazamiento de pendientes y desecación de marjales en la colonización cristiana del territorio valenciano." In *Por una arqueología agraria: Perspectivas de investigación sobre espacios de cultivo en las sociedades medievales hispánicas,* edited by Helena Kirchner, 157–172. Oxford: Archaeopress, 2010.

Torró, Josep, and Enric Guinot. "De la *madîna* a la ciutat. Les pobles del sud i la urbanització dels extramurs de València (1270–1370)." *Saitabi* 51–52 (2001–2): 51–103.

Trillo San José, María Carmen. "A Social Analysis of Irrigation in Al-Andalus: Nazari Granada (13th–15th Centuries)." *Journal of Medieval History* 31, no. 2 (2005): 163–183.

Unger, Richard W. "Introduction: Hoffmann in the Historiography of Environmental History." In *Ecologies and Economies in Medieval and Early Modern History: Studies in Environmental History for Richard C. Hoffmann,* edited by Scott G. Bruce, 1–24. Leiden: Brill, 2010.

Very, Francis George. *The Spanish Corpus Christi Procession: A Literary and Folkloric Study.* Valencia: Tipografía Moderna, 1962.

Vila, Soledad. *La ciudad de Eiximenis. Un proyecto teórico de urbanismo en el siglo XIV.* Valencia: Diputació de Valencia, 1984.

Wessell Lightfoot, Dana. *Women, Dowries and Agency: Marriage in Fifteenth-Century Valencia.* Manchester: Manchester University Press, 2013.

White, Lynn. "The Historical Roots of Our Ecologic Crisis." *Science*, new ser., 155, no. 3767 (1967): 1203–1207.

White, Sam. *The Climate of Rebellion in the Early Modern Ottoman Empire*. Cambridge: Cambridge University Press, 2011.

——. *A Cold Welcome: The Little Ice Age and Europe's Encounter with North America*. Cambridge, MA: Harvard University Press, 2017.

Wing, John T. *Roots of Empire: Forests and State Power in Early Modern Spain, c. 1500–1750*. Leiden: Brill, 2015.

Wolff, Philippe. "The 1391 Pogrom in Spain: Social Crisis or Not?," *Past and Present* 50 (1971): 4–18.

Worster, Donald. *Dust Bowl: The Southern Plains in the 1930s*. New York: Oxford University Press, 1979.

INDEX

Page numbers in *italics* indicate maps, tables, and figures.

Printed in the USA
CPSIA information can be obtained
at www.ICGtesting.com
LVHW052205141223
766376LV00016B/398/J